DATE DUE

ADVANCED PLACEMENT EXAMINATION
IN
AMERICAN HISTORY

ADVANCED PLACEMENT EXAMINATION IN AMERICAN HISTORY

John W. Crum, Ph.D.

Social Studies Department
Mount Pleasant High School
Wilmington, Delaware 19809

ARCO
New York

Second Edition

 ARCO

Simon & Schuster, Inc.
15 Columbus Circle
New York, NY 10023

DISTRIBUTED BY PRENTICE HALL TRADE SALES

Manufactured in the United States of America

1 2 3 4 5 6 7 8 9 10

Library of Congress Cataloging-in-Publication Data

Crum, John W.
    Advanced placement examination in American history / John W. Crum.
—2nd ed.
        p.   cm.
    Includes bibliographical references.
    ISBN 0-13-012998-4
        1. United States—History—Examinations, questions, etc.
    I. Title.
    E178.25.C78   1990
    973′.076—dc20   89-48960
                                                    CIP

Table of Contents

Acknowledgments

Thanks are due to the following for permission to reprint copyrighted material:

The Art Institute of Chicago, for reprint of *American Gothic*, by Grant Wood. Reprinted by courtesy of the Art Institute of Chicago. All rights reserved.

The Atlantic Monthly, for quotes from "What Substitute for War," by Charles Lindbergh, *The Atlantic Monthly*, February, 1940; and "The Road Not Taken," by David Cohen, *The Atlantic Monthly*, March, 1940. Copyright © 1940 by The Atlantic Monthly Co. Reprinted with permission.

The University of Chicago Press, for the quote from *An American Primer*, edited by Daniel Boorstin. Copyright © 1966 by Daniel Boorstin. Reprinted by permission of The University of Chicago Press.

The College Board, for statistics from *The History Examinations of the College Board* 1980/82. Copyright © 1980 by College Entrance Examination Board; and for quotes from *Advanced Placement Course Description: History*. Copyright © 1990 by College Entrance Examination Board, New York. Reprinted by permission of The College Board.

The Curtis Publishing Company, for the cartoon from the *Saturday Evening Post*, January 8, 1938. Reprinted from the *Saturday Evening Post* © 1938 by The Curtis Publishing Company.

E. P. Dutton, Inc., for quotes from *Seventy Years of Life and Labor: An Autobiography* by Samuel Gompers. Copyright © 1925 by E.P. Dutton, Inc., © 1953 by Gertrude Gleaves Gompers. Reprinted by permission of E.P. Dutton, Inc.

Herblock, for the cartoon from Herblock Cartoons, *The Washington Post*, October 6, 1966. Copyright © 1966 by Herblock in *The Washington Post*. Reprinted by permission of Herblock Cartoons.

Michael Katz, for the chart from *The Irony of Early School Reform*, by Michael Katz. Copyright © 1968. Reprinted by permission of Michael Katz.

Richard P. McCormick, for charts from "New Perspectives on Jacksonian Politics," by Richard P. McCormick, *American Historical Review*, LXV, January, 1960. Reprinted by permission of Richard P. McCormick.

Prentice-Hall, Inc., for the chart, "Population Composition of Major Cities, 1910," from *The Evolution of American Urban Society*, by Howard P. Chudacoff. Copyright © 1975. Reprinted by permission of Prentice-Hall, Inc.

Reader's Digest, for quotes from "Pro and Con: Should We Act to Curb Aggressor Nations?" March, 1939. Reprinted by permission of *Reader's Digest* © 1939.

Arthur M. Schlesinger, Jr., for the map, "The Populous States in 1890," from *The Rise of the City*, by Arthur M. Schlesinger, Sr. Copyright © 1933. Reprinted by permission of Arthur M. Schlesinger, Jr.

Stanford University, for the quote from *The Man in the Street*, by Thomas A. Bailey. Copyright © 1948. Reprinted by permission of Stanford University.

James T. Stewart, for quotes from "America Looks at War," by Raoul de Roussy de Sales, *The Atlantic Monthly*, February, 1940. Reprinted by permission of James T. Stewart.

TIME, Inc., for quotes from "1939 Is Not 1914," by Walter Millis, *Life*, November 6, 1939. Reprinted by permission of TIME, Inc.; and for quotes from "Story of a Tide," and "Shift of Opinion," *Time*, 1940. Copyright © 1939, 1940 TIME, Inc.

Barbara White Walker, for quote from *The Autobiography of William Allen White*, by William Allen White. Copyright © 1946. Reprinted by permission of Barbara White Walker, *Emporia Gazette*.

Michael S. Henry and *The Social Studies*, for quotes and a chart from, "The Advanced Placement American History Examination: How Has It Changed?" *The Social Studies*, July/August, 1987. Reprinted with permission of the Helen Dwight Reid Educational Foundation. Published by Heldref Publications, 4000 Albemarle St., N.W., Washington, D.C. 20016. Copyright © 1987.

Preface

As a teacher I owe a great debt of gratitude to several sources of inspiration. I have worked with hundreds of fellow AP teachers from all over the United States. Over the years I have encountered a deep devotion to scholarship and teaching and a high degree of competence.

I have been most fortunate to teach at Mount Pleasant High School, a public high school in Wilmington, Delaware. Our school is well-known for the strength of its academic program, the quality of the faculty, and the friendly interaction between the students and the faculty. I must thank the thousands of students who have challenged and stimulated me in the classroom. I am especially grateful to my longtime colleagues in the Social Studies Department—Robert Emrich, David Menser, and Albert Clark—for their advice, support, and congeniality over the years. It would be difficult to imagine three more stimulating and supportive fellow workers.

Most of all I want to thank my wife and our two daughters for their faithful encouragement, patience, and toleration. My debt to them is beyond mere words. They have sacrificed much to support my academic pursuits. I have won many awards and much recognition as a teacher, but no joy compares to that which has come from being a husband and father. For all these reasons I want to thank my wife, Karen, and our daughters, Laurette and Leslie.

J.W.C.

INTRODUCTION

The College Board Advanced Placement Program is an opportunity to achieve excellence. The AP program provides high school students the opportunity to earn credit and advanced standing from the college of their choice. The College Board contracts with Educational Testing Service to construct, administer, and grade the advanced placement examinations. The tests are scored as 5, 4, 3, 2, or 1. Most colleges and universities grant college credit for scores of 3, 4, or 5.

The College Board estimates that perhaps a fourth of all the nation's college-bound high school students are able to do freshman-level work. It takes more effort than the usual high school course, but the results are well worth it. Such work can enrich your mind and boost your self-confidence. In the final analysis it is your education, your opportunity, your achievement, and your reward. Don't shortchange yourself in effort or in achievement.

AMERICAN HISTORY
AP EXAMINATION:
WHAT TO EXPECT

Structure of the Examination

The American History AP examination is a rigorous three-hour examination. It will be one of the most difficult examinations you will ever prepare for. Whereas almost every college course you will take is a semester course, the AP examination covers a year's worth of effort and content. This is not meant to scare you; thousands and thousands of students have done very well on the American History AP examination. It is, however, an examination that demands and deserves your best effort.

Part One of the examination consists of 100 multiple-choice questions. You have 75 minutes for Part One. The multiple-choice questions and your machine-scored answer sheet are collected at the end of the 75-minute period. You are not able to refer to the multiple-choice questions for facts and ideas to include in your essays.

Part Two, the essay section, is divided between one document-based essay question (DBQ) and one essay question that you select from a list of five. Every student must answer the DBQ, which is question number 1. You are given 6 to 12 documents to analyze in order to answer a question relating to a particular historical circumstance, event, issue, or theme. For your second essay you select one question to answer from a field of of five, numbered 2 to 6. You have a total of 1½ hours to write your two essays. You also have 15 minutes to read the documents, analyze them, outline your essays, etc. The entire examination takes three hours: the 75-minute multiple-choice section, the 15-minute reading period, and the 90-minute essay section.

Specifications for the Examination

The specifications for the multiple-choice questions are arranged by topic as follows: 42% are political history and government questions; 13%, economic history; 12%, social history; 17%, diplomatic history; and 16%, intellectual and cultural history. The chronological specifications are as follows: 15% from 1607–1789; 45%, 1790–1916; 30%, 1917 to the present, and 10% cross between these time periods. No topic before 1607 appears in the multiple-choice questions.

The document-based essay question is limited to the period from the American Revolution to shortly after the Second World War. The College Board American History test development committee, which makes up the examination each year, is well aware of the difficulties AP teachers have trying to cover adequately the history of the U.S. from the Second World War to the present. You should be aware, however, that the committee is interested in extending the range of the essay question through the 1960s.

Of the five essay questions that follow the DBQ on each AP examination you select one to answer. Generally speaking, one essay question comes from each of the topical categories used to describe the multiple-choice questions: political and governmental history; economic history; social history; diplomatic history; and intellectual or cultural history. An essay question is rarely concerned only with the colonial era or the period after 1960. An unwritten rule seems to be that no more than half an essay question falls before 1763 or after 1960. For example, you may be asked to illustrate the assertion that presidents are rarely successful in both domestic and foreign policies. The instructions direct you to write on one 20th century president and one 19th century president. (A question recently appeared on the rise and decline of the Puritans, however, and another on the characteristics of religion in the colonial era.) You should be aware that the colonial era is defined as ending in 1763. A question on the causes of the American Revolution is not a "colonial" question.

Grading the Examination

The American History AP examination is a tough, discriminating examination. It is designed to differentiate among the students who take the examination. The average score for the multiple-choice section is 55 to 60% correct. You must prepare for the psychological shock of taking a test and feeling that you probably correctly answered only 6 out of every 10 questions. Most students think themselves failures if their scores are 60%. On this AP examination 60% may be just fine. After you read the 300 multiple-choice questions in this book you will understand! Each AP examination contains equators, multiple-choice questions that have been given on previous exams. The equators tell the statisticians how this year's group of test-takers compares with those from previous years. That information is included in the eventual decision on where to draw the lines to determine a score of 5, 4, 3, 2, or 1.

Each multiple-choice question is worth .9 points for a total of 90 points for the 100 questions. The document-based essay and the second essay are each graded on a scale of 0–15. The two essay scores are each multipled by 3 for a 0–45 scale. The 45 potential score on the first essay, the 45 potential score on the second essay, and the 90 potential score on the multiple-choice section add up to a 0–180 scale. Based on what the statisticians tell College Board officials about the comparison of this year's group of test-takers with those of previous years, plus information gathered during the week-long grading of the essays by a group of AP high school teachers and college professors, the Chief Reader in American History (employed by the College Board, not ETS, Educational Testing Service) decides where to draw the lines on the 0–180 scale to determine the 5, 4, 3, 2, or 1 score. His primary concern is to maintain the high standards historically associated with the AP examination.

The grading process begins long before the 200 American History graders gather to grade the essays. Experienced graders meet for several days to determine the standards for grading each essay. The 0–15 scale is condensed to a working scale of 0–3, 4–6, 7–9, 10–12, and 13–15. For example, the essay standards delineate the desired qualities of a 10–12 essay. A grader recognizes an essay as a 10–12 essay and then decides whether it is a fair, good, or well done essay within that range; in other words, 10, 11, or 12.

This oversimplified look at the essay grading procedure is intended to illustrate several points. First, the person grading your essay is well qualified. Second, you are judged against a standard; this is not the place for creating a new form of written communication. Third, you are competing with established national standards of excellence; the harder you work to prepare, the better you will do. Don't think of the 0–3, 4–6, 7–9, 10–12, and 13–15 categories as F, D, C, B, and A. The average document-based essay score is 7 to 7½. The average score for the second essay is 6½ to 7. A different grader grades each essay. The 0–15 scale is not a bell-shaped curve, but a pear-shaped curve. Therefore, anything you do to improve your writing of essays is certain to reap dividends. The standards are established on the 0–15 scale to string out the scores of the students taking the examination. As in many endeavors in life the top is less crowded than the bottom! Work toward putting yourself in the top. Expect a difficult examination, and prepare diligently.

After the Examination

The AP examinations are given in May. At your first AP examination for that year you receive a booklet containing your identification number and information about reporting AP scores to your college. You may at that time designate which colleges you wish to receive your scores. If you are not a senior you must initiate the procedure for reporting your scores the following year.

Give careful consideration to the AP policies at colleges you wish to attend. Each academic department within the college or university sets its own standards and policies. Every college catalog contains the school's AP philosophy policy statement, but each department controls that department's policy. Check with the departments concerned to substantiate the disposition of your hard-earned AP scores.

The AP program was designed by secondary schools and colleges to prevent duplication of introductory-level courses. It stemmed from student and university complaints that the first-year college courses repeated the content of high school courses. The AP program established a means by which to validate the achievement of freshman college-level knowledge. When a college receives your score, it determines what that score means within the context of its programs and requirements. Depending upon the college or university, there are eight different approaches to your AP score:

1. credit given in the major field of the examination
2. credit given; you must take an upper-level course in that department
3. credit given; you must pay for the credit hours
4. credit given; the credits are subtracted from the total needed for graduation; in essence, the credits come from your electives outside your major and minor fields
5. credit given for only one introductory course in the major but not for both; e.g., credit given for U.S. History to 1877 or U.S. History Since 1865 but not for both
6. no credit given
7. no credit given, advanced standing given; you must take an upper-level course in that department
8. combining three or four AP scores gives you sophomore standing; you skip the freshman year and begin college as a sophomore

CLEP Examination

If your AP score is too low to qualify for college credit, you have another opportunity before you enroll in the appropriate college introductory course. The College Board also offers the College-Level Examination Program, or CLEP. This program was originally designed for the older student entering college. Through individual reading and experience such a student may feel that he already knows the level of material offered in the introductory course. CLEP provides a test to determine proficiency. If you feel that you just missed qualifying for an acceptable AP score, investigate the possibility of taking the American History CLEP examination at your college or university. The examinations are administered early in the semester. Each college establishes its own procedures, fees, etc. A few summer hours each day with a good American history textbook to complement your AP course work may bring success. Don't be afraid to ask, and don't be afraid to risk the effort.

AP COURSE
SURVIVAL SKILLS

Getting the Facts

You need two tools for studying and writing history: facts and concepts. No shortcut exists for acquiring a body of factual information. You must work at it! You need facts about individuals, ideas, relationships, groups, conditions, and major societal forces to support the arguments you present. Because history suffers from too many facts, you as a student must select only the appropriate and significant ones to support your concepts.

Always cluster your facts around a concept. A concept is an idea, scheme, or design used to group facts. Be able to elaborate upon each concept with at least three to five factual supports. Don't just touch upon a concept or compile a list of facts. Synthesize the facts and concepts. Use the concept as a frame for a canvas and the facts as details to create the painting.

Use concepts to organize your thoughts toward achieving high-level thinking skills of analysis, synthesis, evaluation, and interpretation. Most essay questions invite or force you to answer within the concepts raised in the question. "The Populist Party foolishly sought political solutions to economic problems. Assess the validity of this statement." What were those economic problems, what were the political solutions proposed, and how does the element of foolishness fit in?

One approach to answering the question is the following outline, which first describes the political solutions before addressing the economic problems. This question divides into two major conceptual areas, political and economic. The wording of the question asks you to comment on the foolishness of the political solutions and why these political solutions did not solve the farmers' economic problems.

I. Political Solutions

    A. Sought political reforms designed to make government more responsive to the people

        1. Direct election of senators
        2. Referendum
        3. Initiative
        (Foolishness: They assumed that their demands would lead to a more sympathetic hearing for their problems, yet farmers were becoming a smaller percentage of the population. Farming was changing from a way of life to a business.)

    B. Sought political reforms to break the close alliance between the government and big business and the favoritism shown by the government for the rich and powerful

        1. Governmental ownership of railroads, telephones, telegraphs
        2. Municipal ownership of public utilities
        3. Long haul, short haul discrimination
        4. Morgan rescue of the U.S. Treasury
        5. Income tax amendment

C. Political reforms to ease the farmers' economic plight
   1. Reduce mortgage rates
   2. Easement for debt
   3. Free silver
   4. Stop favoritism of high tariff
      (Please remember that this is only a conceptual outline. All or most of the following facts fit under the concept of free silver: Civil War inflation, greenbacks, Granger Movement, Greenback Party, bimetallism, demonetization of silver, Crime of '73, Gresham's law, Bland-Allison Act, cheap money, 16–1, Cross of Gold speech, Bryan vs. McKinley).

II. Economic Problems

A. Expansion of agriculture
   1. Acreage cultivated doubled
   2. Increased number of farms
   3. Great increases in production
   4. Increased number of tenant farmers
      (Yet paradoxically the percentage of farmers relative to the rest of the population declined. There were too many marginal farmers, and their political, social, and economic status declined.)

B. Application of machinery to farming
   1. New sources of machines and power
   2. Costs too high for marginal farmers

C. Application of science to farming
   1. New methods for fertilizing
   2. Prior tradition of government aid for farmers: Morrill Act, Hatch Act
      (Farming changed from a way of life to a business. The farmers were victims of their own success. They grew too much, overproducing for the new expanded world market in which they now sold their goods.)

III. Conclusion

Society was changing, the agriculturally based society and isolated island communities were disappearing, farmer becoming seen as a hayseed, Jefferson's noble yeoman gone. Federal government had played a role in the expansion of agriculture, and therefore the farmers' demand for governmental aid did not suggest a new departure. The new image (not reality) of laissez-faire, however, worked against the farmers' hopes for political solutions.

In addition, by the 1890s the farmers' problems were unsolvable by political proposals. The 1890s was a period of party realignment that ended the third party system. Farmers counted for less politically in the new party system emerging.

You may look at the concepts roughed out in this outline, and think that you could never duplicate it. You can with practice, practice, practice! Study to master both facts and concepts. After reading an assignment, think about the concepts involved. The key to answering any essay question is to organize it conceptually. The way to be prepared to organize an essay is to have *already* thought in terms of the concepts surrounding the topic. The first step in answering an essay question is to decide what concepts apply and how you are going to organize an answer. Outline your answer conceptually and fill in the facts to support your concepts. Part of the judgment of your essay is the quality and quantity of factual support. Note that quality of facts is listed first because appropriate and significant facts count more than related facts.

A historian doing research builds from the empirical to the conceptual to the general. He (or she) assembles a collection of facts based upon detective work. Then he brainstorms through the material, conceptualizing it first one way, then another, and selects the method that presents the story best. After sufficiently digesting and analyzing the facts and concepts, he recounts the history in his own words.

A student must answer an essay question in the opposite way that a historian researches history. Identify the concepts and generalizations in the question, then assemble the appropriate facts. Unlike the historian doing research, you select the facts and concepts. The essence of answering an essay is to provide a firm conceptual framework with adequate factual support.

When you encounter an essay question, decide what concepts are appropriate. "The North didn't win the Civil War, the South lost it. Explain." How many ways can a nation lose a war? The South could have lost for political, economic, diplomatic, or military reasons. Politically the South suffered a lack of cohesion, a bad governmental structure for waging a war, poor leadership, division of goals and means, and the burden of simultaneously creating a new government. Economically the South suffered from a lack of resources, the overwhelming might of the North, too few banks, mismanagement of resources, too little industry, and structural defects such as a poor railroad system. Diplomatically the South proved unable to gain allies, to find an outlet for its cotton, or to receive recognition as a nation. Militarily the South may have pursued outdated military strategy and tactics, lacked a unified command structure, and been hampered by too little attention to organization and discipline. You ideally should select at least three to five major concepts for answering the question with three to five facts supporting each concept. Which concepts you select is determined by which concepts you understand well enough to write about and which concepts you feel you have sufficient facts to support. A conceptually sound essay without factual support is inadequate. A conceptually weak essay with excellent facts is also inadequate. Always ask yourself: What are my conceptual arguments and are they factually supported?

You might consider some of the following economic concepts for an essay question dealing with economics: competition, scarcity, supply and demand, resource allocation, opportunity cost, technology, invention, industrialization, interdependence, conservation, and land use patterns. A question concerning an increasing or decreasing economic role for the federal government should include a consideration of the simple question of who gained and who lost from the shift in policy. Which individuals, classes, sections, regions, leaders, parties, ideas, or forces won? The decision to create the Interstate Commerce Commission in 1887 was a victory for something over something even if it was a hollow victory. Think and analyze before you write. You otherwise run the risk of writing the following: "And so, to solve some kind of problem they created the ICC, and lived happily ever after." What problem? Who is they? Lived happily ever after? Such writing is so easy to grade!

You might include some of the following concepts for a question concerning beliefs and ideas: values, sovereignty, equality, liberty, natural rights, attitudes, ideology, cultural conflict, liberty versus order, religion, myth, individualism, and moral beliefs.

Decide what political concepts apply to a political question. Three great ideas—liberty, equality, and fraternity—dominated both the French Revolution and its subsequent historiography. One cannot write anything on the French Revolution that ignores these ideas. An American historian once reduced the period of the Confederation and Constitution to four concepts: nation-making, federalism, the creation of a new colonial system (Northwest Ordinance, equal status for new states), and the reconciliation of liberty and order. Suppose you were asked the political significance of the era of the Articles of Confederation and the Constitution. Any essay including these four concepts backed by strong factual support certainly captures the significance of the Confederation and Constitution period. After you know what concepts to organize your answer around, no essay question is difficult. You may not get the highest grade, but you are certain to pass, and pass high.

If a question asks for the causes of something, be aware of the diverse explanatory concepts that surround the general concept of causation. Differentiate between long and short run causes. Remember that most events have multiple causes, and assign relative weight or significance to a few. That is, identify one as the major cause, a second as the second most important, and lump the rest together as contributing causes. Don't forget failure as a cause, since the new in history often springs from the defects of the old. Certainly one of the causes of the adoption of the Constitution was failure of the Articles of Confederation.

Cause questions implicitly or explicitly invite elaborating on results. Try to define how the results relate to the causes. Did the causes change over a period of time so that the results were influenced by new factors? One difficulty with cause and result questions is the problem of success. Don't make the mistake of reading history backwards. Try to evaluate the results against the goals and intentions. Sometimes the situation changes, and creates new problems or new goals. Towards the end of the Vietnam War, for example, the United States refused to agree to a ceasefire until the North Vietnamese agreed to return all our prisoners of war. The safe return of our POWs was not a goal at the beginning of the war! During the course of the war we redefined what we considered an acceptable ending of our involvement in Vietnam.

Many subconcepts are attached to the concept of change, a frequent theme in history essay questions. First, don't forget the power of the twin forces of stability and inertia. Continuity characterizes human society more than change. Use the concept of continuity to refine and specify the elements of change you discuss. There are many types of change: social, political, economic, cultural, policy; different speeds of change, such as revolutionary and evolutionary; and planned and unplanned change. Be aware of the possibility of different reactions for different aspects of society to events and ideas. Liberty and equality moved the Founding Fathers to independence, but not to freeing their slaves. Change implies the word new. Identify the consequences of change, new policies, new goals, and new organizations. Change occasionally throws off the new, and returns to a former policy or accents features of an older policy. Change can look backward as well as forward.

Finally, be alert to apply a model of change. Throughout your study of American history you will encounter various models to explain historical phenomena. The most famous is probably Crane Brinton's *The Anatomy of Revolution*. Brinton studied the English, American, French, and Russian revolutions, and identified stages and events common to all of them. In the initial stages of each revolution the intellectuals transfer their allegiance from the old government to a new revolutionary ideal. For example, in the American Revolution the ideal is liberty and independence. Each revolution contains a period during which two governments co-exist, the old authority (British colonial authorities) and the new revolutionary government (Sons of Liberty and Continental Congress). The uninterested citizen is torn between the two governments whereas the dedicated revolutionary easily gives his allegiance to just one. This period in a revolution is called *dvoevlastie*, an untranslatable Russian word that means dual power and dual sovereignty, two governments, both powerful and both legitimate. This aspect of Brinton's model makes the 1773–1776 period much clearer. Don't superficially and indiscriminately apply models, however. Make sure your model applies and illuminates or don't use it.

Reading a Textbook

Your textbook is the chief source for the building blocks, the facts and concepts of American history. A good knowledge of American history provides the background for seeing how people, events, and ideas fit into the larger picture. There is no easy way to acquire a body of factual knowledge. The process is initially frustrating, but as you learn more history you begin to be able to relate ideas and events to one another. You might study the New Deal reforms of the 1930s as if something like this had never happened before in American history, or you can recognize that attacks on the money trust, attempts to regulate big business, and efforts to mitigate the suffering of the poor are all concepts with deep roots in American history. The first approach is like beginning the study of a foreign language. The second is like curling up on the sofa with an old friend.

Read your textbook assignments as soon as they are assigned. Many students make the mistake of thinking that since only reading is involved they can read two or three chapters at once. Reading a chapter is not the same as studying a chapter, and not the same as understanding a chapter. Look for generalizations, explanations, and interpretations as you read. Textbook authors do not hide their topic sentences; they are usually the first sentence in each paragraph.

Never simply begin reading a textbook. First look through the entire assignment—notice the chapter title, the subheadings, and all the picture captions, cartoons, graphs, etc. Become familiar with the topic before you read. Second, skim the assignment. Put a piece of white paper or a card on the page and go down a column in ten seconds. You will pick up a few words or phrases. Now read the assignment. You might even read one subsection at a time. Next, skim it again. This approach is preferable to reading the entire assignment twice. Concentrate when you read. Reading only words is a waste of time. If someone asks you what you have read when you finish you should be able to say more than simply "fifteen pages." You might as well have read it backwards!

Recent research on reading comprehension indicates that those who learn material keep going over and over it until they understand. Don't get discouraged. Comprehension rates differ from student to student. Another technique is to read the first and last paragraphs of the assignment. Still another is reading the first sentence of each paragraph before or after reading the assignment. Teachers do students a disservice by calling it a "reading assignment." For the student it is a "study and mastery assignment."

Reading a Secondary Source

You will occasionally encounter a secondary source: a journal article, a monograph, or an interpretation. The author usually hits you between the eyes with his thesis: "This author believes that. . ." "In this article I will prove that. . ." "One cannot escape the conclusion that slavery was an unprofitable economic burden on the South."

Ask yourself: What is the author trying to prove? Most secondary source arguments are so emphatically stated that they are overstated. What are the author's assumptions, what is his point of view? How does this source compare to other sources you have read? Teachers assign secondary sources to illustrate a point of view on a disputed concept. Ask yourself what the concept is and what point of view is represented. This is the stuff from which essay questions spring.

An article that concludes that colonial Boston was becoming less economically and socially democratic as the Revolution approached states only that. Rural Massachusetts may well have been quite democratic in land distribution, social democracy, political rights, etc. The first source does not exclude the second interpretation. Of course, both points of view enliven an essay, "How Democratic Was Colonial America?" Be critical as you read; be an active participant in the study of history.

Taking Lecture Notes

Use a pen; pencil notes smear.

Read all textbook assignments and additional reading before, not after, the lecture. A lecture organizes the material around a particular theme with specific factual support. The emphasis and organization may be new to you, but the facts and the topic should not be. You run the risk of missing significant points while you puzzle over what a Sacco and Vanzetti is (a new car, camera, book?). Listen intently to the beginning and end of the lecture for a restating of the thesis and how it relates to the other history you have been studying. Ask yourself: What are the major concepts around which the lecture is based? For example, most textbooks do not discuss the First, Second, Third, etc., Party Systems. The presidential candidates and the parties obviously do not change, just the organizational scheme.

As soon as possible after the lecture, read your notes to see if they make sense. You will probably find that you left holes, intending to go back to fill in the material later. Notetakers often write furiously as the lecturer says, "There are three main reasons for the failure of the Articles of Confederation." You write down only two! He moved on to another topic before you finished all three. It will do little good to open your notebook the night before an examination if you discover gaps in your notes. By going over your notes within a few hours you forestall many potential problems. Leave spaces periodically to allow room for amplification and for facilitating a visual retention of the material. Check the spelling of historical terms immediately. To believe a student is doing his best is difficult when his essay on Gilded Age politics spells the word as "Guilded" or "Gilted."

At the end of each lecture you should summarize the lecture in your notebook in a three by five inch box. The outline for the Populism essay question, "What are Facts and Concepts," ("The Populist Party foolishly sought political solutions to economic problems. Assess the validity of this statement.") would look as follows:

```
pol reforms a)  more dem, dir of sen, ref, init
           b)  anti big bus, RR, tel, tel (govt owned) pub util,
               long,sh, Morgan Bonds, income tax
           c)  eco-mort, debt, 16-1, lo tariff, inflation, B-A Act,
               Granger laws

eco probs  a)  expan-acreage, farms, production, tenants
a business b)  new costs-mach, hurt marginal farmers
           c)  new use of science-govt sponsored Morrill, Hatch

changes        TJ's quote, hayseed, la-faire att, 3rd Party System ending,
               symbol, election of 1896, free silver
```

Reread your notes again and again; commit the boxed summary to memory. Specific numbers regarding the increase in farm acreage and the number of farms are impressive when you use them to support the concept of an overexpanded agricultural system. A boxed summary links quality facts to quality concepts. Periodically review as if you were studying for an examination. In preparing for essay exams concentrate on understanding the concepts. When studying for multiple-choice questions you need more precise knowledge. One key to multiple-choice is to ask yourself as you study: "What is the significance of. . . ." It is not enough to know what the Morrill Act did; what was the significance of the Morrill Act?

Pay attention to chronology. Anchor your knowledge with a few dates and be able to place events, people, and ideas in proper chronological order.

HOW TO WRITE AN ESSAY

The Essay as an Opportunity

An essay examination is an opportunity to display thinking, organizing, and writing skills. Practice thinking when you study. Only through effort do you learn the highest forms of intellectual activity: generalizing, analyzing, interpreting, and evaluating.

An essay gives you the freedom to make a statement in a unique way, but first you must have an argument worth writing and reading. Avoid the temptation to write everthing you know or to tell a pleasant story.

An essay allows you to demonstrate your ability to organize material. Everyday conversation is disorderly; writing should not be. Think through and organize answers to practice essay questions. Take a second look at your creation the next day. While working on a project we frequently feel profound, but Monday's masterpiece is often Wednesday's drivel. If possible, give yourself time to reflect on your written work.

The words used in an essay must do more than just communicate. Don't write *about* a subject; write to persuade. Be careful of abstract words such as democracy, progress, success, and individualism. Certain abstract words carry a wide range of definitions and connotations. Take the time to define an abstract word to yourself even if you do not incorporate the definition into your essay. It helps you focus on that aspect of the word the essay question intends.

Use adjectives to convey the amount of generality or specificity needed for a particular sentence. "Merchants led the revolt against Great Britain." "Urban merchants extensively engaged in imperial trade led the revolt against the newly enforced British navigation acts." The first of these two sentences is vague, the second specific. Now look at another sentence. "The U.S. has a democratic government." You could have written that sentence in fourth grade! Is it a parliamentary democracy, representative democracy, direct democracy, or imperfect democracy? Do you mean political, economic, social, or religious democracy? Do you mean democratic in results or in opportunity? Often a single adjective sufficiently describes a noun, e.g., "fascist leaders," or "marginal farmers."

The third opportunity offered by essay tests is the opportunity to write. Watch the adults in your life. A major difference between those who are successful and those who are not is their ability to express themselves by written means. Learning how to write concisely gives you an advantage, and the only method of learning how to write is to write. Mastering writing is hard work, and must be redone each generation. Even the children of Ph.D's must learn punctuation and vocabulary usage. Concentrate on mastering the basics. Nothing you ever learn matches the supreme sense of self-confidence you feel knowing that you know how to write. Knowledge is power; mastering the communication of knowledge is exhilarating power.

Rules to Follow in Writing Essays

After you have decided what you want to write, the writing of an essay is a race among the amount of paper you have, the clock on the wall, the ink in your pen, and the muscles in your hand. First, know your history; second, organize your thoughts; third, present your arguments; fourth, support them.

Taking a test is scary. Allay those fears by adequate study. If you have studied you know more than you think, and your initial sense of panic is unjustified. Budget your time, for you have plenty. Delay writing your essay for approximately one-fifth to one-fourth of the allotted time. (For a fifty minute test do not write for at least ten minutes.) If you have more than one essay, outline all your answers before you write a single essay. If you are given a choice, choose your questions carefully after reading the directions and the wording of each question. Think about the question. Do you understand it? Watch for absolute words—never, all, only, every, etc. Quickly begin to jot down ideas and facts about all the questions you are answering. Don't forget to number your answers correctly.

Make conceptual arguments in your essay, provide factual support, and move on. Some students pound a single point, believing that constant restating adds to an essay. Avoid lengthy discussion of minor or peripheral material.

When you are finished, briefly read your essay and check for grammatical errors and misspellings. The omission of a single word may change the meaning of your essay. A student occasionally begins an essay with one argument, realizes he has better support for the opposite viewpoint, and changes the remainder of the essay without changing the introduction. For example, he answers an essay on slavery as the sole cause of the Civil War by agreeing with the statement in the introduction and proving that there were multiple causes in the body of his essay.

ORGANIZING YOUR ESSAY

The first rule of organizing an essay is understanding that there are no standard patterns of organization to follow in cookbook fashion. The nature of the material, the purpose of the essay, and the potential grader determine the pattern of organization. Many teachers insist upon a five paragraph format—introduction, three well developed paragraphs, and a conclusion. The wording of some questions, however, does not fit the five paragraph pattern. "In the 1790s the infant United States was confronted by the hostile policies of the two European superpowers. Assess the validity of this statement." You might organize your answer around at least three broad conceptual points, being careful to include both Great Britain and France. Or you could use a four paragraph format, one for each nation in the body of your essay, and incorporate some concepts within the introduction and the conclusion.

Organize your answer according to the key words in the question—list, compare, contrast, define, discuss, illustrate, explain, defend, differentiate, outline, summarize, assess. An essay is written in the form of a thesis or argument defending a position or point of view. Substantiate concepts with specific facts. Concrete details should fit in with one another and with the appropriate concepts. Stalin died March 5, 1953. Broke your train of thought, didn't it? An inappropriate fact thrown into an essay in order to impress a grader with your depth of knowledge usually has the opposite effect.

A question often permits choice in organization. "In the 1790s Great Britain and France interfered with our domestic politics, violated our neutral rights, and prevented us from achieving our foreign policy goals. Assess the validity of this generalization." One approach is to write three paragraphs in the body of your essay, one for each conceptual generalization concerning domestic politics, neutral rights, and foreign policy goals. Suppose you feel weak in one area, though, such as violation of our neutral rights. Do you want a skimpy, two sentence paragraph sandwiched between two healthy paragraphs? An alternative organizes the answer around the two countries rather than the three concepts.

In the first approach you discuss the concept itself, and trace it through British and French policies. Along the way you should introduce distinctions between these nations and explain shifts in policy. This organization is an effective method to emphasize differences between something that initially seemed similar. For example, the degree of French interference in our domestic affairs far exceeded Great Britain's. Be careful to remember to focus constantly on the concept.

In the second approach the focus is on France rather than on French violations of our neutral rights or on French interference with our domestic politics. You should treat the three concepts in the same order within both your French and British paragraphs. If you begin the French paragraph with the violation of our neutral rights, begin the British paragraph the same way. A disadvantage of this organization is that it may leave the grader wondering if you answered the question.

Answering an essay question requires a plan. In order to answer an essay you must first understand what is being asked. The first five things to do in answering an essay are to read the question, read the question, read the question, read the question, and read the question. Like reading problems in mathematics, the phrasing is what gives students trouble. Underline the key words or phrases in the question.

Approach an essay with this format: "It is suggested that . . . however . . . because. . . ." Suppose you were asked, "Slavery was the sole cause of the Civil War. Assess the validity of this statement." In your analysis, say to yourself, *it is suggested* that slavery was the sole cause of the Civil War; *however,* this is only partially true (or is true, or isn't true) *because* of the following reasons. Address the validity of the statement conceptually and support your *however* with *because* concepts and facts.

Outline an answer before writing. Use a topic, phrase, or sentence outline, whichever you prefer, but watch the time. If you are unorganized, jot down on scrap paper all the concepts and facts pertaining to the answer, and then organize the essay. The final picture doesn't emerge by itself; you must outline because otherwise your essay will resemble the transcript of a monologue. In conversation you keep talking until the listener gets your point. In writing you don't have the advantage of watching facial expressions to determine if the reader understands.

The sequence of conceptual points should be carefully planned. Put conceptual assertions in their approximate order of difficulty, with the most complex or interesting either at the end, to finish your essay on a high note, or at the beginning, to get the grader's attention.

Each one of your conceptual points should reveal something about the central topic. Your basic assumptions must be as explicit as possible. Be sure not to contradict assumptions.

Test generalizations by thinking of exceptions and counterarguments. The essay grader knows the counterarguments; therefore, you must address them. Either explain the counterarguments fully or put them in a subordinate clause. "The argument that slavery would have died naturally west of the 100th meridian is a hypothesis that assumes slavery was primarily tied to cotton culture. It was instead a racial institution. . . . " This proves that you understood, considered, and dismissed that argument because you had a better explanation.

THE BEGINNING PARAGRAPH

Introductory paragraphs are difficult to write. A good beginning paragraph has a clear, precise topic sentence that unequivocally states your main idea. Precision is crucial in the beginning paragraph. Don't be too broad, including ideas that the essay will not address, or too narrow, omitting ideas or limiting your eventual scope. Let your introduction lead into the body of your essay. You may state your thesis by rewording the question in the form of an argumentative statement.

History students frequently link their essay to inappropriate, if authoritative, historiography. If the question asks what caused the Civil War, do not build your essay around the remark that the Civil War began with the initial arrival of blacks in 1619 because you have assumed the responsibility for filling in the years between 1619 and 1861. Argue instead that the institution of slavery created political and economic differences too profound for compromise, or that the existence of blacks, emphasizing slavery as a racial system rather than a system of labor, was the root cause of the war. Either statement is more precise than the mere arrival of blacks. Historians who begin with that argument continue to develop it; students usually have difficulty filling in the intervening years. Constantly ask yourself: What does the question ask, what is my thesis, is my thesis manageable?

THE CONCLUDING PARAGRAPH

The concluding paragraph is your last impression on the grader. A conclusion should strengthen your essay, not undermine it. Don't hastily throw a conclusion together. Think about what you have written. If the essay is long, write a brief summary of your main points. Avoid a mere recapitulation of your essay, but don't introduce new ideas. Another possible ending is to elaborate briefly on your thesis in the introduction.

You may introduce new material in a conclusion if you are not making a new conceptual point. After carefully describing specific causes of the Civil War, you might make some short comments on the causes of war in general. Move from the specific to the general. "The Civil War, like all wars, illustrates man's inability to compromise. Emotion renders compromise either impossible to achieve or impossible to sustain. Moral righteousness and practical politics cannot coexist."

Another exception to the rule against introducing new material is the essay which describes the aftermath or result of something. An essay describing the achievements of blacks during Reconstruction might end on a negative or positive note. For instance, racial equality was written into the Constitution although later ignored. "The civil rights laws represented a deferred promise of equal rights. The South slumbered until injustices awakened the North to effective intervention to give blacks minimum legal equality. What might have been in the 1860s was achieved by the bitter struggles of the 1960s. The second Reconstruction completed the promise of the first."

End an essay strongly. Don't confess that your essay probably is not worth reading. A conclusion is not the place for apologies for inadequate preparation, acknowledgement of exceptions to your thesis, or concession to opposing ideas. Deal with possible contradictions to your thesis in the body of the essay. Leaving objections to the end suggests that you just thought of the points and threw them in, like a cook throwing a missing ingredient on top of a half-baked cake. Don't end an essay with a smiley face, "The End," or a dramatic signature. These give the impression you are trying to get by on personality instead of knowledge.

NINE SAMPLE
STUDENT ESSAYS
WITH GRADER COMMENTS

American History AP examination essays are graded on a scale of 0 to 15. In actual practice the scale is divided into categories: 0–3, 4–6, 7–9, 10–12, and 13–15. Do not think that the categories correspond to F, D, C, B, and A. Categories assist the graders in quickly assessing an essay and then judging where that essay fits within the category. For example, if the essay falls in the 7–9 category, is it a 7, 8, or 9? This scale is used to string out the total number of essays in order to differentiate in the final analysis between the good student and the truly outstanding student. The graders consider a 10 to be an excellent essay, but not as well written or well organized or sophisticated as a 13–15 essay.

No matter what skills you have at this moment, you can learn to write essays in the upper range of the 7–9 category. If you know your history you will write an acceptable essay by following the rules and guidelines. If you do not know your history, no level of style or grammar will hide your ignorance.

The first three student essays that follow were written to answer the question below. Read the essays, then the grader's comments and explanation of essay standards.

"Theodore Roosevelt and Woodrow Wilson differed greatly, but both were effective presidents." Assess the validity of this statement by comparing Theodore Roosevelt and Woodrow Wilson as presidents.

First Student Essay

(1)   Woodrow Wilson and Theodore Roosevelt were both good presidents, but in their own ways. They both avoided certain things which could cause controversial and hazardous situations or pressure. They both started out as conservatives, but as things went on, they went their own ways. They didn't necessarily turn away from conservativism, though just taking their own separate parts.

(2)   The Presidents were somewhat equal as conservatives. Both spent their early lives in a relatively secure family, although Wilson went through a long spell of poverty and frustration. They both went along with their party tradition of laissez-faire. Both of them stood for the general good welfare of the country—the middle class. Both were against, though they didn't come right out and say it, labor and the Populist movements. They were suspicious of the trusts because they were a problem to politics, but either didn't know exactly what to do. They eventually converted to the progressive views.

(3)   Even though Wilson and Roosevelt were both conservative and eventually progressive, the difference was in their way of doing it. Wilson, as an early

conservative, was a man who believed in reasoned philosophy of politics. As opposed to Wilson, Roosevelt without much patience pressed toward violence. The early Wilson left himself enough room for reform in his philosophy, though nothing more than a shift of emphasis. Roosevelt on the other hand, didn't leave himself a "reform cause." Roosevelt stuck with what had been there with him, he was not a man of many changes. Wilson went forward with the new, though at the same time he combined the old with the new.

(4)   In the end, they both switched to progressivism because that philosophy had more opportunity for their political careers. They both reached progressivism from different ways. Roosevelt was prompted by ambition to a violent change in language. Wilson simply used his "reform cause."

(5)   All in all, they were two men who were alike as far as conservativism and progressivism were as concepts. But how it was done, was a different story. Roosevelt, who seemed like the stubborn type, for instance fighting against trusts, who muscled through things, though stayed out of sticky situations. Wilson was a man of reason, who could sit down and figure it out, but he could be tough, when needed.

COMMENTS ON THE FIRST STUDENT PAPER

1st Paragraph: The question doesn't ask if the two were "good" Presidents. Use "effective," "innovative," or "ineffective"; that is, any word is more powerful than "good." You are free to agree, to disagree, or to agree partially with the wording of a question. This paper does not take a strong stand; it has no thesis statement. The writer suggests differences between the two, but "own ways," "certain things," and "as things went on" do not present the differences as concepts. This paragraph illustrates the weakness of using too many pronouns in writing. The essay writer knows what the pronouns refer to, but the grader does not. If this student knows what he means, he is not communicating this knowledge. You will not get the benefit of the doubt from the grader.

A grader assumes a grade of 7 when he begins to read an essay. This first paragraph gives the impression that this is no more than a 1–3 range essay. Do first impressions count? Of course they do!

2nd Paragraph: This paragraph illustrates a fatal trap of writing—a pleasant story pleasantly told. "Once upon a time there were two presidents who loved their mothers, believed in goodness, the middle-class, and the American way, and so they became Progressives." There is no transition from the first paragraph to the second. After concluding that the two had taken "their own separate parts," he begins by labeling them "somewhat equal," a contradiction. Their early lives are insignificant unless the student relates them somehow to their later careers as presidents, which he does not. The student has a weak understanding of their differing economic philosophies, the New Nationalism and New Freedom, and no sense of change over time in their economic thinking. If both men were for the middle class, anti-labor, and anti-Populist, the student should explain apparent contradictions such as the Clayton Act and the Coal Strike of 1902. He displays no sophistication on the antitrust issue. This is an excellent opportunity to bring up the question of the degree to which Roosevelt's trustbusting reputation was deserved. He doesn't.

3rd Paragraph: Once again a grader senses a missed opportunity. Where is the sense of growth and change over time for the two politicians? This is also an opportunity to address the question of how conservative the Progressive movement was. Was it a liberal or conservative movement? Based on this paper we shall never know. This student suggests that the two differed in methods but not goals, but this difference could be much more fruitfully developed. "Violence" is a poor word choice for describing Roosevelt. Wilson's "reasoned philosophy of politics" looks interesting conceptually, but this point is not supported factually. As shown by what? Wilson is credited as being more innovative, a man who "combined the old with the new." As shown by what, where, how? Here is a missed opportunity to emphasize their respective policies toward tariffs, banking, trusts, and leading Congress. The writer implies that Roosevelt was more conservative in his methods, but the point is undeveloped.

4th Paragraph: This paragraph repeats much of the earlier drivel. Does the writer really believe that these two presidents embraced Progressivism only to help their political careers?

5th Paragraph: The writer never defines or describes conservatism or Progressivism. At the end of the essay the grader must wonder if the student understands these two concepts. He does seem to know that Roosevelt avoided sticky issues such as the tariff, currency, and banking, but they are not stated. The description of Wilson as a leader who "could be tough, when needed" deserves examples as illustrations.

The grade for this paper is a 3 only because the writer understands too much to put him in the 1—2 range. It is a poor essay. Please note that the numbers in the margin are used only to help you coordinate the student essay and the grader's comments. Never number your paragraphs.

Second Student Essay

(1)   In analyzing the similarities and differences of foreign and domestic policies of Theodore Roosevelt and Woodrow Wilson, one invariably finds that there were many more differences than similarities in their ideas and actions.

(2)   Comparing the ideas of these two men as Presidents, one finds that they didn't agree on too much. However, there were two important things they did agree on. First, in domestic policy, both these men tried desperately to be extreme trust-busters. They were very against the big companies ruling everything and running the "little guy." However, instead of "trust-busting" they ended up more regulating them. On the subject of foreign policy, they both wanted to get rid of the man who called himself President of Mexico, Huerta. They felt he was only hurting the common masses and Wilson even went so far as to support the constitutionalists (Presidential rebels) to try to build a new, more solid Mexican government.

(3)   Between these two men, the differences were enormous. First, in domestic policy, Woodrow Wilson acted on issues that Teddy Roosevelt wouldn't touch because they were "too much trouble." Wilson attacked the bankers and started the Federal Reserve and he wanted lower tariffs through the Underwood-Simmons Act. He was very economy-minded. Roosevelt however, was more into things like conservation that weren't such a public issue. Also, Roosevelt was into New Nationalism to regulate monopolies while Wilson was into New Freedom to destroy them.

(4)   In foreign policy, Roosevelt was a vicious go-getter. He frequently used his "big stick" and violently jumped right into foreign affairs. In his corollary to the Monroe Doctrine, he showed this by stating the U.S. should play "policeman" and use intervention in foreign affairs and he acted on this by being the mediator in the Russo-Japanese War. On the other hand, Wilson was thoroughly disgusted

by "big stickism." He believed in "watchful waiting" and a foreign policy of helpfulness to more than 30 other nations. We can see their ideas on foreign policy and how to handle sticky situations were oceans apart.

(5)   In conclusion, seeing the results of the work of these two men, it is a matter of opinion whether one favors Roosevelt's "go get' em" attitude or Wilson's conservative waiting. These two men, who had basically the same background, obviously had many differences. However, it seems these differences benefited America's domestic and foreign policies at the time in innumerable ways. Both men felt they were doing the right thing and truly worked for the good of America. One cannot say Wilson's or Roosevelt's policies were better because they were just too different. No matter how different they were, though, they seemed to have come to good ends.

COMMENTS ON THE SECOND STUDENT PAPER

1st Paragraph: This student begins with an excellent thesis statement that promises to address both domestic and foreign policies and to prove that there were more differences than similarities. She will support this thesis by referring to specific ideas and actions. What a positive beginning!

2nd Paragraph: The euphoria fades because of the awkward organization of the second paragraph. It has a thesis, which is preferable to having none. After finishing the first paragraph by stating that there were more areas of disagreement, though, she begins the second paragraph by stating the areas of agreement. The student seems to understand Wilson's eventual adoption of Roosevelt's regulatory approach toward trusts, but supplies no specifics. Mixing domestic and foreign policies is an awkward organizational scheme, but it is within the student's premise that their ideas differed. Their respective Mexican policies are poor choices for illustrating differences in foreign policy. The student's knowledge of Roosevelt's comments on Mexico is quite impressive, since this information is not found in most textbooks. The ultimate weakness of this paragraph is the student's use of only two factual supports to prove major areas of agreement existed between the two men.

3rd Paragraph: The organizational awkwardness continues. This paragraph addresses the differences between the two. The factual quality has improved. The student knows that Wilson attacked issues Roosevelt backed away from. The specifics are much better than the first essay, but one wonders what "economy-minded" means to the student. Roosevelt did emphasize conservation, but calling conservation not much of a public issue is incorrect. Finally, the succinct characterization of the New Freedom and the New Nationalism is accurate, but deserves elaboration on the eventual outcome after Wilson won in 1912. The wording detracts from the facts; politicians are not "into" their programs.

4th Paragraph: This paragraph compares the methods used by the two presidents to achieve their foreign policies. The factual support is correct, but it is handled with only minimum adequacy. The U.S. added the Roosevelt Corollary to the Monroe Doctrine. But where, why, for what reasons, how was it received, what other issues did it raise? Wilson pursued "watchful waiting" in regard to Mexico. Does the student believe it aptly describes Wilson's foreign policy everywhere? It could be so used, but she misses the opportunity.

5th Paragraph: In the conclusion, as in the rest of the essay, there are too many fuzzy general statements and too few specific facts. The student fails to take a definite stand. This paper illustrates what graders call "a touch." The student "touches" on facts and concepts without development and explanation. The following lists the factual points the student "touched" without elaborating on them or weaving them together: trustbusting, Huerta, banking and

Federal Reserve, lower tariffs and the Underwood-Simmons tariff, conservation, the New Nationalism and the New Freedom, big stick, Roosevelt Corollary, Russo-Japanese War, and watchful waiting.

The grade for this paper is a 6.

Third Student Essay

(1)   In comparing the foreign and domestic policies of Theodore Roosevelt and Woodrow Wilson, while in office, the general evidence seems to prove that the policies of these two men greatly differed from one another and the similarities between the two were minimal.

(2)   Domestic policy was one of Woodrow Wilson's strong points. He passed much legislation and was very aggressive. Theodore Roosevelt on the other hand passed only a mere amount of legislation and was rather withdrawn. When Roosevelt took office a sweeping reform movement had just begun, it went from stamping out corruption at the municipal level to solving the great national problems growing out of the industrialization and urbanization of the nineteenth century. Roosevelt sought to head the movement while at the same time tempering it with "sane leadership." Legislation passed under Roosevelt consisted of the Hepburn Act in 1906 which increased the power of the Interstate Commerce Commission to regulate the nation's railroads. The Pure Food and Drug Act of 1906 prohibited the manufacture and sale of adulterated foods. A federal Meat Inspection Act was also passed. Roosevelt created the Inland Waterways Commission in 1907 and he also enforced the Sherman Antitrust Act against major corporations. Roosevelt never touched three areas while in office: banking, tariff, and antitrust.

(3)   On the contrary Woodrow Wilson not only attacked these three but solved them. He did so with such legislation as the Underwood-Simmons Tariff Act of 1913 which effected the first sizable reduction of custom rates since the Civil War and provided for a permanent graduated income tax. The Federal Reserve Act of 1913 reorganized the American banking and currency systems and placed them under the control of the Federal Reserve Board appointed by the President. The Clayton Antitrust Act of 1914 legalized labor unions, peaceful pickets, boycotts, and strikes while it limited the use of labor injunctions. The Federal Trade Commission Act was also passed under Wilson in 1914. It provided for the supervision and regulation of interstate trade.

(4)   As for foreign affairs the situation is the reverse. Roosevelt was the aggressor. He was quick to take sides and he liked other countries to be aware of the power of the U.S. and the fact that the U.S was ready and willing to fight to protect itself and its possessions. Woodrow Wilson conversely took the stand of neutrality. He preferred peace and did not intervene unless absolutely necessary and then only if compromise was not possible. While Roosevelt was in office he strengthened the army and navy and started construction of the Panama Canal. He added a corollary to the Monroe Doctrine making the U.S. virtually responsible for seeing that the Latin American countries met international obligations. Roosevelt demonstrated strength by the diplomatic method he used to get the Panama Canal, by U.S. actions during the Venezuela blockade in 1902, by the Alaskan boundary dispute in 1903, and also by sending the Great White Fleet on a peaceful tour of the world. Roosevelt did mediate twice, once he intervened and

it resulted in the Treaty of Portsmouth between Russia and Japan in 1905. The second was in the 1906 dispute between European powers at the Algeciras Conference. Roosevelt won the Nobel Peace Prize in 1906.

(5)   While Wilson was in office he kept the U.S. neutral for his entire first term even though World War I had broken out. Wilson watched and waited. He was moderate and considerate. His main desire was to maintain peaceful relations with foreign countries without the threat or use of violence. He displayed this through his willingness to submit differences with Mexico to mediation and his demand for repeal of the Panama Canal toll exemptions and by his proposal to apologize to Colombia and to pay an indemnity of $25,000,000 for the seizure of the Panama Canal Zone. This last was defeated by the Senate. Even when the U.S. had to enter World War I Wilson wanted not only "victory" but world peace. Wilson made a proposal for world peace which included a League of Nations. For this idea and effort he was awarded the Nobel Peace Prize in 1919.

(6)   In conclusion the foreign and domestic policies of these two men greatly differed based on the above information. Roosevelt was much more aggressive in foreign than in domestic policies. He was not afraid of war and liked to make his military strength known. Wilson on the other hand was much more domestically aggressive rather than foreignly aggressive. He worked on solving domestic problems such as tariffs, banking, and antitrusts while remaining neutral as much as possible on foreign affairs. The two men were similar in only a few ways; both had strong ambition, steady nerves, flexible scruples, and tenacity. Both men won Nobel Peace Prizes which dealt with keeping peace.

COMMENTS ON THE THIRD STUDENT PAPER

1st Paragraph: Compare this thesis statement with the first two papers; it is much stronger.

2nd Paragraph: This paragraph begins by correctly labeling Wilson as a stronger legislative leader than Roosevelt. The student makes the common mistake of stating that the president passes legislation, which detracts somewhat because Congress passes our laws. The president may be for, against, or lukewarm towards a piece of legislation. Roosevelt is correctly called cautious in style and tone. While he was the first Progressive president, the student realizes that the Progressive movement predated him. He realizes that the Progressive movement was a response to problems generated by urbanization and industrialization. Roosevelt did proudly congratulate himself for bringing sane leadership to Progressivism. Remember, he used the derisive term "muckrakers" even though the public accepted the term without his connotation. The Hepburn Act is an example of an impressive quality fact; the date and specifics are included. The other factual support is correct and equally impressive. The student is aware of Roosevelt's caution in banking, tariff, and antitrust. The only flaw in this otherwise excellent paragraph is that the first two sentences give the impression that the paragraph will center on Wilson rather than Roosevelt.

3rd Paragraph: Note the excellent transition from the second to the third paragraph. This whole paragraph presents impressive factual range and depth, especially the detailed knowledge of the Clayton Act.

4th Paragraph: The student sees a reversal in the positions of two men in foreign affairs. Roosevelt is characterized by aggression and Wilson by neutrality. This paragraph contains too many generalizations, e.g., "the U.S. was ready and willing to fight to protect itself and its possessions." As shown by? Quickly glance at the third paragraph. Specific facts in the fourth paragraph are fewer, but the paragraph is still well done. The student is aware that

Roosevelt built up the army as well as the navy. Every student knows the Great White Fleet, but few know Elihu Root's contributions and the subsequent reorganization of the army. The remainder of the paragraph is well done. It needs only a few more specifics.

5th Paragraph: This is an excellent paragraph. The student details Wilson's methods and goals with quality and quantity facts. The Mexico policy could be developed in more depth. The Panama Tolls dispute and the apology to Columbia is impressive, as is the understanding of the larger implications in the League and world peace issues.

6th Paragraph: The concluding paragraph is awkwardly written. It could be strengthened by returning to the original question and emphasizing the effectiveness of the two presidents in domestic affairs and foreign policies. Instead, the student emphasizes the "aggressiveness" of the two, and concludes the essay around a concept that he used to organize his thoughts to differentiate between the two men. The original question asked for both differences and effectiveness. The student should have addressed both briefly in his conclusion.

The grade for this paper is a 12. It was a 13 or 14 before the concluding paragraph.

Grading Standards

The grading standards for this essay question are as follows:

"Theodore Roosevelt and Woodrow Wilson differed greatly, but both were effective presidents." Assess the validity of this statement by comparing Theodore Roosevelt and Woodrow Wilson as presidents.

13–15   well balanced treatment of both presidents
        excellent coverage of foreign and domestic policies
        3–4 concepts, each supported by 4–5 facts
        analyzes the question by focusing on events, personalities, programs, and
          political philosophies
        explains similarities and differences
        well written, well organized, sophisticated

10–12   balanced treatment of both presidents
        good coverage of foreign and domestic policies
        3–4 concepts, each supported by 4–5 facts
        focuses on events, personalities, programs, and political philosophies
        explains similarities and differences

7–9   some imbalance, but deals with both presidents
        may emphasize either foreign or domestic more, but mentions both
        2–3 concepts or 2 done very well, with 2–3 facts for each
        mentions some events, personalities, programs, or political philosophies
        attempts to explain similarities and differences
        may contain a few errors

4–6   imbalance, generalized treatment of both presidents, with weakness in
          regard to one president
        little consideration of either domestic or foreign for one (or both)
          presidents

little or poor conceptualization—few specific facts, weak facts, or inappropriate facts
similarities and differences muddled or not addressed
major errors—puts Federal Reserve under Roosevelt, Northern Securities under Wilson

0–3   generalized discussion, a rambling essay
conceptualization missing, few facts, little substance
major errors
rather inept

Errors startle an essay grader and raise doubts about the student's level of knowledge. Because of errors the grader no longer assumes that a general statement means what the grader had previously been giving the student credit for without explaining. An accident of haste is easy to recognize. Writing 1812 instead of 1912 is not a major error. Writing "the Guilded Age" instead of "the Gilded Age" causes chuckles. Every grader recognizes that a student is under extreme pressure.

Major errors are significant, however, and keep a student from getting above the lower end of the 7–9 category at best. Confusing the Underwood-Simmons Tariff and the Payne-Aldrich Tariff is significant if you are using the tariff issue to illustrate a major point. If you are just mentioning Wilson's attack on the "triple wall of privilege" and mislabel the tariff, the damage is less significant. Errors are evaluated within the total context of the argument in your essay. Incorrect dates, faulty chronology, and factual mistakes are not as significant as an incorrect emphasis.

A grader wonders about the student who claims that the La Follette Seamen's Act was a major part of Wilson's Progressive legislation. The grader says to himself, "Is that all you are going to mention?" The student need not worry if he or she mentions the La Follette Seamen's Act as typical of the era, as part of the Wilson administration, or as an example of Progressive legislation pushed through without strong presidential support. All three descriptions are accurate enough.

In short, there are errors and there are errors. Minor errors are not held against you, but they slow the adding of points for you. Major errors cast doubts on the essay, and cause the grader to wonder how much the student really understands. You no longer get the benefit of the doubt. Reduce your potential for errors by adequate study and clear writing.

The first set of essays contained only three essays, this one contains six. By carefully studying the differences and nuances between the six essays, you can get a better understanding of what separates an average essay from a poor one, and the excellent essay from the average.

The six essays that follow were written to answer the question below. Read the essays, then the grader's comments and the explanation of the essay standards.

"What have been the issues, successes, and failures for the women's movement since 1945?"

Fourth Student Essay

(1)   Since the 1920s, the women's movement has been a typical American reform movement and like many others, it has shared the same triumphs, setbacks, and heavy opposition. From the days of Lucretia Mott and Susan B. Anthony, the women's movement has taken different goals and routes to amend its aims. In the early 20th century, women marched in the streets just as civil rights marchers did in the 1960's amid obscentities being yelled at them, violence being perpertrated on them, hate-filled policemen and sexists cursing and kicking them, etc., however they kept pursuing at it. The methods that each of the women's movements have used have ranged from having patrons sign petitions and trying to influence high and powerful VIPs to speak on behalf of the cause just as many labor and other special interest movements have, to marching and protesting in the streets as all other groups have. The goals of the women's movement have been to achieve better and equal status in American society. They have done this by lobbying for admendments similar to the 19th admendment which gave them the right to vote. The tactics that have been common for this group have been to play off powerful opponents, in this case powerful male chauvanists and sexists to increase there own stance just as a few astute civil rights officials played off conservative Democrats and Republicans to augment their own programs and purposes. The tactics suceeding in some cases that are somewhat in concurrence with the women's movement like the 1973 Roe v. Wade decision that legalized abortion by a divided supreme court.

(2)   However, for the women's movement opposition has been a huge adversary. There are many women as well as men who feel that a women cannot and should not be granted certain priviledges as men have. Phyllis Schlafly, one of the leading anti-feminist crusaders in the country today has joined thousands of conservative men and women that have been successful enough to block ERA ratifications by the Senate more than once. Along with Schafly there were those who argued that if this women's movement was enacted, that means private facilities meaning men and women would be no more and other arguments that come into play against this movement. Overall, the women's movement like all of the other movements has as the Virginia Slims advertisement says, "come a long way, baby" but women still have many doors that are still closed off to them. But has gained much freedom that at one time was denied to them and to the movement itself.

COMMENTS ON THE FOURTH STUDENT PAPER

1st Paragraph: The student begins by digging a hole for himself. Why waste so much time on introductory material before 1945? Does the student not know enough to write on the question itself? A flag comes up in the second sentence, "to amend its aims." Whatever he means by this, it isn't clear. Oh, my, two misspellings—obscenities and perpetrated. What is "it" that women "kept pursuing at it"? Marching? Was marching an issue, success, or failure? He is straying too far from the question. The sentence on the methods of the women's movement and the previous sentence combine to suggest that this student intended to write on any reform question by generalizing about all reform movements.

Finally, a hint of substance in the sentences on goals and the Nineteenth Amendment, although he misspells amendment. The last two sentences in this paragraph are gibberish. Note the "there" and "suceeding." He seems to know that Roe v. Wade (the date is impressive) came out of a divided court, but says nothing about what this has to do with the tactics of the movement, let alone its successes or failures.

My initial reaction to this essay was to ask myself, and by implication the student, "Does it matter that you took a course in American History or that you read the textbook?" Is this not an essay you could have written the second day of school? Other than three names, a well-known court case, and the Nineteenth Amendment, what is in here that shows more than the general knowledge of any reasonably intelligent person?

It is clear that this student has basic knowledge about the topic, but little else.

2nd Paragraph: Now on to the opposition. Is opposition the same as failure? You might write the topic sentence for the paragraph using a portion of the wording of the question: "However, opposition to the women's movement doomed many of its goals to failure." The ERA was blocked in state legislatures, not in the U.S. Senate. He doesn't understand how amendments are ratified, or how to spell privileges.

Knowing Phyllis Schlafly is impressive, although he may mean two different people, based on the changing spelling. The final sentence, the last opportunity to make an impression, doesn't even have a subject! Overgeneralized and trite, this essay falls into the 1–3 range, probably a 2 because he knows some specifics.

Fifth Student Essay

(1)   The women's movement of today is very strong and very positive, however, their movement in 1945 and the 1950s had it's weak points. During the decade between the 1940s and 1950s the women's movement digressed. Fewer women were enrolled in college, fewer women were becoming Ph.D.'s. The United States, unlike many other countries, did not put a great deal of value on our children. This greatly affects the women's fight for equality because they are the sex which produces children and the child is therefore naturally linked with women. This situation is carried to a less severe case today because we know that children are the responsibility of both parents and we acknowledge this, early Americans did not. The child was the mother's.

(2)   The women's movement was helped and hindered by the feminists. Many feminists organizations were formed to help women achieve their equality, but as time progressed, the groups were beginning to be taken over by the radical feminists. This takeover drove membership down and took away from the feminists' power. The issue of abortion also played a big part in the women's movement. When a women wanted an abortion, she was supposedly killing a human life; this was her right as a woman, and since this was a woman's issue, the feminist groups must have wanted to support it. This was not necessarily true. All of this tended to drive a wedge between the feminist groups, diminishing their power and their drive to achieve equality for women. Equality for women is very important to women, but to others it was not and therefore did not receive a great deal of support.

(3)   The women's movement of today is aided greatly because of the longer life expectancy of women. In earlier years women would become old enough to have children and barely get them through college when they died. Today women have their children and get them through college and still have twenty or more years to do whatever they would like. Some pursue a career and a few even go back to

school themselves. The role of the female, as well as, her equality has come a long way since 1945, Jimmy Carter even brought up the issue of drafting women for non-combat purposes, but was turned down.

COMMENTS ON THE FIFTH STUDENT PAPER

1st Paragraph: If you learn nothing else from reading these essays and comments, please remember to answer the question that was asked. Is this paragraph an introduction to an answer, or does it focus on issues, failures, or successes? The grader can't be sure. Some facts on the women's movement are interwoven with some very elementary biology lessons, but there is little here of substance. The facts need concepts to put them in touch with the question. This paragraph gives the impression that the student may know something about this topic. She may not, however, understand the topic conceptually.

2nd Paragraph: This paragraph illustrates the essay's lack of a sense of change over time. It is almost as if the years since 1945 all have the same characteristics. There were differences among women over tactics, but this essay doesn't develop or explain them. He seems to just take them for granted. She hints that abortion was not initially an important issue for the women's movement, but he never develops the consequences for the drive for the ERA. The split among the movement's advocates was not as significant as the rise of a solid opposition bloc, the grass roots Right-to-Life Movement, which linked with anti-feminists to end the ERA just short of success. The defeat of the ERA has to be the movement's greatest failure, but we shall never know from this essay.

3rd Paragraph: This paragraph ends the essay, but it doesn't conclude the essay. Was President Carter's proposal a success or failure for the women's movement? Actually, it was never an issue for women. They never advocated the draft for women, but after the issue was raised, women's groups reluctantly supported it. So does that make it a success or failure, or a nonissue? The other information is roughly correct, but how does it relate to any concept in regard to the question?

The grade for this essay is a 4.

Sixth Student Essay

(1)   The women's movement since 1945 has gone through several stages and has often become very confused. After the Second World War, many women still worked or wanted to work, but the baby boom often led to the return of women to their homes. In the 1950s, people like Doris Day glorified and honored the housewife with her sweetness and innocence. At the same time, Marilyn Monroe convinced everyone to be as curvaceous and flirtatious as possible. Freud tried to convince women to stay home with the children, as did Dr. Spock. So many confused images for women to follow!

(2)   In the 1960s, more and more women went to college. Unfortunately, most dropped out before graduation to marry. It seems that college was the place to find a promising man for a husband.

(3)   Women had the right to vote now, and most of the everyday American women were satisfied. Of course, there are always radicals, and as was the case of Black Americans, radicals began to stir things up and the women's movement was split.

These new radical women wanted to erase the distinction between men and women. Women won the right to be drafted. This failed when President Carter called a draft and Congress wouldn't let women be drafted after Russia invaded Afghanistan. Women won the right to murder fetuses in Roe v. Wade when the Supreme Court legalized abortion. The abortion issue caused Phyllis Schafley and her anti-ERA movement to join with the Right-to Life anti-abortion movement.

(4)   By this time, most American women had dropped out of the women's movement. They had only wanted equal pay for equal work. The movement lost its momentum and is basically nonexistent today.

COMMENTS ON THE SIXTH STUDENT PAPER

This concise essay teasingly displays more understanding than it develops. This is a student who studies hard, understands the women's movement, and knows how to say much in a short space, however, this student never ties the conceptual points together. The general chronological framework is the organizational theme more than the issues, successes, or failures of the women's movement. The worst feature is the emotional reference to murder in regard to abortions. A good essayist keeps himself and his own emotions out of an essay. Think of an essay as a reasoned argument rather than an emotional argument, especially if you do not know the grader well. A good grader also keeps his emotions out of the grading process. Help him. I hope Phyllis Schlafly knows how to spell her name. Most of us do not!

This essay has too much information for the 4-6 category. It is just barely a 7.

Seventh Student Essay

(1)   The women's movement can be seen to have had its roots in the civil rights' movement activity of the 1950s and 1960s. The objective of the women's movement was by liberation a woman would gain influence and power. The way the women would gain influence and power is through their job standing. Women discovered that men, both white and black, obtained the top policy positions while women were delegated to the menial types of chores. They recognized the importance of militant, well-publicized pressure groups in an effort to bring about change. Beginning in the 1940s, America witnessed a period of transformation and readjustment. Men were being sent home from war. This conflicted with women's new task of working outside of the home. Men returned with the ideas of the wife in the home while the husbands returned back to their normal jobs. Women had enjoyed working outside of the home and many women remained in the workforce. *Generation of Vipers* stated that women in the household were stripping men of their masculinity and *Lost Generation* was stating that more women were not staying at home. Freud, on the other hand, stated that the only way women could achieve satisfaction was through childbirth. This is the belief that many women moved away from during the beginning of the women's movement. In the period of the 1950s there was the outstanding baby boom. With more children in the household, this made the decision easier for women to remain in the household. There was a large emphasis in this time period on housewife and motherhood. Some 60% of all women attending college dropped out before earning their degree. The emphasis was to go to school and find a husband. After early

marriage the women were expected to have children, and support their husbands' careers. Magazines and movies in this time period also depicted women's innocence. Women like Doris Day portraying innocence and Debbie Reynolds' sweetness was the typical stereotype of that time. Marilyn Monroe with no character was another famous actress who portrays a popular stereotype. Magazines also emphasized the housewife role. "Good Housekeeping" and "Ladies Home Journal" stressed the housewife as the hero. A new fascination with sex constructed the "Playboy" magazine. A new mode of style for clothing was also emphasized. Straight skirts, suits, shoulder pads, skinny waists, large breasts, and high heels were the new form of fashion. Women still remained at the bottom of the social scale performing their "pink collar" jobs in the clerical and secretarial areas. Women's main purpose in this time period was to play your cards right and land the right man and be his object of desire.

(2)   The 1960s brought about another change in the women's movement. At least half of all women worked. Although working in "women's jobs," they earned only 63¢ to the males' $1. The Civil Rights Act of 1964 started the prohibition of discrimination on the basis of gender. As day care centers emerged more women with preschool children remained in the outside work of the home. The National Organization for Women emphasized fair pay, equal opportunity, and also for the development of a new egalitarian form of marriage. Books like the *Feminine Mystique* offered arguments supporting women by stating that women didn't have the special ability to raise children and women don't have to stay home. The greatest impact on the feminist movement occurred with the invention of the pill. Women could now control their bodies and plan children around their lives.

(3)   The decade of 1970 to 1980 placed even more emphasis on feminism. There was a continuing struggle for existence and equal opportunity; however, the facts told a different story. More women were working but there remained no equal pay for equal work. Women were only earning only 58¢ for every $1 of their male counterpart. With the greater existence of day care, almost 45% of women with preschool children have entered the workforce. Women have also attained some political appointments. G. Ferraro ran for the vice-presidency and the first woman to be appointed to the Supreme Court, Sandra Day O'Connor, among other women in the mayoral and senatorial races. In this time period we also see a deterioration of the movement. Magazines such as MS which placed an emphasis on ideas such as abortion and forums for the improvement in the feminist movement conflicted largely with Good Housekeeping, which stressed domestic issues, house decorating, and often sexual fantasies.

(4)   With the passage of the ERA which stated equal pay for equal work and stated that no one shall be denied any rights by basis of sex the feminists from New York, who became known as radicals got a little out of control. Most of them were lesbians, communists, and socialists. They stressed that fundamental change of the individual's identity was necessary. With the decision like Roe v. Wade, which declared abortions legal, was the final dividing point among the feminists and also the declaration of the equal draft, brought the movement to somewhat of an end. Although the women's movement was never unified, until the decade of 1974 to 1984 women continued to vote their fundamental civil rights and values.

COMMENTS ON THE SEVENTH STUDENT PAPER

1st Paragraph: This verbose essay makes a grader want to get out the scissors. The first paragraph is too long. It is difficult to see the conceptual theme. The student seems to lay the groundwork for the women's movement in the Second World War and the rise of black civil rights activity. Many statements, however, just float over the page. One gets the impression that this paragraph could be cut into individual sentences and pasted together in any order. It is a collection of facts rather than a paragraph. The information is excellent and correct; but a grader can't help but feel sorry for what could have been much better said.

2nd Paragraph: This paragraph repeats the mistakes of the first. The factual information is correct, but the theme of "change" is too weak to form the paragraph around. Change in what direction, toward what, away from what, or led by whom? A much better topic sentence would read as follows: "In the 1960s many factors combined to revitalize the women's movement, with women playing a more significant role." A subtheme of the paragraph would be the accomplishments of the decade: the birth control pill, the Civil Rights Act of 1964, and the formation of the National Organization for Women. Two of these achievements, the pill and the Civil Rights Act, were not due to the women's movement. Better organization would have greatly strengthened this information. As it is, this paragraph is conceptually weak.

3rd Paragraph: The reference to feminism is puzzling. After reading the paragraph it is clear that the student should have written: "In the decade from 1970 to 1980 there was a continuing struggle for equal opportunity; however, the facts told a different story." The reference to more emphasis on feminism was not developed. The student instead paints a picture of some small victories and continuing difficulties. Again, good information in a conceptually weak paragraph.

4th Paragraph: This paragraph unravels and deteriorates. The student leaves the grader guessing. Does he really understand the issues, successes, and failures of the women's movement or has he instead merely listed events and ideas associated with the women's movement? The ERA was passed by Congress but never ratified by the required number of states. There was a New York feminist group which legally took the nickname "The Feminists" and gave the movement a radical image. Internal disputes and division over goals weakened the women's movement. He understands this, but says it poorly. What a sad way to end an essay. Compare this essay with the previous one. If we could combine this information with the previous essay's conceptualization—wow!

The grade for this essay is a 7 or an 8, depending on how the grader valued the quality of the factual information. I would call it a strong 7.

Eighth Student Essay

(1)   The women's movement since 1945 has been a successful reform movement. This can clearly be seen by evaluating the issues, failures, and the degree of success for the women's movement.

(2)   In the 1940s, women were looked upon as being the root of evil in society if they decided to get a job outside of the home. In the 1950s, women were seen as "the perfect housewife" who was willing and able to do whatever her husband and children needed her to do. This ideology has put women back many years, thus the 1960s and 1970s have been major turning points here in the United States.

(3)   Women in the United States have more rights than any other women on the globe. Still though, women have been trying to work towards the goal of "equal opportunity" in the United States. Women, to some extent have achieved this goal with such acts as the Civil Rights Act of 1964. This act was intended to give the black minority the civil rights they deserved with a stipulation of "no discrimination of race, color, or creed." The addition of "sex" gave women the leverage which they needed to band together and fight for equal rights.

(4)   The way in which women have achieved their current status is by banding together and forming organizations. NOW and ERA are both prominent organizations formed to further the advancement of women. NOW is the National Organization of Women and was created with the intent to get legislation passed for equal rights for females. ERA is the equal rights admendment, this is the admendment that was not ratified, and which would have constitutionally guaranteed women equal rights (the 5th and 14th are supposed to already guarantee this).

(5)   The Supreme Court case, Reed v. Reed was a success for women. It dealt with the distribution of an estate of a teenager in Idaho. The mother had custody of the child and therefore wanted to be executor of the estate (instead of the husband, from whom she was separated). The court found in favor of the woman.

(6)   Women have also gotten more rights and have exercised these by becoming directly involved with the political system, such as Geraldine Ferraro as a vice presidential running mate, and some have written books, such as Gloria Steinem, for the advancement of women today.

(7)   There have been hindering effects placed on women from the 1940s up to the ERA movement in present day America. The 1940s placed women at the root of problems if she entered the work force. Followers of Freud stated that women felt inferior to men, not because they didn't have equal rights, but because women wanted to be like men. The only way women could lay this envy of males to rest was to have sons.

(8)   The 1950s brought with it fiction dealing with the housewife heroine and non-fiction literature which dealt with childbearing and cooking and cleaning tips. This era also brought movie stars devoid of character (Marilyn Monroe), sweet and innocent (Debbie Reynolds), or the all-American girl (Doris Day). These stereotypes hindered the advancement from the home to the work force and instead glorified the housewife in her station wagon waiting at the train station for her husband.

(9)   Unfortunately a few left-wing radical groups such as WITCH, Women's International Terrorist Conspiracy from Hell, and COYOTE, Cut Out Your Old Tired Ethics, a group of prostitutes, and other groups called for the destruction of the national government and the family, while still others felt that women should not live with men. One organization, The Feminists, a New York radical group, with this legal nickname, was often confused with feminists who were working towards the advancement of women's issues. The typical female voter is 47 years old, and radical issues are simply not going to attract her support.

(10)   The degree of success of the women's movement has mixed responses. Women have gotten more rights than in the 1940s, both constitutionally and societal, but other incidents in recent years set back the ERA. Abortion legalization in the Supreme Court case Roe v. Wade pitted both pro-lifers and anti-ERAers together to destroy the ERA movement. The Afghanistan crisis in which women would have been drafted also set back the ERA movement. Therefore, the degree of success is mixed. Women have more time to enjoy their life now, not like the

early 1900s when a woman got married at 22, had children until 32 and died at 51. Today woman are finishing college, and instead of trying to marry a doctor, are becoming doctors themselves. In 1950 only about 40% finished college, the rest dropped out and got married. Therefore, the woman's movement since 1945 has been a successful reform movement.

COMMENTS ON THE EIGHTH STUDENT PAPER

1st Paragraph: This paragraph immediately shows this essay's major defect: the paragraphs are too short. The first two paragraphs should be joined together, as they are naturally.

3rd Paragraph: After suggesting in the first two paragraphs that he will follow a chronological approach, the student sets off on a topical approach. What he writes is correct, but it leaves the grader puzzled as to conceptual organization. One should never puzzle a grader!

4th Paragraph: In addition to organizational difficulties, the student needs help with transition. Transition is the smooth flow from one paragraph to the next. Paragraph three and paragraph four could be interchanged. Read them both ways. This should never be. Your paragraphs should logically build toward your conclusion, piling up evidence in a sequential manner. Two small errors—the spelling of amendment, and NOW, which is the National Organization *for* Women—also detract from the paragraph.

5th Paragraph: Now we are degenerating into the pleasant story pleasantly told. "And so a woman named Reed sued a man named Reed over their child's estate." So what? What is the significance of this case? That the wife won? No, no, no! This is the first Supreme Court decision in history which stated that a state law could not discriminate in favor of a male without a compelling reason. You cannot discriminate against a woman because she is a woman. What a missed opportunity to conceptually develop his argument. This paragraph should have been tied together with the second half of the fourth paragraph to develop a superb outline of the changing constitutional position for women in the 1970s. The ERA failed, but there were constitutional victories.

6th Paragraph: What is the tie between more rights and increased political awareness, or political activity, or political visibility. None of these have come about as a result of increased rights. Does this student believe that before Gloria Steinem women were not allowed to write books? Fuzzy thinking and writing fails to get you the benefit of the doubt in the grader's mind. There is no real excuse for a one sentence paragraph. Unless it is a dramatic turning point in your essay, avoid the single sentence paragraph. It belongs more to fiction writing.

7th and 8th Paragraphs: The next two paragraphs drift back to a chronological theme. The information is correct but the writing is conceptually weak. These paragraphs paint a picture more than they argue a position. Rather than "hindering effects" the student should have used stronger language. "Expectations, stereotypes, and self-image hindered the women's movement in the 1940s and 1950s." Merge the two paragraphs with this sentence replacing the first one in paragraph seven. Read it this way—it sounds much better.

9th Paragraph: "Unfortunately" in the first sentence is the only clue that the student feels that the woman's movement took a wrong turn by becoming more radical. At the end of the paragraph the grader clearly understands this, but a grader should not have to wait until the end of a paragraph to catch your conceptual point. Let's replace the single word "unfortunately" with a new sentence: "In the 1960s and 1970s the women's movement unfortunately became more radical, alienating many of its advocates and potential supporters."

10 Paragraph: The first sentence is awkward; almost any rewording will improve it. The rest of this paragraph is good, although it violates the general rule that new information should not be introduced in the concluding paragraph.

This paper is just barely a 10 due to the inconsistency in its conceptual organization. Overall, it is actually stronger.

Ninth Student Essay

(1) The women's liberation movement from 1945 to 1985 faced many issues, successes, and failures. Women were not out to change American society greatly, but were simply seeking equal status, equal pay for equal jobs, and the right to have equal access to jobs as well.

(2) In the late 1940s and early 1950s women were seen as solely housewives and mothers. Those women who wanted to leave their homes and work were looked down upon. The book, *The Generation of Vipers*, which came out in the early 1940s, said that women were trying to strip men of their masculinity. Law suits involving discrimination were lost in court because women should clearly know that their place was in the home, not outside of it. There was even a book which helped women to plan all of their household duties in such a way that they were still able to pick up their husbands at the commuter railroad station. Many women went to college to drop out and get married. In 1950, 50% of the women enrolled in college dropped out to get married. They went to college to get their MRS degree. However, at the same time there were women who left their homes to work and even liked it.

(3) One of the major forces for change in any society is technology. In the 1960s the birth control pill brought about big changes. For the first time women were able to organize and plan when they wanted to have children. They no longer had to plan their life around surprises, birth could be prevented, and this allowed a new freedom for women. Simultaneously society's morals were changing outside of marriage and sexual activity lost its former bad connotations. Women began taking advantage of the new means of birth control and many women lived alone and worked outside of the home.

(4) The women's movement achieved occasional goals in conjunction with the civil rights movement. In 1964 the Civil Rights Act passed, and this seemed to be a step in the right direction for females. Southern conservatives inserted the word "sex" into the Civil Rights Act as an amendment to the original bill to make the bill so ridiculous that it would never pass. If black civil rights couldn't be stopped, then link it to female civil rights and doom the whole idea! However, the bill passed. The Civil Rights Act gave the "go-ahead" for many cases to go to court for inequality. For example, Sally Reed was separated from her husband and was living with and taking care of their son. The son died, and the small estate went to her husband according to Idaho law. She fought this, and the U.S. Supreme Court ruled that such a law was unconstitutional. This was the first Supreme Court case that ever ruled that discrimination against women was unconstitutional.

(5) A new awareness arose among women with many new magazines emerging such as MS, which was highly feminist. Gloria Steinem, the editor of MS magazine, went as far to say that "marriage is a form of prostitution." These magazines contributed to a radicalization in the women's movement.

(6)   In 1979 President Jimmy Carter tried to pass a law which would allow the United States to draft women into the army. If women wanted to be equal, then we might as well take them up on it. Here is another example where women started to get themselves into issues which they did not initiate, and once again, as with Roe v. Wade, the women's movement started to lose many followers. The draft was not passed, but it initiated a change of heart in more conservative women.

(7)   By the mid 1960s the women's movement started to become a radical movement, just like what happened to the blacks, and many conservative women dropped out. Radical groups such as COYOTE, Cut Out Your Old Tired Ethics, WITCH, Women's International Terrorist Conspiracy from Hell, and the New York Radical Women, who were nicknamed "The Feminists," were started. It seemed that the women's movement had turned into a movement of lesbians, socialists, and radicals.

(8)   A curious characteristic of the women's movement was that many of its successes and failures had little to do with the actions of the organized women's movement. For example, abortion had never been much of an issue. But, once the Supreme Court ruled in Roe v. Wade that women had the right to abortions during the first six months of pregnancy, the movement had to endorse the ruling because it philosophically fell under their abstract assertions that women had the right to control their own lives. Out of the opposition to the abortion decision emerged the Pro-Life Movement which linked up to Phyllis Schlafly's anti-ERA organization to create a formidable opponent for the now narrowly defined and radical women's movement.

(9)   Yes, women have come a long way, but it is still a fact that college graduates who are women receive less income than high school graduates who are men. And, furthermore, for the same job, the same qualifications, men receive higher incomes than women. Overall, women had many successes, then faced with unexpected issues the movement turned radical, and radicalism, simply, isn't the answer.

COMMENTS ON THE NINTH STUDENT PAPER

1st Paragraph: This introductory paragraph needs to be strengthened and lengthened somewhat. He gives the impression that he will concentrate on equal status, equal pay, and equal access. But the following paragraphs do not develop these themes. Instead, the next three paragraphs emphasize self-image, the role of technology, and the parallel influence of the civil rights movement. This paragraph needs one more sentence, such as: "The early women's movement fought off the image of the dutiful housewife and was stimulated by two concurrent but unrelated developments: the invention of the birth control pill and the growth of civil rights for blacks."

2nd, 3rd, and 4th Paragraphs: Some excess verbiage pads these paragraphs, but they are well done.

5th Paragraph: This looks like the paragraph of a student who has just panicked because he glanced at the clock. This paragraph would be better joined to the seventh paragraph. Note the similar themes of the radicalization of the movement.

6th Paragraph: Buried in the middle of this paragraph is a profound concept that should have been the conceptual focus. It is the idea that the women's movement became entangled in issues not on their agenda. Both abortion and the draft were two such issues that alienated many conservative and moderate supporters. This paragraph is poorly constructed. Before you write any paragraph always ask yourself—what is my conceptual point and how am I going to prove it?

8th Paragraph: This paragraph and paragraph six should be merged. Note the clear conceptual statement alluded to in paragraph six.

9th Paragraph: Not a bad ending; he sees some successes, some failures, and yet some issues remain.

This is clearly the best paper. It is a strong 12. A few small improvements would have easily pushed it into the 13-15 category.

Grading Standards

The grading standards for this essay question are as follows:

"What have been the issues, successes, and failures for the women's movement since 1945?"

13-15   well balanced treatment which explicitly addresses all three concepts—issues, successes, and failures
uses 4-5 facts to support each concept
analyzes the question by focusing on changes over time and cause and effect and nuances in successes and failures
comprehensive coverage of the whole period
well written, well organized, sophisticated

10-12   balanced treatment which addresses all three concepts—issues, successes, and failures
uses 4-5 facts to support each concept
focuses on changes over time, cause and effect
covers the whole period

7-9   may be imbalanced, may explicitly or implicitly address all three concepts
uses 2-3 facts
limited awareness of changes over time and cause and effect
may superficially cover some parts of the 1945-to-the-present period
may contain minor errors of fact not significant to the essay

4-6   imbalanced, generalized treatment of the question
may not address, even implicitly, one of the concepts
conceptually weak
few specific facts, weak facts, or inappropriate facts
major errors of fact

1-3   generalized discussion of the question
conceptualization missing, few facts, little substance
major errors
rather inept

Don't make the mistake of assuming that an essay grader merely counts the number of facts in an essay. The standards use phrases such as "2-3 facts." But some facts are better than others. Some are more appropriate than others. Some illustrate a point better than others.

What counts is the way in which the facts support the particular conceptual argument you are making in that paragraph. An essay is an argument. A paragraph is part of your overall argument. A fact is a descriptive illustration to buttress that particular part of your overall argument. An essay grader does not simply count the facts in an essay. Each fact is evaluated within the context of the paragraph. Don't assume that the grader will understand the connection between the Boston Massacre and the beginning of the Revolutionary War. You assume that responsibility.

THE NINE TYPES OF
HISTORY ESSAY
QUESTION

1. Change Over Time

Example: "The period from 1783 to 1815 was a period of evolution to economic maturity for the infant United States. Assess the validity of this view."

This type of question asks you to measure the degree of change over a period of time. First ascertain what you are assessing. Next identify the key words. Did other major events occur within these dates that had an impact on the period? Why did the question select these dates? Do they mark turning points, beginnings, ends, dramatic shifts, or a convenient time period? Remember to cover the entire period of the question. If it asks for 1783–1815, do not concentrate on the 1790s. Change over time assumes that something changed over the time period. It is possible some ideas or policies did not change.

Example: "Between 1790 and 1870 the economic growth of the United States was significantly stimulated by governmental aid. Assess the validity of this statement."

What is meant by governmental aid—tariffs, internal improvements, public land policy, land grants to railroads, subsidies, Bank of the U.S., etc.? The key words are the dates, economic growth, stimulated, and governmental aid. Why pick these dates? What is meant by stimulated? What governments are involved—state, local, or national? What does the phrase, economic growth, mean? Was the stimulus uneven, sporadic, or even counterproductive? Why the use of "significantly?" Could the governmental aid have been insignificant? Were factors at work stimulating the economy other than governmental aid?

2. Cause and Effect

Example: "Why did the United States enter the First World War?"

In this question be sure to balance immediate and long range causes. How are the causes related? Can you group them under broad ideas? An essay on the American entry into the First World War should not begin with the German resumption of unrestricted submarine warfare in January, 1917, but do not find causes too far back in history. If you blame the initial arrival of blacks in 1619 for the Civil War, you have given yourself the responsibility for filling in the years between 1619 and 1861.

Nothing is so simple that it has one cause. Always answer cause and effect questions with multiple causation. Rank the relative importance of the causes and explain your choice. Include the consequences of ideas, actions, and events to emphasize the effect. A discussion of the causes of the Civil War should conclude that it resolved the dilemma of slavery in the territories. Remember feedback from the effect to the cause. The original system for electing the president produced the tie vote in the electoral college of 1800. The procedure changed. The 1800 election result ended that cause of a tie in future electoral college votes.

Example: "What caused the Civil War?"

Think of broad categories for causes and decide which categories to emphasize and which facts to emphasize within each category. A good answer considers the following: slavery in the territories; the clash of economic systems; Southern nationalism versus Northern dominance; race, slavery, and the future of blacks in America; Northern abolitionism and Southern reaction; and the failure of democracy or the triumph of democracy. Conclude your essay with a look at the broad issues resolved by the Civil War and a peek at new issues raised by the struggle.

3. Compare and Contrast

Example: "Compare and contrast Jacksonian Democracy and Jeffersonian Democracy."

To contrast is to compare with respect to differences. "Compare" emphasizes likenesses over differences. In a sense, therefore, "compare and contrast" is redundant. No matter how the question is phrased, though, the student must include both similarities and differences in a "compare," "contrast," or "compare and contrast" question. Often students concentrate on only half of the question. Ask yourself what is comparable among the choices given. Are there obvious differences or similarities? Do you organize the answer by developing a description of each separately or by linking both for each concept? A fresh approach is needed if the question is phrased in a manner you never considered. For example, compare Jacksonian Democracy and Populism, or compare and contrast colonial immigration with 19th century immigration.

Example: "Compare and contrast three colonies—Virginia, Pennsylvania, and Massachusetts."

Create a list of conceptual comparisons. Decide which are the most important and defend them well. You should consider the following: motives of the founders; influence of climate and geography; economies; political systems; closeness to the British colonial ideal; religions; morals; social structure; and education systems. All of these conceptual ideas are significant enough to require a separate paragraph. Some should be grouped together, however, according to the wording of the question, your degree of knowledge, and the amount of time. Two paragraphs that cover religion and the economy merely introduce the subject. Strive for a broad range of concepts to compare and contrast.

4. Define and Identify

Example: "Discuss Jacksonian Democracy."

Ask yourself what were the traits, leaders, characteristics, origins, results, or issues involved. A define and identify question is often worded as "describe" or "discuss." "Discuss Jacksonian

Democracy" does not mean telling a series of pleasant stories about Jackson. Zero in, and define and identify Jacksonian Democracy through its origins, leaders, characteristics, issues, and policies. Sometimes a define and identify question is limited to one or two qualities. To answer the question, "What were the characteristics of colonial religion?" you must identify, define, and explain the characteristics. In response to the question, "What were the results of Reconstruction?" you should carefully define Reconstruction, and include the issues that had an impact on the results of Reconstruction.

Of all the possible wordings that are used, "define and identify" most easily degenerates into a pleasant narrative. Remember that defining and describing means ranking and explaining the traits, characteristics, results, issues, origins, or leaders. Jackson's attack on the Bank of the United States may be a symbol of Jacksonian Democracy or an aberration. To write that Jackson attacked the Bank is not enough. Why did he, what did he or his supporters gain, and what beliefs did the attack illustrate?

5. Statement, React to It

Example: "Presidents are rarely successful in both foreign and domestic policy. Assess the validity of this statement."

These questions are usually worded as statements followed by either "explain," or "assess the validity." You may react to the statement as valid, invalid, or partially valid. Avoid the trap of the simplistic answer which blandly declares with little support the statement valid or invalid. The best answers select the partially valid choice, address the opposite position, or state a strong support.

Example: "Slavery was the sole cause of the Civil War. Evaluate this statement."

If you defend the statement, define slavery broadly and consider its ramifications broadly. The best essays discuss slavery as one cause and then discuss other causes. Remember to look for key words in the statement. In this example it is "sole." If you disagree with the statement, do not write an analysis of the causes of the Civil War and ignore the issue of slavery. You may justify other causes, but do not neglect slavery as a cause.

6. Evaluation

Example: "Pick three of the following and evaluate their effectiveness as political leaders.

George Washington	Henry Clay
John C. Calhoun	John Quincy Adams
Thomas Jefferson	Daniel Webster"

Evaluation questions are worded as "evaluate," "assess the significance," or "assess the validity." You control your answer because you determine the conceptual criteria and factual support. A quick path to an "F" on this essay is to write in the "it was good, it was really good, or it was bad" mode. "Evaluate" or "assess" demands an evaluation, not an evasion. "Evaluate Jacksonian Democracy" means that you decide what criteria to use to evaluate Jacksonian Democracy. Do not glibly stamp Jacksonian Democracy as "good."

Example: "Was colonial society democratic?"

You must first deal with the ambiguous word democratic. Carefully create a workable definition of democracy. Next, identify conceptual categories for your evaluation of colonial democracy—religious, political, social, economic. A good essay suggests that some aspects of colonial society were democratic, some were not, and changes occurred throughout the colonial period.

7. A Statement From a Particular Viewpoint

Example: "Defend British policies during the period from 1763 to 1776."

The secret to this question is to place yourself in the asked-for position. In order to do that you must clearly understand the view stated and be able to defend it. These questions frequently confuse students momentarily because the question may be worded in a manner that the student has never considered.

Example: "According to a radical historian, what have been the foreign policy objectives of the United States in the twentieth century?"

Do you know the basic tenets of the radical critique of American foreign policy? If so, this may be easy; otherwise . . . ! An answer to this question emphasizes the aggressive, expansionist, and imperialistic nature of our foreign policy, the elite control of decision making, our anti-democratic posture, and our internal oppression of workers and minorities. Even if you disagree with the radical critique of our foreign policy, do not forget that your primary purpose is to answer the question. The question tests your knowledge, not your patriotism. Do not make the mistake of writing a critique of the radical critique instead of answering the question. Add a statement to your conclusion that gives your opinion in a discreet manner if you wish. For example, write, "The radical critique of 20th century foreign policy more aptly applies to communist nations than to the United States."

8. Given Framework

Example: "The powers of the President grew because of war and foreign crises. Evaluate this statement."

A given-framework question limits your range of conceptualization because you must write within the defined framework. Otherwise, a long essay proudly submitted may be returned with a single terse comment, "You failed to answer the question." You may disagree with the statement that the powers of the President have expanded because of war and foreign crises, but that places upon you the burden of showing that war and foreign crises did *not* cause the growth of presidential power. You cannot answer the question by stating the opposite, that domestic problems are the primary cause for the growth of presidential power. That approach fails to address the question.

Example: "The United States displayed all the typical characteristics of a new nation during the early republic, 1789–1823. Assess the validity of this view."

This framework suggests that the experiences of the infant United States have a modern counterpart in the nascent nations of the Third World. Either make a brief reference to new Third World nations in your conclusion or introduction or sprinkle remarks throughout your essay. An adequate answer includes the attempts to avoid superpower struggles, to expand the economy, to achieve neutrality, to spread our unique ideology, and to expand our territory.

9. Problem–Solution

Example: "What causes of the Civil War were resolved by the Civil War and Reconstruction?"

In a problem–solution question a defined problem leads to a proposed solution that then resolves the problem, generates new problems, or both. The chief difficulty for a student is accurately identifying the relationship between the problem and the solution. The second difficulty is judging if the solution resolved the issue.

Example: "The Progressive movement solved problems that rose from industrialization. Discuss this statement."

What aspects of the Progressive movement concerned themselves with industrialization? An adequate answer includes political manipulation of legislatures, inspection of products, safety of workers, maldistribution of wealth, neutrality in labor disputes, control of Wall Street, antitrust, etc. In an essay you should evaluate the solutions, and identify those that were successful and those which led to new problems, such as meat inspection laws aiding the consolidation of the meat-packing industry.

HISTORIOGRAPHY AND
THE ESSAY

Two historians using the same facts may come to two different interpretations of a historical event. Contemporary British and American views of the battles of Lexington and Concord would obviously differ because the two sides held different assumptions. Any two historians several years later also hold different assumptions, and produce different historical accounts. Decades later other historians declare that the previous historians only perceived part of the truth. Generation after generation rewrites history, and theoretically comes closer to the truth. In actuality each historian reflects his time. The study of changing historical interpretations, shifting emphasis, and different methodologies is called historiography.

Students in survey courses need to know some historiography, but should never sacrifice a firm grounding in the fundamental facts and concepts of American history for more depth in historiography. You run the risk of name-dropping in your writing, and of citing authoritative sources as a substitute for your own analysis. To explain the breakdown of the federal political system in the 1850s is better than to state, "Craven blames the coming of the Civil War on the breakdown of the political system." How? When? Where? As shown by?

Historiography helps you to understand the assumptions behind the conceptual statements made by historians. For instance, many intellectuals were distressed by the inability to secure a peaceful world after the First World War. Disillusioned by war as a means of obtaining any political or diplomatic goal, they reasoned that war itself was often unnecessary and counterproductive. Historians with these assumptions found in the 1850s a "blundering generation" of politicians who were too stupid and petty to avoid the needless tragedy of the Civil War. The Second World War taught a different lesson. Some evils are so monstrous, they stated, that society is justified in suffering great numbers of casualties in order to eradicate the evil. Hitler was such an evil, and slavery was also. The Civil War tragedy of 600,000 dead soldiers, formerly perceived as having died needlessly, became the triumph over a monstrous evil. They did not die in vain. Nothing about the ending of slavery was unnecessary or blundering.

The summaries that follow explain the chronology and assumptions underlying three schools of historiography concerning domestic politics (Progressive, Consensus, and New Left), and three schools of historiography for foreign policies (Nationalist, Realist, and Radical). Be leery of a fatal trap for students: Summarizing a historian's viewpoint in one or two sentences is impossible. Include historiography in your writing if you wish, but don't substitute it for your own analysis. Use historiography to support your arguments. Remember that historians hold varying opinions of the correctness of other historians' ideas. Unless the question directly asks about historiography, make it a minor part of your essay if you use it at all.

Progressive Historiography

Three different schools of historians have emerged in the 20th century. The first, the Progressive school, named for the Progressive reform era, dominated historiography from the early 20th century to the end of the Second World War. Like the writings of most intellectuals, the themes of the Progressive historians reflected the issues and concerns of their time. The Progressive movement was a collection of reforms designed to adjust to changes brought on by industrialization and urbanization. A second influence upon these historians was the rise of the social sciences—economics, sociology, psychology, etc.—as separate fields of study. Historians borrowed heavily from these new fields for insights into history, correcting what they saw as the overemphasis on political history. Progressive historians hoped for the social and political betterment of the society of their time, and made no effort to hide their loyalties. They championed liberal, democratic, and progressive ideas and causes. The solution to almost every problem was more democracy, and the way to the golden age was through the secret ballot. The people would prevail because they were the embodiment of goodness. Finally, to the basic assumptions of the Progressive historians add one philosophical characteristic of the era, a belief in progress.

Progressive historians stressed the differences between competing groups, sections, and classes. American society was an arena of competing social and economic forces. First one, then the other gained control in cycles of reform and reaction. The dominant theme was class and sectional conflict. Clearly defined turning points marked the ascension of one group and the defeat of the other. All of the following were used to represent our polarized history: rich vs. poor, interests vs. people, haves vs. have-nots, privileged vs. less privileged, aristocracy vs. democracy, debtors vs. creditors, East vs. South and West, labor vs. big business, Jeffersonianism vs. Hamiltonianism, democracy vs. oligarchy, liberalism vs. conservatism, and agrarianism vs. capitalism.

The central role in American history was played by the frontier or by social forces or by economic forces. Historian Frederick Jackson Turner stressed "The Significance of the Frontier in American History." Carl Becker argued that the American Revolution was a question of home rule and who shall rule at home. The colonists revolted from Great Britain and fought among themselves for control of the new American governmental institutions. The Constitution marked the temporary victory of the conservatives over the democrats, temporary in the sense that the struggle was to resurface in American history again and again.

The most famous Progressive historian was Charles Beard. In 1913 Beard shocked conservatives with his *An Economic Interpretation of the Constitution*, which asserted that the Constitution represented the triumph of large property interests over the interests of small farmers. The Constitution that every school child was taught to revere was antidemocratic. No scholarly historical book had ever provoked the debate Beard's did. He carefully worded the title of his book, using "An" rather than "The." He accepted the possibility that he may not have researched and written "The" definitive economic explanation of the origins of the Constitution. Therefore he used "An," allowing "The" for future use. Whatever definitive explanation a future historian would make would be economic. Of that Beard was certain.

Consensus Historiography

After the Second World War a new school emerged of historians who stressed that the shared ideas of Americans were more important in our history than conflicts among them. They believed that Americans possessed a much narrower range of divisive issues and conflicts compared with other peoples of the world. We had had conflicts, but our domestic disputes had never approached the nastiness of European uprisings and revolutions. The bloody reign of terror in the French Revolution had no comparable American counterpart. Patriots battled Tories during the American Revolution, but not with guillotines.

The Consensus historians, or Neoconservatives as they were sometimes called, unabashedly celebrated the accomplishments and achievements of American democratic capitalism. A key word used to describe them is continuity. They rejected much of the periodicalization of American history, and studied ideas that crossed over the typical political periods. Consensus historians saw in American culture common traits, expressed in the longevity and durability of our institutions. In a world of constantly changing political ideas, governments, and constitutions, they asked, why has our political system endured? Dumb luck? No, features in the American national character have shaped our history, and given it a unique stability and homogeneity. The cement holding us together is our widespread prosperity and universal acceptance of the principles succinctly summarized in the first parts of the Declaration of Independence and the Constitution.

Consensus historians believed that American society by the 1950s had achieved an unmatched state of widely dispersed affluence. In short, we had no have-nots, or so few that they were insignificant in our history. Political power had always been widespread because of liberal suffrage laws. Americans fought through the ballot, not to achieve the ballot. As a people we all endorse the same egalitarian fundamentals, they said. Our political struggles have always been within the center rather than between left and right extremists.

Consensus analysis of economic forces ignored the emphasis by Progressive historians upon the role of individuals. For them institutional factors shaped and molded our economy. The Robber Barons became entrepreneurs, innovators in new fields. Men like Rockefeller and Carnegie brought order to the chaos of oil refining and steel production. Their methods may have led to monopoly, but they also led to efficiency. Carnegie, for example, lowered the price of steel from seventy-five dollars a ton to fourteen dollars. What passes for conflict between the haves and have-nots in American history is really competition between competing groups of businessmen or entrepreneurs.

For the Progressive historian the struggle for political power was the struggle for control of the one institution, the federal government, capable of giving one group of entrepreneurs an advantage over another. Raising or lowering the tariff helped or hurt depending upon your economic interests. Approaching from a different level of economic analysis, Consensus historians ignored individuals to concentrate upon the larger economic factors such as the growth of urban markets, the rise of research and development, the rise of the corporate organization, and the rise of advertising.

Much of their political writing directly or indirectly tried to address a perplexing question of American society. Every industrial nation has developed a strong worker, labor, or socialist political party or parties. Why not us? Louis Hartz suggested that American political development took place within the framework of the ideas of European politics but outside their actual conditions. The debates between our liberals and conservatives were really debates among liberals because we had never had the extreme conservatives and leftists of Europe. We don't have deeply felt political issues, he said, because we don't have deep political thought on either end. In this past year, how many evenings did you spend intensely discussing political issues? Constant political discussion sharpens differences, clarifies thinking, and leads to more deeply held convictions. Our political culture doesn't generate truly divisive issues, because we disagree on only minor questions of ends or means, according to Hartz. Daniel Boorstin has suggested that Americans are not an idea-oriented people. The key to understanding American society is pragmatism. We don't think, we do.

Critics disliked several features of Consensus historiography. Their writings perpetuated the myth of American uniqueness that carried with it the implication of superiority. There was little need to study other nations. The history of the United States developed the way it did only because of Americans. In defense of the Consensus historians, consider the impact of both the Second World War and the rise of the Cold War upon intellectuals. Without our superb arsenal of industry we would have never won the Second World War. Thank God for

Rockefeller and Carnegie. Our moral and economic superiority over the communists was a self-evident truth in the 1950s.

In the Consensus view ideas of pragmatism, abundance, and liberalism had a life of their own. They never sprang from, or were associated with, any class struggle or decisive event. The interesting parts of American history were missing. The peaks and valleys of American history were smoothed out by the single-theme emphases.

Finally, if man is not influenced by economic needs and desires, what motivates him? What causes him to join a group to contest the control of the political apparatus? Richard Hofstadter's *The Age of Reform* suggested that concern over rising or declining status, or "status anxieties," lay behind the irrational addiction to Populism, Prohibition, and McCarthyism. Consensus historians borrowed from the social sciences even more than had the Progressives to explain motives. They occasionally selected complex and controversial theories upon which to base their explanations. Many psychologists do not share Hofstadter's faith in borrowed theories of status. Even a lifetime may not be enough to master an academic field such as history. Borrowing from another academic field carries risks, but also may offer unusual insights.

New Left Historiography

Great changes accompanied America's transition into the 1960s. The 1950s had been characterized by a general agreement on national goals, by a secure self-confidence, and by an easy categorization of other nations into good guys and bad guys. In the late 1950s our smug self-assurance dissolved in successive waves of polarization over the issues of racism, imperialism, and poverty. The seeming reemergence of conflict in current events stimulated a reexamination of conflict in American history.

The new champions of the theme of conflict in our history constituted an approach termed the "New Left." The "new" theoretically differentiates them from the unimaginative, Socialist Party orientation of the old left of the 1930s and 1940s. The "left" signifies an orientation towards methods and concepts that focus on the masses and their experiences, "history from the bottom up," as it is called. Unlike the old left, the New Left avoids the preconceived molds of Marxist theories, which distorted the facts to fit a foreign doctrine. The historians of the New Left demand the inclusion of those features of our history that explain how we came to be a violent, racist, repressive society. We don't need imported 19th century theories to find what is discreditable in our history because we have plenty if we don't mince words. We need a "usable past," one that realistically includes all of our bad features. We need to break from the textbook view of American history. Otherwise we can't begin to understand and deal with the poverty, racism, and repression of today.

The renewed emphasis on conflict and polarization was fed by the civil rights struggle. Early New Left historians wrote on the depth of American racism and the pervasiveness of slavery. The rediscovery of poverty and the War on Poverty of Lyndon Johnson's administration both stemmed from the same source, Michael Harrington's *The Other America,* a detailed look at scenes unknown to most middle- and upper-class Americans. Unrest over the draft and the war in Vietnam, impatience with the pace of civil rights, and the examples of political assassinations combined to produce explosions of violence in the cities in the 1960s. The final ingredient convulsing American society was the emergence of the women's movement. Women and minorities destroyed the homogenized image of "consensus" America. The new emphasis was on our pluralism, the existence of many different peoples, ethnic groups, and races. Each aspect of this pluralism deserved representation in our history. We are not a melting pot, but a stew of race, class, gender, and ethnicity.

Diplomatic Historiography: Nationalists

All nations pursue foreign policy objectives consistent with their own self-interest. Foreign policy is normally an offshoot of domestic policies, needs, and goals. You are already familiar with the Nationalist approach, for it is found in almost every textbook. Nationalist historians believe that American foreign policy combines a realistic concept of self-interest with generous support of other nations' goals of democracy, self-determination, and economic prosperity. A commitment to high ideals characterizes a successful foreign policy, a record of which we should be proud.

After the American Revolution Lafayette returned to France with a framed copy of the Declaration of Independence. He placed it off center on a wall. The empty space was reserved for a hoped-for French document granting similar rights. In similar fashion our Declaration of Independence and Constitution have inspired people all over the world and well they should, for these documents epitomize the aspirations of all mankind, not just Americans. Our foreign policy has given expression and substance to these ideas, a record of unselfish idealism unequaled in the history of the world.

We have, admit the Nationalists, made a few mistakes in our foreign policy, such as taking the Philippines and keeping it as a colony. But we rectified our error by generously preparing it for independence and economic stability. We built roads, bridges, schools, etc. Independence came on July 4, 1946, symbolizing the aspiration of all people of the world for self-rule. We may have been an imperialist power, but we were a good imperialist power, prepared from the start for the eventual end of our control.

The assumptions underlying the Nationalist evaluation of American foreign policy were succinctly summarized by a European newspaper during the celebration of the United States bicentennial. The newspaper confessed that although it had often been critical of the United States, what the world needed was more rather than fewer countries like the United States of America.

Diplomatic Historiography: Realists

The Realist school of historical interpretation emerged as a criticism of what it saw as wide swings in 20th century foreign policy. We sought to "make the world safe for democracy" during the First World War. Ten years later we rejected world leadership and withdrew into a cocoon of isolationism. Both extreme swings, say the Realists, were not in our best self-interest. The United States has too often regarded itself as a special nation not bound by the same rules and consequences as others. Our victory in the Spanish-American War was due to God, claimed McKinley and many history books. Realist historians are more apt to accept Bismarck's contemporary analysis, "God watches over fools, drunks, and the United States of America." We were lucky!

Realists criticize both the assumptions behind American foreign policy and the mechanism for conducting it. The American people have mistakenly assumed that much of our history turned out the way it did because we wanted it to. We avoided European wars in the 19th century because we chose to stay out. Actually, none were fought. The long period of peace in our history is abnormal, considering the history of other nations. The safe 19th century and the security of two oceans gave us the erroneous opinion that war was abnormal and peace normal. Therefore, any interruption of peace is due to evil people, nations, or isms.

We don't fight wars; we cleanse the world of evil. For foolish, idealistic, and moral reasons we periodically go on crusades like the knights of old. Our success rate is better than theirs, but the consequences may be worse.

Realists castigate American foreign policy for ignoring the timeless lessons of history. The key element preserving the peace among nations is a balance of power, in which every nation's existence is maintained in a shifting, interlocking stability of conflict and tension. Wars occasionally break out, but they are always limited to a nation's foreign policy objectives, which stem from her self-interests. A nation goes to war to gain territory, protect markets, etc., not just to win. War is not the same as the World Series. The United States, claim the Realists, too often goes to war to win, and forgets objectives consistent with its own self-interest.

One of the great mistakes of war is unconditional surrender. It creates power vacuums and sucks us into future conflicts. Before the Second World War Japan kept order in the Far East. Since the Second World War we have, in Korea, in Vietnam, in Taiwan, and with mammoth military defense budgets. Has Japan suffered from no longer shouldering this burden? Please notice what is missing in this analysis. There are no statements of right and wrong, moral and immoral, good and evil. Realists reject this line of thought. We can't right every wrong, defend everyone, and correct all injustice. So we simply do what is best for us. A chastised Japan would have been better for the U.S. than a defeated Japan.

Our sense of specialness has led us to believe that we are an example to the world. Our political practices, economic prosperity, and eternal ideals place us above the normal fray of shortsighted nations. For example, the Soviet Union speaks for the Soviet Union only; we speak for all mankind. We have been shocked on occasions in the 20th century to discover that some people did not understand how special we are. Stung by criticism, we have withdrawn. This vacillation between intense moralistic crusades and indifferent, self-righteous isolation characterizes our foreign policy. The only way to avoid such swings is to remove the masses and emotion from the decision-making process.

Realists boldly assert that foreign policy is not a matter for public debate. The self-interest goals of any nation clearly establish themselves. The conduct of foreign policy should rest in the hands of professional diplomats who coldly assess the immediate and the long-range consequences of potential policies, and keep in mind the self-interest goals of all the nations involved in a dispute. Realists accept the world as it is and suggest realistic policies. The difficulty for Realists lies in the fact that democracies do occasionally become emotionally aroused. Sometimes the leaders of a government mold public opinion, but sometimes they are moved by it.

Diplomatic Historiography: Radicals

Radical diplomatic historians believe that American foreign policy is controlled by our industrial and economic elite who guide our foreign policies in order to gain new economic markets and resources. In the process the public is manipulated, misled, or propagandized into believing that foreign policy objectives are matters of national rather than corporate or elite concern. The rallying cry of democratic ideals and national security masks the real purpose. The masses fight; the elite gains.

In the 19th century the blood lust for land and resources swept away Mexicans, Indians, and Spaniards. The enlargement of national territory was imperialism, the grabbing of colonies, in disguise. As the 20th century dawned, a new type of imperialism sought to establish economic hegemony over the Caribbean and Latin America. Occasionally U.S. military might has protected American business adventures abroad. By the middle of the 20th century the United States expanded, and influenced or controlled vast areas of the world for markets and resources. Businessmen do not like instability. Thus, say Radical historians, the economic power elite has enlisted the United States government in its efforts to prevent small nations from controlling their own resources or from keeping these resources to themselves. The United States, claim the Radical historians, is now the opposite of what it was in its beginning. It is now the most antiprogressive and antirevolutionary nation in the world. The Declaration of Independence has been shelved.

What has caused the United States to assume this stance? Foreign policies stem from domestic needs, goals, and images. Radical historians feel primarily that our foreign policies mirror our domestic policies and distract attention from the real issues. What we need is a domestic policy that seeks solutions to the plight of our deprived and disadvantaged classes. We must reduce the power of the elite to provide more for the lower classes. By redistributing income within the United States the domestic economy could absorb the goods produced by our economy for foreign markets, and make much of our imperialism unnecessary.

Radical historians are not Marxists, but they accept the tone and direction of leftist writers. The raw power of the upper classes within American domestic politics is muted, but shines through in the execution of our foreign policy; they say. If you seek the extent to which the power elite will go to enhance or maintain their position, study American foreign policy; it reveals the worst features of the elite control of American society.

As students of history it is important that you understand the difficulties facing Radical historians. To my knowledge no Radical historian has ever found a letter or document written by a member of the power elite establishing a clear relationship between the adoption of a specific foreign policy and the economic objectives of a specific corporation or business. Their case would benefit greatly from a 1940 letter, say, to the stockholders by a major steel corporation urging a flood of letters to their congressmen asking for war in order to increase stock dividends. An old adage among historians is "no documents, no proof, no history." Without documents history writing cannot be supported on the minute, footnote level.

Radicals, however, sense an overall tone and orientation toward American society which is expressed in most of our institutions such as churches, corporations, governments, universities, foundations, etc. It is this larger feel for American society upon which their historical assumptions rest.

Radical historians have been influenced by Lenin's adaptation of Marx's theory of class struggle. Marx postulated a capitalist society in which the capitalists would progressively squeeze the workers through longer hours and lower pay, which would lead to more and more dissatisfaction. Eventually the workers would revolt in a great socialist revolution, end capitalism, and inaugurate socialism. This two-sentence summary of Marx's writings is quite oversimplified! In many ways Marx was a prisoner of his time, the mid 19th century. What he did not foresee was the rise of the middle class, the development of labor unions, and the growth of the welfare state, all of which undermined Marx's prophecy.

Early in the twentieth century, Lenin, who later led the Russian communist revolution, added to Marx's scenario of revolution. Lenin theorized that the capitalists, sensing a rising cauldron of trouble, would try to divert domestic dissatisfaction by pursuing an imperialistic foreign policy in the hope that nationalism would suffocate worker dissatisfaction. Imperialism therefore is not just the greedy thrust of the power elite, but represents the dying gasp of the capitalist class who clutch at straws as they sink lower and lower into the consequences of the mess they themselves created and into a defeat they cannot avoid. To a sincere Marxist capitalist imperialism is an encouraging sign that the capitalist society can no longer sufficiently suppress its own workers. Now you understand why so much communist propaganda criticizing the United States uses the phrase "imperialist."

Hardly any American Radical historian is a Marxist. As a group, however, they do share a belief that American society has been too little concerned with the disadvantaged and too much concerned with an aggressive foreign policy. The key word is aggressive. Firm believers in protecting American society and protecting American interests, they argue that a more peaceful, understanding, and cooperative foreign policy must replace the policies we have historically pursued. Their general criticisms of our foreign policy are clearer than their specific prescriptions for what they would do if they could determine our foreign policy. Only a small number of historians of American foreign policy are Radical historians, but their influence exceeds their number. They force all students of history to think, to defend, to analyze, and to reexamine. Any scholar must understand the arguments of the other side. Understanding the assumptions of Radical historians doesn't make you a radical, just as understanding a football playbook doesn't make you a football player.

Always be alert to the philosophical assumptions an author may have. This short summary of the schools of historiography will help you analyze writings by historians.

THE ESSENTIALS
OF
AMERICAN HISTORY

How To Use This Chapter

The units that follow break American history into ten chronological time periods: 1607–1763, 1763–1783, 1783–1800, 1800–1840, 1840–1877, 1865–1900, 1900–1920, 1920–1940, 1940–1960, and 1960 to the present. An additional unit discusses the Constitution.

Each unit begins with the *Major Themes and Ideas* for that period. These themes come from former AP essay questions and the traditional essay questions historians associate with the era. You should be able to write an essay on at least three or four themes under each subsection of the *Major Themes and Ideas*. The themes and ideas are the concepts you must understand in order to be able to grasp the significant issues of the era.

Next comes the *Major Terms and Concepts* for the unit. This is the key factual information for the period. Learn these terms, but not in a mere recognition manner. To know that Langston Hughes was a black poet is not enough. When did he write? What did he write? What is his significance? Constantly ask questions as you go through each term under the *Major Terms and Concepts*. Your goal is to acquire enough understanding and knowledge to be able to organize your thoughts and to explain a point of view in an essay. Few of the AP multiple-choice questions are recognition questions. Most require extensive knowledge and understanding of the terms and concepts involved.

The next section gives brief summaries of the *Supreme Court Cases to Know*. The Court cases often focus on the issues of the era, and illuminate these issues because of the Court's need to come to a decision.

Readings for Depth and Historical Interpretation provides a short bibliography of readings. You do not have time for an extensive list. This carefully developed list balances depth and interpretation. It was not compiled in the same manner as a bibliography for a term paper. These lists give you the depth needed for a deeper understanding of the conceptual issues for the period under study. Neither extensive nor exhaustive, the list is just very useful.

Each unit ends with a *Sample Outline* that illustrates what to do in order to prepare for an essay question on some part of that topic. As you work your way through the chapter you will realize that the outlines differ greatly. Some are more conceptual, others more factual. The difference is deliberate, and is designed to show the range of approaches of studying for a major essay examination.

Unit One: 1607 to 1763

MAJOR THEMES AND IDEAS

Colonization

1. How careful European plans for various colonies were altered by the reality of the American environment
2. Compare and contrast three colonies.
3. Explain and illustrate the growing differences between the Southern, New England, and Middle colonies.
4. There were two Souths: the Chesapeake society and the Carolinas.

Puritans and Religion

1. Characteristics of the Puritan experiment
2. How successful were the Puritans as a "City upon a Hill"?
3. Characteristics of religion in colonial America

Slavery and Indians

1. Interaction between Europeans and Native Americans (Indians)
2. Origins of slavery

Great Britain and the Colonies

1. Nature of the British political heritage we inherited
2. Events in Great Britain that had an impact on the colonies

3. The slow evolution from separate colonies to unity by 1763
4. Economic and political relationships between Great Britain and the colonies to 1763
5. British control through economic and political measures to 1763
6. Competition between Great Britain and France: causes, strengths of each, consequences
7. Impact of the Colonial wars on the colonies and on their relationship with Great Britain

Colonial Institutions

1. Role of slavery and indentured servanthood in the colonial economy
2. Mercantilism and the colonies
3. The great issues of the 17th century were theological, those of the 18th political.
4. Between 1607 and 1763 Americans gained control over their own economic and political institutions.
5. Growth of democracy in the colonial era: social, political, economic, and religious
6. Social mobility in the colonial era
7. The intellectual life of the colonies was more American than European.
8. Benjamin Franklin as a perfect example of an 18th century American

MAJOR TERMS AND CONCEPTS

Discovery

best known explorers, countries they sailed for, areas explored
Columbus, reasons
Spanish Armada, 1588
know the order of colonization of the colonies in North America

New England

Mayflower Compact
William Bradford

contrast Pilgrims and Puritans
Massachusetts Bay colony
Cambridge Agreement
Puritan migration
Church of England
John Winthrop, his beliefs
Separatists, Non-Separatists
Calvinism
Congregational church, Cambridge Platform
contrast Puritan colonies with others
Anne Hutchinson, antinomianism
Roger Williams, Rhode Island
covenant theology

voting granted to church members, 1631
Half-Way Covenant
Brattle Street Church
Thomas Hooker
Saybrook Platform
Fundamental Orders of Connecticut
Massachusetts school law
Harvard founded
New England Confederation, 1643
King Philip's War
Dominion of New England
Sir Edmund Andros

Southern Colonies

joint stock company
Virginia: purpose, problems, failures, successes
headright system
John Smith
John Rolfe, tobacco
slavery begins
House of Burgesses
Cavaliers
Bacon's Rebellion
Culpeper's Rebellion
Georgia: reasons, successes
James Oglethorpe
Carolinas
John Locke, Fundamental Constitutions
Charleston
staple crops in the South

Middle Colonies

Pennsylvania, William Penn
liberal land laws in Pa
Holy Experiment
1701 Frame of Government
New York: Dutch, 1664 English
patroon system
Peter Stuyvesant
Five Nations
crops in the middle colonies
New York City and Philadelphia as urban centers
Leisler's Rebellion
Benjamin Franklin
John Bartram

Religion in the Colonies

Pennsylvania, Maryland, Rhode Island—founders
established churches

Great Awakening
Jonathan Edwards, *Sinners in the Hands of an Angry God, A Careful and Strict Enquiry into . . . That Freedom of Will*
George Whitefield (pronounced Whitfield)
William Tennent
Gilbert Tennent
Old Lights, New Lights
Lord Baltimore
Maryland Act of Toleration
deism
Huguenots
SPG, Society for the Propagation of the Gospel (in Foreign Parts)

The Colonial Economy

mercantilism: features, rationale, impact on Great Britain, impact on the different colonies
North–South economic differences
Navigation Acts of 1650, 1660, 1663, 1696
admiralty courts
triangular trade (it wasn't very triangular!)
merchants/markets
consignment system
Molasses Act, 1733
Woolens Act, 1699; Hat Act, 1732; Iron Act, 1750
Currency Act, 1751 (applied to Massachusetts)
Currency Act, 1764 (extended to all the colonies)

Colonial Society

Salem witch trials
primogeniture, entail
quitrents
indentured servants
Poor Richard's Almanac(k)
Phillis Wheatly
Ann Bradstreet

Colonial Politics

Magna Carta, 1215
Petition of Right, 1628
Habeas Corpus Act, 1679
Bill of Rights, 1689
Board of Trade (of the Privy Council)
Robert Walpole
"salutary neglect"
the Enlightenment
theories of representative government in legislatures: virtual representation, actual representation

rise of the lower house
proprietary, charter, and royal colonies
colonial agents
town meetings
John Peter Zenger trial
Glorious Revolution, 1688
John Locke, his theories
a democratic society or not?

Great Britain versus France

land claims, squabbles in North America: where, why, over what
changes in land claims of 1689, 1713, 1763
differences between French and British colonization

why Great Britain eventually won
Queen Anne's War (War of Spanish Succession)
Treaty of Utrecht, 1713
War of Jenkin's Ear
King George's War (War of Austrian Succession)
French and Indian War, Seven Years War, Great War for Empire
Francis Parkman
Albany Plan of Union, Benjamin Franklin
General Braddock
William Pitt
Fort Pitt, Fort Duquesne
Wolfe, Montcalm, Quebec—the Plains of Abraham
Treaty of Paris, 1763
Pontiac's Rebellion
Proclamation of 1763

READINGS FOR DEPTH AND HISTORICAL INTERPRETATION

Democracy in Colonial America

1. James A. Henretta, "Economic Development and Social Structure in Colonial Boston," *William and Mary Quarterly*, January 1965, pp. 75–92. Henretta uses two Boston tax lists—for 1687 and 1771—and quantitatively compares the two Bostons. He concludes that the 1771 Boston was decidedly less democratic.

2. Kenneth A. Lockridge and Alan Kreider, "The Evolution of Massachusetts Town Government, 1640–1740," *William and Mary Quarterly*, October 1966. The authors dispute the traditional view of the town meeting as the citadel of democracy. Until the end of the colonial era the town meeting was run by the selectmen through consensus politics, not democracy.

3. Charles Sydnor, chapter on "County Oligarchies" in *Gentlemen Freeholders: Political Practices in Washington's Virginia*. Sydnor deems the Virginia of George Washington's era an oligarchy run by church vestries and county courts. Who served in the legislature didn't matter.

4. Robert E. Brown, *Middle-Class Democracy and the Revolution in Massachusetts, 1691–1780*. Brown's thesis is in his title. Massachusetts in the colonial era was a middle-class democracy. The land ownership requirement for suffrage, inherited from the Old World to restrict voting, actually

gave suffrage to eighty percent of the adult male population because land ownership was so widespread. The colonists fought Great Britain in the revolution to preserve the democratic society they already possessed.

5. Oscar Handlin, "The Significance of the Seventeenth Century," in James Smith, ed., *Seventeenth Century America: Essays in Colonial History*. Handlin explains the 17th century development of a decentralized, mobile society with a sense of mission which led to an institutional looseness and the creation of a new social order.

Origins of Slavery

1. Oscar and Mary Handlin, *Race and Nationality in American Life*, pp. 7–28. The Handlins see the Southern need for a labor supply as the primary reason for the institution of slavery.

2. Carl N. Degler, Chapter 1, "Black Men in a White Men's Country" in his *Out of Our Past*. Degler sees the existence of prejudice as the significant attitudinal source in the early development of slavery.

3. Winthrop Jordan, chapter 2, "Unthinking Decision, Enslavement of Africans in America to 1700" in his *The White Man's Burden*; or see the longer book, *White Over Black*. (One has the footnotes, one doesn't.) The enslavement of

blacks was an "unthinking decision" resulting from a variety of factors—racism, labor need, a general debasement of blacks, English concepts of blackness, and the African's heathen status.

Religion in the Colonies

1. Edmund S. Morgan, *The Puritan Dilemma: The Story of John Winthrop*, pp. 84-95. Gives the political thought of John Winthrop and the conversion of the charter into a government in 1631.

2. Daniel J. Boorstin, "A City Upon A Hill: The Puritans of Massachusetts Bay" in his *The Ameri-cans: The Colonial Experience*. Boorstin sees the Puritans as a practical people, community builders who were not preoccupied with religious dogma.

3. Carl Degler, section from chapter 1, "Were the Puritans 'Puritanical'?" in his *Out of Our Past*. Degler finds a different group than that found by 19th century moralists.

4. Richard Bushman, "Awakening," in his *From Puritan to Yankee: Character and the Social Order in Connecticut, 1690–1765*. The chapter on the Awakening helps explain the transition of the Puritan into a Yankee as the old social and religious order broke down in the face of economic and social changes.

SAMPLE OUTLINE

What were the chief characteristics of religion in colonial America? Since this question doesn't set a terminal date for the colonial period, you must decide the chronological end of your outline. You may use 1763, 1775, 1783, or 1789. Be sure to carry your outline to a conclusion chronologically. Your outline should prepare you to be able to answer any question about any aspect of colonial religion.

RELIGION IN THE COLONIAL ERA

I. **Characteristics of Religion**

    A. Important motive behind several colonies

        1. Freedom from religious persecution (not religious freedom)
          a. Pa: Penn, 1682, Quakers
          b. RI: Roger Williams, from Massachusetts
          c. Md: Lord Baltimore, Catholics
          d. SC and NJ experiments
        2. Combat spread of Catholic powers Spain and France
        3. French Huguenots

    B. Colonial religion part of the continuing debate dating from the Reformation

        1. Role of ministers, number of sacraments, organization of the church, liturgical service, hierarchy, Presbyterians, Congregationalists, Quakers, antinomianism, Arminianism
        2. Changes in England: Bishop Laud, Charles I, 39 Articles, Civil War, Levellers, Puritan Commonwealth, Test Act (1673), Toleration Act (1689), Glorious Revolution

    C. Influence of Puritanism

        1. Source of significant ideas—education for Bible reading, Harvard—ministers, higher law, moral codes
        2. City upon a hill, an example of a sense of mission
        3. Covenant theology: boost to the idea of a covenant between government and governed

D. Union of church and state

   1. Established churches in 9 colonies (tax supported)
     Anglican: NY, Md, Va, NC, SC, Ga
     Congregational: Mass, Conn, NH
     Quakers: Pa (for all practical purposes)

   2. Roger Williams: RI separate to preserve the purity of church, not state

   3. Fear of tyranny of church and state, SPG (Society for the Propagation of the Gospel in Foreign Parts) seen as a conspiracy

   4. Anne Hutchinson exiled for doctrinal belief that faith more important than good works

E. Overwhelmingly Protestant

   1. Of 3142 church buildings in 1775 only 56 Catholic churches and 5 Jewish synagogues—more than 98% Protestant

   2. Called "Penal Period" by Catholic historians; all colonies had anti-Catholic laws at one time

   3. U.S. now more than 20% Catholic, 3% Jewish

II. Changes in the Colonial Period

A. Multitude of religions

   1. Too many for any one church to control, although Mass and Pa significant; Roger Williams, Anne Hutchinson, Mary Dyer

   2. Four largest, Congregational, Presbyterian, Anglican, Baptist, were only 21%, 19%, 16%, and 16% of total population.

B. Calvinistic

   1. Emphasis on evangelical Calvinism

   2. The individual's direct personal relationship to God rather than the church's corporate one

   3. Emotion, not doctrine

C. Influence of the Great Awakening

   1. Reinvigorated Calvinistic influence—society seen as egalitarian

   2. Jonathan Edwards, *Sinners in the Hands of an Angry God . . . Freedom of Will*

   3. William and George Tennent

   4. George Whitefield from Great Britain

   5. Colleges established to train ministers

   6. Controversies within denominations—New Sides, Old Sides; New Lights, Old Lights

   7. Missionaries to Indians

D. Many unchurched

   1. Many never attended church (in Phila only 18 churches in 1776 for 40,000 people)

   2. Few churches or missionaries in backwoods areas

   3. Deism widespread among upper classes

E. Colonial religion contributed to the rise of political liberty.

   1. James I: "No Bishop, No King." Democratic churches led to a demand for democratic governments.

   2. Puritan franchise to church members seemingly restrictive, but was very democratic

3. Concept of natural laws, natural rights fed by deism
4. Weak church organization and control spurred individualism. Calvinism emphasized significance of individual rather than corporate body.
5. Disestablishment came only because it proved too difficult to establish a single church. Disestablishment came with Revolutionary War, Va Declaration of Rights (1776); Va Act for Establishment of Religious Freedom (1785) after much debate and effort to establish an official church.
6. Religious freedom not original desire (Md Act of Toleration for only those who believed in the Trinity) but ended up as such. (Don't confuse religious freedom and freedom from religious persecution.)

Unit Two: 1763 to 1783

MAJOR THEMES AND IDEAS

The Coming of the American Revolution

Be aware that it is possible to think of the "Revolution" in three ways: the War for Independence, 1775–1783; the period from 1763 to 1783; or the period from 1763 to the writing of the Constitution. Be sure your essay fits the meaning of the wording of the question.

1. The victory over France led to the American Revolution.
2. The long and short run causes of the American Revolution
3. Colonial assemblies as leaders against Great Britain
4. The revolution fomented by changes in British colonial policy in the 1763–1776 period
5. The revolution was brought on by tight economic controls and loose political controls.
6. Economic factors caused the Revolution.
7. The ideas and accusations in the Declaration of Independence
8. Support two different interpretations by historians on the causes of the American Revolution.

The American Revolution

1. The American Revolution as an event in European history
2. Was the Treaty of Paris (1783) a victory for the U.S.?
3. What did the participants in the American Revolution seek to preserve in American society?
4. In what ways and how had the thirteen separate colonies become similar by the time of the revolution?
5. There were 21 British colonies in the New World. Why didn't all of them revolt?
6. The American Revolution as a democratic revolution turned into an aristocratic government by the Constitution
7. Why did great political thinkers and leaders develop in the slave South?
8. The American Revolution as a question of home rule and who should rule at home
9. The American Revolution as a revolutionary event: consider the economic and social changes associated with the revolution.
10. Was the revolution avoidable?

MAJOR TERMS AND CONCEPTS

Great Britain versus France

Review Unit One terms and concepts on this topic.

Coming of the American Revolution

writs of assistance
James Otis
Pontiac's Rebellion
Proclamation of 1763
Paxton Boys
Navigation Act, 1651 (a temporary act)
Navigation Act, 1660: renewed the provisions of the 1651 act; trade in English ships; enumerated articles to be sold only to England
Navigation Act, 1663: European trade through England first, then to colonies; strengthened in 1673

Navigation Act, 1696: created Board of Trade and Plantations to enforce navigation acts
Grenville's program
Sugar Act, 1764: modified Molasses Act, 1733
Currency Act, 1764: extended Currency Act of 1751, that applied only to Mass, to all the colonies
vice-admiralty courts
non-importation
virtual, actual representation
Stamp Act
Virginia Resolves
Stamp Act Congress, 1765
Patrick Henry
Sons of Liberty
internal taxes
external taxes
Declaratory Act, 1766

Quartering Act (called the Mutiny Act by the British)

Townshend Acts, reaction

John Dickinson, "Letters From a Farmer in Pennsylvania"

Massachusetts Circular Letter

Sam Adams

The Association

repeal of the Townshend Acts, except tax on tea

Boston Massacre, 1770

Crispus Attucks

John Adams

Carolina Regulators

Battle of the Alamance

Gaspee incident

Governor Thomas Hutchinson of Mass

committees of correspondence

Lord North

Tea Act, East India Company

Boston Tea Party, 1773

Coercive Acts (or Intolerable Acts, or Repressive Acts)

  Boston Port Act

  Massachusetts Government Act

Quebec Act

First Continental Congress, 1774

Suffolk Resolves

Galloway Plan

Continental Association

Lexington and Concord, April 19, 1775

Paul Revere, William Dawes

Second Continental Congress

George Washington

Battle of Bunker Hill (Breed's Hill)

Olive Branch Petition

Thomas Paine, *Common Sense*

natural rights philosophy

John Locke, *Second Treatise of Government*

George III

Richard Henry Lee's Resolution of June 7, 1776:

"These united colonies are, and of right ought to be, free and independent states."

Committee on Independence: Thomas Jefferson, Benjamin Franklin, John Adams, Roger Sherman, and Robert Livingston

July 4, 1776 and the Declaration of Independence. Read it and know the ideas in the preamble.

Somerset case (in Great Britain)

Quock Walker case—Mass

Revolutionary War

John Adams

Abigail Adams

Mercy Otis Warren

Edmund Burke

Lafayette

George Rogers Clark

Benedict Arnold

Robert Morris

John Paul Jones

"Bonhomme Richard" and the "Serapis"

Conway cabal

French Alliance of 1778, reasons for it

major battles: Saratoga, Valley Forge

Yorktown, Lord Cornwallis

League of Armed Neutrality

Treaty of Paris, 1783

  negotiators: Benjamin Franklin, John Adams, John Jay

  French and British intrigue over U.S. boundaries

social impact of the war

primogeniture, entail

disestablishment, Virginia Statute of Religious Freedom

new state constitutions (Mass new constitution adopted by popular vote)

Newburgh conspiracy

Articles of Confederation: powers, weaknesses, successes

READINGS FOR DEPTH AND HISTORICAL INTERPRETATION

The American Revolution and the Civil War are two of the most studied and least understood events in American history. We know what happened; what we don't know is why both happened and what they mean in the broader context of American history. Additional readings on the American Revolution provide *some* depth and understanding. Complete understanding takes more than a lifetime.

American Revolution

1. Robert B. Downs, "Clarion Call for Revolution: Thomas Paine's *Common Sense*," in *Books That Changed America*. Downs calls *Common Sense* "the American best seller of all time in relation to population." Probably every fifth American owned a copy of *Common Sense*. This source

summarizes Paine's ideas and place in American history.

2. Carl Becker, "Provincial Parties and Party Politics, 1700–1769," in his *The History of Political Parties in the Province of New York, 1760–1776*. Becker sees the American Revolution as two struggles—one against the British for independence and another between the privileged and the unprivileged for control of the state government. "The first was the question of home rule; second was the question . . . of who should rule at home."

3. J. Franklin Jameson, *The American Revolution Considered as a Social Movement*. Originally published in 1926, Jameson sees accompanying the revolution deep and permanent social and economic changes in the patterns of landholding, church-state relations, restrictions on slavery, changes in inheritance laws, etc.

4. Crane Brinton, *The Anatomy of Revolution*. This 1938 book uses four revolutions—the American, French, English, and Russian—to study the phenomenon of revolutions. It is difficult reading, but immensely rewarding for the serious student of history.

5. Gordon S. Wood, "Rhetoric and Reality in the American Revolution," *William and Mary Quarterly*, 1966. Wood reviews the various interpretations for the causes of the American Revolution, and discusses the difficulty involved in trying to link ideas and behavior.

6. Robert E. Brown, *Middle-Class Democracy and the Revolution in Massachusetts, 1691–1780*. Brown claims that Massachusetts in the colonial era was already a middle-class democracy because the land ownership requirement for the right of suffrage gave the right to vote to over eighty percent of the adult white males. Because the colonists fought against Great Britain to preserve the already existing democratic society, ours was a conservative revolution.

SAMPLE OUTLINE

THE AMERICAN REVOLUTION AS AN INTELLECTUAL AND IDEOLOGICAL REVOLUTION

I. Looking Backward, 1776 to 1760 in Retrospect

A. John Adams: "There seems to be a direct and formal design to enslave America."

B. Thomas Jefferson in 1774: "[though] single acts of tyranny may be ascribed to the accidental opinion of a day . . . a series of oppressions begun at a distinguished period and pursued unalterably through every change of ministers too plainly proves a deliberate and systematical plan of reducing us to slavery."

C. Changes in self-perception and changes in our image of Great Britain

1. America seen as the citadel of natural rights
2. Long American identification with and sympathy for the Whig opposition to the British government
3. America was the last defense of traditional English liberties and rights. (Note that early appeals were to Parliament until the colonists realized that Parliament sided with the stupid, corrupt, or evil ministers. Then the appeal was to the king until the colonists realized the king, the ministers, and Parliament were all of a single mind.)
4. The entire British government and society increasingly seen as corrupt; America viewed as crude, but morally superior; slow realization that our inferiority was really our superiority.

II. Specific British Acts of Tyranny (part of the long "series of oppressions" and the "direct and formal design")

A. The early acts

1. Writs of assistance widely thought to be illegal (Mass high court had to ask if they were legal because the court was uncertain itself. Almost all colonial lawyers thought them to be unconstitutional.)

2. Proclamation of 1763 a logical British answer to Pontiac's Rebellion, but had adverse impact on land speculators and colonial land claims in a society that increasingly thought of itself as crowded

3. Revenue laws
   a. Sugar Act, 1764, cut rates of Molasses Act of 1733, but now strictly enforced
   b. Currency Act, 1764, forbade issuing of paper money by colonies, hindering trade
   c. Stamp Act, 1765, to be affixed to 54 different types of documents, from 1¢ to $10 to set a precedent for internal taxes. (The amounts to be raised were small, why did the British push for it?)
   d. Stamp Act Congress: Unity forced England to back down; Declaratory Act passed, ignored by colonists

4. The attack on the principle of representative government
   a. Suspension of the NY legislature for protesting against the Quartering Act
   b. Suspension of Mass legislature for circular letter urging resistance to Townshend Acts

B. Corruption in Great Britain

1. John Wilkes: a radical denied his seat in Parliament after election and imprisoned

2. His supporters gathered at St. George's Fields, beside King's Bench Prison, to protest and see him; British army dispersed mob (attacked by a standing army)

3. Wilkes's friend, Colonel Barre, condemned government's action. (Wilkes-Barre, Pa was named for them.)

4. Paoli, leading a revolution in Corsica, asked England for aid, and was instead lured from his revolution by British money and gifts (Paoli, Pa named for him).

5. Significance of these events: British government opposed to representative government and republican ideals; preferred old monarchical principles

6. Boston Massacre (1770) similar to St. George's fields massacre (Note the terminology. A few deaths become a massacre when fighting tyranny.)

C. Confirmation of prior suspicions

1. 1770–1773 a period of calm with isolated events—Alexander McDougall, NYC, Sons of Liberty leader imprisoned; Gaspee burned, British revenue ship

2. Committees of correspondence active

3. Slow development of *dvoevlastie* (see p. 10)

4. Boston Tea party, 1773, 342 chests of tea

5. British response: Coercive Acts (Intolerable Acts or Repressive Acts)
   a. Closed port of Boston
   b. British troops could be quartered anywhere at colonial expense.
   c. Mass town meetings restricted to one a year
   d. British officials to be tried in English rather than American courts

6. Quebec Act passed to appease Canadian French Catholics and retain their loyalty (very successful in long run); angered Americans, extended Canada's border

to Ohio River, jeopardized colonial land claims and extended area of hated Catholicism. (The colonists unfairly linked the Quebec Act to Intolerable Acts.)

7. Intolerable Acts led to First Continental Congress.

III. Reflections on Events Since 1763

A. First Continental Congress asked for redress of grievances, yet they denounced every British action taken since 1763.

B. Church of England's SPG sent missionaries to Indians, yet they stayed in Boston area where there had been no Indians for 100 years.

C. Since 1763 there had been a large increase in the number of British officials in the colonies—why?

D. New policy of tenure for judges caused reduced effect of popular pressure on judges.

E. Vice-admiralty courts to try violation of navigation acts (no longer a jury of your peers, your fellow anti-Britishers)

F. Shift of location of trials from Mass to Nova Scotia

IV. The Revolution in American Thinking

A. The Revolution erupted at the end of a long period culminating in the development of uniquely American political, social, and intellectual ideas.

B. The intense political debate from 1763 to 1776 convinced Americans that American society and institutions were not only different from, but better than their British counterparts.

C. Americans became convinced that traditional English liberties could only survive on the pure American republican continent.

D. Thus, the commitment to a moralistic, optimistic, regenerative republic

E. All that was left after this realization was for the Second Continental Congress to assume the power to govern, which it did.

The Constitution

DIVIDING POWER BETWEEN THE FEDERAL GOVERNMENT AND THE STATE GOVERNMENTS

Federal Powers Only

1. Regulate foreign commerce
2. Regulate interstate commerce
3. Coin money
4. Establish post offices
5. Control naturalization and immigration
6. Grant patents and copyrights
7. Declare war and peace
8. Admit new states
9. Fix standard weights and measures
10. Raise and maintain an army and navy
11. Govern the District of Columbia
12. Conduct foreign relations
13. Set uniform laws for bankruptcy

Federal and State Powers

1. To tax, to borrow, and to spend money
2. To control the militia
3. Both governments could now act directly on individuals

Limitations on the Federal Government

1. Bill of Rights guarantees for individuals
2. No ex post facto laws
3. No bill of attainder
4. Appropriation for the military limited to two years
5. May not suspend habeas corpus except in a crisis
6. May not favor one port over another

7. No taxes on exports
8. May not grant titles

State Powers Only

1. Conduct elections
2. Establish qualifications for voters
3. Provide local governments
4. Ratify amendments to the Constitution
5. Regulate contracts, wills
6. Regulate intrastate commerce
7. Provide education
8. Levy direct taxes (before the Sixteenth Amendment permitted the federal government to levy direct taxes)
9. Exercise police power over the public's health, safety, and morals
10. Maintain integrity of state borders—no change without approval of states involved

Limitations on State Governments

1. No ex post facto laws
2. No bill of attainder
3. May not enter into a treaty, alliance, or confederation
4. May not grant letters of marque and reprisal
5. May not impair contracts
6. May not print money or emit bills of credit
7. May not levy export or import taxes
8. May not wage war (unless invaded)

FEDERALISM

Federalism is composed of two independent levels of government, the federal and the state. The powers granted to the federal government are called delegated or enumerated powers. All powers not granted to the federal government and not specifically prohibited to the states are reserved powers belonging to the states.

The elastic clause, Article I, section 8, clause 18, is the source of the debate over loose and strict construction of the Constitution. The Founding Fathers inserted the elastic clause into the Constitution because they realized that they could not think of everything. The Constitution clearly grants the power to print money. Does that include the power to purchase ink and paper? The elastic clause solved that problem. But what of questions in more ambiguous areas? The federal government may collect taxes. Can it create a national bank to deposit its tax revenues? Or build a warehouse to house merchandise before customs duties are collected? Defining the edges of federal and state intrusions upon one another is a never-ending process. In some new areas the federal and state governments have expanded the scope of their shared powers through grants such as federal aid for building highways.

It's interesting to learn what the Founding Fathers did not argue about. The areas of agreement are rarely mentioned, and yet, probably nowhere else in the world would a group of government makers have accepted the following without at least serious argument:

1. The principle of representative government
2. A single executive (Plural executives are common in history. Within a short time the French Revolution produced a multiple executive, the Directory.)
3. A bicameral legislature (Many national legislatures are unicameral, and almost all products of revolutions are unicameral. Franklin wanted a unicameral legislature, since Pennsylvania had one.)
4. A means to amend the Constitution in the future (This was a confession that their work was imperfect.)
5. A fixed time for elections, limiting terms of office
6. Two governments, a federal and a state, with overlapping powers and each having a legislature, an executive, and a judiciary
7. The supremacy of the national government over state governments (Perhaps the Articles of Confederation could have been strengthened.)

SECTIONS OF THE CONSTITUTION

Preamble

It gives the purposes of the Constitution although it is not technically part of the Constitution. Read it.

Article I: Legislature

TERMS—KNOW THE FOLLOWING:

  logrolling
  riders
  quorum
  seniority
  committee system
  majority leader
  majority whip
  minority leader
  minority whip
  gerrymander

YOU SHOULD KNOW:

  how a bill becomes a law
  that each House judges the qualifications of its members
  that members of Congress may not hold another federal office
  that members of Congress are free from arrest for anything said on the floor of Congress

HOUSE OF REPRESENTATIVES

  2-year terms, 25 years old at least, 435 members, based on population
  Speaker of the House presides
  limited debate because of size, except that they may reorganize themselves into the Committee of the Whole (technically a committee) for long debate
  brings impeachment charges
  All money bills must originate in the House.

SENATE

  6-year terms, 30 years old at least, two per state
  Vice-president is presiding officer, and may vote in a tie.
  President pro tempore normally presides.
  unlimited debate, filibuster, closure (cloture)
  originally elected by state legislatures
  serves as a court and jury for impeachment
  approves or rejects presidential nominations
  approves or rejects treaties

Article II: Executive

  4-year term, no limit on reelection, 35 years old at least, citizen for at least 14 years
  Twenty-second Amendment limited the president to two terms.

The president and the vice-president were elected by the electoral college, which was designed to insulate the selection process from the people. Electors were selected by state legislatures, and each state had the same number of electors as it had total senators and representatives. The winner was the man (or woman) with the most votes named on over one half of the electoral ballots. The vice-president was the one with the second highest number of votes, provided that he (or she) was also named on over one half of the ballots. If no one received a majority the House of Representatives, voting by states, selected the president; the Senate selected the vice-president. Note that in either case the states are equal in power. The Founding Fathers expected four out of every five presidential elections to end in the House of Representatives. If each elector independently selected his choice for the two best men for president, the chances of a majority of electors naming one of the same choices would be very slim. Thus most elections would go to the House of Representatives. The rise of political parties altered the operation of the electoral college. Electors began to pledge that they would vote for a certain candidate if selected as an elector. Party loyalty negated the original intention of the electoral college mechanism.

The electoral college system has come under criticism from many sides. It has many advantages, though, and should not be hastily abandoned. It produces a clear winner. If we depended on a national popular vote the recounting might drag through courts for years. The electoral college also reminds us that this is a federal system. States do count for something other than serving as administrative units for the federal government's programs.

The president's powers, as described by Clinton Rossiter in *The American Presidency*, are as follows:

CONSTITUTIONAL RESPONSIBILITIES

Chief of state—the ceremonial head of the government

Chief executive—responsible for carrying out laws

Commander in chief—commander of the armed forces

Chief diplomat—As Truman said in 1948, "I make American foreign policy."

Chief legislator—presents a legislative program to Congress and exerts leadership, signs legislation

UNOFFICIAL RESPONSIBILITIES

Chief of party—leads his party as a politician

Voice of the people—the molder and voice of public opinion

Protector of the peace—responds to emergencies with aid and comfort

Manager of prosperity—the Employment Act of 1946 gives the president the responsibility for the state of the economy. (Even if this law didn't, the voters would.)

World leader—the leader of the coalition of free nations

Article III: Judiciary

The Constitution established the Supreme Court and described its powers, but left all the details to Congress. The Judiciary Act of 1789 created the federal court system with district courts and circuit courts. Section 2 of Article III describes the original jurisdiction cases for federal courts. These suits begin in the federal courts. Another jurisdiction the courts possess is over appellate cases, which are appealed from lower court decisions. This article specifically defines treason as an overt act witnessed by two other persons. The Founding Fathers were well aware of the ease with which the charge of treason had been used to smear in the past. Treason is such an odious crime that the accused is popularly convicted by just the accusation. The Founding Fathers wanted a clear act, not a thought or a profane expression, with two witnesses. You may, in this country, discuss many ideas with impunity as long as you don't actually do something. Discussing the ease and desirability of overthrowing the government might get you some strange glances from your neighbors. Discussing the same ideas while loading your shotgun will get you in deep trouble.

TERMS—KNOW THE FOLLOWING:

common law
statute law
civil law
equity law
admiralty and maritime law
martial law
international law
canon law
majority opinion
minority opinion or dissenting opinion
concurring opinion

Article IV: Interstate Relations

Section 1 is the "full faith and credit" clause. This clause means that court decisions and legal actions in one state are valid in others. Once married, you do not have to remarry if you move to another state. A corporation chartered in one state is a corporation in the other 49 states. This article provided for the extradition of criminals and runaway slaves and the reciprocal exchange of the benefits of citizenship. New states may be added to the original 13. This sounds so logical to us today that we do not appreciate how revolutionary it was. The Northwest Ordinance of 1787 and the Constitution admitted new states on equal footing with the older states and guaranteed that the power and influence of the original states would be diluted. Virginia had one-thirteenth of the vote in the first Senate and 10 of the 65 members of the first House of Representatives. Virginia's power in the present Congress is much less. This article also guarantees a republican form of government for each state and federal protection against invasion and domestic violence.

Article V: The Amendment Process

Amendments can be *proposed* by a two-thirds vote of each house of Congress or by a special convention called by Congress upon the request of two-thirds of the state legislatures. Amendments can be *ratified* by three-fourths of the state legislatures or by conventions in three-fourths of the states. Only the Twenty-first Amendment (repeal of prohibition) was ratified by the latter method. The Seventeenth Amendment passed Congress only after it became clear that the states would actually use the convention method to propose an amendment. Since the Articles of Confederation demanded unanimous consent for amendments, the Founding Fathers wanted to make amending the Constitution easier but still prevent emotional issues from easily changing the supreme law of the land.

Article VI: Supremacy Clause

All federal and state judges and officials must take an oath to support the Constitution. According to the Constitution, it is the supreme law of the land, followed by treaties, federal laws (and now federal regulatory agency directives), state constitutions, state laws, and local laws. For example, if a treaty and a state law conflict, the treaty takes precedence.

Article VII: Ratification

The Constitution went into effect when it was ratified by special conventions in nine states. Rhode Island and North Carolina disapproved of the Constitution. You should take a long look at the order of ratification and the closeness of the vote in many states. As the ninth state to ratify approached, the crux of the ratification vote lay in Virginia and New York. If they did not join, the whole endeavor was in jeopardy.

1.	Delaware	unanimous	Dec. 7, 1787
2.	Pennsylvania	46 to 23	Dec. 12, 1787
3.	New Jersey	unanimous	Dec. 18, 1787
4.	Georgia	unanimous	Jan. 2, 1788
5.	Connecticut	128 to 40	Jan. 9, 1788
6.	Massachusetts	187 to 168	Feb. 7, 1788
7.	Maryland	63 to 11	Apr. 28, 1788
8.	South Carolina	149 to 73	May 23, 1788
9.	New Hampshire	57 to 47	June 21, 1788
10.	Virginia	89 to 79	June 26, 1788
11.	New York	30 to 27	July 26, 1788
12.	North Carolina	194 to 77	Nov. 21, 1789
13.	Rhode Island	34 to 32	May 29, 1790

AMENDMENTS TO THE CONSTITUTION

THE BILL OF RIGHTS—FIRST–TENTH AMENDMENTS, all passed in 1791
FIRST AMENDMENT: freedom of religion, speech, press, assembly, and freedom to petition the government
SECOND AMENDMENT: right to bear arms (in order for states to maintain a militia. This was not meant to guarantee an individual's right to bear arms.)
THIRD AMENDMENT: no quartering of troops in private homes

FOURTH AMENDMENT: specific search warrants required
FIFTH AMENDMENT: rights of the accused, indictments required, double jeopardy, self-incrimination, due process, just compensation
SIXTH AMENDMENT: speedy and public trial, to be confronted by witnesses, ability to call your own witnesses
SEVENTH AMENDMENT: trial by jury
EIGHTH AMENDMENT: excessive bail, cruel and unusual punishment

NINTH AMENDMENT: All rights not enumerated are retained by the people.

TENTH AMENDMENT: All powers not delegated are retained by the states.

ELEVENTH AMENDMENT, 1798: Individuals may not sue states.

TWELFTH AMENDMENT, 1804: Electors cast separate ballots for president and vice-president. If there is no winner the House selects the president and the Senate the vice-president. (This amendment prevented the recurrence of the results of the election of 1800.)

CIVIL WAR AMENDMENTS—THIRTEENTH, FOURTEENTH, FIFTEENTH

THIRTEENTH AMENDMENT, 1865: abolishes slavery

FOURTEENTH AMENDMENT, 1868: Blacks became citizens. Confederate leaders were not eligible for public office; Confederate debt was void; and (Southern) states would have their representation in Congress reduced proportionately if they denied (blacks) voting rights. This amendment confers dual citizenship—you are a citizen of the United States and of your state. Section 1 has been interpreted as applying all the rights in the Bill of Rights, which applied only to the federal government, to the state governments. The "due process" clause and the "equal protection of the laws" clause have been part of many significant court suits.

FIFTEENTH AMENDMENT, 1870: Black suffrage guaranteed.

PROGRESSIVE AMENDMENTS—SIXTEENTH, SEVENTEENTH, EIGHTEENTH, NINETEENTH

SIXTEENTH AMENDMENT, 1913: legalizes the income tax

SEVENTEENTH AMENDMENT, 1913: direct election of senators, instead of by state legislatures

EIGHTEENTH AMENDMENT, 1919: Prohibition

NINETEENTH AMENDMENT, 1920: women's suffrage

TWENTIETH AMENDMENT, 1933: Lame duck sessions of Congress were abolished, and inauguration date was changed from March 4 to January 20. Under the older timetable newly elected congressmen did not meet until thirteen months after their election in November. This amendment eliminated the session of Congress that met from December to March, after the November elections had possibly replaced some congressmen.

TWENTY-FIRST AMENDMENT, 1933: repealed prohibition

TWENTY-SECOND AMENDMENT, 1951: two-term limit for the president

TWENTY-THIRD AMENDMENT, 1961: presidential electoral votes for the District of Columbia

TWENTY-FOURTH AMENDMENT, 1964: poll taxes prohibited

TWENTY-FIFTH AMENDMENT, 1967: presidential disability and succession

TWENTY-SIXTH AMENDMENT, 1971: suffrage for eighteen-year-olds

SEPARATION OF POWERS

The separation of powers and the checks and balances system prevent any person or group from gaining control of all three branches of government. They diffuse power. In addition, the federal nature of our government puts us under two executives, the president and a governor; two legislatures, Congress and a state assembly; and two judiciaries, the federal and state courts. As an ambassador once said, "Anyone who thinks he knows exactly how and where a decision is made in America is crazy." The levels of government and the diffusion of power and responsibility do exactly what they were intended to do—prevent centralization and dilute authority. The

three most important powers of government are lodged mainly in three separate branches: legislative power—power to make laws; executive power—power to enforce laws; and judicial power—power to interpret laws.

One of the most difficult concepts for students to understand is that the Founding Fathers intended to create a slow, deliberate government. They valued debate and rational decisions more than haste. The popular will is often frustrated by the slow machinery, but the Constitution is the oldest continuous form of government in the world. The government doesn't work quickly, but it seems to work well.

Checks and Balances

PRESIDENT VERSUS CONGRESS		CONGRESS VERSUS JUDICIARY	
PRESIDENT	**CONGRESS**	**CONGRESS**	**JUDICIARY**
1. May veto legislation	1. May override a veto by a two-thirds vote	1. Creates inferior courts and their jurisdiction	1. Interprets laws and treaties
2. Suggests legislation	2. Investigates executive branch	2. Determines the number of Supreme Court judges	2. Judicial review of laws (when the issue comes up in a court case)
3. Party leader	3. Has control over appropriations	3. May specifically restrict court review of a piece of legislation*	3. Lifetime tenure
4. Molds public opinion	4. Declares war	4. May propose a constitutional amendment to negate a court decision	
5. May call a special session	5. House only may impeach President.	5. House only may impeach judges.	
6. Commander in chief	6. Senate only is court and jury for impeachment.	6. Senate only is court and jury for impeachment.	
7. Chief diplomat	7. Senate only ratifies appointments.	7. Senate only ratifies presidential appointments of judges.	
8. Salary may not be raised or lowered.	8. Senate only ratifies treaties.		

JUDICIARY VERSUS PRESIDENT	
JUDICIARY	**PRESIDENT**
1. Interprets laws and treaties	1. May pardon
2. Judicial review of presidential actions (when the issue comes up in a court suit)	2. Appoints judges (with Senate approval)
3. Lifetime tenure	3. May refuse to enforce a court order

CONGRESS AND VOTING

Study the following list. Students often confuse the majorities needed for legislative actions.

ACTIONS REQUIRING ONLY A MAJORITY VOTE
   raising taxes
   appropriations
   declaring war
   adding to the national debt
   instituting a draft
   House only—impeachment charges

ACTIONS REQUIRING A TWO-THIRDS MAJORITY
   overriding a presidential veto
   proposing amendments to the Constitution
   expelling a member of Congress (a two-thirds vote in only that one house of Congress)
   Senate only—ratifying treaties
   Senate only—acting as a jury for impeachment
   Senate only—ratifying presidential appointments to executive branch positions, the judiciary, and federal agencies

ACTIONS REQUIRING A THREE-FOURTHS MAJORITY
three-fourths of the states must approve a proposed constitutional amendment

* Several colleagues inquired about the basis for number three. The reference is to "the exceptions clause of the Constitution," Article III, Section 2, Clause 2, " . . . the supreme Court shall have appellate Jurisdiction, both as to Law and Fact, with such Exceptions, and under such Regulations as the Congress shall make." In the debate over the repeal of the Judiciary Act of 1801, following Jefferson's victory over John Adams, the Federalists in Congress never denied the right to use this clause to modify the Supreme Court's appellate jurisdiction. The best example of a decision under this clause occurred on March 27, 1868, when the Radical Republicans in Congress repealed an 1867 law which conferred upon the Supreme Court the right to hear certain appeals involving habeas corpus. In Ex Parte McCardle (also spelled McArdle), 1869, the Supreme Court acknowledged Congress' right to define and to limit its appellate jurisdiction by unanimously declaring that no appeal from a federal Circuit Court under the repealed act of 1867 was reviewable.

Scholars still argue over the meaning of "the exceptions clause" within the context of the whole Article III and the subsequent evolution of constitutional law and practice. See Raoul Berger, *Congress v. The Supreme Court*, 1969, and section four of Sarah Baumgartner Thurow, editor, *E Pluribus Unum: Constitutional Principles and the Institutions of Government*, 1988.

Unit Three: 1783 to 1800

MAJOR THEMES AND IDEAS

Confederation and Constitution

1. Enlightenment concepts and the Constitution
2. How critical was the "critical period"?
3. Compare and contrast the Declaration of Independence, the Articles of Confederation, and the Constitution.
4. Did the Constitution reject the principles of the Declaration of Independence?
5. The Constitution came from American experiences.
6. The Constitution came from European ideas and concepts.
7. Origins of the ideas of separation of powers, written constitutions, and federalism
8. Areas of agreement at the Constitutional Convention
9. Amendments, reasons for them
10. Historiography of the Constitution
11. Bill of Rights: Provisions and meanings
12. Slavery and the Constitution

Domestic Issues of the 1790s

1. Failure of the Constitution led to political parties.
2. Development of political parties
3. Liberty versus order in the 1790s
4. U.S. as a typical new nation

5. Hamilton's economic program
6. Thomas Jefferson versus Alexander Hamilton
7. Differences between the Democratic-Republicans and the Federalists
8. Different concepts of the role of government in the 1790s
9. Compare 1763–1776 with 1783–1800 in regard to the relationship between the central government and the colonies or states.
10. Significant elections: 1796, 1800
11. The Revolution of 1800
12. Loose versus strict construction as a matter of sectional or political interest
13. Why is George Washington ranked as a great president?

Foreign Policy Issues in the 1790s

1. Trace relations with France to 1800.
2. Trace relations with Great Britain to 1800.
3. Trace relations with Spain to 1800.
4. Basis of our foreign policy: economic motives, moral principle, or political motives
5. Was our foreign policy successful?
6. This period as the beginning of isolationism
7. Foreign policy differences: Federalists and Democratic-Republicans
8. Motives and nature of westward expansion in the 1790s

MAJOR TERMS AND CONCEPTS

Articles of Confederation

Maryland, cession of western land claims
strengths, weaknesses of the Articles of Confederation
new state constitutions during the Revolutionary War and after
primogeniture, entail
disestablishment
Pennsylvania militia routs Congress, 1783
Northwest posts
Land Ordinance of 1785
Northwest Ordinance, 1787
proposed Jay-Gardoqui Treaty, 1785

Shays's Rebellion
Annapolis Convention, 1786
1780s depression
Noah Webster

Writing the Constitution, Ratification

Philadelphia Convention
delegates: Alexander Hamilton, George Washington, Benjamin Franklin
Montesquieu, *The Spirit of Laws*
John Locke, *Second Treatise of Government*
Hobbes

James Madison, "Father of the Constitution"
Great Compromise
Va Plan, NJ Plan, Conn Compromise
checks and balances—examples
North-South compromises
slavery and the Constitution: slave trade, three-fifths
  clause
procedures for amendments
Beard thesis, his critics
Fiske, *The Critical Period of American History*
Antifederalists
supporters of the Constitution
opponents of the Constitution
Patrick Henry
Sam Adams
George Mason, Bill of Rights
the ratification fights, especially in Mass, NY, and
  Va
The Federalist Papers, Jay, Hamilton, Madison
The Federalist, number 10

Politics in the 1790s

Bill of Rights adopted, 1791
President George Washington
Vice-president John Adams
Judiciary Act, 1789
Secretary of the Treasury Hamilton
Secretary of State Jefferson
Secretary of War Knox
Attorney General Randolph
Hamilton's program: ideas, proposals, reasons for it
Tariff of 1789
Bank of the U.S.
national debt, state debt, foreign debt
excise taxes
Report on Manufactures
implied powers, elastic clause, necessary and proper
  clause
loose, strict interpretation of the Constitution
location of the capital: logrolling, D.C.
Residence Act
Major L'Enfant, Benjamin Banneker
Whiskey Rebellion
Washington's Farewell Address

election of 1796: President Adams, Vice-president
  Jefferson
new states: Vt, Ky, Tenn
Federalists and Democratic-Republicans (Demo-
  crats) or Jeffersonians or Republicans
  party leaders and supporters
  programs
  philosophies
  foreign proclivities
Society of the Cincinnati
Democratic Societies
Alien and Sedition Acts
Virginia and Kentucky Resolutions
doctrine of nullification
election of 1800, tie, Jefferson and Burr
Revolution of 1800
Jefferson's Inaugural Address
Twelfth Amendment
second Great Awakening
Gilbert Stuart
Charles Willson Peale

Foreign Affairs in the 1790s

French Alliance of 1778
French Revolution
Citizen Genêt
Neutrality Proclamation
XYZ affair, Talleyrand
undeclared naval war with France
Convention of 1800
British seizure of American ships
"Rule of 1756"
Northwest posts
Jay's Treaty
Washington's Farewell Address
Pinckney's Treaty (San Lorenzo), right of deposit at
  New Orleans
Spanish intrigue in the Southwest
James Wilkinson
"Mad" Anthony Wayne, Battle of Fallen Timbers
Treaty of Greenville, 1795
Barbary pirates

COURT CASES TO KNOW

The first three cases are significant because they all dealt with judicial review before the Constitution was written. Many constitutional scholars believe that the Founding Fathers understood and approved of the con- cept of judicial review, but some believe the opposite. These cases are extensively discussed in Gordon S. Wood, *The Creation of the American Republic, 1776– 1787*. The quotes below are from Wood's book.

1. *Rutgers* vs. *Waddington*, 1784

This case involved a clash between a legislative law and common law, which includes the law of nations, the prevailing international law. The New York Trespass Act of 1783 prohibited military authorization of the use of abandoned property. The prevailing law of nations permitted using abandoned property during wartime. In addition, in the Treaty of Paris of 1783, which ended the Revolutionary War, the two sides renounced all previous damage claims. The judges in the case carefully skirted the issue of ruling the New York Trespass Act illegal. When the legislature passes a law that is unreasonable the duty of the court is "to give their *intention* its proper effect." After all, the judges concluded, the legislators did not really mean to void the law of nations because they never said they intended to do so.

2. *Trevett* vs. *Weeden*, 1786–1787

The Rhode Island legislature passed legislation to force merchants to accept paper money. The merchants closed their shops in protest. In his arguments for Weeden, a merchant, the defense attorney asserted that the judge's responsibility was to "reject all acts of the legislature that are contrary to the trust reposed in them by the people." Since the people themselves are the source of the creation of the legislature, the responsibility of the judiciary, itself a creation of the people, is to prevent the legislature from exceeding their original responsibilities. The people may constitutionally change the legislature's responsibilities; the legislature may not constitutionally change the legislature's responsibilities.

3. *Bayard* vs. *Singleton*, 1787

This court case preceded the Philadelphia Constitutional Convention. In this North Carolina case the North Carolina Supreme Court declared a state law void. It is the clearest application of judicial review in this period.

SUPREME COURT CASES TO KNOW

The abbreviation for versus in Supreme Court cases is (v.). The abbreviation for versus in all other cases is (vs.).

1. *Chisholm* v. *Georgia*, 1793 (individuals suing states)

Two citizens of South Carolina sued Georgia in the Supreme Court. The court accepted the case and handed down a decision for the South Carolinians, who were acting as agents for a British creditor. Georgia refused to participate in the case. The case angered many, who saw it as an infringement on the sovereignty of the states. According to English common law a sovereign power (Georgia) could not be sued without its permission. The Eleventh Amendment ended such suits.

2. *Ware* v. *Hylton*, 1796 (treaties and state laws)

This case involved a conflict between the 1783 Treaty of Paris and a 1777 Virginia statute hindering British creditors in their attempt to recover debts owed by Americans. In the treaty the United States pledged not to impede British attempts to secure payment of debts. The court ruled that, as specified in the Constitution, treaties overruled state laws.

READINGS FOR DEPTH AND HISTORICAL INTERPRETATION

Constitution

1. Richard Hofstadter, "The Founding Fathers: An Age of Realism," *The American Political Tradition*. Hofstadter surveys the political and economic thinking of the Founding Fathers, and finds them to be realistic in their appraisal of their fellow man and astute in devising a form of government to serve as an arena for economic self-interest.

2. Charles A. Beard, *An Economic Interpretation of the Constitution*, 1913. Beard argued that economic interests and motives led the Founding Fathers to create a Constitution to protect and to

promote their own economic interests. Read the summary of his argument in the last few pages of the book.

3. Gordon S. Wood, "The Worthy Against the Licentious," and "The Federalist Persuasion," in his *The Creation of the American Republic, 1776–1787*. Wood sees fundamental social differences between the Federalist and Antifederalist visions of society. In many respects this is an updating of the Progressive era dichotomy.

4. Cecelia Kenyon, "Men of Little Faith: The Anti-Federalists on the Nature of Representative Government," *William and Mary Quarterly*, January 1955. Kenyon focuses her attention on the opponents of the ratification of the Constitution. She does not see the Antifederalists as democratic defenders against a conservative aristocratic group favoring centralized authority. They were men with little faith in majority rule, a large country, representative democracy, etc.

5. John P. Roche, "The Founding Fathers: A Reform Caucus in Action," *American Political Review*, December 1961. Roche sees the members of the Constitutional Convention as "superb democratic politicians" who understood the political realities of their day. Practical politics and compromise rather than abstract theory hammered out a consensus on what should be in the Constitution.

Politics in the 1790s

Three decades in American history you must understand. The 1790s is the first. If you understand the events and issues of the 1790s you understand much of American history preceding this decade and many subsequent developments. The other two decades are the 1850s and the 1930s.

1. J.A. Carroll, "George Washington," Stephen G. Kurtz, "John Adams," and Morton Borden, "Thomas Jefferson," in Morton Borden, ed., *America's Eleven Greatest Presidents*. This book looks at eleven presidents and their times, and is worth having to facilitate understanding of this complex decade.

2. Richard Hofstadter, "Thomas Jefferson: The Aristocrat as Democrat," *The American Political Tradition*. A thorough brief discussion of Jefferson's political philosophy in theory and in practice.

3. John C. Miller, "The Quarrel Between Hamilton and Jefferson," in his *The Federalist Era, 1789–1801*. An excellent summary of the dispute between Hamilton and Jefferson. Upset by the early quarrel between Hamilton and Jefferson, Washington asked the two men to explain the reasons for their dispute. They both replied in letters written on September 9, 1792. They are reprinted in Frederick Prescott, ed., *Alexander Hamilton and Thomas Jefferson: Representative Selections*, published in 1934. A local college library should have a copy.

4. James MacGregor Burns, *The Deadlock of Democracy: Four-Party Politics in America*, pp. 27–46. This contains an analysis of Jefferson and Madison as political party leaders in and out of the presidency. Madison was the weaker president because he was constrained by his political theories. Jefferson was the better practical politician in the presidency.

SAMPLE OUTLINE

DEVELOPMENT OF POLITICAL PARTIES IN THE 1790s

I. **Continuity from the Revolutionary War?**

    A. Revolutionary War organizations tended to be ad hoc interest groups and factions more certain of what they didn't want than what they did.

    B. Radical and conservative labels make little sense—not much of a range

II. **Political Parties in the 1790s**

    A. Essentials of a political party

        1. Elaboration of *ideology* in platforms and newspapers

        2. Growth of a party structure, *organization* within the states

3. Recruitment of party *leadership* at different levels
4. Enlistment of a *cadre* of faithful party workers
5. Development of party *loyalty* among the electorate
6. All this provided an institutional complexity and stability that earlier political forms lacked.

B. Issues

1. Great consensus on the basic tenets of American republican ideology
2. Men and their policies were at fault, not the Constitution.
3. Each party believed the other threatened the survival of its vision of the future of the U.S.
4. The disputes centered around the dramatic personalities of Hamilton and Jefferson.
5. Those in office regarded themselves as the embodiment of the national will.
   a. Federalist approach was plebiscitarian.
   b. Federalists called Republicans "Democrats" as a smear tactic. Republicans proudly accepted the name.
6. Disputes arose over basic constitutional, economic, and diplomatic policies, and the relative powers of the states and the federal government.

C. A period of trials for the new nation revealed sharp disagreements and accented differences. Examples include the Whiskey Rebellion, undeclared naval war, Alien and Sedition Acts, Va and Ky Resolutions, Jay's Treaty, and disunion schemes in the West.

III. Hamilton's Program

A. Nonpartisan beginnings

1. Madison, in *The Federalist Papers,* stated, "Among the numerous advantages promised by a well constructed Union, none deserves to be more accurately developed than its tendency to break and control the violence of faction (party). The friend of popular governments never finds himself so much alarmed for their character and fate, as when he contemplates their propensity to this dangerous vice."
2. Hamilton: The "poison" of faction would menace the republic.
3. Washington: "A frightful despotism" would be erected "on the ruins of Public Liberty" if parties ever developed in this country.
4. Jefferson: "If I could not go to heaven but with a party, I would not go there at all."

B. Debt—foreign, national, state

1. Hamilton's proposal to refinance at par to present bondholders; Madison opposed—original owners
2. Refinancing of state debt to strengthen union and increase centralization. State position depended on size of debt and if already paid off, but division tended to be North-South.
3. Assumption of state debts traded for Northern support for national capital located on the Potomac River after ten years in Philadelphia

C. Bank proposal

1. Sectional voting, North 33-1, South 6-19
2. On this issue, Hamilton and Jefferson wrote explanations of loose and strict construction.

D. Excise tax on whiskey

    1   25% of net price, North 28-6, South 7-15

    2. To raise revenues, impress westerners with Federal power

    3. Eventually led to Whiskey Rebellion; 12,600 man army raised to put down rebellion

    4. Jefferson: "An insurrection was announced and proclaimed and armed against, but could never be found."

E. Hamilton wanted a protective tariff; revenue tariff passed.

F. Report on Manufactures

G. Arguments over Hamilton's program form the first ingredients in the platforms of the parties.

IV. Split over Foreign Policy

A. French Revolution: dominating event of the decade

    1. Initial enthusiasm waned as excesses and terror appeared; disagreement over what the French Revolution symbolized.

    2. John Adams: "Ours was resistance to innovation; theirs was innovation itself."

    3. Jefferson: "The liberty of the whole earth was depending on the issue of the contests, and . . . rather than it should have failed, I would have seen half the earth devastated."

B. Complications caused by the Treaty of 1778

    1. Citizen Genêt

    2. Washington's Neutrality Proclamation, 1793

C. Great Britain: Northwest posts, neutral commerce rights violated, impressment

D. Jay's Treaty: event around which differences crystallized

    1. Provisions of the treaty: posts surrendered by June 1796; East Indian ports opened to U.S. ships; minor and limited concessions on U.S. trade with West Indies (so offensive that this part was removed before ratification); acceptance of paper (unenforced) blockades; commissions in the future to resolve border disputes

    2. Senate controlled by Federalists; treaty passed

    3. House controlled by Dem-Reps tried to block treaty by withholding appropriations ($90,000). (The first congressional caucus in history was a Republican meeting for strategy on this issue.)

E. Election of 1796: caucus used to select candidates for president (note: initial organization is at top); Washington's Farewell Address warns against parties. Adams, president; Jefferson, vice-president

V. Alien and Sedition Acts

A. XYZ affair

    1. Negotiators sent: Charles Pinckney, Elbridge Gerry, John Marshall, bribes, Talleyrand

    2. A Republican disaster when they forced the president to make public the negotiations; war fever; undeclared naval war with France. Federalists gain twenty seats in next election.

B. Alien and Sedition Acts

1. Most immigrants joined Republican Party, most famous Albert Gallatin.
2. Naturalization Act: 5 to 14 years for citizenship
3. Alien Friends Act: remove aliens in wartime
4. Alien Act: president may order out of the country all aliens suspected of "treasonable activities."
5. Sedition Act: illegal to falsely criticize the government
   a. For example, two Republican newspaper editors wrote, "No Stamp Act, No Sedition, No Alien Bills, No Land Tax; downfall to the tyrants of America, peace and retirement to the President, long live the Vice-president and the Minority; may moral virtue be the basis of civil government."
   b. One convicted for violating the Sedition Act received 6 hours in jail and a $5 fine; the other, 18 months and a $400 fine
6. Virginia and Kentucky resolutions protested. Written by Madison (Va) and Jefferson (Ky), the resolutions are an overreaction to the Alien and Sedition Acts, not a party doctrinal statement in favor of nullification and states' rights. The issue was liberty, not constitutional doctrine.

C. Federalist Party hurt by two factors:

1. Adams's peace with France in undeclared naval war
2. Adams pushed Hamilton's supporters out of the cabinet in a split between Hamilton and Adams.

D. Election of 1800: crystallization of the party platforms, established party organizations

1. The "tie": Jefferson, 73; Burr, 73
2. House controlled by Federalists decided winner.
3. 35 ballots before tie was broken. Federalists finally accept Jefferson because of distrust for Burr.

E. The election of 1800 is seen as the acceptance of the decision of the electorate and the toleration of an opposition. In truth, both parties pursued an approach to become the only party and only embodiment of the national will (which each believed themselves to be).

VI. Parties in the 1790s

A. Each feared tyranny, but expected it from a different source.

1. Federalists: mobs, the majority in the House
2. Republicans: executive branch and Senate

B. Party debate clarified thinking and sharpened policies, and led to policies and institutions in the 1790s that were well thought out.

Unit Four: 1800 to 1840

MAJOR THEMES AND IDEAS

Politics

1. Did Jefferson out-federalize the Federalists by stealing their ideas?
2. Decline and death of the Federalist Party
3. Era of Good Feelings
4. Forces for nationalism
5. Marshall and his Supreme Court decisions
6. Supreme Court as a partisan body, acting in the interests of one party, section, or ideology
7. Differences and similarities between Jeffersonian and Jacksonian Democracy
8. Compare Jefferson and Jackson in regard to courts and criticism of the judiciary.
9. What was Jacksonian Democracy?
10. What caused Jacksonian Democracy to develop?
11. Compare the Second Party System with the First.
12. Rise and development of political parties in the Jacksonian era—economic, social, and geographical characteristics and leaders
13. Immediate and long range consequences of the split between Jackson and Calhoun
14. The issues that divided the supporters and opponents of the Constitution divided the Whigs and the Jacksonian Democrats.
15. Hamilton's economic program created the political issues for the next fifty years.
16. Loose or strict interpretation of the Constitution was used to defend the economic, political, and constitutional positions of various regions between 1800 and 1840.
17. Trace sectional tensions, 1800–1840.
18. Give the positions, rationale, issues, and spokesmen for the sections on the following political topics: tariff, banking, internal improvements, expansion, and slavery.
19. The Federalists and the Whigs represented the same classes, ideologies, attitudes, sections, and political philosophies.
20. Clay, Calhoun, and Webster reflected the interests of their sections between 1810 and 1850.
21. Significant elections: 1824, 1828, 1832, and 1840.

Foreign Policy

1. Trace relations with Great Britain and France from 1800 to 1815.
2. Trace our relations with Spain to 1824.
3. War of 1812 as a second War for Independence
4. Foreign policy united and divided Americans between 1800 and 1824.
5. Explain the changes in the historiography of the War of 1812.
6. The interests of the West were satisfied by neither the Jeffersonians nor the Federalists between 1789 and 1815.
7. Our border adjustments, 1800–1824
8. Provisions and impact of the Monroe Doctrine

Economy

1. Clay's American system
2. Was Jacksonianism an attack on privilege?
3. Bank War: its enemies and defenders, veto message, laws from 1800 to 1865 on banking
4. Changes in federal land laws and policies
5. Role of state and federal governments in promoting economic growth, 1800–1860
6. Changes in the economy in transportation, labor, and industrialization
7. Impact of changes and improvements in transportation on the direction and extent of population movement and trade patterns
8. United States as an underdeveloped nation in 1840

Reform and Intellectual Movements

1. Identify the motives, methods, leadership, goals, and accomplishments for any reform.
2. Status and goals of the women's movement
3. An era of the common man?
4. Transcendentalism: why, what was it, leaders
5. Reform characterized by perfectionism, distrust of established institutions, and uncompromising impatience
6. Social mobility in American society
7. Era was one of the establishment of political, economic, and cultural independence from Europe.
8. Compare the First and Second Great Awakenings.

MAJOR TERMS AND CONCEPTS

Jeffersonians and Period to the War of 1812

election of 1800

Revolution of 1800

President Jefferson, Vice-president Burr, Secretary of Treasury Gallatin

Jefferson's inaugural address, "We are all Federalists, we are all Republicans."

Federalist control of courts and judges, midnight judges

Justice Samuel Chase

Tripolitan War

Treaty of San Ildefonso

Louisiana Purchase: reasons, Jefferson and loose construction

Toussaint L'Ouverture

Federalist opposition to Louisiana Purchase

Hamilton-Burr duel

Burr expedition, treason trial

Lewis and Clark, Pike, Major Long, their observations

Berlin Decree, 1806; Milan Decree, 1807

Polly case, Essex case

orders-in-council

impressment

Chesapeake-Leopard affair

Embargo of 1807, opposition

Nonintercourse Act

Erskine Agreement

Macon's Bill No. 2

Tecumseh

War Hawks

causes of the War of 1812

why war against Great Britain rather than against France

Federalist opposition to the War of 1812, why?

naval engagements in the War of 1812

Fort McHenry, Francis Scott Key, Star Spangled Banner

events of the war: Perry, Lake Erie, D.C., New Orleans

Jackson's victory at New Orleans

New England's merchants, critics of the war, Essex Junto

Hartford Convention, resolutions

treaty negotiators: John Quincy Adams, Albert Gallatin, Henry Clay

Treaty of Ghent, provisions

neutral rights issues end with the defeat of Napoleon

Nationalism and Sectionalism to 1828

war increased nationalism, economic independence

second Bank of the U.S. a reversal of Jeffersonian ideas

Tariff of 1816 protective

Bonus bill veto

Rush-Bagot, Great Lakes

Convention of 1818

panic of 1819

West Florida, 1810

Jackson in Florida, Rhea letter

purchase of Florida

Transcontinental Treaty (Adams-Onis Treaty or Step Treaty or Florida Treaty)

Quadruple Alliance, Holy Alliance

George Canning

Monroe Doctrine: origins, provisions, impact

era of good feelings

Chief Justice John Marshall: decisions

Missouri: Tallmadge Amendment, Thomas Amendment, Missouri Compromise, provisions

Clay's American System, ideas

growth of industry in New England, textiles

Samuel Slater

Robert Fulton, Clermont

Eli Whitney, cotton gin, interchangeable parts

Boston Associates, Lowell, Mass

Daniel Webster

National (Cumberland) Road

internal improvements

Erie Canal, DeWitt Clinton

new states

federal government's land policy: 1796, 1800, 1804, 1820

New England's opposition to cheap land

John Quincy Adams as Secretary of State: Fla, Monroe Doctrine

election of 1824: popular vote, electoral vote, House vote: Jackson, Adams, Crawford, Clay

"corrupt bargain"

Panama Conference

Tariff of Abominations

Vice-president Calhoun: South Carolina Exposition and Protest, nullification

Jacksonian Democracy

Jacksonian Revolution of 1828

age of the common man

Jacksonian Democracy: characteristics
franchise extended
spoils system
National Republicans
caucus system, national nominating conventions
kitchen cabinet
Cherokee Indian removal, trail of tears
Worcester v. *Georgia*, 1832; and *Cherokee Nation* v. *Georgia*, 1831
Whigs: origins, policies
Maysville Road veto
election of 1832, Anti-Masonic Party
Clay, bank recharter bill, Nicholas Biddle
veto message
Jackson's removal of deposits, Roger B. Taney, pet banks, Loco-Focos
Chestnut Street to Wall Street
Foote Resolution, Webster-Hayne Debate
Peggy Eaton affair
Calhoun resigns as vice-president
South opposes protective tariffs (Tariff of Abominations) nullification, SC Exposition and Protest
Jefferson Day dinner: toasts and quotes
Clay: Compromise Tariff of 1833, Force Bill
Calhoun splits with Jackson
Martin Van Buren, the Albany Regency
Specie Circular, 1836
Charles River Bridge decision, Chief Justice Roger B. Taney, general incorporation laws
panic of 1837
Dorr's Rebellion
Independent Treasury Plan
election of 1840: candidates, characteristics
rise of the second party system
Pre-emption act, 1841
Tariff of 1842

Reform: Social and Intellectual

Transcendentalism
Transcendentalists
Ralph Waldo Emerson
Henry David Thoreau, *Walden*, "On Civil Disobedience"
Orestes Brownson
Margaret Fuller, *The Dial*

authors and their works
James Fenimore Cooper, *The Last of the Mohicans, The Spy, The Pioneers*
Herman Melville, *Moby Dick*
Nathaniel Hawthorne, *The Scarlet Letter*
Edgar Allan Poe
Washington Irving
Henry Wadsworth Longfellow
Walt Whitman, *Leaves of Grass*
Hudson River school of art
Alexis de Tocqueville, *Democracy in America*
millennialism, Millerites
"the burned-over district"
Charles G. Finney
Mormons, Joseph Smith, Brigham Young, Utah
Brook Farm, New Harmony, Oneida Community, Shakers, Amana Community
lyceum movement
some reforms successful, some not—why?
Dorothea Dix, treatment of the insane
rise of labor leaders
National Trades Union
Commonwealth vs. *Hunt*
criminal conspiracy laws and early unions
Oberlin, 1833; Mt. Holyoke, 1836
public education, Horace Mann
American Temperance Union
Ten Nights in a Bar-Room, Timothy Shay Arthur
Maine law, Neal Dow
Irish, German immigration
nativism; Samuel F.B. Morse, *Imminent Dangers to the Free Institutions of the United States through Foreign Immigration, and the Present State of the Naturalization Laws*
women, their rights, areas of discrimination
Lucretia Mott
Elizabeth Cady Stanton
Seneca Falls, 1848
Emma Willard
Catherine Beecher
"Cult of True Womanhood": piety, domesticity, purity, and submissiveness
women's movement, like others, overshadowed by antislavery movement
American Peace Society
prison reform: Auburn system, Pennsylvania system

SUPREME COURT CASES TO KNOW

1. *Marbury* v. *Madison,* 1803 (judicial review)

In March 1801, Secretary of State James Madison refused to give William Marbury a commission as a justice of the peace for Washington, D.C. after the previous presidential administration had authorized the commission. Marbury sued under a writ of mandamus to obtain his commission. The Court's decision, written by Chief Justice John Marshall, dismissed Marbury's suit because he had sued under a writ of mandamus, and the Constitution did not include such writs within its listing of the powers of the Supreme Court. The Judiciary Act of 1789 authorized the Supreme Court to issue a writ of mandamus, but, claimed Marshall, Congress could not enlarge the powers of the Supreme Court. Therefore, Section 13 of the Judiciary Act of 1789 was unconstitutional. This case is significant because it is the first time the Supreme Court declared an act of Congress unconstitutional. The second did not occur until the Dred Scott case.

2. *Fletcher* v. *Peck,* 1810 (contracts and state laws)

This case was the first to declare a state law void as a violation of the Constitution. Influenced by bribes the corrupt Georgia legislature sold land to speculators. The outraged public elected virtually a new legislature at the next election, and the new legislature rescinded the previous sale. The case involved the legality of the sale of a tract of land made before the second legislature rescinded the original transaction. Chief Justice John Marshall wrote the decision. The Georgia legislature could not interfere with a lawfully executed contract. No matter how the original land speculators had obtained the land grant, Fletcher had made a legal, contractual purchase with which the legislature could not interfere. The contract clause of the Constitution overrode the state law.

3. *Martin* v. *Hunters Lessee,* 1816 (federal appellate jurisdiction over state courts)

This case asserted that the Supreme Court had appellate jurisdiction over state court decisions. Concurrent federal and state jurisdiction did not make the state and federal courts equal, and state judges must decide cases according to "the supreme law of the land," the Constitution. Supreme Court appellate jurisdiction of state court cases ensures a uniformity of constitutional decisions.

4. *Dartmouth College* v. *Woodward,* 1819 (contracts and state laws)

In 1816 the state legislature of New Hampshire took over Dartmouth College. The board of trustees sued to regain control. Was the original charter granted in 1769 a contract within the meaning of the contract clause of the Constitution? The Supreme Court ruled that it was. The charter of a private corporation was protected by the Constitution and could not be altered by the people through their legislature.

5. *McCulloch* v. *Maryland,* 1819 (the elastic clause and federal state relations)

The state of Maryland levied a tax on the Baltimore branch of the Bank of the United States. The cashier of the Bank refused to pay the tax. The case raised the question of the constitutionality of the 1791 act of Congress which created the Bank, and the question of whether a state could tax the federal government. Marshall's opinion supported the loose construction theory of the Constitution. "Let the end be legitimate, let it be within the scope of the Constitution, and all means which are appropriate, which are plainly adapted to that end, which are not prohibited, but consist with the letter and spirit of the Constitution, are constitutional." The act of Congress creating the Bank was constitutional. In answering the second question the Court ruled that "the power to tax is the power to destroy." Think of the logic of taxation. The annual tax on the Baltimore branch was $15,000. Once the principle of state taxation of the Bank was admitted, though, what is the difference, in principle, between a $15,000 tax and a $483 billion dollar tax? A tax is a tax, but the second tax puts the bank into bankruptcy! Therefore, the Maryland tax was unconstitutional.

6. *Cohens* v. *Virginia,* 1821 (federal jurisdiction over state cases involving federal rights)

The Cohens were arrested and fined for selling lottery tickets in Virginia. They had sold Washington, D.C. lottery tickets authorized by Congress, the government for the District of Columbia. The Cohens appealed their conviction. Marshall rules that the Supreme Court possessed the power to review state court decisions to see "whether that judgment be in violation of the Constitution or the laws of the United States," in this case the act of Congress authorizing the D.C. lottery.

7. *Gibbons* v. *Ogden*, 1824 (federal control of interstate commerce)

This is the first case decided under the commerce clause. Two steamboat operators clashed over their respective charters to control steamboats in New York City harbor. One had a charter from the federal government; the other had a monopoly grant from the state of New York. The decision affirmed exclusive federal control of interstate commerce even in the absence of federal legislation or action.

8. *Cherokee Nation* v. *Georgia*, 1831; *Worcester* v. *Georgia*, 1832 (state laws, treaties, and Indians)

These two cases are part of the long struggle by Georgia to push the Cherokee Indians westward. The federal government had much earlier promised to support Georgia's efforts. The Cherokee tried to stop a Georgia declaration that the laws of the Cherokee were null and void. The Court ruled in the first case that while it lacked jurisdiction, the Cherokee Nation was a "domestic, dependent, nation" possessing some sovereignty, and not a foreign nation. In the second case Marshall ruled that the laws of Georgia had no force within the territorial boundaries of the Cherokee Nation. President Jackson, no admirer of Marshall, reportedly said, "John Marshall has made his decision, now let him enforce it." In this clear clash between state law and the federal government the president sided with the state of Georgia.

9. *Charles River Bridge* v. *Warren Bridge*, 1837 (contracts and the community's rights)

The Charles River Bridge Company sued to prevent the state of Massachusetts from authorizing the construction of a new bridge across the Charles River. Was its original charter a contract, an implied, vested, perpetual agreement? Chief Justice Roger B. Taney, in his first significant decision, ruled that no charter granted to a private corporation permanently vested rights that might harm the public interest. Taney wrote, "the continued existence of a government would be of no great value, if by implications and presumptions, it was disarmed of the powers necessary to accomplish the ends of its creation; and the functions it was designed to perform, transferred to the hands of privileged corporations." (Try to imagine the situation if the Charles River Bridge Company still owned the only permitted bridge across the Charles River.)

The rights of the community supersede a broad interpretation of the private rights of a corporation. "While the rights of property are sacredly guarded, we must not forget that the community also have rights. . . ." It is not the duty of the legislature to specify what the corporation charter does not say.

10. *Commonwealth* vs. *Hunt*, 1842 (a union's right to organize)

This Massachusetts decision ruled that trade union organization and strike tactics were legal. Traditional interpretations considered unions illegal under the conspiracy laws of English common law. This decision did not immediately open a new era for labor unions; many judges continued to consider unions to be illegal.

READINGS FOR DEPTH AND HISTORICAL INTERPRETATION

Foreign Policy

For issues in diplomatic history you are advised to concentrate on reading for depth rather than for acquiring various historical interpretations. Read for better understanding of the chronology and the complexities of foreign policy. Almost every student in American history can write in an essay that prior to the War of 1812 the British violated our neutral rights. How many include a paragraph on the "Rule of 1756," detailing one aspect of British violations? Strengthen your understanding of diplomatic history by reading relevant sections in standard diplomatic history textbooks.

Diplomatic History Textbooks

1. Samuel Flagg Bemis, *A Diplomatic History of the United States.* Thomas Bailey, *A Diplomatic History of the American People.* Robert H. Ferrell, *American Diplomacy.*

2. Dexter Perkins, *A History of the Monroe Doctrine.* The author is considered the authority on the Monroe Doctrine. The first two chapters describe the origins and meaning of the Monroe Doctrine.

Overviews of the Period

1. Marcus Cunliffe, *The Nation Takes Shape: 1789–1837*. An excellent survey of the period, it focuses on conflicts such as nationalism and sectionalism, conservatism and democracy, etc.

2. Alexis de Tocqueville, *Democracy in America*. This is a classic in American literature. Bear in mind as you read *Democracy in America* that it is an aristocratic Frenchman's sympathetic analysis of democracy rather than of America. Read sections of the book or see the selections and commentary in Robert B. Downs, *Books That Changed America*.

Jackson and Jacksonian Democracy

With some misgivings I recommend books and articles for Jackson and Jacksonianism. If you read everything written about this subject you will add to your knowledge but not necessarily to your understanding. This period is confusing. No historical interpretation or emphasis seems to exclude other interpretations, but simply piles on top of them. This period aptly exemplifies the old adage, "History is what historians say it is." Part of the source of the confusion is that Jackson and Jacksonian Democracy may be two separate entities having little to do with one another.

1. John William Ward, *Andrew Jackson: Symbol for an Age.* Ward uses three ideas—Nature, Providence, and Will—to study the period and to describe how Jackson came to symbolize these concepts in myth and fact. Intellectual history at its liveliest; you will never forget the images of Jackson.

2. Marvin Meyers, "The Old Republic and the New: An Introduction," and "The Restoration Theme: On Jacksons's Message," in his *The Jacksonian Persuasion: Politics and Belief*. Myers claims that Jacksonian Democrats in this era yearned for earlier republican virtues such as integrity, morality, frugality, and simplicity. They looked backward, not forward.

3. Richard P. McCormick, Chapter 7 in his *The Second American Party System: Party Formation in the Jacksonian Era*. A thoughtful analysis of the forces behind the creation of political parties in this period, it separates reality from the myths of Jacksonian politics.

4. Arthur M. Schlesinger, Jr., *The Age of Jackson*, especially the chapters "Jacksonian Democracy as an Intellectual Movement" and "Traditions of Democracy," which include a discussion of Jeffersonian Democracy. Schlesinger defines liberal reform as the periodic attempt by "other sections of society to restrain the power of the business community." He sees the origins of Jacksonian Democracy in the lower economic classes, and challenges Frederick Jackson Turner's theme of Jackson as a western revolt.

5. Bray Hammond, Chapters 12–15, *Banks and Politics in America From the Revolution to the Civil War*.

   Richard Hofstadter, "Andrew Jackson and the Rise of Liberal Capitalism," in his *The American Political Tradition*.

   These two selections argue that Jacksonian Democracy was the successful struggle by one group of entrepreneurs against an entrenched, privileged business group identified with the Bank of the United States. Hammond summarizes it as a struggle between Wall Street and Chestnut Street, the Philadelphia site of the Bank.

6. Edward Pessen, *Jacksonian America: Society, Personality and Politics*. A very readable survey of the period, it includes his studies of social mobility in Jacksonian America. He found increasing inequality, not a rise in democracy. See also Edward Pessen, "The Egalitarian Myth and the American Social Reality: Wealth, Mobility, and Equality in the 'Era of the Common Man'," *American Historical Review*, 1971.

Reform

1. Barbara Welter, "The Cult of True Womanhood: 1820–1860," *American Quarterly*, Summer 1966. Welter describes the creation of the image of the ideal middle-class woman complete with the four cardinal virtues—piety, purity, submissiveness, and domesticity.

2. John L. Thomas, "Romantic Reform in America, 1815–1865," *American Quarterly*, Winter 1965. In his analysis of the reform impulse Thomas emphasizes the reliance upon individual conversion as a method for achieving reform. Difficult reading but insightful.

SAMPLE OUTLINE

THE AGE OF REFORM

I. **Defining Reform**

   A. Reform and revolution: Revolution implies a thorough revision of the institutions of society; reform is more of a patching approach to the ills of society.

   B. Heredity and environment: Reforms tend to come in periods of greater faith in environment as an influence on individuals.

   C. Perfectibility: A key characteristic of this reform era was the belief in the perfectibility of man and the doctrine of progress, a desire to perfect human institutions, a belief in the worth of the individual, and a compassionate humanitarianism.

II. **Characteristics of the Reform Impulse**

   A. Part of the Romantic literary stress on the natural, the simple, the ordinary

   B. Reformers tended to be optimists.

   C. Reformers displayed an extraordinary sense of obligation and stewardship and religious conviction.

   D. They saw science and reason as complementing religion, not contradicting it, but did not have the supreme faith in reason characteristic of the Enlightenment.

   E. Catholic in their concerns and interests, they recognized the complexity and interdependence of modern society, and were well aware of similar reforms in Europe.

   F. Reformers tended to come from well-to-do and middle-class. Politically they tended to be old Federalists, Whigs, and anti-Jackson.

   G. This was a period of institutional instability. (Colonial society had been balanced, with measured economic development, a slow trend toward equality, and social order and stability.) Economic individualism eroded this, and led to instability and to the proliferation of the chief mechanism of reform—the voluntary association.

   H. An emphasis on institutional solutions to social problems—the asylum, the custodial school—in an urban society that was deteriorating. What was needed was regimentation, punctuality, precision.

   I. Not all reform aimed toward progress and goodness. 1. Nativism: an attempt to Americanize a newly pluralistic society 2. Temperance: leaders narrow and bigoted, Dow

   J. Variety of reforms: Reformers sometimes fought one another for attention, funds, workers, etc.

   K. They may have worked in a local area, but their goals were national in vision.

   L. Motivation? a displaced elite? a displaced class without function? impose their values?

III. Example: Education Reform

A. Prior to the 1830s
   1. Colonial schools: high literacy rate, few public schools, dame schools, transitory teachers
   2. Schools: little preparation for world of work
   3. English tradition: nondenominational charity schools designed to build character
   4. Sunday school: Their emphasis and purpose changed from 1815 to 1840 from teaching fundamental skills to teaching religion, from serving the poor to serving everyone.
   5. Lancaster system, monitorial school
   6. Regular schools: sixty-plus kids per room

B. Behind the impulse for educational reform

   1. Change in the conception of childhood, from miniature adults to children in a plastic, malleable stage
   2. Education seen as the key to progress, to democracy, and to individual fulfillment
   3. Changes in the family and the role of the wife due to Industrial Revolution

C. Issues of educational reform

   1. Tuition: Does it make one a better parent? How to attract the lower classes (formerly the "rate schools" were free but for special tax on parents)?
   2. Great concern for the future of urban society, how to break the cycle of poverty
   3. Social control: the breakdown of institutional controls, the school as a custodial institution, discipline (in one school in Boston—65 floggings per day out of 400 students in the school). Should these methods continue?
   4. Local control versus larger (state), the benefits of uniformity versus local control
   5. Teaching teachers–unspecialized schools?
   6. Separate schools for blacks? Roberts case in Boston. In St. Louis the black schools had numbers, not names, and no black teachers.
   7. Since no compulsory attendance laws yet, how to attract the middle class? What range of subjects offered in the high school?
   8. Male or female teachers? A feminization of the teaching faculty. Mann quote: "The greater intensity of the parental instinct in the female sex, their natural love of the society of children, and the superior gentleness and forebearance of their dispositions—all of which lead them to mildness rather than severity, to the use of hope rather than fear as a motive of action, and to the various arts of encouragement rather than to annoyances and compulsion, in their management of the young."
   9. Catholics: How to attract them into the public school? In NYC—from 2% to 19% of the population; which Bible to use? Differences found in St. Louis: Catholic schools, foreign-born teachers, emphasis on absolute values; public schools, native-born teachers, emphasis on a functional education. In 1844, NJ was the first state to put secular education in its constitution.

D. Horace Mann, the father of public education

   1. Appointed Secretary to the Mass State Board of Education in 1837; influential through his twelve annual reports—little regard for educational theory, practical and useful information
   2. "I have faith in the improvability of the race—in their accelerating improvability."

3. The means of education: "On schools and teachers I rely more than on any other earthly instrumentality, for the prosperity and honor of the state, and for the reformation and advancement of the race. All other reforms seek to abolish specific ills; education is preventive." The public common school is "the greatest discovery ever made by man."

4. Moralistic, he believed that most problems were moral. Favorite words: Man, Duty, God. One of his last statements was, "Be ashamed to die until you have won some victory for humanity."

E. Results

1. Reformers could not imagine a workable pluralistic society of different cultures, values, and traditions.

2. Gains not uniform: Of 320 high schools in 1860, 167 were in just three states—NY, Ohio, and Mass

3. Laid the basis for great expansion after Civil War

Unit Five: 1840 to 1877

MAJOR THEMES AND IDEAS

Slavery and Abolitionism

1. Trace the history of blacks and slavery from 1619 to the Fifteenth Amendment.
2. "Mind of the South" (Wilbur Cash wrote a book by that title, *The Mind of the South.*)
3. Slavery from the viewpoint of the slave, the slaveholder, and the nonslaveholding white Southerner
4. The issue of slavery in the territories involved an imaginary slave in a place not suited for slavery.
5. Slavery as a threat to white Northern labor
6. Compare the black struggle to achieve freedom with the abolitionist struggle to free slaves.
7. Southern justifications for slavery
8. Blacks in the North, 1790–1860
9. William Lloyd Garrison: hero or villain of the antislavery movement?
10. South fought to keep from becoming what the North had become, a democratic society.
11. Trace sectionalism from 1810–1850 through the careers of Clay, Calhoun, and Webster.
12. Northerners objected not to slaves but to the political and economic power and influence slavery gave the slaveholder in the national government.
13. There were many reforms in the 1830s; by the 1850s abolition was the only reform.
14. Why was abolition disreputable in the 1830s and acceptable by the 1850s?
15. Slavery dominated all aspects of Southern life: political, economic, social, and intellectual.

Civil War and Reconstruction

1. Event, person, or place as a symbol of North-South division, such as bleeding Kansas, John Brown, or the Crittenden Compromise
2. Role of the Supreme Court in the Civil War and Reconstruction
3. Breakdown of both the Whig and Democratic parties in the 1850s and the rise of the third party system
4. Struggle between the president and Congress for dominant political power within the federal government, 1850–1868
5. Accomplishments and failures of Reconstruction

6. States' rights from 1790—1860 for all the sections
7. Civil War: triumph of American democracy over European aristocracy
8. Why did black male suffrage come before white female suffrage?
9. The 1850s: a decade of political sectionalism and economic nationalism
10. When did the Civil War become inevitable and why?
11. What causes of the Civil War were resolved by the Civil War and Reconstruction?
12. The North and the South compromised in 1820, 1833, 1850, and 1877. Why was compromise impossible in 1860?
13. Did the North win the Civil War or the South lose it?
14. Outline events of the 1850s.
15. Historiography of the causes of the Civil War
16. Compare the elections of 1852, 1856, and 1860.
17. Was the Republican Party consistent in its policies from the 1850s to 1877?
18. Decade of the 1850s as a period of major battles within rather than between parties
19. The issues of the Civil War were similar to those of the American Revolution.
20. Lincoln: a hero to blacks?
21. Why is Lincoln ranked as a great president?
22. Why did Lincoln, who opposed social and political equality for blacks, eventually free the slaves?

Economy

1. Role of the state and national governments in promoting economic growth
2. Trace land policy changes.
3. Trace changes in the economy in transportation, money, labor, banking, sectionalism, and commerce.
4. Republican legislation passed during the Civil War—triumph of Clay's American System and beginnings of industrial growth
5. Economic changes in American society drew the Northeast and the Northwest closer while driving the South from both.
6. Industrialization in the United States
7. Trace the history of the corporation as a business institution.

8. Compare Southern black slavery and Northern wage slavery.
9. The South: an underdeveloped economy in the antebellum period
10. Southern economic grievances against the North
11. North-South economic differences before the Civil War that continued unresolved after it
12. Trace the history of the union movement from 1790 to 1860.

Expansion and Foreign Affairs

1. Principles that caused territorial expansion between 1815 and 1860
2. Slavery and territorial expansion as causes of the Civil War
3. Impact of Manifest Destiny on both foreign affairs and domestic politics
4. U.S. policy toward Latin America was dishonorable, but produced good results.
5. The Civil War began with the Mexican War.
6. Principles of the Monroe Doctrine and how these principles were put into practice from 1823 to 1895
7. Compare policies toward California, Texas Cuba, and Oregon.

8. Manifest Destiny grew out of Jacksonian Democracy.
9. Why was Oregon annexed peacefully, but not Texas?
10. Trace the history of the Oregon Territory to annexation.
11. Use Texas to illustrate the characteristics and consequences of American foreign policy from 1830 to 1850.
12. Trace relations between Great Britain and the United States from 1830 to 1875.
13. The diplomacy of the Civil War was based on consistent principles.
14. The opening of trade relations with China and Japan illustrates significant themes in American foreign policy.

Black History

1. Supreme Court, Congress, and the president and the position of blacks in American society, 1850–1900
2. Compare the social and political gains made by blacks during Reconstruction with those during the second Reconstruction, and during the 1950s and 1960s.
3. Outline developments in the history of blacks between 1865 and 1912.

MAJOR TERMS AND CONCEPTS

Manifest Destiny

Great American Desert
"Manifest Destiny"
Horace Greeley
Senator Thomas Hart Benton
Stephen Austin
Texas War for Independence
Santa Anna
Alamo
San Jacinto
Sam Houston
Republic of Texas
annexation of Texas, joint resolution under President Tyler
election of 1844: candidates, issues, third party's impact, Liberty Party
reoccupation of Texas and reannexation of Oregon
54° 40′ or Fight!

James K. Polk
Slidell mission to Mexico
Rio Grande, Nueces River, disputed territory
General Zachary Taylor
Mexican War: causes, results
spot resolutions
Stephen Kearny, John C. Fremont, General Winfield Scott
Nicholas Trist
Treaty of Guadelupe Hidalgo provisions
All Mexico movement
Mexican Cession
Webster-Ashburton Treaty
Caroline and Creole affairs
Aroostook War
John Jacob Astor
Oregon fever
Willamette Valley
Oregon territory

49th parallel
election of 1848: Cass, Taylor
Wilmot Proviso
Joseph Smith
Brigham Young, Mormons, Great Salt Lake
Gadsden Purchase
hegemony

Economy

Samuel Slater
"transportation revolution"
Eli Whitney, interchangeable parts
cotton gin (short for engine)
Erie Canal
National Road (Cumberland Road)
Commonwealth vs. *Hunt* (Mass case)
Boston Associates
Lowell factory, factory girls
Cyrus McCormick, mechanical reaper
Elias Howe
ten-hour movement
clipper ships
Cyrus Field
Robert Fulton, steamships
Samuel F.B. Morse, telegraph
Walker Tariff, 1846
Independent Treasury system, Van Buren and Polk

Slavery and South

American Colonization Society
cotton gin
abolitionism
sectionalism
William Lloyd Garrison
The Liberator
American Antislavery Society
Theodore Weld
Theodore Parker
the Grimké sisters
Elijah Lovejoy
Wendell Phillips
Nat Turner's insurrection
David Walker, *Walker's Appeal*
Sojourner Truth
Gabriel Prosser
Denmark Vesey
Frederick Douglass
Tredegar Iron Works, Richmond, Virginia
mountain whites in the South
Prigg v. *Pa*, 1842

personal liberty laws
"King Cotton"
Free Soil Party

The 1850s

John Sutter
forty-niners
California applies for admission as a state
Compromise of 1850: provisions, impact
Fugitive Slave Law
Anthony Burns
Ableman v. *Booth*
Webster's 7th of March speech
Nashville Convention
Henry Clay
John C. Calhoun
underground railroad
Harriet Tubman
Uncle Tom's Cabin, Harriet Beecher Stowe
election of 1852: end of the Whig Party
Perry and Japan
Ostend Manifesto
Kansas-Nebraska Act, 1854
birth of the Republican Party
Stephen A. Douglas
popular sovereignty
36° 30′ line
election of 1856: Republican Party, Know-Nothing
  Party
"bleeding Kansas" and Lawrence
"Beecher's Bibles"
John Brown's raid
Pottawatomie massacre
New England Emigrant Aid Company
Sumner-Brooks affair
Lecompton Constitution
Dred Scott decision
Chief Justice Roger B. Taney (pronounced Tawny)
Lincoln-Douglas debates of 1858 during Illinois
  senatorial campaign
Freeport Doctrine
panic of 1857
George Fitzhugh, *Sociology for the South, or the Failure*
  of Free Society
Hinton Helper, *The Impending Crisis of the South*
Lincoln's "house divided" speech
John Brown, Harpers Ferry raid
election of 1860: candidates, parties, issues
Democratic Party conventions: Baltimore, Charleston
John Bell
John Breckinridge

Republican Party: 1860 platform, supporters, leaders
Buchanan and the secession crisis
Crittenden Compromise proposal

Civil War

border states
South's advantages in the Civil War
North's advantages in the Civil War
Fort Sumter
Bull Run
Monitor and the Merrimac
Lee, Jackson
Grant, McClellan, Sherman, Meade
Vicksburg, Gettysburg, Antietam, Appomattox
Jefferson Davis, Alexander Stephens
Northern blockade
cotton versus wheat
Copperheads
Congressman Clement L. Vallandigham
suspension of habeas corpus
Republican legislation passed in Congress after Southerners left: banking, tariff, homestead, transcontinental railroad
conscription, draft riots
Emancipation Proclamation
Charles Francis Adams
Great Britain: Trent, Alabama, Laird rams, "continuous voyage"
election of 1864: candidates, parties
financing of the war effort by North and South
Clara Barton

Reconstruction

Lincoln's ten percent plan
assassination of April 14, 1865
John Wilkes Booth
Ex parte Milligan
Radical Republicans

Wade-Davis bill, veto, Wade-Davis Manifesto
Joint Committee on Reconstruction (Committee of Fifteen)
Reconstruction acts, 1867
state suicide theory
conquered territory theory
the unreconstructed South
black codes
Texas v. White, 1869
Thaddeus Stevens
Charles Sumner
Andrew Johnson
Freedmen's Bureau
General Oliver O. Howard
Ku Klux Klan
Civil Rights Act
Thirteenth Amendment
Fourteenth Amendment and its provisions
Fifteenth Amendment
Tenure of Office Act
impeachment
Chief Justice Chase
Secretary of War Stanton
scalawags, carpetbaggers
purchase of Alaska
Secretary of State William Seward
Napoleon III
Maximilian in Mexico
Monroe Doctrine
Ulysses S. Grant
Treaty of Washington
Secretary of State Hamilton Fish
election of 1872; Liberal Republicans, Horace Greeley
election of 1876: Hayes and Tilden
Compromise of 1877 provisions
Solid South
sharecropping, crop lien system
segregation
Hiram R. Revels
Blanche K. Bruce

SUPREME COURT CASES TO KNOW

1. *Prigg* v. *Pennsylvania,* 1842 (fugitive slaves and federal-state powers)

Pennsylvania tried to prohibit the capture and return of runaway slaves within the state, a direct challenge to the federal government's fugitive slave law of 1793. The state law was declared unconstitutional because the return of fugitive slaves was a federal power as specified in Article IV, section 2 of the Constitution. Many Northern states responded by prohibiting state officials from assisting anyone pursuing runaway slaves (called personal liberty laws).

2. *Dred Scott* v. *Sandford,* 1857 (citizenship and slaves)

This complex case raised three questions: 1) Was Dred Scott a citizen? If he wasn't, he could not sue in a federal court. In other words, did the Supreme Court have jurisdiction to hear the case? 2) Could Congress exclude slavery from the territories? Since territories are controlled by Congress, who exercised a responsibility to represent all the people of the United States, could Congress restrict citizens of one section from taking their slaves into the territories? 3) If slaves are property, is the owner not protected by the Fifth Amendment from being deprived of his property without compensation?

Dred Scott was owned by an army doctor who took Scott into Illinois and part of the Wisconsin territory. Slavery had been outlawed in these two areas by the Northwest Ordinance and Illinois law and by the Missouri Compromise of 1820. Scott sued for his freedom based on the argument that residence on free soil made him a free man. The case quickly became a test case, with the doctor's widow selling Scott to her brother, Sanford, in New York (misspelled Sandford in official legal documents). The involvement of two different states forced the case into the federal courts.

All the judges wrote separate opinions in the case, which caused the debate to go on long after the decisions. The majority held that Scott was not a citizen; free blacks or slaves could not be citizens of the United States. They could be granted state citizenship. (The Fourteenth Amendment clearly granted dual citizenship to abolish this aspect of the case.) The judges could have ended their explanation here, and they hoped to do so. Two Northern Supreme Court judges, however, announced their intention to write long dissenting opinions against the majority, and the majority was forced to refute the hostile dissents. But the majority itself was so divided in its reasoning that all the majority judges wrote separate opinions. In answering the other two questions the Taney court declared the Missouri Compromise null and void because it prohibited a citizen of the United States from taking his property (slaves) into the territories. Southerners smiled; Northerners bristled with contempt. Dred Scott's owner freed him and his family.

3. *Ableman* v. *Booth,* 1859 (a state challenge to federal authority)

Booth, a Wisconsin abolitionist editor, was arrested by the federal government for helping a fugitive slave escape from the custody of a federal marshall. The Wisconsin Supreme Court issued a writ of habeas corpus to release him. The federal authorities refused to recognize the validity of the writ of habeas corpus.

Chief Justice Taney wrote the unanimous decision asserting that a court or judge which goes beyond the limits of its jurisdiction exercises "nothing less than lawless violence." The issue was now federal supremacy, not the fugitive slave laws. Northern reaction paralleled the earlier Virginia and Kentucky Resolutions.

4. Ex parte Merryman, 1861 (president's war powers)

This is not technically a Supreme Court case. Early in the Civil War an unruly Baltimore mob attacked Union soldiers passing through the city. Under President Lincoln's orders the army suspended habeas corpus and declared martial law. John Merryman, a Southern sympathizer, was among those arrested. The federal circuit judge, who happened to be Chief Justice Roger B. Taney, issued a writ of habeas corpus which the army refused to accept. The only recourse left to Taney was to write to the president criticizing his usurpation of the power of Congress (Article I, section 9). Lincoln never directly replied. When Merryman was no longer a potential threat to the war effort he was quietly released.

5. Prize Cases, 1863 (president's war powers)

In April 1861, Lincoln declared a blockade of Southern ports before Congress met to react to secession. Captured ship owners sued to recover their property, and claimed that in the absence of a declaration of war by Congress the president was powerless. The Court by a 5-4 margin upheld the blockade from the date it was first proclaimed. Under his powers as commander in chief the president had to respond to an insurrection which had become a war "without waiting for Congress to baptize it with a name."

6. Ex parte Milligan, 1866 (constitutional rights during war)

Lambdin Milligan, a citizen of Indiana, was arrested for subversive activities in support of the Southern cause during the Civil War. He was tried, convicted, and sentenced to die by a military court in Indiana in spite of the fact that the Indiana civilian court system was functioning. Milligan's appeal to the Supreme Court raised the question of the dividing line between civil and military control over civilians during wartime. The Supreme Court ruled that while the Constitution permitted the suspension of habeas corpus, it did not suspend the judicial powers of federal courts. Military tribunals could be established, but when the federal courts were "open and ready" no other court could claim jurisdiction. "The Constitution of the United States is a law for rulers and people, equally in war and in peace, and covers with the shield of its protection all classes of men, at all times, and under all circumstances." Milligan sued for damages for false imprisonment. A jury awarded him five dollars.

7. *Mississippi* v. *Johnson,* 1867 (separation of powers)

This case involved the attempt by the state of Mississippi to force the president to stop enforcing the Reconstruction acts on the grounds that the acts were unconstitutional. Can the Supreme Court stop the president from carrying out an act of Congress?

"The Congress is the legislative department of the government; the President is the executive department. Neither can be restrained in its action by the judicial department; though the acts of both, when performed, are in proper cases, subject to its cognizance."

The Court had earlier issued the doctrine of political question to avoid involvement in Dorr's Rebellion (*Luther* v. *Borden,* 1849). This doctrine simply stated that the issue was a political question to be resolved at the polls or in the legislature.

8. *Texas* v. *White,* 1869 (nature of the Union)

This case involved the legality of the sale of U.S. federal government bonds in the possession of the Texas government, which were sold after the state seceded. The case hinged upon the question of whether or not a state could leave the Union. The Court said secession was constitutionally impossible. "The Constitution, in all its provisions, looks to an indestructible Union, composed of indestructible states.

"When, therefore, Texas became one of the United States, she entered into an indissoluble relation. All the obligations of perpetual union and all the guarantees of republican government in the Union, attached at once to the State. The act which consummated her admission into the Union was something more than a compact; it was the incorporation of a new member into the political body. And it was final. The union between Texas and the other states was as complete, as perpetual, and as indissoluble as the union between the original States."

READINGS FOR DEPTH AND HISTORICAL INTERPRETATION

Slavery

1. Kenneth Stamp, *The Peculiar Institution.* An early attack on Ulrich B. Phillip's older view that slavery would have died eventually if left alone and was a benign paternalistic institution, a schoolhouse of civilization for primitive Africans. Stamp painted a picture of rebellious slaves, and destroyed the myth of the contented happy slave.

2. John Blassingame, *The Slave Community,* especially the revised and enlarged edition. Blassingame looks at slavery through the eyes of black slaves, history seen from the bottom up. He studies the "African heritage, culture, family, acculturation, behavior, religion, and personality."

3. Herbert G. Gutman, *The Black Family in Slavery and Freedom, 1750–1925.* This attacks the myth of the maternalistic black family existing in and coming out of slavery. Considering the impedi-

ments, slave families were remarkably durable and resilent.

4. Eugene D. Genovese, *The World the Slaveholders Made.* Or see "The Slave South: An Interpretation," *Science & Society,* December 1961, pp. 320-337, which is also in *The Political Economy of Slavery.* A Marxist scholar, he sees a precapitalist society in the South dominated economically, politically, and socially by an aristocratic class of planters. Within the context of the master-slave relationship the slaves fought back to the best of their ability.

5. Richard Hofstadter, "John C. Calhoun: The Marx of the Master Class," in *The American Political Tradition.* A good explanation of the political thought of America's most original political thinker. Hofstadter explores the economic foundations of Calhoun's ideas.

6. Stanley Elkins, *Slavery, A Problem in American Institutional Life.* See also the introduction in Ann J. Lane, *The Debate Over Slavery: Stanley Elkins and His Critics.* Elkins explains the Sambo image of slaves as arising out of the no-exit situation of slavery, which caused slaves to revert to infantile behavior patterns.

Economy, 1790–1860

1. George R. Taylor, *The Transportation Revolution, 1815–1860.* Uses changes in transportation to illustrate fundamental changes in the American economy in this period.

2. Louis Hartz, *Economic Policy and Democratic Thought: Pennsylvania, 1776–1860.* Using Pennsylvania as a case study, Hartz shows that state governments often intervened in the economy to direct economic affairs. He destroys the myth that laissez-faire aptly describes governmental policy in this era.

3. Douglass C. North, "Acceleration of U.S. Economic Growth, 1815–1860," in his *Growth and Welfare in the American Past: A New Economic History.* See also North's *The Economic Growth of the United States, 1790–1860.* North uses the newer approach of statistical analysis to look at economic growth.

4. Richard Hofstadter, "Andrew Jackson and the Rise of Liberal Capitalism," in *The American Political Tradition.* Hofstadter covers the Bank War and introduces students to the entrepreneurial school of interpretation.

The 1850s and the Coming of the Civil War

1. Charles and Mary Beard, *The Rise of American Civilization.* The war was caused by competition between economic interest groups fighting for control of the federal government. The two major economic groups—industrialists and planters— just happened also to be divided geographically.

2. James G. Randall, "The Blundering Generation," *Mississippi Valley Historical Review,* June 1940. The 1850s generation blundered into a needless and unnecessary war because they were not intelligent political leaders. They played on emotions to gain votes rather than face the issues.

3. Avery Craven, *The Coming of the Civil War,* or "The 1840s and the Democratic Process," *Journal of Southern History* XVI, 1950. Agitation over slavery led to mistaken and false sectional images. The fanaticism of the abolitionists was critical in causing the war (as well as irresponsible).

4. Arthur M. Schlesinger, Jr., "The Causes of the Civil War: A Note on Historical Sentimentalism," *The Partisan Review,* October 1949. The needless war and the blundering generation critics miss a major point. Some moral evils are so great that their destruction is worth the deaths of thousands. Slavery was such a moral evil. Schlesinger had been influenced by the experiences of the Second World War.

Reconstruction

1. Kenneth Stamp, "The Tragic Legend of Reconstruction," *Commentary,* January 1965. Summarizes the Dunning school interpretation of Reconstruction and shows how the revisionists have challenged the older interpretation. Places the older interpretation within the context of that era's intellectual thought.

2. Carl Degler, "Dawn Without Noon," in *Out of Our Past,* latest revised edition. Summarizes the recent revisionist historical views of Reconstruction.

3. William A. Dunning, *Essays on the Civil War & Reconstruction.* A reprint of the 1897 book. The original statement by one who saw Reconstruction as a tragic era.

4. John Hope Franklin, *From Slavery to Freedom.* Black history by a noted black historian. He emphasizes the positive black achievements during Reconstruction.

5. C. Vann Woodward, *The Strange Career of Jim Crow,* third and revised edition. Woodward links the first Reconstruction to the second, the civil rights movement in the 1950s and 1960s. He sees segregation as a product of the politics of the Populist revolt, not the Reconstruction era.

6. E. Merton Coulter, *The South During Reconstruction, 1865–1877.* A more modern (1947) summary of the Dunning interpretation.

SAMPLE OUTLINE

Reconstruction confuses students. This period in American history can be organized around many different themes. One theme is the North versus the South, or the Civil War continued. Among the salient points in this emphasis are the triumph of Northern economic interests; the North first aiding blacks in the South and then losing interest and commitment; and the question of which came first, Southern intransigence or Radical Republican laws. A second theme looks at Reconstruction as either a success or a failure, with an emphasis on the differing viewpoints of the Dunning school of historians and the revisionist historians. A third view concentrates on the South, seeing the essence of Reconstruction in the ongoing struggle between Southern whites and the former slaves. A fourth method for viewing Reconstruction is through the contest between Congress and the president over the issue of civil rights for blacks. This viewpoint is outlined below.

MEANING OF RECONSTRUCTION

CONGRESS VERSUS PRESIDENT OVER ISSUE OF CIVIL RIGHTS

Two concepts are central to Reconstruction: 1) the demand of Congress that the president recognize the prerogative of Congress (the powers of Congress are listed first in the Constitution because legislative power is paramount); and 2) the demand of Congress to somehow guarantee civil rights for blacks

I. **Presidents Take Charge**

 A. The relationship between Lincoln and Congress created a residue of ill will.

 1. Beginning of the Civil War: Lincoln did not call a special session of Congress from April to July.
 2. President suspended habeas corpus, suppressed newspapers, and issued arrest order for Congressman Vallandigham.
 3. President issued Emancipation Proclamation, Jan 1, 1863.
 4. Question of Lincoln's commitment: once spoke of colonizing blacks outside the U.S., and of letting South work out details of black-white relations after the war
 5. President's Reconstruction Plan
 a. When 10% of all ex-Confederates take oath of allegiance and agree to support Thirteenth Amendment, states may set up a state government.
 b. Tenn, Ark, and La did.
 6. Congressional reaction—Wade-Davis bill, July 1864—asserted Congressional control of Reconstruction, pocket vetoed by Lincoln. Wade-Davis Manifesto, August 1864, blasted Lincoln.
 a. Majority (not 10%) must take loyalty oath,
 b. must repudiate Confederate debt.
 c. Similarities to Lincoln's: accept Thirteenth Amendment, high Confederate officials disenfranchised
 Quote from Wade-Davis Manifesto: The President "must understand that our support is of a cause and not of a man; that the authority of Congress is paramount and must be respected; that the whole body of the Union men of Congress will not submit to be impeached by him of rash and unconstitutional

legislation; and if he wishes our support, he must confine himself to his executive duties—to obey and execute, not make the laws—to suppress by arms armed rebellion, and leave political reorganization to Congress."

B. Election of 1864 and Andrew Johnson

1. Republican Party dissolved; Union Party with former Republican from North as President, former Democrat from South as Vice-president
2. Second Inaugural Address conciliatory
3. Lincoln assassinated April 14, 1865. Johnson takes over.
4. Johnson's Reconstruction Plan: South abolish slavery, accept Thirteenth Amendment, repudiate Confederate debt, disavow secession.
5. Congress not in session April to December 1, 1865
6. All but Texas accepted Johnson's terms for return
7. South unrepentant in spirit: black codes
8. In November election for Congress, South elected many ex-Confederate leaders, who arrogantly demanded Congressional seniority back. Congress kicked them out.

II. Congress Takes Charge

A. Seized control of Reconstruction policy

1. Joint Committee on Reconstruction (Committee of Fifteen): Thaddeus Stevens, Benjamin Wade, Charles Sumner
2. Theoretical question of control over South: territorial status or state suicide theory
3. Motives: protect program of Republican Party (banking, tariff, RR, Homestead Act) to ensure its future
4. "Radical" tag a misnomer; all but handful opposed Johnson
5. Thaddeus Stevens, September 6, 1865, advocated 40 acres and a mule.
6. General Sherman issued Order No. 15: 40,000 land titles to freedmen for 485,000 acres seized
7. Southern Homestead Act, July 1866 (expired January 1, 1867) extended principle of 1862 Homestead Act to public lands of Ala, Miss, Ark, La, and Fla. It was open to all who did not support the Confederacy. It failed; their land was inferior, and freedmen lacked capital for equipment.

B. Congress and president fight over civil rights and Reconstruction policies

1. February 1866: Freedmen's Bureau extended, vetoed, and passed over veto.
2. April 1866: Civil Rights Act passed, vetoed, and passed over veto.
3. Fourteenth Amendment proposed, and sent to states. All Southern states but Tenn refused to ratify.
4. In the Congressional elections of 1866, Radicals won over two-thirds of seats.

C. Congress in control

1. March 1867 Reconstruction Act: Ten Southern states divided into five military districts (the "sinful ten" who rejected the Fourteenth Amendment).
2. To reenter the Union they had to write new state constitutions, guarantee black suffrage, and ratify the Fourteenth Amendment.
3. By election of 1868, only three had not accepted these terms—Va, Tex, Miss.
4. In 1868 election Republican Grant narrowly wins. Democrats win two Southern states, La and Ga; Radicals claimed only because blacks were not allowed to vote.
5. Fifteenth Amendment proposed to guarantee black vote.

D. Congress handcuffs Supreme Court

1. No appeals to courts allowed under Reconstruction acts
2. Number of SC judges reduced to prevent Johnson from appointing one if vacancy occured

E. Assuring a Republican Party future

1. Impeachment part of Congress vs. president battle over civil rights
2. Tenure of Office Act: Secretary of War Stanton was in charge of five military districts, and therefore control of this office meant control of Reconstruction policy.
3. Trial ended 35-19; failed by one vote, two-thirds needed.
4. Pliant Grant wins presidency.
5. Va, Tex, and Miss accepted Fifteenth Amendment and were readmitted.
6. Ga readmitted after being put again under military rule for anti-black measures

F. After 1870

1. Southerners and Conservatives gradually regained control of individual Southern states.
2. General Amnesty Act, 1872, issued for all but 500 top ex-Confederates.
3. Republicans still worked to protect blacks and civil rights: Ku Klux Klan Acts, Civil Rights Act, 1875.

III. Reconstruction and Civil Rights

A. Putting the commitment to equal rights in perspective

1. The U.S. was the first major nation to commit itself to equal rights for all.
2. In later quest for equality blacks appealed to the national government to obey established national laws rather than to change them.

B. Reasons for the failure to secure civil rights

1. The push for black equality required interference with local governments on a massive scale. The weakness of the Radical program was this dependence on national intervention.
2. Black vote supported on principle and on Republican dependence on black vote. As the second weakened, so did the first.
3. Difficult to ensure legal and constitutional racial equality in a society that did not popularly believe in the equality of the races in any sense. The popular belief in the equality of the races is a mid-20th century concept.

Unit Six: 1865 to 1900

MAJOR THEMES AND IDEAS

Politics in Late 19th Century

1. Characteristics of the third party system
2. Characteristics of politics in the late 19th century
3. Compare and contrast Democratic and Republican parties: base of support, policies, successes, etc.
4. Relative powers and influence of Congress, presidents, and Supreme Court
5. History of political reform movements and why they failed
6. Who in this period deserves to be called a statesman, and why?
7. Compare Cleveland with any other period politician.
8. Presidents are rarely successful in both foreign policy and domestic policy. Assess this statement in regard to Johnson and Grant.
9. Pivotal election of 1896

Business

1. Is the Robber Baron nickname deserved?
2. Changes in the economy from 1865–1900 in transportation, agriculture, labor force, and industry
3. Did the Civil War stimulate or retard industrialization?
4. Rise of corporations, trusts, pools, and holding companies
5. Social mobility and businessmen (their origins)
6. Antimonopoly movement to the 1930s
7. The 1890s as a decade of economic, political, and social crises
8. Factors that promoted industrialization
9. Which shaped the economy more, individual businessmen or market forces?
10. Trace shifting Supreme Court decisions in regard to the regulation of railroads and industry.
11. Money question as an economic and political problem
12. This period, 1865–1900, as a period of governmental intervention in the economy, not of laissez-faire.

Labor

1. Characteristics of different unions—NLU, Knights, AFL, ARU—differences, successes, failures, leaders, reasons for directions they took
2. Changing workplace conditions: wages, hours, safety
3. Compare and contrast the Haymarket Square riot, the Homestead strike, and the Pullman strike.
4. Why were American workers unreceptive to socialist doctrines?
5. Attitude of government, state and federal, toward labor unions to 1914

Urbanization

1. Explain the location and growth of specific cities.
2. Impact of new immigrants on cities
3. Rise of spectator sports
4. Explain James Bryce's observation that city governments were "the one conspicuous failure of the United States."
5. Advantages and disadvantages of urban life
6. Gilded Age as an era of "conspicuous consumption" (Thorstein Veblen's phrase)
7. Reciprocal relationship between technology and urban growth
8. Reformers' attempts to address problems of poverty, housing, and health
9. Municipal governments: why were they so bad, why so frustrating to reformers?
10. Women's Movement, 1848 to 1900
11. Churches' attack on social and economic problems
12. Rise of urban transportation
13. Reactions to immigration: pre-Civil War, Civil War to 1920s
14. Urbanization reflected in art and literature

Social and Intellectual Movements and Ideas

1. What did intellectuals criticize in American society?

2. Darwinism and church leaders
3. Darwinism created and justified new thought.
4. Impact of Darwinism on scientific thought
5. Compare and contrast Henry George and Edward Bellamy.
6. Higher education: role of individuals and governments
7. *Progress and Poverty* and *Uncle Tom's Cabin* were two of the three top selling books of the 19th century. Evaluate their themes and impact.
8. Competition and laissez-faire as ideals and as realities
9. Characteristics of literature and art in the late 19th century
10. The Social Gospel as a religious movement.
11. Causes of the increasing inequality of wealth and solutions proposed by intellectuals

Blacks

1. Outline developments in the history of blacks, 1865–1912.
2. Compare and contrast the treatment of immigrants, blacks, and Indians.
3. Race as the central issue in Southern life, 1865–1900
4. Southern whites reestablished political control after Reconstruction and modernized the Southern economy.

5. Rise of Jim Crow
6. Booker T. Washington versus W.E.B. DuBois

The West and Populism

1. Populism urged political solutions to economic problems.
2. Why did Populism fail, or did it?
3. Problems facing farmers
4. Compare and contrast the Grange, the Farmers' Alliance, and Populism.
5. Compare Populism and Jacksonianism or Jeffersonianism.
6. Connect Southern Populism and the rise of racism.
7. Compare the Southern agricultural systems before and after the Civil War.
8. Why was the Great Plains settled last?
9. What brought a speedy end to the frontier?
10. Economic and political consequences of the closing of the frontier
11. Theories of Frederick Jackson Turner
12. Myth of the cowboy
13. What factors removed the Plains Indians?
14. Evolution of federal land policy toward Indians to 1924
15. Farmers versus the railroads and industry

MAJOR TERMS AND CONCEPTS

Politics in Late 19th Century

Ulysses S. Grant
Whiskey Ring
"waving the bloody shirt"
Ku Klux Klan
Secretary of State Hamilton Fish
Treaty of Washington, 1871
Liberal Republicans: Carl Schurz, Horace Greeley
panic of 1873, depression
election of 1876: candidates, electoral commission
Compromise of 1877
Solid South
greenbacks
Ohio Idea
Legal Tender Cases
Specie Resumption Act
Greenback-Labor Party
Pendleton Civil Service Act
Chester A. Arthur

election of 1884: James G. Blaine, Grover Cleveland
Stalwarts
Roscoe Conkling
Half-Breeds
Mugwumps
"Rum, Romanism, and Rebellion"
high tariffs
treasury surplus
pensions, GAR
secret ballot (Australian ballot)
Cleveland's 1887 annual address
election of 1888: candidates, issues
Benjamin Harrison, Billion Dollar Congress, Czar Reed
McKinley Tariff
election of 1892: candidates, issues
Morgan bond transaction
Wilson-Gorman Tariff
Pollock v. Farmers' Loan and Trust Co.
Dingley Tariff

Business

laissez-faire
Adam Smith, *The Wealth of Nations*
Union Pacific Railroad, Central Pacific Railroad
Crédit Mobilier
"Robber Barons"
John D. Rockefeller
Standard Oil Company
horizontal consolidation
Andrew Carnegie
Henry Clay Frick
vertical consolidation
Charles Schwab
Thomas A. Edison
Alexander Graham Bell
Leland Stanford
James G. Hill, Great Northern Railroad
Cornelius Vanderbilt, New York Central Railroad
Bessemer process
United States Steel Corporation, Elbert H. Gary
Mesabi Range
J. Pierpont Morgan
Gustavus Swift
Philip Armour
James B. Duke
Andrew Mellon
"stock watering"
Jay Cooke Co.
Jay Gould and Jim Fiske
pools, trusts
rebates
depression of 1873
holding companies
Fourteenth Amendment's "due process clause"
Munn v. Illinois, 1877
Wabash Railroad Case, 1886
Interstate Commerce Act, Interstate Commerce Commission
long haul, short haul
Sherman Antitrust Act, 1890
E.C. Knight case

Labor

National Labor Union
William Sylvis
Knights of Labor: Uriah Stephens, Terence Powderly
American Federation of Labor (AFL)
Samuel Gompers
collective bargaining
injunction
strikes
boycotts
closed shop
blacklist
yellow dog contracts
company unions
Great Railroad strike, 1877
Haymarket Square riot
John Peter Altgeld
Homestead strike
Pinkertons
American Railway Union
Pullman strike, 1894
Eugene V. Debs
Richard Olney
In re Debs
Danbury Hatters strike

Urbanization

George Washington Plunkitt
"honest graft"
Boss Tweed
Tammany Hall
Thomas Nast
"new immigration"
Dillingham Commission Report, 1911
streetcar suburbs
tenements
Jane Addams, Hull House
Denis Kearney
Chinese Exclusion law, 1882
American Protective Association
literacy tests
James Bryce, *The American Commonwealth*
John A. Roebling, Brooklyn Bridge
Louis Sullivan
Frank Lloyd Wright
Ashcan school
Armory Show, 1913
Anthony Comstock

Social and Intellectual Movements and Ideas

Charles Darwin, *Origin of Species*
Social Darwinism
Andrew Carnegie, *The Gospel of Wealth*
Herbert Spencer
William Graham Sumner, *What Social Classes Owe to Each Other*
Henry Ward Beecher
Rev. Russell Conwell, "Acres of Diamonds"
Dwight L. Moody

Rev. Josiah Strong
Lester Frank Ward
Social Gospel
Salvation Army, YMCA
Walter Rauschenbusch
Washington Gladden
Rerum Novarum, 1891
Charles Sheldon, *In His Steps*
Mary Baker Eddy
Chautauqua movement
Johns Hopkins University
Charles W. Eliot, Harvard
Josiah Willard Gibbs
Morrill Act, 1862
land grant colleges, A&M, A&T, A&I
Hatch Act, 1887
Edward Bellamy, *Looking Backward, 2000-1887*
Henry George, *Progress and Poverty*
the single tax
"Gilded Age"
nouveau riche
William James
pragmatism
E.L. Godkin, editor of *The Nation*
William Dean Howells
Henry James
Stephen Crane
Hamlin Garland
Bret Harte
Mark Twain
The Gilded Age, Mark Twain and Charles Dudley
  Warner
Horatio Alger's books for youth
James McNeill Whistler
Winslow Homer
Joseph Pulitzer
William Randolph Hearst
Susan B. Anthony
Elizabeth Cady Stanton
Carrie Chapman Catt
Alice Paul
Women's Christian Temperance Union (WCTU)
Francis Willard
Carry A. Nation
Clara Barton

Blacks

Mississippi plan
Bourbons or Redeemers
New South, Henry Grady
Joel Chandler Harris

Slaughterhouse Cases
Civil Rights Act, 1875
Civil Rights Cases, 1883
sharecropping, crop lien laws
lynching
Booker T. Washington, Tuskegee Institute
Atlanta Compromise
George Washington Carver
W.E.B. DuBois
"talented tenth"
Plessy v. *Ferguson*, "separate but equal"
Jim Crow laws
disenfranchisement, *Williams* v. *Mississippi*, 1898
grandfather clause
Niagara Movement
Springfield, Ill riot, 1908
NAACP
The Crisis

The West and Populism

Great American Desert
Homestead Act, 1862
Oliver H. Kelley
Granger Movement
Granger laws
barbed wire, Joseph Glidden
Indian Appropriations Act, 1871
Plains Indians
Chivington massacre
Battle of the Little Big Horn
Chief Joseph
Battle of Wounded Knee
Helen Hunt Jackson, *A Century of Dishonor*
Dawes Severalty Act, 1887
Frederick Jackson Turner, frontier thesis
safety valve thesis
Comstock Lode
"Crime of 1873"
Bland-Allison Act
Sherman Silver Purchase Act
bimetallism
"Coin" Harvey
free silver
16 to 1
depression of 1893
Coxey's army, 1893
repeal of the Sherman Silver Purchase Act, 1893
Farmers' Alliance
Ocala Demands, 1890
Populist Party platform, Omaha Platform, 1892
Tom Watson

James B. Weaver
"Pitchfork" Ben Tillman
Mary Ellen Lease
"Sockless" Jerry Simpson
Ignatius Donnelly

William Jennings Bryan
"Cross of Gold" speech
election of 1896: candidates, issues
Marcus Hanna
Gold Standard Act, 1900

SUPREME COURT CASES TO KNOW

1. Legal Tender Cases, 1870, 1871 (federal monetary powers)

During the Civil War the Union government issued paper money, called greenbacks, and made them legal tender, meaning that they were considered money for all public and private debts. Even if one refused to accept a greenback when it was offered, the debt was still legally considered to have been paid. (Read a modern dollar bill.) Many in this period believed that paper money had to be backed by specie. When the first case, *Hepburn v. Griswold,* was decided in 1870 a 5-4 Court majority ruled the Legal Tender Acts of 1862 and 1863 unconstitutional in regard to contracts made before the passage of these acts. The decision implied that later contracts might be invalid, and jeopardized the circulation of $350,000,000 in greenbacks. Within a year President Grant appointed two new judges to the Supreme Court. The two new judges joined three of the dissenters from *Hepburn v. Griswold* to declare the Legal Tender Acts constitutional in a new suit for all debts, whether previous or subsequent to the first Legal Tender Act. The cases involved in the 1871 second suit were *Knox v. Lee* and *Parker v. Davis.* Grant was incensed at the Hepburn decision and frankly solicited the opinions of his new appointees before submitting their names to the Senate for confirmation. These cases clearly illustrate how the Supreme Court can become involved in current political issues.

2. Slaughterhouse Cases, 1873 (the privileges and immunities clause)

The three suits in the Slaughterhouse cases were the first under the Fourteenth Amendment. Both the majority opinion and dissenting opinions molded the interpretation of the Fourteenth Amendment for decades. The Louisiana Reconstruction state government granted a monopoly to one corporation for butchering livestock in New Orleans, and put over one thousand butchers out of business. The butchers claimed this act violated the Fourteenth Amend-

ment, abridging their "privileges and immunities" as citizens of the United States. In a 5-4 decision the Court ruled a sharp distinction between state privileges and rights and federal privileges and rights. The Fourteenth Amendment protected only the latter; it offered no protection against state infringement. Most rights of citizenship are state, not national. The Court narrowly interpreted the Thirteenth, Fourteenth, and Fifteenth amendments as designed solely for freeing slaves and establishing citizenship rights for blacks.

The dissenting opinions of two judges foreshadowed the future emphasis of the first clause of the Fourteenth Amendment. The due process and equal protection clauses became the heart of the amendment's later interpretations, which made the guarantees in the Bill of Rights applicable to the states. Read the first section of the Fourteenth Amendment.

3. *Minor v. Happensett,* 1875 (suffrage for women)

Mrs. Virginia Minor sued in federal court in St. Louis claiming that she had been deprived of one of her "privileges and immunities" by being denied suffrage. In a unanimous decision the Court ruled that suffrage was not a right of citizenship.

4. *Munn v. Illinois,* 1877 (state regulation of business)

This case involved an Illinois state law limiting maximum rates for the storage of grain in privately owned grain elevators. One of the so-called Granger laws, it grew out of the 1870 revision of the state constitution, which empowered the legislature to regulate the storage of grain. Munn and his partner were fined $100 for charging higher rates and for operating without a license. He sought relief from his conviction on the grounds that it violated the due process and equal protection clauses of the Fourteenth Amendment and on the grounds of exclusive federal regulation of commerce. Chief Justice Waite wrote the 7-2 majority opinion asserting that the public has always had a right to regulate business operations in which the public has an interest.

"Property does become clothed with a public interest when used in a manner to make it of public consequence, and affect the community at large. When, therefore, one devotes his property to a use in which the public has an interest, he, in effect, grants to the public an interest in that use, and must submit to be controlled by the public for the common good, to the extent of the interest he has thus created. He may withdraw his grant by discontinuing the use; but, so long as he maintains the use, he must submit to the control. . . ." Justice Waite recognized that all regulation carries the potential for abuse, but cautioned, "For protection against abuses by legislatures the people must resort to the polls, not to the courts."

5. Civil Rights Cases, 1883 (discrimination against individuals)

In a decision consistent with the Slaughterhouse Cases the Supreme Court narrowly defined the civil rights guaranteed by the Fourteenth Amendment in the Civil Rights Cases. The Civil Rights Act of 1875 made it a crime for any individual to deny full and equal use of public conveyances and public places such as hotels, trains, railroads, theaters, and restaurants. The Court declared that the Fourteenth Amendment protected individuals from state action, not individual action. "The wrongful act of an individual unsupported by any such state authority, is simply a private wrong, or a crime of that individual. . . ." Discouraged, Congress did not pass another civil rights act until 1957.

6. Wabash, St. Louis & Pacific RR Co. v. Illinois, 1886 (states and the commerce clause)

Popularly known as the Wabash Case, this decision is significant because it added to the push for the Interstate Commerce Act of 1887. An Illinois law prohibited the infamous practice of different rates for long and short haul traffic. The Court ruled that states could only regulate intrastate commerce, not interstate commerce. Since the federal government had not yet begun to regulate railroads crossing state lines, the railroads were legally beyond control. Compare this decision to the Munn case.

7. U.S. v. E.C. Knight Co., 1895 (monopolies, manufacturing, and commerce)

This was the first significant case under the Sherman Antitrust Act. The E.C. Knight Co. controlled 98% of the nation's manufacture of sugar. The Court ruled that monopoly control of manufacturing was not the same as monopoly control of commerce. The Sher-

man Antitrust Act restricted commerce, not manufacturing. Within a short time the Court broadened the definition of commerce by introducing the concept of "stream of commerce."

8. Pollock v. Farmers' Loan and Trust Co., 1895 (the income tax)

Actually several cases, the Pollock suit challenged the constitutionality of the income tax imposed by the Wilson-Gorman Tariff, 1894. Income taxes had been in use for thirty years, but the Court now found them to be a violation of the Constitution, which requires direct taxes to be apportioned by population. The Court decided that a tax on rental income and a tax on personal property were both direct taxes. The Sixteenth Amendment negated this decision, and specifically permitted income taxes.

9. In re Debs, 1895 (labor and injunctions)

During the Pullman strike in 1894 the Pullman Company obtained an injunction under the Sherman Antitrust Act. After refusing to comply, the union's leader, Eugene V. Debs, was arrested for contempt of court. Debs' writ of habeas corpus to the Supreme Court was denied on the basis of a broad interpretation of the commerce clause and the federal government's obligation to deliver the mail. Justice Brewer wrote, "The strong arm of the national government may be put forth to brush away all obstructions to the freedom of interstate commerce or the transportation of the mails." Critics and cynics wondered why "the strong arm of the national government" did not move as swiftly against monopolies.

10. Plessy v. Ferguson, 1896 (separate but equal)

One-eighth black, Homer Plessy was fined for refusing to leave a railroad car restricted to only whites. Louisiana state law required "separate but equal" facilities. The Fourteenth Amendment ensured political equality, not social equality. "We consider the underlying fallacy of the plaintiff's argument to consist in the assumption that the enforced separation of the two races stamps the colored race with a badge of inferiority. If this be so, it is not by reason of anything found in the act, but solely because the colored race chooses to put that construction upon it." According to the Court, separate was not second-class citizenship. The legislature could only do so much to ensure civil rights. "Legislation is powerless to eradicate racial instincts or to abolish distinctions based upon physical differences, and the attempt to do so can only result in accentuating the difficulties of the present situation. If the civil and political rights of both races be equal one cannot be inferior to the other civilly or politically. If one race be inferior to the other socially, the Constitution of the United States cannot put them upon the same plane."

In a stinging dissent Justice Harlan laid the foundation for the arguments that overturned the Plessy decision in *Brown* v. *the Board of Education of Topeka, Kansas,* 1954. "Our Constitution is color-blind, and neither knows nor tolerates classes among citizens. In respect of civil rights, all citizens are equal before the law. The humblest is the peer of the most powerful. The law regards man as man, and takes no account of his surroundings or of his color when his civil rights as guaranteed by the supreme law of the land are involved. It is, therefore, to be regretted that this high tribunal, the final expositor of the fundamental law of the land, has reached the conclusion that it is competent for a state to regulate the enjoyment by citizens of their civil rights solely upon the basis of race."

READINGS FOR DEPTH AND HISTORICAL INTERPRETATION

Politics and Overviews of Period

1. Robert H. Wiebe, *The Search for Order: 1877–1920.* A good introduction to the link between economic issues and politics. Wiebe also assesses the impact of the expanding transportation system upon social values. He sees the destruction of the small town "island communities."

2. Vincent P. De Santis, "The Republican Party Revisited, 1877–1897," in H. Wayne Morgan, ed., *The Gilded Age: A Reappraisal.* De Santis analyzes the strengths and weaknesses of the two major political parties. He finds not a disgusting period devoid of values but "an era of party stalemate and equilibrium."

3. Ari Hoogenboom, "Spoilsmen and Reformers: Civil Service Reform and Public Morality," in H. Wayne Morgan, ed., *The Gilded Age: A Reappraisal.* Hoogenboom dispassionately looks at the Gilded Age's reputation for corruption. Its sordid image was due as much as anything else to the articulate and quotable reformers of the era who often took part in the "political corruption" of the spoils system.

4. Richard Hofstadter, "The Spoilsmen: An Age of Cynicism," in his *The American Political Tradition.* This is the traditional view of the era's politics. Woodrow Wilson summarized the politics as "No leaders, no principles: no principles, no parties."

5. Richard Hofstadter, "William Jennings Bryan: The Democrat as Revivalist," in his *The American Political Tradition.* This is a good source for the confusing politics of free silver and the election of 1896.

Business

1. Matthew Josephson, *The Robber Barons,* pp. 264-280. Josephson popularized the "Robber Baron" nickname in his 1934 book. The date is significant, for businessmen were not popular in the 1930s. In this section Josephson portrays John D. Rockefeller as a ruthless, conspiratorial businessman who callously brushed away competitors.

2. John Tipple, "The Robber Baron in the Gilded Age: Entrepreneur or Iconoclast?" in H. Wayne Morgan, ed., *The Gilded Age: A Reappraisal.* Tipple weaves together the Robber Baron image and the rise of the corporation as an instrument to conduct business activities. The corporation was "a supralegal abstraction above the traditional laws of the land," which undermined "American institutions and individualistic values by rendering them impotent. . . ."

3. Harold Livesay, *Andrew Carnegie and the Rise of Big Business.* Livesay looks at Carnegie the businessman and finds the secret of his success in his obsession with cutting costs. The key to profits was not high prices, but efficient production and lower prices. This book presents an image that certainly differs from *The Robber Barons.*

4. Alfred D. Chandler, Jr., "The Beginnings of Big Business in American Industry," *Business History Review,* Spring 1959, or *The Visible Hand: The Managerial Revolution in American Business.* Market forces—marketing, purchasing, processing—and changes in the structure of industry—the corporation with its autonomous divisions—molded and shaped industrial expansion. Few

individuals are mentioned in Chandler's analysis. Not only is the Robber Baron image incorrect, he states, it is not even applicable.

Labor

1. Stephan Thernstrom, "Newburyport and the Larger Society," in his *Poverty and Progress: Social Mobility in a Nineteenth Century City,* or "Urbanization, Migration, and Social Mobility in Late Nineteenth-Century America," in Barton J. Berstein, ed., *Towards a New Past: Dissenting Essays in American History.* Thernstrom introduces the concept of social mobility, movement up or down the social class ladder. Before Thernstrom historians too frequently assumed easy movement up the ladder. This study found a more static society.

2. Harold Livesay, *Samuel Gompers and Organized Labor in America.* Livesay's book portrays Gompers as an effective labor leader but only for elite skilled workers. Gompers stuck to his union principles, and generally ignored the plight of the unskilled mass production workers.

3. Carl Degler, the last two sections of "Machines, Men, and Socialism," in *Out of Our Past.* Degler summarizes the rise of unions and addresses the intriguing question of the absence of a strong socialist movement among American workers. We are the only industrial nation without a viable socialist movement.

4. Herbert G. Gutman, "Work, Culture, and Society in Industrializing America, 1815–1919," *American Historical Review,* June 1973. This article is difficult reading but full of insight. During this one-hundred-year period successive waves of immigrants shaped the culture of American workers and determined our business values.

Urbanization

1. Oscar Handlin, *The Uprooted,* or *Boston's Immigrants. The Uprooted* is a more general account of immigration, which includes the European background. *Boston's Immigrants* treats the Irish in Boston: their arrival, economic and social adjustment, conflicts, and group identity.

2. Jane Addams, *Twenty Years at Hull House.* This autobiographical account by America's premier social worker covers the years from 1889 to 1909. She presents an insider's look at immigrant life,

municipal corruption, and urban poverty in Chicago.

3. Carl Degler, *Out of Our Past.* The first half of the chapter, "Alabaster Cities and Amber Waves of Grain," is devoted to developments in the cities in the late 19th century.

Social and Intellectual Movements and Ideas

1. Edward Bellamy's *Looking Backward, 2000–1887* in Robert B. Downs, *Books That Changed America.* Bellamy's *Looking Backward* inspired millions of readers in the late 19th century. He offered hope that the vicious cycle of unending competition between individuals would somehow be replaced by a more cooperative society.

2. Michael Zuckerman, "The Nursery Tales of Horatio Alger," *American Quarterly,* 1972, or John G. Cawelti, "From Rags to Respectability: Horatio Alger," in his *Apostles of the Self-Made Man.* Either of these two articles help put Horatio Alger into perspective. Alger's message was never rags to riches. His heroes achieved respectability and exhibited the virtues of what we would call the team player and the organization man.

Blacks

1. Booker T. Washington, *Up From Slavery,* and W.E.B. DuBois (he Anglicized the pronunciation, so don't pronounce DuBois as if it were French), *The Souls of Black Folk.* (Both these books are in a paperback, *Three Negro Classics,* along with James Weldon Johnson's *The Autobiography of an Ex-Colored Man.*) The dispute between Booker T. Washington and W.E.B. DuBois is best followed by reading their philosophies in their own words to compare their differences.

2. C. Vann Woodward, "Capitulation to Racism," in his *The Strange Career of Jim Crow.* Woodward details the rise of extreme Southern racism due to the decline of three restraining forces in the late 19th century: "Northern liberalism, Southern conservatism, and Southern radicalism."

The West and Populism

1. Walter Prescott Webb, "The Frontier as a Modifier of Institutions," in his *The Great Frontier,* which summarizes significant points in his famous

book, *The Great Plains*. Webb's *The Great Plains* illustrated the impact of environment upon institutions. The Plains region changed and modified settlers as much as they modified it. Among changed institutions were the six-gun, fences, transportation, and laws about water usage.

2. Dee Brown, *Bury My Heart at Wounded Knee*. This is a popular history of the Indian wars as seen from the Indian point of view.

3. Frederick Jackson Turner, "The Significance of the Frontier in American History," in Robert B. Downs, *Books That Changed America*. Frederick Jackson Turner is considered one of America's preeminent historians. His essay on the significance of the frontier has dominated historical writing on the West since 1893. He revolutionized the writing of history by reversing the emphasis on the "germ theory" on the European origins of American institutions. To him frontier experience shaped America's institutions more than our ancient political and constitutional principles.

4. Paolo E. Coletta, "Greenbacks, Goldbugs, and Silverites: Currency Reform and Policy, 1860–1897," in H. Wayne Morgan, ed., *The Gilded Age: A Reappraisal*. This is an excellent short summary of a topic that mesmerizes students—the money question.

5. John D. Hicks, *The Populist Revolt*, especially the chapters entitled, "The Grievances" and "The Populist Contribution." This 1931 book still remains the most comprehensive and sympathetic treatment of the Populists. You should also find a copy of the 1892 Omaha Platform of the Populist Party and read it carefully.

6. Richard Hofstadter, "The Folklore of Populism," in his *The Age of Reform*. Hofstadter is critical of the Populists and balances Hick's sympathetic portrayal. Hofstadter paints a picture of status anxieties and harebrained schemes instead of genuine economic problems confronting the Populists.

7. Carl Degler, *Out of Our Past*. The second half of the chapter entitled, "Alabaster Cities and Amber Waves of Grain" summarizes the plight of the farmers and describes the Populist Party revolt.

SAMPLE OUTLINE

Urban America changed dramatically between 1850 and 1900. Waves of immigrants flooded the cities; mass transit systems sorted the population; and industrialization created new and different types of employment. The modern city emerged from this interaction between mass man and mass technology. One word of caution; Urbanization and industrialization occurred at the same time in the United States, but they are different, if parallel, historical movements. The fact that they occurred at the same time had momentous consequences for the nature of our cities. European cities differ drastically from American cities because urbanization preceded industrialization in Europe.

Much of the information in this outline is from Howard P. Chudacoff, *The Evolution of American Urban Society*, an excellent survey of our urban history.

URBANIZATION

I. **The Old City**

   A. Until the 1850s the compact city centered around the waterfront.

   B. Walking city up to the 1850s

   C. Land use was mixed; commercial, residential, industrial—all intermingled.

   D. People relatively integrated, little segregation by immigrant or occupational group

E. Lure of the city

1. Easy reception to novel ideas
2. A person could lose his past.
3. Tendency of urbanites to look the other way when ambition took a dishonest turn
4. Even today the average age of farmers is in the fifties.

II. Changing the Old City: Growth of Mass Transit

A. Omnibus: By 1833, 80 in NYC, each drawn by two horses, capacity of twelve passengers; 180 in 1837; 260 in 1847; 683 in 1853 serviced 120,000 daily.

B. Commuter railroad, 1859, 40 trains daily between Philadelphia and Germantown at a cost of 15¢ to 25¢ (too much for laborers who made only $1 a day).

C. Streetcars from horse-drawn to mechanical by 1873; cable cars in Chicago and San Francisco featured a continuous wire cable (a break halted the whole system); trolley cars: Frank Sprague, Richmond in the 1880s. By 1890, 5,700 animal-powered, 500 cable, 1,260 electric. By 1902, 250 animal, 22,000 electric.

D. Streets getting too crowded

1. Elevated railroads came into use because 600 died in accidents in Philadelphia in just one year. 8,000 railroad street crossings existed in Philadelphia alone.
2. Subway; 1897 in Boston; 1904 in NYC

E. Streets were mostly unpaved. In 1880 NYC, Boston, and Philadelphia combined didn't have 10 miles of asphalt. By 1900 extensive roads existed. (Revulsion over power of urban transit systems and political corruption led to cries of reform, one feature of the Progressive movement.)

F. Consequences

1. Transit sorted people and land uses. In 1850 the borders of Boston were 2 miles from the central business district; in 1900, 10 miles.
2. Decentralization of economic functions, with multiple commercial districts
3. Fine social and economic distinctions between neighborhoods; the ideal of the single-family dwelling and the small community setting. Note such pastoral names as Woodside and Shipley Farms.
4. Emergence of rings or zones around the city; central business district, poor, middle class, wealthy suburbs
5. Speed and punctuality became urban habits, and mobility made the ideal of the stable community impossible.

III. Changing the Old City: Industrialization

A. Economic specialization, mass production, mass consumption, and mass distribution of goods and services

B. Urban imperialism, the drive for hinterland economic markets; competition between cities such as St. Louis and Chicago; NYC, Philadelphia, and Baltimore; San Diego and LA

C. Specialization among industrial cities

1. Large unskilled labor force led to mass production industries. Philadelphia, textiles; NYC, clothing (At one time NYC had 10% of the nation's manufacturing total.)

2. Exploited nearby industries: Milwaukee, beer; Minneapolis, flour
3. Nearby resources: Cleveland, coal and iron; Dallas, oil; Denver, minerals
4. Technological advances: Akron, tires; Detroit, automobiles; Dayton, cash registers

IV. Changing the Old City: Immigration

A. From 1860 to 1920, population living in U.S. cities rose from 6.2 million to 54.3 million.

B. Internal immigrants: Rural Americans, or "buckwheats," escaped the isolation and loneliness of farms.

C. First wave of immigrants: 1840s to peak in 1880s; Irish Catholics, German Catholics and Protestants, English, some Scandinavians
   1. Drinking habits: beer, ale, wine were introduced. (Rum and whiskey were traditional American drinks.)
   2. Religion; 1840–90 5½ million Catholics entered. Of 3142 church buildings in 1775, only 56 were Catholic; by 1870, 40% of all churchgoers were Catholic.
   3. American innovation of the ethnic parish for Catholics
   4. Squabbles: Know-Nothings; Bible reading in public schools

D. Second wave from 1880s to 1920, like earlier wave, featured mostly poor and peasants, but the numbers were greater. Catholics from Italy and Poland, Jews from Russia and Eastern Europe (Russian draft for the army was for 21 years' service.)
   1. Larger numbers: 1880–1890, 5.2 million; 1900–1910, 8.8 million
   2. Much ethnic conflict among Catholics
   3. Jews: conflict between German and Russian Jews, and between Orthodox, Conservative, and Reform Jews

E. Characteristics of immigrants
   1. Loss of self-identity led to emphasis on nationalism after arrival.
   2. Many came only to earn money, and hoped to return home. From 1900-1910 an estimated 30-40% went home.
   3. Lived in older urban areas, such as NYC's lower East Side

F. Blacks: In 1890, 90% lived in rural South; by 1900, 32 cities in the North and West had more than 10,000 blacks.

G. Social Mobility: much outmigration and great turnover. Between 1870 and 1880 56% left Atlanta; 1910–1920, 59% left Boston. In one decade in Boston, 138,000 families moved out and 158,000 moved in.

H. Housing
   1. NYC set standard lot size of 25' by 100' in 1811.
   2. In 1860s and 1870s tenements appeared, featuring 4-6 stories, 16 to 24 families, and as many as 150 per building. Number of tenement houses in 1879 were 21,000; 1888, 32,000; 1900, 43,000.
   3. Dumbbell tenement invented as a reform, not considered as such by 1900
   4. Problem of fires: Chicago, 1871
   5. Public health: In 1877 Philadelphia had 82,000 cesspools; Washington, D.C., 56,000.

I. Park Movement: Frederick Law Olmsted, architect of Central Park, NYC

V. Rev. Josiah Strong, *Our Country: Its Possible Future and Present Crisis* (1885) illustrated attitudes toward the cities.

"The city is the nerve center of our civilization. It is also the storm center. The fact, therefore, that it is growing much more rapidly than the whole population is full of significance.

"The city has become a serious menace to our civilization. . . . It has a peculiar attraction for the immigrant.

"Because our cities are so largely foreign, Romanism finds in them its chief strength.

"For the same reason a saloon, together with the intemperance and the liquor power which it represents, is multiplied in the city.

"Not only does the proportion of the poor increase with the growth of the city, but their condition becomes more wretched. The poor of a city of 8,000 inhabitants are well off compared with many in New York; and there are no such depths of woe, such utter and heart-wringing wretchedness in New York as in London. . . .

"Socialism not only centers in the city, but is almost confined to it, and the materials of its growth are multiplied with the growth of the city. Here is heaped the social dynamite; here inequality is the greatest."

Population Compositions of Major Cities, 1910

	Total	Foreign Born White		Native Born of Foreign or Mixed Parentage		Black	
		Number	%	Number	%	Number	%
New York	4,766,883	1,927,703	40.4	1,820,141	38.2	91,709	1.9
Chicago	2,185,283	781,217	35.7	912,701	41.8	44,103	2.0
Philadelphia	1,549,008	382,578	24.7	496,785	32.1	84,459	5.5
St. Louis	687,029	125,706	18.3	246,946	40.0	43,960	6.4
Boston	670,535	240,722	35.9	257,104	38.3	13,564	2.0
Cleveland	560,663	195,703	34.9	223,908	39.9	8,448	1.5
Baltimore	558,485	77,043	13.8	134,870	24.1	84,749	15.2
Pittsburgh	533,905	140,436	26.3	191,483	35.9	25,623	4.8
Detroit	465,766	156,565	33.6	188,255	40.4	5,741	1.2
Buffalo	423,715	118,444	30.0	183,673	40.4	1,773	0.4
San Francisco	416,912	130,874	31.4	153,781	36.9	1,642	0.4
Milwaukee	373,857	111,456	29.8	182,530	48.8	980	0.3
Cincinnati	363,591	56,792	15.6	132,190	36.4	19,639	5.4
Newark	347,469	110,655	31.8	132,350	38.1	9,475	2.7
New Orleans	339,075	27,686	8.2	74.244	21.9	89,262	26.3
Washington	331,069	24,351	7.4	45,066	13.6	94,446	28.5

Unit Seven: 1900 to 1920

MAJOR THEMES AND IDEAS

Foreign Policy

1. Organize U.S. foreign policy from 1865 to 1900 by 1) geographic region—Far East, Latin America, Caribbean, Europe; 2) American motives—economic, moral, Monroe Doctrine, balance of power among European nations, dominance in the Caribbean; 3) influence of domestic politics on foreign policy.
2. Imperialism: characteristics, sources, nature, causes, impact, results, compared to European imperialism
3. Link Reconstruction, Populism, and imperialism.
4. Compare and contrast the old and new Manifest Destiny.
5. Debate over the Treaty of Paris
6. Open Door: myth or reality?
7. Roosevelt's foreign policy
8. Wilson's foreign policy
9. U.S. policy toward Mexico and Cuba, 1890s to 1930s
10. The U.S. pushed around smaller nations, 1865 to 1914.
11. U.S. policy in the Far East: Balance Japan and protect China.
12. Causes of U.S. entry into the First World War and its attempts to remain neutral
13. Give several contrasting interpretations of U.S. entry into the First World War.
14. Defeat of the Versailles Treaty; immediate and long-run consequences
15. Who was responsible for the defeat of the Versailles Treaty?
16. War and the threat of war united and divided Americans in the 1898 to 1920 period.

Progressive Movement

1. Compare and contrast the Populist and Progressive movements.
2. Compare Progressivism and Jacksonianism.
3. Social, economic, political, and intellectual sources of Progressivism
4. Goals of Progressivism; successes, failures
5. Compare the political philosophies of Progressivism, Conservativism, and Socialism.
6. Progressives as the new Federalists: Compare Hamilton's program and Progressivism.
7. Progressivism as an answer to the problems raised by immigration and urbanization
8. Progressivism as the have-nots against the haves: role of labor unions, immigrants, blacks, women and urban poor
9. Charles Beard's *An Economic Interpretation of the Constitution* as a reflection of its times
10. There was not one but many parallel "Progressive movements."
11. What did Progressivism seek to preserve in American life?
12. Corporations and unions both wanted governmental protection but not governmental regulation.
13. Trace the regulation of big business and court interpretations from the Interstate Commerce Act to *U.S.* v. *United States Steel Corporation* in 1920.
14. Trace the long history of a reform such as prohibition, women's rights, or banking.
15. Supreme Court interpretations and changing economic and social conditions, 1890–1920
16. Significant elections: 1900, 1912, 1920
17. Struggles within the parties, 1900 to 1912
18. Compare and contrast the programs and administrations of Theodore Roosevelt and Woodrow Wilson: banking, railroads, trusts, tariffs, etc.
19. Presidencies of Taft, Roosevelt, and Wilson: real differences or differing philosophies of the office of the president
20. Compare Congress versus Johnson with Congress versus Wilson.
21. First World War both helped and hurt blacks and labor.
22. Compare the domestic impact of the First and Second World War.
23. Progressivism—a liberal or conservative movement?

MAJOR TERMS AND CONCEPTS

Imperialism

James G. Blaine, Pan-Americanism
Venezuelan boundary dispute
Bering Sea seal controversy
"yellow journalism"
Josiah Strong, *Our Country*
Captain Alfred Thayer Mahan
Samoa, Pago Pago
Virginius
reconcentration policy
de Lome letter
Maine explodes
Assistant Secretary of Navy Theodore Roosevelt
Commodore Dewey, Manila Bay
Cleveland and Hawaii
Queen Liliuokalani
annexation of Hawaii
Rough Riders, San Juan Hill
Treaty of Paris, 1898
American Anti-Imperialist League
Philippines, Guam, Puerto Rico
Walter Reed
Insular Cases
Teller Amendment
Platt Amendment
protectorate
Aguinaldo, Philippine insurrection
Secretary of State John Hay, Open Door Notes
spheres of influence
Boxer Rebellion
extraterritoriality
most favored nation clause
election of 1900: candidates, issues
Roosevelt's Big Stick diplomacy
U.S.S. Oregon
Clayton-Bulwer Treaty
Hay-Pauncefote Treaty
Hay-Herran Treaty
Hay-Bunau-Varilla Treaty
Panama revolution
Pamana Canal
Goethals and Gorgas
Venezuelan crisis, 1902
Drago Doctrine
Roosevelt Corollary
"Colossus of the North"
Dominican Republic

Russo-Japanese War, Treaty of Portsmouth
San Francisco School Board incident
Elihu Root
Gentleman's Agreement
Great White Fleet
Root-Takahira Agreement
Lansing-Ishii Agreement, 1917

Progressivism

democracy, efficiency, pragmatism
"muckrakers"
Henry Demarest Lloyd, *Wealth Against Commonwealth*
Thorstein Veblen, *The Theory of the Leisure Class*
Jacob Riis, *How the Other Half Lives*
Lincoln Steffens, *The Shame of the Cities*
Frank Norris, *The Octopus*
Ida Tarbell, *History of the Standard Oil Company*
John Spargo, *The Bitter Cry of the Children*
David Graham Phillips, *The Treason of the Senate*
Charlotte Perkins Gilman, *Woman and Economics*
John Dewey, *The School and Society,* "progressive education," "learn by doing"
Oliver Wendell Holmes, Jr., Supreme Court
Margaret Sanger
Edward Ross
Richard Ely
initiative, referendum, recall
direct primary
Australian ballot (secret ballot)
Tammany Hall
Sixteenth, Seventeenth, Eighteenth, and Nineteenth amendments
Charles Evans Hughes
Triangle Shirtwaist Co. fire
WCTU, Women's Christian Temperance Union
Anti-Saloon League
Square Deal
Newlands Reclamation Act, 1902
Forest Reserve Act, 1891
anthracite coal strike, 1902, George F. Baer
Elkins Act, 1903, rebates
Hepburn Act, 1906
Mann-Elkins Act, 1910
"trustbuster"
Northern Securities Co. case
Meat Inspection Act
Upton Sinclair, *The Jungle*

Pure Food and Drug Act
conservation conference, 1908
panic of 1907
election of 1908: candidates, issues
Mark Hanna
scientific management, Frederick W. Taylor
Wisconsin, "laboratory of democracy"
Robert M. La Follette
regulatory commissions
Jane Addams, Hull House
Florence Kelley, consumerism
home rule for cities
Tom Johnson, Sam (Golden Rule) Jones, Brand Whitlock, Hazen Pingree
city manager plan, commission plan
William Howard Taft
Department of Labor (from 1903 Department of Commerce and Labor, Bureau of Corporations also in 1903)
Payne-Aldrich Tariff, 1909
Ballinger-Pinchot controversy
Uncle Joe Cannon, Old Guard
Senator George Norris
rule of reason: Standard Oil case, American Tobacco case
"dollar diplomacy"
Secretary of State Knox
Manchurian railroad scheme
Roosevelt's Osawatomie, Kansas speech
Taft-Roosevelt split
Bull Moose Party
Woodrow Wilson, New Freedom
Theodore Roosevelt, New Nationalism
Herbert Croly, *The Promise of American Life*
election of 1912: Wilson, Roosevelt, Taft, Debs—issues
Eugene V. Debs, Socialist Party
Daniel DeLeon, IWW, Wobblies, "Big Bill" Haywood
Pujo Committee
Federal Reserve Act
Underwood-Simmons Tariff
income tax
Federal Trade Commission, cease and desist orders
Clayton Antitrust Act, labor's Magna Carta (?)
Secretary of State William Jennings Bryan
arbitration treaties
Panama Tolls dispute
Colonel House
Louis Brandeis, "Brandeis brief"
La Follette Seaman's Act
Federal Highways Act, 1916

Adamson Act, 1916
Smith-Lever Act, Smith-Hughes Act
Vigin Islands purchased
Jones Act, 1916 (Philippines)
Jones Act, 1917 (Puerto Rico)
Mexican Revolution, Diaz, Huerta, Carranza
Mexican migration to the U.S.
"watchful waiting"
ABC Powers
Pancho Villa, General Pershing
Archangel expedition

First World War

"sick man of Europe", Ottoman Empire, Balkan Wars
Triple Entente: Allies
Triple Alliance: Central Powers
loans to the Allies
British blockade
Lusitania, Arabic pledge, Sussex pledge
election of 1916: Hughes, Wilson, issues
unrestricted submarine warfare
Zimmermann Note
Russian Revolutions, 1917, March and Bolshevik
war declared, April 1917
"Make the world safe for democracy."
Creel Committee
bond drives
War Industries Board
Bernard Baruch
Herbert Hoover, Food Administration
Espionage Act, 1917; Sedition Act, 1918
Eugene V. Debs imprisoned
AEF
selective service
black migration to Northern cities
aims of Allies and U.S. at peace conference
wartime manpower losses
Fourteen Points
congressional elections of 1918
Versailles Conference, Versailles Treaty
U.S. Versailles delegation
Big Four: Wilson, George, Clemenceau, Orlando
League of Nations
collective security
new nations, self-determination
reparations
mandate system
Article 10 (often written Article X) of the Versailles Treaty
Article 231 of the Versailles Treaty

Senate rejection, Senator Henry Cabot Lodge, reservations
"irreconcilables": Borah, Johnson, La Follette
Red Scare, Palmer raids

strikes: 1919, coal, steel, police
inflation during the First World War
election of 1920: candidates, issues
brief depression, 1920–1921

SUPREME COURT CASES TO KNOW

1. Insular Cases, 1901, 1903, 1904 (constitutional rights in territories)

Three appeals to the Supreme Court—*Dorr* v. *U.S.*, *Downes* v. *Bidwell*, and *Hawaii* v. *Mankichi*—raised questions concerning the extent to which constitutional rights were bestowed automatically upon the natives in newly acquired territories. The Supreme Court slowly worked out a new judicial position for the Constitution. Some rights are fundamental and applied to all American territory. Other rights are procedural and should not be imposed upon those unfamiliar with American law. Congress must determine which procedural rights applied in unincorporated territories. The Constitution did not follow the flag.

2. Northern Securities Case, 1904 (antitrust laws)

At the turn of the century three financial giants, J.P. Morgan, James J. Hill, and E.H. Harriman fought for control of the railroads running west from Chicago to the Pacific coast. Frustrated in their separate efforts, they joined forces to create the Northern Securities Company, which owned a majority of the stock in both the Northern Pacific and the Great Northern railroads, which together owned enough stock to control the Burlington Railroad. A single holding company thus controlled the entire transportation network for one quarter of the nation. The Supreme Court ruled 5-4 that the Northern Securities holding company violated the Sherman Antitrust Act. The company was a "trust," not just a stock company. Owning the stock of competing railroads violated the Sherman Antitrust Act.

3. *Lochner* v. *New York*, 1905 (due process and state police power)

The state of New York passed a law to limit bakery and confectionary workers to only sixty hours a week or ten hours per day. Lochner, who owned a bakery in Utica, was arrested for violating the law. The case involved a contest between the due process clause of freedom of contract and the state's police power to guard the health, safety, and morals of its people. In a

5-4 decision the Court held that the Fourteenth Amendment protected individuals against "an unreasonable, unnecessary and arbitrary interference with the right of the individual to his personal liberty." These criteria put judges in the position of legislators. Unreasonable and arbitrary laws are easier to identify than unnecessary laws, which are a matter of philosophical opinion. "Due process" had historically meant procedures to guarantee a fair trial. The Supreme Court now used "due process" to protect property from unreasonable, unnecessary, and arbitrary legislation.

Justice Holmes's dissent became the majority viewpoint after the 1937 case of *West Coast Hotel* v. *Parrish*. He said in 1905, "This case is decided upon an economic theory which a large part of the country does not entertain. . . . The Fourteenth Amendment does not enact Mr. Herbert Spencer's [a famous proponent of Social Darwinism] *Social Statics*. . . . A constitution is not intended to embody a particular economic theory, whether of paternalism and the organic relation of the citizen to the State or of laissez faire. It is made for people of fundamentally differing views, and the accident of our finding certain opinions natural and familiar or novel and even shocking ought not to conclude our judgment upon the question whether statutes embodying them conflict with the Constitution of the United States."

4. *Muller* v. *Oregon*, 1908 (due process and state police power)

This case is famous for the novel arguments presented by Louis Brandeis, who was later appointed to the Supreme Court. Oregon limited women to only ten hours of labor in factories and laundries. Curt Muller owned a laundry in Portland, and based on the Lochner decision he refused to comply with the law. His appeal eventually reached the Supreme Court. In defense of the Oregon law Brandeis presented only two pages of legal arguments and over one hundred pages detailing statistics and opinions from various commission reports on the adverse impact of long hours on the health of women. In a unanimous decision the Court accepted the economic and social arguments in the "Brandeis brief." Brandeis argued that the law must come out of facts, not abstract logic. The majority opinion in Lochner cited the "common knowledge" that baking was not a difficult occupation. Brandeis undermined any potential opinion that the health of a nation's female population was not a legitimate governmental concern. The Court found that "in order to preserve the strength and vigor of the race . . . [a] woman's physical structure, and the functions she performs in consequence thereof, justify special legislation restricting or qualifying the conditions under which she should be permitted to toil."

5. Danbury Hatters' Case, 1908 (*Loewe* v. *Lawlor*) (antitrust laws and labor unions)

Unable to secure union recognition at the Danbury Hatters Company owned by Loewe and others, the hatters' union instituted a boycott against the company's hats. The unanimous Supreme Court decision held the boycott to be a violation of the Sherman Antitrust Act, and required triple damages against the union for the amount of normal income lost due to the boycott. Labor unions were shocked. They found partial exemption from antitrust laws in the Clayton Act.

6. *Standard Oil of New Jersey* v. *U.S.*, 1911; *U.S.* v. *American Tobacco Co.*, 1911; and *U.S.* v. *United States Steel Corporation*, 1920 (antitrust laws)

In three cases the Supreme Court differentiated between a "good" trust and a "bad" trust, putting into interpretation a widespread popular view that bigness was not synonymous with badness, and that large corporations were part of modern society. The Court took responsibility for determining if a specific trust was good or bad, the "rule of reason." Standard Oil of New Jersey was dissolved under the Court's "rule of reason." The American Tobacco Company was bad, but not too bad, and so it was forced to reorganize to stimulate competition. The United States Steel Corporation didn't have to be dissolved; it was a "good" trust. The antitrust laws applied only to "bad" trusts.

7. *Hammer* v. *Dagenhart*, 1918 (child labor laws)

The Keating-Owen Act of 1916 tried to stop child labor by excluding the products produced by child labor from interstate commerce. Dagenhart sued, asking for an injunction to permit his two sons to continue working to supplement the family's income. The Court ruled 5-4 that Congress had overstepped its authority. The Court narrowly defined the

commerce power of Congress. "Over interstate transportation, or its incidents, the regulatory power of Congress is ample, but the production of articles intended for interstate commerce is a matter of local regulation." The Court evoked a doctrine that came to be known as "dual federalism," the idea that Congress could not intrude into the powers reserved to the states by the Tenth Amendment. "In interpreting the Constitution it must never be forgotten that the nation is made up of states, to which are intrusted the powers of local government. And to them and to the people the powers not expressly delegated to the national government are reserved."

8. *Bailey* v. *Drexel Furniture Co.*, 1922 (child labor laws)

Unable to use the commerce clause to prohibit child labor, Congress used its power to tax in order to impose a heavy fine upon the profits of companies employing child labor. In an 8-1 decision the Court decided that the tax attempted to regulate an area reserved for the states rather than to tax to raise revenue. Not until *U.S.* v. *Darby* in 1941 were child labor laws found to be constitutional.

9. *Schenck* v. *U.S.*, 1919 (radicals and the First Amendment)

Schenck, an official of the Socialist party, was arrested and convicted for violation of the Espionage Act of 1917 because he and other socialists had distributed leaflets to draftees urging them to resist. One side of the leaflet was a copy of the Thirteenth Amendment, which outlawed slavery or involuntary servitude. Schenck claimed he was protected by the First Amendment freedom of speech and press. The opinion by the unanimous Court announced Justice Holmes's "clear and present danger" test. Every act must be judged according to the circumstances. No freedom is absolute; First Amendment questions were a matter of "proximity and degree," and the nation was at war. He included his often quoted remark that freedom of speech "would not protect a man in falsely shouting fire in a theatre and causing a panic."

10. *Abrams* v. *U.S.*, 1919 (radicals and the First Amendment)

The Abrams case involved the Sedition Act of 1918, an amendment to the Espionage Act of 1917. Five Russian immigrants were convicted for distributing antiwar propaganda. Justice Holmes, who wrote the opinion in the Schenck case, dissented from the 7-2 decision. Holmes recognized that "the United States constitutionally may punish speech that produces or is intended to produce a clear and imminent danger that it will bring about forthwith certain substantive evils that the United States constitutionally may seek to prevent. The power undoubtedly is greater in time of war than in time of peace because war opens dangers that do not exist at other times." In a brilliant plea for freedom of speech and press he wrote, "when men have realized that time has upset many fighting faiths, they come to believe even more than they believe the very foundations of their own conduct that the ultimate good desired is better reached by free trade in ideas—that the best test of truth is the power of the thought to get itself accepted in the competition of the market, and that truth is the only ground upon which their wishes safely can be carried out."

READINGS FOR DEPTH AND HISTORICAL INTERPRETATION

Origins and Essence of Progressive Movement

1. George E. Mowry, "Political America," and "The Progressive Profile," in his The Era of Theodore Roosevelt and the Birth of Modern America, 1900–1912. Mowry describes the intellectual political currents in the Progressive era.

2. Richard Hofstadter, "The Status Revolution and Progressive Leaders," in his The Age of Reform. Both Mowry and Hofstadter see the Progressive movement as a revolt by the middle class. Hofstadter added the view that the middle class was primarily motivated by status anxieties over their relative decline in American society.

3. J. Joseph Huthmacher, "Urban Liberalism and the Age of Reform," Mississippi Valley Historical Review (now the Journal of American History), 1962. Huthmacher argues that lower-class immigrant urbanites formed a significant source for the Progressive impulse. They knew from experience the evils that needed correction.

4. David P. Thelen, "Social Tensions and the Origins of Progressivism," Journal of American History, 1969. The Progressive movement grew out of the railroad and corporate arrogance of the 1890s and the social tension generated by the depression of the 1890s. He attacks Hofstadter's status revolution thesis.

5. Lincoln Steffens, The Shame of the Cities; Upton Sinclair, The Jungle; Jane Addams, Twenty Years at Hull-House; and Frederick Winslow Taylor, The Principles of Scientific Mangement in Robert B. Downs, Books That Changed America. Four of the twenty-five books Downs identified as influential were written in the Progressive era. This provides a quick look at these influential works.

6. Gabriel Kolko, "Introduction" and the first section of the "Conclusion," in his The Triumph of Conservatism. Kolko sees a different perspective in the Progressive movement, the fight against "political capitalism," the effort by big business to use governmental power to protect and to expand their profits. The interventionist government served business, not reform. This argument represents a different and unusual perspective for students.

7. Jill Conway, "Women Reformers and American Culture, 1870–1930," Journal of Social History, V, 1971–1972, pp. 164–175. Conway shows the persistence of stereotypes among women which hindered women reformers and reform for women.

Theodore Roosevelt and Woodrow Wilson

1. Richard Hofstadter, "Theodore Roosevelt: The Conservative as Progressive," and "Woodrow Wilson: The Conservative as Liberal," in his The American Political Tradition. An excellent introduction to these two progressives.

2. Richard Lowitt, "Theodore Roosevelt" and E. David Cronon, "Woodrow Wilson," in Morton Borden, ed., America's Eleven Greatest Presidents.

3. Arthur S. Link, "The New Nationalism Versus the New Freedom," in his Woodrow Wilson and the Progressive Era, 1910–1917.

Foreign Policy

1. Alfred T. Mahan's The Influence of Sea Power upon History, 1660–1783, in Robert B. Downs, Books That Changed America. Mahan is credited with popularizing the idea that sea power lies behind every great nation.

2. Frederick Merk, "The Rise and Fall of Insular Imperialism," and "Mission," in his *Manifest Destiny and Mission in American History*. Merk compares the two thrusts of Manifest Destiny.

3. Walter La Feber, *The New Empire: An Interpretation of American Expansion, 1860–1898*. Chapter one, "Years of Preparation, 1860–1889," summarizes American foreign policy in this period. Pages 407–417 summarize his basic argument that American foreign policy was primarily economically motivated, as contemporary socialists charged.

4. George F. Kennan, *American Diplomacy, 1900–1950*. Chapters one, two, and three criticize the Spanish-American War and American policy in the Far East. Kennan belongs to the Realist school of foreign policy historians who criticize the crusading morality of our foreign policy.

5. Dexter Perkins, "The Policeman of the West: The Evolution of the Roosevelt Corollary," in his *A History of the Monroe Doctrine*. Provides a look at the Caribbean policies of Roosevelt.

First World War and Versailles

1. Arthur S. Link, *Woodrow Wilson and the Progressive Era, 1910–1917*. The chapter entitled, "From Peace Without Victory to War," covers the U.S. entry into the First World War.

2. George F. Kennan, *American Diplomacy, 1900–1950*, gives the Realist historians' view of the mistakes made by U.S. foreign policy in regard to the First World War and the Versailles Treaty.

3. Thomas A. Bailey, *Woodrow Wilson and the Great Betrayal*. "The Supreme Infanticide" puts most of the blame for the defeat of the Versailles Treaty on Wilson's failure to make adjustments in his creation.

4. Selig Adler, *The Isolationist Impulse: Its Twentieth Century Reaction*. The first chapter traces the history of isolationism since the Revolutionary War. The second chapter summarizes the factions which formed the basis for the isolationist sentiment after the First World War.

SAMPLE OUTLINE

POLITICAL PHILOSOPHIES IN THE PROGRESSIVE ERA

I. **Political Climate in 1900**

A. World of change: economic and technological, new scientific and religious ideas, growth of big business and organized labor, urbanization

B. Various political ideological groups developed. Two had been present in politics for previous 25 years.

C. The third felt the full impact of the new ideas and intellectual forces and rapidly changing conditions. This group came to be called the Progressives.

D. Differentiating political philosophies
   1. Radical (Socialist in this era) refers to advocating drastic revolutionary changes in society and in the government.
   2. Conservative refers to preserving the existing order; that is, conserving rather than changing.
   3. Reactionary refers to desiring to move society backwards into a past society, usually idealized.
   4. Liberal refers to advocating changes in society's institutions to reflect changing conditions.
   5. These terms refer to means as well as ends; one can pursue radical goals by conservative means, e.g., socialists running for political office in a democratic political system.

II. Conservative Creed

A. Nature of man

1. Frail creatures unable to withstand evil impulses. Life was a "succession of pitiful compromises with fate."
2. With the present uncertain and the future unknowable, the only way to prevent anarchy, chaos, and disaster was to cling to the time-tested methods of the past. "God Almighty made men and certain laws which are essential to their progress in civilization and Congressmen cannot break these natural laws without causing suffering."
3. Inequality: Interested in protecting the rights of the outstanding contributor to society; inequality was natural because the average man contributed little to progress.
4. The masses were political junk. Democratic systems of goverment led to demagogues.

B. Nature of progress

1. Application of natural (divine) laws was the key to progress. It was beyond the capacity of mankind to devise improvements.
2. Reason could not solve any political problem because the reasoner never gets all the premises into his thinking.
3. Man could only discover God's laws, not change them—Social Darwinism. Progress was God's process, which took generations, not years or days. The quest for property was man's progress.

III. Radical Rationale

A. Nature of man

1. Nothing was evil in human nature.
2. Society was the teacher, creating the experiences for each individual's life; tabula rasa.
3. Man was a mirror which reflected his environment, chiefly his material environment. (This is pre-1917 socialist thinking.)

B. Nature of progress

1. Scientific: Man was a creature of his economic class, which had evolved according to the scientific laws of evolution.
2. Inevitable: It was only a matter of time before progress instituted the classless society. 1904 Socialist Party platform: "The Socialist program is not a theory imposed upon society for its acceptance or rejection, it is but the interpretation of what is sooner or later inevitable."

IV. Progressive Profile

A. Nature of man

1. The conservative was pessimistic, the Progressive optimistic.
2. Deep faith in man and his ability to better his station on earth; used phrases like, "the beautiful people," "the essential nobility of man." "In the end the people are bound to do the right thing, no matter how much they fail at times."
3. A free individual: Man must be free to develop to his fullest capacity as an individual and to bring benefits to society. Many Progressives opposed all organizations hampering the free individual—parties, unions, big business, etc.

4. Democracy: not just a belief, but a faith; the right to choose more important than the ability to choose wisely. "Democracy is a soul satisfying thing." The solution to most problems was more effective democratic methods.

5. Dichotomy of economic beliefs:
   Some Progressives favored a return to laissez-faire economics; feared the federal governmental bureaucracy as well as trusts; aim was to preserve individualism: Wilson, New Freedom. (Its original philosophy was to break up the industrial system with antimonopoly laws.)
   Other Progressives wanted to face the economic realities of the time and have national regulation of national industries to preserve and protect individualism: Roosevelt, New Nationalism. (Accept the industrial system and regulate it.)

6. Christian ethics: In attacking society's problems the solution was to amend the system. In dealing with the individuals who need reform the solution was to preach Christian ethics and to tolerate no exceptions: juvenile courts, juvenile offenders, Judge Benjamin Barr Lindsey. The movement had a righteous and evangelical character, "a political carnival of purity."

B. Nature of progress

1. Man was neither chained to his past (as the conservative believed) nor riding automatically into the predetermined future (as the socialist believed).

2. Man was a free agent who controlled his own destiny.

3. Inequality caused injustice and most of the evil in the world. If inequality could be wiped out the result would be a more honest, neighborly, helpful, and capable individual. (Read the Boy Scout oath, for the BSA was founded in this period.)

4. By improving the basic building block of society, the free individual, society as a whole would improve and progress.

5. Malleable homo sapiens: Central to the Progressives was the idea that man, more good than evil, had the power through his moral sense and intellect to change his environment and himself.

Unit Eight: 1920 to 1940

MAJOR THEMES AND IDEAS

The Twenties

1. Harding and the Twenties as the end of Progressivism
2. What aspects of Progressivism survived into the Twenties?
3. Were the Twenties "golden" for agriculture, labor, and business?
4. Coolidge's quote in regard to union-business relations: "The man who builds a factory builds a temple; the man who works there worships there."
5. The Twenties as an age of nonconformity: blacks, feminists, literary criticism, sexual customs
6. The Twenties: an assault by rural and small-town America against urban America
7. The dark side of the Twenties: immigration, KKK, Scopes, prohibition
8. Alienation as a literary theme in the Twenties
9. The Twenties as an era of transition
10. Individuals that best exemplify the Twenties
11. The issues and results of the presidential elections of 1920, 1924, and 1928
12. Causes of the Great Depression

The Thirties

1. Compare Hoover's and Roosevelt's response to the Depression.
2. Compare the role of the federal government in the economies of the Twenties and Thirties.
3. The Twenties were pro-business; the Thirties were anti-business.
4. Compare Progressivism and the New Deal.
5. Compare and contrast the first and second New Deals.
6. Relate aspects of the New Deal to previous reform movements in regard to antimonopoly, labor, banking, agriculture, taxation, and relief.
7. The New Deal was revolutionary.
8. The New Deal was a conservative program.
9. The New Deal helped the rich more than the needy.
10. Successes and failures of the New Deal
11. Supreme Court and the New Deal
12. Impact of the Depression on segments of the economy; corporations, workers, farmers, middle class, etc.
13. Impact of various New Deal programs and agencies on American society
14. Rise of the welfare state
15. Countervailing powers theory: Big government and big labor checked big business.
16. Explain the critics: Townsend, Coughlin, Long, leftists, conservatives.
17. What ended the reform effort by the late 1930s?
18. Reform would have come without a depression because reform in American history is the periodic readjustment of aspects of the economy.
19. Compare the labor movement of the 1930s with the labor movement of the late nineteenth century.
20. Why did the Socialist Party fail to become a serious factor in American politics?

MAJOR TERMS AND CONCEPTS

The Twenties

election of 1920: candidates, issues, vice-presidential candidates
Normalcy
Esch-Cummins Transportation Act
Harding scandals: Charles Forbes, Harry Daugherty, Secretary of Interior Fall, Teapot Dome, Harry Sinclair
Harding's death, Coolidge takes over
Bureau of the Budget
Secretary of Treasury Mellon, tax cuts
Senator George Norris, Muscle Shoals
election of 1924: candidates, Robert La Follette, Progressive Party
McNary-Haugen Bill, vetoes
Federal Farm Board
election of 1928: candidates, personalities, backgrounds
Bruce Barton, *The Man Nobody Knows*, 1925

H. L. Mencken, editor of the magazine, *The American Mercury*
"the Lost Generation"
F. Scott Fitzgerald, *The Great Gatsby*
Sinclair Lewis, *Main Street, Babbitt*
Theodore Dreiser, *An American Tragedy*
Ernest Hemingway, *A Farewell to Arms*
T.S. Eliot, *The Waste Land*
Sigmund Freud's theories
KDKA, Pittsburgh
Prohibition, Volstead Act, Al Capone
KKK
fundamentalists
Immigration Acts, 1921, 1924, quota system
Sacco and Vanzetti case
Leopold and Loeb case
Billy Sunday
Scopes trial, Clarence Darrow, William Jennings Bryan
Henry Ford, the Model T, Alfred P. Sloan
Cecil B. de Mille
The Jazz Singer
Rudolph Valentino, Charlie Chaplin
new woman, flappers
Harlem Renaissance, Langston Hughes
James Weldon Johnson
Marcus Garvey, Universal Negro Improvement Association
Charles Lindbergh, *Spirit of St. Louis*
Babe Ruth, Jack Dempsey

Foreign Policy

Twenty-One Demands
Lansing-Ishii Agreement
Versailles Treaty
Washington Disarmament Conference
Five Power Treaty, Four Power Treaty, Nine Power Treaty
5–5–3–1.75–1.75 ratio
World Court
reparations
Dawes Plan, Young Plan
Kellogg-Briand Treaty

Hoover Administration

causes of the Depression
Depression as an international event
Fordney-McCumber Tariff, 1922
Hawley-Smoot Tariff, 1930
Reconstruction Finance Corporation, RFC

Bonus Army
"Hooverville"
Clark Memorandum
London Naval Conference
Hoover Moratorium, 1931
Manchuria, Hoover-Stimson Doctrine
Mexico's nationalization of oil
Ambassador Morrow
Good Neighbor Policy
Norris-La Guardia (anti-injection) Act, 1932
election of 1932: candidates, issues

Roosevelt and New Deal

Twentieth Amendment
Wickersham Commission
Twenty-first Amendment
"bank holiday"
Hundred Days
"relief, recovery, reform"
Brain Trust
Emergency Banking Relief Act, 1933
Glass-Steagall Banking Reform Act, 1933
Gold Clause Act, 1935
Federal Deposit Insurance Corporation (FDIC)
National Industrial Recovery Act (NIRA)
National Industrial Recovery Administration (NRA), "The Blue Eagle," Hugh Johnson
Agricultural Adjustment Act (AAA), second AAA, 1938
Soil Conservation and Domestic Allotment Act, 1936
Civilian Conservation Corps (CCC)
Federal Emergency Relief Administration (FERA)
Civil Works Administration (CWA)
Public Works Administration (PWA), Harold Ickes
Works Progress Administration (WPA), Harry Hopkins, Federal Arts Project
Home Owners' Loan Corporation (HOLC)
Federal Housing Authority (FHA)
Securities and Exchange Commission (SEC)
Tennessee Valley Authority (TVA), Senator Norris
Rural Electrification Administration (REA)
National Youth Administration (NYA)
Indian Reorganization Act, 1934
recognition of the USSR, 1933
section 7a of the NRA
Wagner Act, 1935
National Labor Relations Board (NLRB)
Fair Labor Standards Act: maximum hours and minimum wage

Congress of Industrial Organizations (CIO), John L. Lewis

sit down strikes

dust bowl, Okies, John Steinbeck, *The Grapes of Wrath*

Frances Perkins, Secretary of Labor

Eleanor Roosevelt

Keynesian economics

deficit spending

monetary policy, fiscal policy

Revenue Act, 1935

Liberty League

coalition of the Democratic Party: blacks, unions, intellectuals, big city machines, South

Huey Long, Share the Wealth, Gerald L.K. Smith

Father Charles Coughlin

Dr. Francis Townsend

election of 1936: candidates, issues

Literary Digest poll

second New Deal

Social Security Act

"court packing" proposal

Chief Justice Charles Evans Hughes

"conservative coalition" in Congress

Robinson-Patman Act, 1936

Miller-Tydings Act, 1937

Hatch Act, 1939

SUPREME COURT CASES TO KNOW

1. *Adkins* v. *Children's Hospital,* 1923 (minimum wage laws)

From the 1890s to the 1930s the Supreme Court frustrated congressional and state regulatory efforts. It invalidated many acts under the freedom of contract doctrine and the due process and equal protection clauses of the Fourteenth Amendment. As the government for the District of Columbia, Congress passed an act in 1918 creating a Minimum Wage Board, authorized to establish minimum wages for women and children working within the District of Columbia. Several female employees at Children's Hospital were fired because the hospital did not want to pay the minimum wage for these jobs. Their suit claimed that their individual freedom of contract had been abridged; the Court agreed, 5-3. "In making . . . contracts, generally speaking, the parties have an equal right to obtain from each other the best terms they can as the result of private bargaining. . . . There is, of course, no such thing as absolute freedom of contract. It is subject to a great variety of restraints. But freedom of contract is, nevertheless, the general rule and restraint the exception; and the exercise of legislative authority to abridge it can be justified only by the existence of exceptional circumstances." Chief Justice Taft's dissent challenged the Court's assumption of legislative powers.

2. *Gitlow* v. *New York,* 1925 (radicals and the First Amendment)

This case involved the arrest of Benjamin Gitlow, an official of the Communist Party, for the violation of New York's criminal anarchy law. The Court upheld the conviction, 7-2. The real significance of the case is that the majority asserted for the first time that the guarantees in the Bill of Rights also apply to the states because of the Fourteenth Amendment.

3. *Schechter Poultry Corp.* v. *U.S.,* 1935 (constitutionality of New Deal programs)

This "Sick Chicken Case" unanimously found the National Industrial Recovery Act unconstitutional. Under the act the NRA was directed to establish codes for each industry in partnership with industries and unions. If the industry did not establish its code, the NRA could impose one. This last feature of the law violated the Constitution because it granted legislative powers to the executive branch. The act also exceeded the government's interstate commerce authority by attempting to regulate the killing of chickens for market, which the Court found to be a intrastate activity. Chief Justice Hughes rejected the argument that a national emergency justified the NRA. "Extraordinary conditions do not create or enlarge constitutional power. The Constitution established a national government with powers deemed to be adequate, as they have proved to be in war and peace, but these powers of the national government are limited by the constitutional grants. Those who act under these grants are not at liberty to transcend the imposed limits because they believe that more or different power is necessary."

4. *U.S.* v. *Butler,* 1936 (constitutionality of New Deal programs)

This decision was the second to declare an important New Deal program, in this case the Agricultural

Adjustment Act, unconstitutional. The law used the federal government's taxing power as a means to regulate production. As such, it exceeded the powers of the federal government by invading state jurisdiction. In this decision the court resurrected the doctrine of "dual federalism," the concept that the states and the national government were equals, and that the Tenth Amendment limited the delegated powers given to Congress. In his dissent Justice Stone blasted the conservatives on the Court. "Courts are not the only agency of government that must be assumed to have capacity to govern."

5. *NLRB* v. *Jones and Laughlin Steel Corp.*, 1937 (interstate commerce and control of labor)

Many students mistakenly believe that most bitter strikes involve wage demands. The most disruptive strikes have involved union recognition, the industry's acquiescence in the union's right to represent the workers and to engage in collective bargaining. The National Labor Relations Board was established to supervise and conduct elections for workers deciding upon union representation. In a 5-4 decision the Court upheld the constitutionality of the Wagner Act creating the NLRB. The Court broadly defined commerce, asserting Congress's right to legislate broadly in the "stream of commerce" because commerce was more than mere transportation. "Although activities may be intrastate in character when separately considered, if they have such a close and substantial relation to interstate commerce that their control is essential or appropriate to protect that commerce from burdens and obstructions, Congress cannot be denied the power to exercise that control."

6. *West Coast Hotel* v. *Parrish*, 1937 (due process and state police powers)

This 5-4 decision upheld state regulation of wages and hours for women and children. The Court reversed the decision in *Adkins* v. *Children's Hospital* by putting the contract clause into a different perspective. "The Constitution does not speak of freedom of contract. It speaks of liberty and prohibits the deprivation of liberty without due process of law. In prohibiting that deprivation the Constitution does not recognize an absolute and uncontrollable liberty. Liberty in each of its phases has its history and connotation. But the liberty safeguarded is liberty in

a social organization which requires the protection of law against the evils which menace the health, safety, morals, and welfare of the people. Liberty under the Constitution is thus necessarily subject to the restraints of due process, and regulation which is reasonable in relation to its subject and adopted in the interests of the community is due process."

7. *U.S.* v. *Darby Lumber Co.*, 1941 (commerce and wages and hours)

This case expressly overruled *Hammer* v. *Dagenhart.* The Darby Lumber Company was charged with violating the federal Fair Labor Standards Act of 1938, which established minimum wages and maximum hours for workers engaged in interstate commerce. The unanimous decision enlarged the definition of interstate commerce to include the production of goods for commerce, not just the transportation of goods. "The motive and purpose of a regulation of interstate commerce are matters for legislative judgment upon the exercise of which the Constitution places no restriction and over which the courts are given no control."

8. *U.S.* v. *Curtiss-Wright Export Corp.*, 1936 (president's control over foreign policy)

In 1934 Congress empowered the president to prohibit the sale of military supplies to Bolivia and Paraguay, who were engaged in a war which threatened the peace of the whole of South America. Bolivia purchased her entire air force of thirty-four planes from the Curtiss-Wright Export Corporation prior to the congressional resolution. In violation of President Roosevelt's proclamation the Curtiss-Wright Corporation tried to smuggle fifteen airplane machine guns into Bolivia. When the case reached the Supreme Court the key question involved the legality of the congressional grant of legislative power to the President. The previous year the NIRA had been declared unconstitutional in the Schechter sick chicken case on the same grounds. In a 7-1 majority opinion the Court differentiated between domestic and foreign policy. The Court ruled that the president has a "degree of discretion and freedom from statutory restriction which would not be admissible were domestic affairs alone involved." As President Harry Truman later said, "I am American foreign policy."

READINGS FOR DEPTH AND HISTORICAL INTERPRETATION

The Twenties

1. Frederick Lewis Allen, "The Revolution in Manners and Morals," in his *Only Yesterday*. This contains delightful comments and examples of the social revolution of the Twenties.

2. H.L. Mencken's *Prejudices* in Robert B. Downs, *Books That Changed America*. Mencken, the supreme iconoclast in American journalism, gives you a new definition of satire. He was called "the most powerful private citizen" in the nation by *The New York Times*. He had a great impact on the literary giants and intellectuals of his era and much later.

3. Arthur S. Link, "What Happened to the Progressive Movement in the 1920's?" *American Historical Review*, 1959. Link argues that many features of Progressivism survived into the 1920s.

4. Irving Bernstein, "The Worker in an Unbalanced Society," in his *The Lean Years: A History of the American Worker, 1920–1933*. Bernstein destroys the image of the Twenties as a golden age for workers; "the serious maladjustments within the economic system fell upon them with disproportionate weight."

5. William E. Leuchtenburg, "Epilogue," in his *The Perils of Prosperity, 1914–1932*. Leuchtenburg summarizes the decade of the Twenties.

6. John Kenneth Galbraith, "Cause and Consequence," in his *The Great Crash, 1929*. Galbraith explains the causes and consequences of the 1929 crash, which ushered in the Great Depression.

The New Deal

1. Otis Graham, *An Encore for Reform: The Old Progressives and the New Deal*, pp. 172–186. Graham compares the Progressive movement and the New Deal by asking what old Progressives thought of the New Deal. He found most Progressives opposed to the New Deal, suggesting significant differences between the two reform movements.

2. Richard Hofstadter, "Herbert Hoover and the Crisis of American Individualism," and "Franklin D. Roosevelt: The Patrician as Opportunist," in his *The American Political Tradition*. Hofstadter compares Hoover and Roosevelt as political leaders.

3. James MacGregor Burns, "President of All the People?" and a section of chapter 18 subtitled, "Roosevelt as a Party Leader," in his *The Lion and the Fox*. These two sections address the subject of FDR as a political leader.

4. Arthur M. Schlesinger, Jr., "The Ideology of the Second New Deal," "The Politics of the Second New Deal," and "The Roosevelt Coalition," in his *The Politics of Upheaval*. Schlesinger compares the First and Second New Deals. Major characteristics, "the techniques employed, the economic presuppositions, the political style, the vision of the American future itself" all changed.

5. Douglass C. North, "War, Prosperity, Depression, and War, 1914–1945," in his *Growth and Welfare in the American Past: A New Economic History*. North looks at statistical data to ask the question: "Was the New Deal a Social Revolution?" His investigation of its policies in regard to employment, economic growth, and income redistribution indicates that it was not revolutionary.

6. Carl Degler, "Was It a New or Old Deal?" in his *Out of Our Past*. Degler surveys historical opinions and offers his own assessment "that traditional as the words may have been in which the New Deal expressed itself, in actuality it was a revolutionary response to a revolutionary situation."

7. Richard Hofstadter, "The New Departure," and "The New Opportunism," in his *The Age of Reform*. Hofstadter sees the New Deal as unlike any previous reform movement in American history, "different in its ideas and its spirit and its techniques." The New Deal was a "drastic new departure" in American reform.

8. William E. Leuchtenburg, "The Roosevelt Reconstruction: Retrospect," in his *Franklin D. Roosevelt and the New Deal, 1932–1940*. Leuchtenburg looks at FDR and the New Deal and pronounces the New Deal to be a "half-way revolution."

9. Paul Murphy, "Franklin Roosevelt," in Morton Borden, ed., *America's Eleven Greatest Presidents*. Murphy looks at the New Deal and FDR's leadership in the Second World War, an often neglected area in assessing FDR.

SAMPLE OUTLINE

One theme around which to organize the 1920s is the urban-rural cultural conflict. Urban values and institutions triumphed in the Twenties. The 1920 census revealed that a majority of Americans lived in urban areas, and rural areas sensed that they were losing out to the new culture, the urban culture. Farmers and small town dwellers by this period thought of themselves as hicks, hillbillies, and hayseeds; they were proud of their rural heritage, yet beginning to feel inferior. In the Twenties rural America fought to reassert its values in an urbanizing nation.

THE TWENTIES AS A DECADE OF CULTURAL CONFLICT

I. Threats to the Old Order

    A. Changing standards of morality

        1. Behavior: new codes for dancing and dress—Charleston, thinner clothes, juvenile look, sleveless dresses

        2. Double standard: A change in attitudes occurred toward expectations for behavior in regard to sexual standards for men and women. Now women began to assert publicly their right to imitate male standards. Only affection was necessary for sex.

    B. Reasons for changing standards

        1. First World War: The maxim "eat, drink, and be merry" often appears after wars. The First World War had the highest ratio of those killed and injured to participants of any war. Small matters of morality seemed less important after this carnage.

        2. Women: greater independence, less parental supervision, 19th Amendment. They joined the labor force in large numbers, and more lived alone.

        3. Impersonality of urban areas

        4. Automobile: sudden capability to escape supervision

        5. Freudian psychology filtered down to the popular level in the 1920s. The message that came down said repressed desires lead to mental illness.

II. Manifestations of Cultural Conflict

    A. Ku Klux Klan: five million members, strong in over twenty states, especially Indiana and Oregon. More of a small-town, fraternal, patriotic defense of the old order than an anti-black organization, they hated Jews, Catholics, blacks, immigrants, and unions. Oregon required all children to attend public schools, not parochial schools.

    B. 1924 Democratic Party Convention in Madison Square Garden: one-hundred three ballots were required to nominate a presidential candidate, John W. Davis, and William Jennings Bryan's brother as vice-president. A huge fight over platform statement denouncing the Klan passed by fewer than five votes.

    C. Fundamentalism: The Scopes trial in Dayton, Tenn concerned the teaching of the theory of evolution. Bryan aided the prosecution, Clarence Darrow, the defense. Bryan testified that the world was created in 4004 B.C. and the flood occurred in 2348 B.C.

D. Nativism: laws of 1921 and 1924, fear of radicals, competition among workers, unions for it, feeling those here insufficiently Americanized, patriotism of First World War, new influx after the war, scientific racism, Army I.Q. tests. First 1910, then 1890 used as a base

E. Al Smith campaign: NYC, Tammany Hall, a wet, Catholic, son of immigrants, accent, strong rural and Southern vote against him

F. Prohibition: WCTU, Anti-Saloon League, 18th Amendment, Volstead Act, job safety, attacks on the urban saloon. Immigrant drinking was seen as a cause of poverty. Anti-union because saloons seen as union meeting places. Anti-German war spirit, speakeasies, bootleg liquor. Al Capone in one year made 110 million dollars and was responsible for 110 deaths.

G. Hero worship: Lindbergh, a small-town boy, beat the corporations as the "Lone Eagle." Individualism was not dead. Babe Ruth was an orphan, a man who didn't follow the organization rules, yet he was successful and an individual.

H. Fear of radicals: Red Scare, Palmer raids. President Coolidge wrote an article for the *Saturday Evening Post,* "Are the Reds Stalking Our College Women?"

I. Marcus Garvey and UNIA. Popularity was a response by urbanized Southern blacks to the harshness of Northern life; Chicago race riot, 1919.

III. **Age of Social Insecurity**

A. Technology caused drastic changes.
1. Car: In 1919, one of every sixteen people owned a car; in 1929, one of five; Model-T.
2. Films: weekly average attendance in 1922, 40 million; by 1930, 115 million
3. Radio: WWJ, Detroit, and KDKA, Pittsburgh; in 1930, 612 stations. In 1920, $10 million in radios & parts; by 1920, $400 million

B. Nicknames for the Twenties: The roaring 20s, The Jazz Age, The Flapper Age, The Golden Age, Normalcy; summarized as "We never had it so good."

C. The verdict of literature was more harsh. "The Lost Generation" was disillusioned with the war and materialism.
1. T.S.Eliot, *The Waste Land*
2. Sinclair Lewis, *Babbitt, Main Street.* In 1930 Lewis gave a scathing Nobel Prize acceptance speech attacking the literary establishment.
3. H.L.Mencken, editor of the magazine, *The American Mercury*
4. Dreiser's *An American Tragedy.* The dream of success slips away.

D. Popular literature not harsh
1. "Confession" magazines have their beginning.
2. Bruce Barton, *The Man Nobody Knows,* popular view of Christ as a super businessman

Unit Nine: 1940 to 1960

MAJOR THEMES AND IDEAS

Foreign Policies

1. Compare isolationism after the First World War with leadership of the Western world after the Second World War.
2. Compare and contrast American foreign policy in the Twenties and Thirties with American foreign policy in the fifteen years after the Second World War.
3. The impact of communism upon both foreign and domestic affairs in the two decades after the Second World War
4. Was the Cold War inevitable?
5. Compare American neutrality before the First World War with American neutrality before the Second World War.
6. Compare and contrast the foreign policies of Truman and Eisenhower.
7. Historiography of the Cold War
8. Was FDR ineffective in his foreign policy from 1933 to 1941?
9. How consistent was U.S. policy toward China from 1900 to 1949?
10. Impact of the Spanish-American War, the First World War, and the Second World War on our commitments and security in Asia and the Pacific Ocean
11. Trace the changes in the Monroe Doctrine in the 20th century.
12. American foreign policy from 1945 to 1960 was controlled by the ghost of Woodrow Wilson.
13. League of Nations, World Court, and United Nations: success and failures

Domestic Policies

1. Compare and contrast the experiences of various groups—labor, blacks, business, farmers—following the First and Second World Wars.
2. Disputes among black leaders over goals, methods, and the degree of integregation
3. 1950s as an era of social anxiety
4. Reasons for and consequences of black migration from the rural South to the urban North in the 20th century
5. Supreme Court and social change in the period from 1920 to 1965
6. Civil rights movement to 1960

Presidency

1. Power of the presidency: foreign crises, economic depressions, and social conflicts
2. Power of the presidency: war and the threat of war
3. Historians love to rank presidents; compare and contrast three presidents since 1928.
4. Analyze the connection between previous administrations and presidential election campaigns and the election results for 1912, 1920, 1932, 1952, 1960, 1968, 1976, and 1980.
5. Why is FDR ranked as a great president?

MAJOR TERMS AND CONCEPTS

Second World War

Montevideo Conference
Rio de Janeiro Conference, 1933
Buenos Aires Conference, 1936
Lima Conference, 1938
Declaration of Panama, 1939
Act of Havana, 1940
Jones Act, 1916

Tydings-McDuffie Act, 1934, Philippines
Nye Committee
"merchants of death"
neutrality legislation: 1935, 1936, 1937
Spanish Civil War, Franco
Ethiopia
Mussolini
Japan attacks China, Chiang Kai-shek
Panay incident

"Quarantine speech", 1937
Hitler, Nazism
Munich Conference, appeasement, Neville Chamberlain
Austria annexed
nonaggression pact between Germany and USSR
invasion of Poland, blitzkrieg
Axis powers
"cash and carry," revision of neutrality
fall of France
America First Committee
isolationism, Charles Lindbergh
Committee to Defend America by Aiding the Allies
Smith Act
Tojo
destroyer deal
election of 1940: candidates, issues
"lend lease," March 1941
Atlantic Charter, August 1941
Pearl Harbor, December 7, 1941
Japanese relocation
bond drives
War Production Board
Office of Price Administration (OPA)
War Labor Board
General Eisenhower, General MacArthur
genocide, "Final Solution"
second front
D-Day, June 6, 1944
Stalingrad
Winston Churchill
Casablanca Conference, 1943
Cairo Conference, 1943
Teheran Conference, 1943
"unconditional surrender"
Okinawa
Battle of the Bulge
Manhattan Project
J. Robert Oppenheimer
atomic bomb
Hiroshima, Nagasaki

Cold War

Yalta Conference
Potsdam Conference
partitioning of Korea, Vietnam, Germany
Charles de Gaulle
Winston Churchill, "Iron Curtain" speech
Stalin
Bretton Woods Conference

Dumbarton Oaks Conference
San Francisco Conference, 1945 and UN Charter
UN: Security Council, General Assembly, Secretary-General
Atomic Energy Commission
superpowers
socialism, communism
satellites
Nuremberg trials
Department of Defense created
Voice of America, CARE
Yugoslavia, Marshall Tito
Czechoslovakian coup
containment, George F. Kennan
Truman Doctrine
Marshall Plan
Point Four
Israel created, 1948
Berlin blockade
North Atlantic Treaty Organization (NATO)
Warsaw Pact
Southeast Asia Treaty Organization (SEATO)
Central Treaty Organization (CENTO)
Australia, New Zealand, U.S. (ANZUS)
collective security
fall of China, Mao Tse-tung
State Department "White Paper," 1949
Chiang Kai-shek, Formosa
Quemoy, Matsu
Korean War, limited war
Truman-MacArthur controversy
Gandhi
Dien Bien Phu
Vietnam, Ho Chi Minh
Bricker Amendment
John Foster Dulles
"massive retaliation"
brinksmanship
preemptive strike
Khrushchev, 1955 Geneva Summit
Hungarian revolt, 1956
Nasser, Suez Canal crisis
peaceful coexistence
Eisenhower Doctrine
Common Market
Organization of American States (OAS)
U-2 incident
Castro's revolution
Bay of Pigs
Alliance for Progress
Cuban missile crisis
ICBM

Domestic, 1940s and 1950s

Revenue Act of 1942
G.I. Bill of Rights, 1944
Office of War Mobilization and Reconversion
extension of OPA vetoed
postwar inflation
baby boom
Employment Act of 1946
Taft-Hartley Act
Sen. Robert A. Taft
"right-to-work" laws
1948 election: candidates, issues
Dixiecrats, J. Strom Thurmond
Progressive Party, Henry Wallace
Fair Deal
Americans for Democratic Action (ADA)
National Security Act, 1947, 1949
House Un-American Activities Committee (HUAC)
McCarthyism, Senator Joseph McCarthy
Alger Hiss
McCarran Internal Security Act, 1950
Julius and Ethel Rosenberg
Twenty-second Amendment
1952 election: candidates, issues
Ike and Modern Republicanism
"fiscal management"
Reinhold Niebuhr
Ayn Rand, *The Fountainhead*
McCarran-Walter Immigration Act, 1952
Department of Health, Education and Welfare (HEW)

Interstate Highway Act
St. Lawrence Seaway
Landrum-Griffin Act
Jimmy Hoffa
AFL-CIO merger
Alaska, Hawaii
Sputnik
National Defense Education Act (NDEA Act)
"military-industrial complex"

Black History

A. Philip Randolph
Fair Employment Practices Committee
Detroit race riots, 1943
Gunnar Myrdal, *An American Dilemma*
rural and Southern to urban and Northern
To Secure These Rights
desegregation of the armed forces, 1948
Korean War
"separate but equal"
Brown v. Bd. of Education of Topeka
Thurgood Marshall
Rosa Parks, Montgomery bus boycott
Rev. Martin Luther King, Jr.
Little Rock, Ark crisis
Civil Rights Act, 1957
Civil Rights Act, 1960
literacy tests, grandfather clause, poll taxes, white primaries

SUPREME COURT CASES TO KNOW

1. *West Virginia State Board of Education* v. *Barnette*, 1943 (flag salute in school)

In a 1940 case, *Minersville School District* v. *Gobitis*, the Supreme Court upheld the expulsion from school of two Gobitas children (misspelled in official legal documents) who refused to salute the flag. The Gobitas family belonged to Jehovah's Witnesses, who believe the First Commandment directs them to worship no other god. The Court upheld the school board, 8-1. Just three years later the Court reversed itself, 6-3, in a similar case from West Virginia. Through various legal contortions students expelled from school for refusing to salute the flag were declared delinquents, subject to imprisonment in reform schools. Many local and state school boards

felt the Gobitis decision sanctioned broadly based attacks on Jehovah's Witnesses, and the members of the Supreme Court were shocked at the consequences of that decision. Thus, their reversal is less dramatic than it seems. (Ironically, the decision was announced on Flag Day, June 14th.) The majority opinion reflected the atmosphere of 1943, which differed from the war preparation and uncertainty of 1940. In 1943 we knew we would eventually win. The Court strongly defended the First Amendment. "If there is any fixed star in our constitutional constellation, it is that no official, high or petty, can prescribe what shall be orthodox in politics, nationalism, religion, or other matters of opinion or force citizens to confess by word or act their faith therein."

2. *Korematsu* v. *U.S.*, 1944 (war powers and civilians)

Korematsu was arrested and convicted for noncompliance with the military order that moved all people of Japanese ancestry from the West Coast into relocation centers after the attack on Pearl Harbor. The Court upheld the action in a 6-3 decision based upon a broad interpretation of the nation's war powers. In his dissent Justice Jackson explained Korematsu's dilemma. He "was convicted of an act not commonly a crime . . . being present in the state whereof he is a citizen, near the place where he was born, and where he lived all his life. Even more unusual is the series of military orders which make this conduct a crime. They forbid such a one to remain, and they also forbid him to leave. They were so drawn that the only way Korematsu could avoid violation was to give himself up to the military authority." Fred Korematsu had tried to enlist in the army, but was rejected because of ulcers. He then spent his life savings of $150 to learn welding to help the war effort. Instead he was arrested.

3. *Smith* v. *Allwright,* 1944 (blacks and voting in primaries)

Texas Democrats limited membership in their political party to only whites. This tactic negated the black vote because whites fought their internecine battles in the party primaries, and then almost all of them voted for the Democratic candidates in the general election. The Court ruled that this practice violated the Fifteenth Amendment. The Texas state government gave parties complete control of the primary procedures, but this attempt to evade state responsibility was unconstitutional. "When primaries become a part of the machinery for choosing officials, state and national, as they have here, the same tests to determine the character of discrimination or abridgment should be applied to the primary as are applied to the general election."

4. *Dennis* v. *U.S.*, 1951 (radicals and constitutional rights)

Decided in the middle of the McCarthy era, this case upheld the conviction, 6-2, of eleven leaders of the Communist Party for violating the 1940 Smith Act. The case revived the division among judges over the "clear and present danger" and the "bad tendency test" in regard to subversive activities. The "clear and present danger" doctrine announced in *Schenck* v. *U.S.* stated, "The question in every case is whether the words used are used in such circumstances and are of such a nature as to create a clear and present danger that they will bring about the substantive evils that Congress has a right to prevent. It is a question of proximity and degree."

The "bad tendency test" formulated in the decision of *Gitlow* v. *U.S.* was based upon a government's inherent right of self-preservation. A government could restrict any freedom of speech or press that had the tendency to injure the government.

In the majority opinion in the Dennis case the Court declared, "Whatever theoretical merit there may be to the argument that there is a 'right' to rebellion against dictatorial government is without force where the existing structure of the government provides for peaceful and orderly change."

5. *Youngstown Sheet and Tube Co.* v. *Sawyer,* 1952 (president's powers)

After a long, bitter dispute between the United Steelworkers Union and the steel companies a strike date was announced. Various federal agencies intervened unsuccessfully to settle the strike. The nation was engaged in the Korean War, a limited war which had not been declared. The Korean War was technically a police action, not a war. Truman ordered Secretary of Commerce Sawyer to take possession of the mills for the federal government. The steel companies sued to regain control, and won in a 6-3 decision. The majority judges wrote six different opinions. Two common threads held that the president received no grant of power from Congress authorizing him to so act, and even in his capacity as Commander in Chief he could not seize property. Neither Congress nor the Constitution supported the seizure, and Truman quickly and quietly complied. The union went on strike.

6. *Sweatt* v. *Painter,* 1950 (blacks and "separate but equal" education)

Several cases over the years foreshadowed judicial disenchantment with the "separate but equal" Plessy doctrine. Two cases were announced the same day in 1950. The first, *McLaurin* v. *Oklahoma State Regents,* ended the segregation against a black student after admission to the state graduate school. He had been assigned his own cafeteria table, his own library table, and an entire row in his classrooms.

Sweatt was denied admission to the University of Texas Law School solely on the basis of race. After he had filed suit the state government hurriedly put together a "separate but equal" law school for blacks.

In a unanimous decision the Court found the two schools unequal, denying Sweatt the equal protection of the laws. The two schools especially differed in "those qualities which are incapable of objective measurement but which make for greatness in a law school. Such qualities, to name but a few, include reputation of the faculty, experience of the administration, position and influence of the alumni, standing in the community, traditions and prestige. It is difficult to believe that one who had a free choice between these law schools would consider the question close."

7. *Brown vs. Board of Education of Topeka, Kansas* 1954 (blacks, education and the equal protection clause)

In 1951 Oliver Brown filed suit on behalf of his daughter, Linda, who was bused to a black school over twenty blocks away. Another elementary school for whites only was five blocks away. Three other cases—from South Carolina, Virginia, and Delaware—were also filed at this time. This is one of the most significant cases ever decided by the Supreme Court. Recognizing the impact of this case the Court entertained arguments from all quarters. Fifty-one *amici curiae*, "friends of the court," briefs were filed along with those involved in the case. The majority opinion, 8–0, relied heavily on sociological and psychological factors as well as legal arguments. Segregation had to end. "We conclude that in the field of public education the doctrine of 'separate but equal' has no place. Separate educational facilities are inherently unequal." The Court did not order immediate compliance, but instead directed lower courts to implement the order "with all deliberate speed." This speed was lacking for a number of years.

READINGS FOR DEPTH AND HISTORICAL INTERPRETATION

Domestic, 1940s and 1950s

1. Richard Kirkendall, "Harry Truman," in Morton Borden, ed., *America's Eleven Greatest Presidents.* This book was originally entitled, *America's Ten Greatest Presidents.* The addition of Harry Truman changed the title. Most known for his foreign policies, Truman avoided the massive economic depression that everyone expected. Truman made decisions that determined our Cold War foreign policy for decades.

2. Arthur M. Schlesinger, Jr., "Introduction," and "Freedom: A Fighting Faith," in his *The Vital Center.* The book was originally written in the late 1940s as a clarion call for liberals to revitalize liberalism in order to confront the challenge of socialism and communism. Schlesinger updated his book in the 1960s.

3. Richard Hofstadter, "The Pseudo-Conservative Revolt—1954," in his *The Paranoid Style in American Politics.* Hofstadter sees McCarthyism as part of the American tradition of the conspiracy theory of history. Status anxieties motivated those behind McCarthyism, which was a reappearance of the same impulses behind Populism.

4. Richard H. Rovere, "What He Was and What He Did," in his *Senator Joe McCarthy.* Rovere gives a hostile assessment of McCarthy and McCarthyism.

5. Norman Graebner, "Eisenhower's Popular Leadership," *Current History,* October 1960. A contemporary assessment of Eisenhower's administration.

6. John Kenneth Galbraith, *The Affluent Society,* in Robert Downs, ed., *Books That Changed America.* Galbraith added a phrase to our economic thinking. In his book Galbraith castigated economists for continuing to emphasize production for personal consumption in a society that neglected public communal needs.

7. Douglass C. North, "Current Economic Problems in Historical Perspective, 1945–1965," in his *Growth and Welfare in the American Past: A New Economic History.* North looks at the historical economic background of the role of government, poverty, balance of trade, full employment, economic growth, etc.

Second World War and Cold War

1. Walter La Feber, "Before Pearl Harbor," *Current History,* August 1969. La Feber traces U.S. Far Eastern policy for the fifty years before the Second World War.

2. George F. Kennan (Mr. X), "The Sources of Soviet Conduct," *Foreign Affairs*, 1947, also in his *American Diplomacy, 1900–1950*. This is the original argument for the policy of containment, written by George F. Kennan under the pseudonym, "Mr. X."

3. Arthur M. Schlesinger, Jr., "Origins of the Cold War," *Foreign Affairs*, October 1967. Schlesinger puts most of the blame for the beginning of the Cold War on the Russians and Stalin.

4. Gar Alperovitz, "How the Cold War Began," *The New York Review of Books*, March 23, 1967. Alperovitz puts most of the blame for the beginning of the Cold War on the U.S. and Truman.

5. William A. Williams, *The Tragedy of American Diplomacy*, pp. 164–177. A leftist critique of the origins of the Cold War, it puts most of the blame on the long-term nature of our capitalist economy.

SAMPLE OUTLINE

SECOND WORLD WAR IN HISTORICAL PERSPECTIVE

I. **Impact of the War on Domestic America**
   The war brought increased coordination between business, labor, and government. Two new institutions were admitted into the inner circle of power—higher education and the scientific community.

   A. Stimulus to the economy

   1. War contracts aided big business.
      a. Introduction of tax write-offs
      b. Cost plus fixed fee contracts
      c. Two-thirds of war contracts (total of 117 billion) went to corporations in the top 100; GM got 8%.
      d. Economic concentration; 500,000 small businesses disappeared during the war.
      e. Number employed in iron and steel rose by 500,000; transportation up 2,600,000.
      f. Big corporations had first option to buy government surplus facilities after the war.

   2. Labor union membership grew from 8.5 million in 1940 to 15 million in 1945.

   3 Agriculture
      a. Total output increased 50% during the war.
      b. Concentration increased.
      c. Value of machinery used increased from 3.1 billion in 1940 to 6.5 billion in 1945.

   B. Permanent changes in government

   1. Numbers in federal bureaucracy grew from 1 million in 1940 to 3 million in 1945.
   2. New agencies: CIA, NRC, Department of Defense

   C. Higher education and the scientific community

   1. Universities received big contracts for scientific research; MIT, 117 million; Cal Tech, 83 million; Others were Harvard, Columbia, U of Cal, Johns Hopkins, U of Chicago.
   2. Higher Ed science joined the military-industrial complex. For example, synthetic rubber; After Japan captured 97% of the source of U.S. supply of rubber, the federal government spent 700 million to develop synthetic rubber, and gave

corporations the patents for small fee. Before the war the U.S. was the largest importer of rubber; after the war it was the largest exporter of synthetic rubber.

D. Social impact of the war

1. Blacks served in large numbers.
2. Same number of women worked in 1950 as in 1945.
3. 14.5 million served in armed forces.
4. The internal movement of our population during the war was greater than the total number of immigrants who entered the U.S.
5. Many day care centers and child care centers
6. Large juvenile delinquency rates in 1950s among those who were young children during the war
7. Pollutants show up for the first time: DDT, plastics, smog in L.A.

II. Second World War in Worldwide Perspective

A. Change from a European-centered world to a world stage; from 1500 to 1945 European nations had dominated the world, but this was no longer true.

B. Change from international balance of power politics to balance of terror. Atomic weapons undermined a viable use of balance of power.

C. Before the war eight nations were considered more or less equal—U.S., Germany, Japan, Great Britain, France, China, Italy, and USSR. After the war three were defeated, three exhausted, and only two were left. (Since 1945 we have seen the slow resurrection of the six defeated and exhausted nations rather than any decline of the U.S.)

D. From alliances to superpowers: Instead of alliances for collective security, superpowers now provide a nuclear shield for their satellites.

E. Superpowers' needs

1. Large land mass
2. Large population
3. Advanced economy and technology (not necessarily a high standard of living)
4. Possession of deliverable atomic bombs
5. Autonomy in foreign policies

F. Confrontation of "isms": Military losses in Second World War were USSR, 7.5 million, U.S. 291,000; The war was primarily fought as a war between the isms of Germany and USSR.

G. From old to new imperialism

1. Old imperialism was political and economic.
2. New imperialism is military and ideological.

H. Resurgence of Africa and Asia

1. End of the old imperialism brought independence to many new nations and much confusion in some (Congo).
2. Soviet propaganda effective as part of anti-imperialism effort; U.S. often unfairly linked to European imperialists.
3. Race as an issue complicated the end of imperialism. (1950s marked the beginning of the popular acceptance of the concept of racial equality.)

I. The speed of technological change has gone from evolutionary to revolutionary, in part speeded up by the war effort.

Unit Ten: 1960 to 1990

MAJOR THEMES AND IDEAS

Foreign Policies

1. Containment policy in the Eisenhower, Kennedy, and Johnson administrations
2. What were the immediate and long range consequences of the Vietnam War?
3. Continuing themes and new departures in foreign policy since 1960
4. Did the "military-industrial complex" lead us into the Vietnam War?
5. Vietnam killed the Great Society.
6. Consistency in American foreign policy in the 1960–1985 period
7. Compare and contrast the foreign policies of two presidents from 1960 to the present.

Social Change

1. New patterns of black leadership since 1960
2. Is American society becoming more egalitarian?
3. Trace the issues, leaders, goals, turning points, successes, and failures of the women's movement.
4. Counterculture movement and changing American values

5. The 1960s as an era of alienation
6. Immigration legislation to the 1980s
7. Leftist criticism since 1960
8. Social issues: crime, elderly, poverty
9. Compare the civil rights movement for blacks in the North and South.
10. Compare the Great Society and the New Deal.
11. Compare the goals and strategies of the women's suffrage movement and feminism since 1945.

Politics and Political Issues

1. Pivotal elections: 1968, 1972, 1976, 1980, 1984
2. Why did presidents from 1960 to 1980 serve less than two full terms?
3. Trace the increase and decrease of military programs and social programs as reflected in the federal budgets since 1960.
4. Federal budget since 1960: Keynesian economics, monetary policy, fiscal policy, deficits, priorities
5. What happened to the antitrust movement in the 20th century?
6. What in the past ten years will become part of future history books and why?

MAJOR TERMS AND CONCEPTS

Blacks

Brown v. Board of Education of Topeka, Kansas
Montgomery bus boycott
Rev. Martin Luther King, Jr.
Southern Christian Leadership Conference
National Association for the Advancement of Colored People (NAACP)
Urban League
Congress of Racial Equality (CORE)
Student Nonviolent Coordinating Committee (SNCC)
sit-ins, freedom rides
"I have a dream" speech
March on Washington, 1963
Medgar Evers
Adam Clayton Powell
H. Rap Brown

Malcolm X
Stokely Carmichael
Black Panthers
Black Muslims
Angela Davis
black power
Twenty-fourth Amendment
Watts, Detroit race riots
Kerner Commission on Civil Disorders
de facto, de jure segregation
white backlash
Robert Weaver
Thurgood Marshall
Civil Rights Act of 1964, public accommodations section of the act
Voting Rights Act, 1965
Civil Rights Act, 1968

Vietnam

geography: Gulf of Tonkin, North Vietnam, South Vietnam, Thailand, Laos, Cambodia
Ho Chi Minh
Viet Cong
Dien Bien Phu
Geneva Conference, 1954
National Liberation Front (NLF)
Gulf of Tonkin Resolution, 1964
demilitarized zone (DMZ)
domino theory
Tet offensive
Kent State incident, Jackson State incident
Daniel Ellsberg, Pentagon Papers
My Lai, Lt. Calley
Hanoi, Haiphong
Senator Fulbright
bombing of Laos and Cambodia
Vietnamization
Paris Accords, 1973

1960s

election of 1960: issues, candidates, "missile gap"
"impeach Earl Warren"
Miranda decision, Escobedo decision
Gideon v. *Wainwright*
Baker v. *Carr*
Rachel Carson, *Silent Spring*
New Frontier
Kennedy and the steel price rollback
Peace Corps, VISTA
Berlin Wall
Common Market
Trade Expansion Act, 1962
Nuclear Test Ban Treaty, 1963
Lee Harvey Oswald, Warren Commission
Bay of Pigs
UN in the Congo
"flexible response"
Cuban missile crisis
Alliance for Progress
Dominican Republic, 1965
Salvador Allende
Panama Canal treaties
Students for a Democratic Society (SDS)
"flower children"
Charles Reich, *The Greening of America*
election of 1964: LBJ, Goldwater
Great Society
Office of Economic Opportunity
War on Poverty

Elementary and Secondary Act
Medicare
abolition of immigration quotas
Department of Housing and Urban Development
John Birch Society
New Left
Robert Kennedy
election of 1968: candidates, issues
Czechoslovakia invaded
Chicago, Democratic Party Convention riot
Richard Nixon's "Southern strategy"
Governor Wallace
moon race, Neil Armstrong
Sunbelt versus Frostbelt
Betty Friedan, *The Feminine Mystique*
National Organization for Women (NOW)
Equal Rights Amendment (ERA)
National Women's Political Caucus
Ralph Nader, *Unsafe at Any Speed*

1970s

Nixon, "New Federalism"
Spiro T. Agnew, his resignation
"revenue sharing"
wage and price controls
Nixon versus Congress
Watergate
Committee for the Reelection of the President
election of 1972: candidates, issues
White House "plumbers"
Sen. George McGovern
Sen. Edmund Muskie
Watergate tapes
H.R. Haldeman, John Ehrlichman, John Dean, John Mitchell
impeachment proceedings
SALT I Agreement
detente
China visit, 1972
recognition of China
War Powers Act, 1973
Six Day War, 1967
Yom Kippur War
Henry Kissinger, "shuttle diplomacy"
Twenty-fifth Amendment
Twenty-sixth Amendment
Chicanos
Cesar Chavez
William Burger appointed, 1969
American Indian Movement (AIM), Wounded Knee

multinational corporations
Arab oil embargo
Organization of Petroleum Exporting Countries (OPEC)
balance of trade, trade deficits
Alaska pipeline
The Imperial Presidency
Gerald Ford
Nixon pardon
"stagflation"
SALT II
election of 1976: candidates, issues
Jimmy Carter
amnesty
Panama Canal Treaty
Camp David Accords
Egypt-Israel Peace Treaty: Menachem Begin, Anwar Sadat
Palestinian Liberation Front, (PLO), Yasser Arafat
Department of Energy
Department of Education
Iranian crisis, the Shah, Ayatollah Khomeini

1980s

Afghanistan, 1979–1989
Olympic boycott, 1980
election of 1980: candidates, issues
Reaganomics
supply side economics
Sandra Day O'Connor
Lech Walesa, Solidarity
Three Mile Island
Love Canal, Niagara Falls, NY
Times Beach, Missouri
EPA, Environmental Protection Agency
"New Federalism" proposals, 1982

deregulation—AT&T, airlines, trucking
NEH, National Endowment for the Humanities
Title 9 of Education Amendments, 1972
Betty Friedan, *The Second Stage*, 1981
defeat of the ERA
Phyllis Schlafly
Falkland Islands War
Grenada, 1983
El Salvador
Nicaragua—Somoza family, Sandinistas, Contras, Ortega
Arias Peace Plan in Central America
Iran-Iraq War
"Star Wars," SDI, Strategic Defense Initiative
Third World debt
election of 1984: candidates, issues
Geraldine Ferraro
AIDS
"Moral Majority"
Rev. Jerry Falwell
Agent Orange
Challenger disaster, 1986
Tax Reform Act, 1986
nuclear freeze movement
Iran-Contra affair, Irangate
Col. North
Tower Commission Report
Panama, Gen. Noriega
South Africa, apartheid
Marcos, Philippines
Duvalier, Haiti
Middle East—Persian Gulf, West Bank
Gorbachev, glasnost, perestroika
Col. Qaddafi, Libya
INF Treaty, 1987
Rev. Jessee Jackson, Rainbow Coalition
election of 1988: candidates, issues
George Bush
holes in the "Iron Curtain"
Berlin Wall opens
Webster v. *Reproductive Health Services*

SUPREME COURT CASES TO KNOW

1. *Mapp* v. *Ohio*, 1961 (Bill of Rights and the states)

This case was the first of a series of decisions that extended the Fourteenth Amendment to protect citizens against state infringement. The Supreme Court used the "due process" clause to make the Bill of Rights apply to state officials. The Mapp case overturned a state court conviction based on evidence obtained by an unreasonable search and seizure. (Since 1914 the Supreme Court had barred federal use of illegally obtained evidence.)

2. *Gideon* v. *Wainwright*, 1963 (right to counsel)

Gideon was arrested in 1961 for breaking into a poolroom. He asked for a court-appointed lawyer because he could not afford one. Florida law provided lawyers for penniless defendants in only capital crimes, which carried a possible death penalty. The Supreme Court decided that legal counsel must be provided for all persons charged with a felony. In 1972 the Court extended the right to counsel to anyone charged with misdemeanors, a lesser category of crimes, in a decision in regard to Jon Argersinger, another Floridian, *Argersinger* v. *Hamlin*. Argersinger was sentenced to 90 days in jail for carrying a concealed weapon.

3. *Escobedo* v. *Illinois*, 1964 (right to counsel)

In a 5-4 decision the Supreme Court ruled that the police must honor an arrested person's request that a lawyer be present during a police interrogation. The constitutional guarantee to be represented by counsel extends to the period prior to actual indictment.

4. *Miranda* v. *Arizona*, 1966 (rights of the accused)

The Miranda decision culminated the 1960s trend toward protecting the rights of the accused. In a 5-4 decision the Supreme Court stated that an arrested person must be told that he has the right to remain silent; that whatever he says may be used against him; that he has the right to be represented by a lawyer; that if he cannot afford a lawyer one will be provided; and finally, that he is permitted one telephone call to obtain a lawyer or to contact someone to make arrangements for him to arrange for a lawyer and bail proceedings. The Supreme Court justices were heavily criticized for coddling criminals. In a rare comment before a convention of chiefs of police, one justice stated that in America it is supposed to be difficult to arrest and convict someone.

5. *Engel* v. *Vitale*, 1962; *School District of Abington Township* v. *Schempp*, 1963 (religion and public schools)

The first case struck down a prayer composed by the New York State Board of Regents, the state public education authority. The second ended the reciting of the Lord's Prayer and the daily reading of ten Bible verses. The Court held that under the Constitution religion is "too personal, too sacred, too holy" for governmental sanction. Religion is a personal matter; government is a public matter.

6. *Baker* v. *Carr*, 1962; *Wesberry* v. *Sanders*, 1964; *Reynolds* v. *Sims*, 1964 (legislative reapportionment)

Beginning with the *Baker* v. *Carr* case, the Supreme Court ended the old practice of apportioning legislative districts to overrepresent rural areas. The boundary lines for both houses of the state legislatures and for congressional districts must reflect the principle of "one man, one vote" as much as possible. Before the *Baker* v. *Carr* case, federal courts avoided reapportionment arguments as "political questions" to be resolved by the legislatures and the voters.

7. *Heart of Atlanta Motel* v. *U.S.*, 1964 (discrimination in public accommodations)

The Civil Rights Act of 1964 outlawed discrimination in schools, employment, and voting. It also outlawed discrimination in public accommodations, or areas frequented by the public. The Supreme Court upheld the constitutionality of this section of the Civil Rights Act of 1964, and ended the argument that a proprietor had the right to refuse service on the basis of race in his own establishment.

8. *Swan* v. *Charlotte-Mecklenburg Board of Education*, 1971 (public schools and integregation)

Southern school districts tried every conceivable method, even closing schools for a year, to avoid desegregating their public schools. In this opinion the Supreme Court sanctioned virtually any method to achieve desegregation, including busing, redrawing district boundary lines, racial balancing, etc. This decision ended seventeen years of Southern legal subterfuge to avoid the Brown decision.

9. *Bakke* v. *Board of Regents*, 1978 (reverse discrimination)

This reverse discrimination case involved a claim by a white, Allan Bakke, that he was the victim of discrimination. The Civil Rights Act of 1965 prohibited discrimination based upon race, but in order to compensate for the collective results of previous discrimination practices, the University of California at Davis reserved sixteen of its hundred openings for medical school specifically for non-whites. Objective scores and measurements of Bakke's potential put him outside the 84 slots for whites, but higher than the successful applicants for the sixteen non-white positions. In a 5-4 decision the Court upheld both Bakke's admission and the university's use of race to ensure a diverse student body.

10. *Reed* v. *Reed,* 1971 (discrimination based on sex)

This case was the first of a series of sex discrimination decisions. Idaho state law prescribed that the father be given preference over the mother in a dispute over administering the estate of a deceased child. The Reeds were separated when their child died, leaving an estate less than a thousand dollars. The Supreme Court ruled that if both parents were equally qualified the state could not give men preferential treatment; state law had to serve "a compelling government interest" in differentiating between men and women.

11. *Doe* v. *Bolton,* 1973; *Roe* v. *Wade,* 1973 (the abortion cases)

These two cases struck down Texas and Georgia state statutes prohibiting abortions. The Court found such laws to be an infringement on rights to privacy protected by the Ninth and Fourteenth Amendments. The Court limited state legislation by defining three stages of pregnancy and specifying when and which state restrictions were legal.

These two cases illustrate a weakness within our political system. Our political system works because it facilitates compromises at many different levels before a policy decision is actually rendered. When the issue involved is a moral issue, however, or is seen by many as a moral issue—abortion or slavery—compromise becomes difficult, if not impossible. Moral right and wrong leave no middle ground for compromise. Half-right is the same as half-sinful; something is either sinful or it is not, especially to those who know that they are morally in the right. Our political system does not handle deeply felt moral issues well.

12. *Diamond* v. *Chakrabarty,* 1980 (patent laws and new life forms)

In a decision with monumental possible consequences for the future the Supreme Court in 1980 declared that a genetically created new bacteria could be patented. Chakrabarty's new bacteria broke down crude oil components to facilitate the control of oil spills. The Supreme Court ruled that man-made forms of life can be patented because they are "not nature's handiwork."

READINGS FOR DEPTH AND HISTORICAL INTERPRETATION

Domestic, 1960s and 1970s

1. Rachel Carson, *Silent Spring,* in Robert Downs, ed., *Books That Changed America.* This book alerted the nation to the disastrous impact of pesticides and insecticides, especially DDT, on the balance of nature.

2. Gunnar Myrdal, *An American Dilemma.* A Swedish scholar, Myrdal was invited to study the status of blacks in American society. The dilemma in our society was the gap between American ideals and racial practices. This book helped the later push for desegregating the armed forces and public schools.

3. John Hope Franklin, "The Postwar Years," and "The Black Revolution," in *From Slavery to Freedom: A History of Negro Americans.* Franklin summarizes the black civil rights movement.

4. Betty Friedan, "The Problem That Has No Name," and "The Happy Housewife Heroine," in *The Feminine Mystique.* This book was the original catalyst for the women's movement.

5. Lois W. Banner, "Feminism Comes of Age: 1945–1974," *Women in Modern America: A Brief History.* Banner summarizes the women's movement.

6. Bill Moyers, "Listening to America," *Harper's,* Dec., 1970, pp. 47–109. This article catches the mood of America in this era—the antiwar demonstrations, the flag-waving patriotism, the intolerance and the widespread uneasiness over the country's future.

7. Christopher Lasch, "The Narcissist Society," *The New York Review of Books,* September 30, 1976. Lasch discusses changes in social relationships within our society.

Foreign Affairs, 1960s and 1970s

1. John W. Spanier, "The Challenges of the 1960s," in *American Foreign Policy Since World War II.* This chapter, a broad introduction to the 1960s, also includes a comparison of the Korean and Vietnam wars, Latin America, Castro, and Africa.

2. C. Vann Woodward, "The Age of Reinterpretation," *American Historical Review,* October 1960. Woodward sees events and changes in the 1945–1960 period as forcing historians to look at previous interpretations of American history. For example, the rise of missiles makes clear the extent to which our history has been shaped by the security provided by two oceans.

3. James Thomson, Jr., "How Could Vietnam Happen? An Autopsy," *Atlantic Monthly,* April 1968. Walter La Feber, "The Last War, the Next War, and the New Revisionists," *Democracy,* January 1981. These two articles put the Vietnam War into historical perspective.

SAMPLE OUTLINE

The organization of this outline comes from two books that are well worth reading: Clinton Rossiter's *The American Presidency* and Theodore Sorensen's *Decision Making in the White House.* You will also benefit from Arthur M. Schlesinger, Jr.'s *The Imperial Presidency.*

THE PRESIDENCY IN THE 20TH CENTURY

I. **Constitutional Responsibilities**

  A. Chief of state

    1. Most nations divide their leadership positions in two: a head of government (prime minister) and a head of state (queen, president). The U.S. combines both positions in the same office.

    2. Figurehead

    3. Symbolic embodiment of the U.S.

B. Chief administrator or chief executive

1. Runs the executive branch of government, executes laws, carries out laws and court directives.

2. Oversees millions working in the executive department (Ballinger-Pinchot controversy under Taft).

3. Hampered and limited by the rise of regulatory agencies—now over 1800 beyond his immediate control—Federal Reserve Board, Interstate Commerce Commission, Federal Trade Commission.

4. Agencies are often controlled by interest groups. An example is Kolko's argument on Meat Inspection Act, 1906. He argues that the Progressive movement included a successful attempt by big business to eliminate competition in the guise of reform.

5. Carter tried to streamline the bureaucracy, but encountered much inertia.

6. Kennedy complained that he spent half of his time trying to get people to do what they were supposed to be doing.

7. Beginning with the 1921 Budget and Accounting Act, many responsibilities have passed from Congress to the president.

8. Nixon: revenue sharing and New Federalism shifted more responsibilities back to the states.

9. Executive Order 8248 (FDR, 1939) created the Executive Office of the President, putting some agencies within the White House—Bureau of the Budget, National Security Council, Central Intelligence Agency, Council of Economic Advisors. (Note that older cabinet organization has become less important.)

C. Commander in chief

1. For all practical purposes the president controls the army, navy, air force, marines, and coast guard.

2. Lincoln expanded original definition to include powers over civilian matters considered to be militarily significant.

3. Second World War greatly expanded scope of CIC powers. FDR claimed the right to "take measures necessary to avert a disaster which would interfere with the winning of the war." Examples: stablized prices by controls, Japanese removal, Truman's dismissal of General MacArthur

4. Congress retains sole power to declare war, but technology and the need for speed puts many military options under the president's practical control: Teddy Roosevelt and Great White Fleet, Manhattan Project, nuclear response.

5. Attempts to restrict the president include Wilson and arming of merchantmen, Ludlow Amendment, Neutrality Acts, Bricker Amendment, two term limitation, War Powers Act, 1973.

6. He is also restricted by budget fights with Congress and the need for two-thirds Senate approval for treaties.

7. Executive orders often are used to implement CIC goals and diplomatic goals. (An executive order is based on the president's authority and theoretically is in force only to the end of that president's term. As a practical matter most executive orders are irreversible.) Examples: FDR and destroyers for bases deal, Truman and desegregation of armed forces.

8. Real change in CIC role came in August 1945. The bomb brought massive retaliation, preemptive strike, and nuclear shield under the president's power.

9. Before the Second World War we had no bases overseas outside of American territory. Now we have over 400.

10. Since 1940 a major long run change in our society is the permanent military presence during peacetime.

D. Chief diplomat or chief of foreign policy

1. The single voice of American foreign policy. As Truman said, "I am American foreign policy." He controls negotiations of treaties, such as SALT I, SALT II, Yalta Conference, and summit conferences.

2. Limited by Congressional control of funds and Senate ratification of treaties. Examples: Roosevelt and Great White Fleet, neutrality acts in 1930s, Wilson and Versailles Treaty

3. May boldly lead: Teddy Roosevelt and Panama Canal, Russo-Japanese War mediation; Truman—Marshall Plan, Point Four, NATO, Cold War, recognition of Israel, decision to intervene in Korea; Carter's peace initiative in the Middle East; Nixon's visit to China; JFK's Alliance for Progress, Peace Corps

4. May follow public opinion rather than mold it: FDR and Quarantine speech; Washington Disarmament Conference in 1920s; FDR in 1940–41; Wilson in 1914–17

5. May ignore public opinion or previous conventional policies: LBJ and Vietnam; Nixon and bombing of Cambodia; Wilson and Watchful Waiting; nonrecognition of USSR from 1917 to 1933

E. Chief legislator

1. Most major pieces of legislation now originate in the White House. The president takes the legislative initiative such as the State of the Union Address, budget message, and presenting a program. Examples: FDR and 100 Days; LBJ and Great Society; Wilson and tariff, banking, and antitrust legislation

2. President rarely gets all he wants: FDR and court packing plan.

3. President has lost historic confrontations with Congress: Truman and OPA extension, Taft-Hartley Act.

F. Chief judicial officer

1. Appoints all federal judges. Memorable examples: Wilson, Louis Brandeis; LBJ, Thurgood Marshall; Reagan, Sandra Day O'Connor

2. Limitations: FDR and court packing plan, Nixon and appointment of Southerners to Supreme Court

3. Length of judicial service means a president's influence may extend for years after his own term.

4. Part of election politics: "Impeach Earl Warren." Wallace in 1968 hoped to throw the presidential election into the House to exchange his support for the power to veto appointment of Supreme Court judges.

II. Unofficial Positions

A. Chief of party

1. Taft's fight with Teddy Roosevelt for control of Republican Party machinery in 1912.

2. FDR was the most successful broker of political coalitions.

3. Kennedy went to Dallas in November of 1963 to smooth over infighting among Texas Democrats.

4. Patronage jobs distributed

5. Involved in Congressional party politics: Taft, Uncle Joe Cannon, Old Guard versus George Norris and Progressive Republican insurgents

B. Molder of public opinion, or voice of the people

1. Commands immediate attention of the media.

2. Successes: LBJ in pushing for civil rights, Reagan's image in news conferences, FDR in fireside chats, Harding as a symbol for Normalcy

3. Failures: Wilson's push for joining the League of Nations; Nixon's attempt to quiet Watergate

4. Especially powerful in foreign affairs: FDR and Atlantic Charter; Carter and Olympic boycott; Wilson and "Make the world safe for democracy."

5. Creates commissions to publicize issues: LBJ and Kerner Commission on Civil Disorders; Truman and civil rights report, To Secure These Rights; T. Roosevelt and conservation conference, 1908

6. Sometimes forced by public opinion to act, e.g., Eisenhower in Little Rock, Ark, 1957

C. Chief of the economy, or manager of prosperity

1. Public has always blamed the president for economic hard times.
   a. Pujo Committee under Taft was established to study financial concentration on Wall Street.
   b. Politics and ideology sometimes dictate response: Hoover and Hawley-Smoot Tariff; T. Roosevelt and Northern Securities case and Anthracite Coal strike, 1902.

2. Hoover was the first to assume responsibility for intervening in the economy to reverse downturns with the RFC; FDR assumed total responsibility; JFK and steel price rollback; Truman lost to steel companies; Bush and Savings & Loan industry

3. Employment Act of 1946 created legislative foundation for giving the president responsibility for maintaining full employment; Council of Economic Advisors.

4. President, Congress, and agencies control through fiscal policy (spending and taxing policies) and monetary policy (controlling the amount of money and credit in circulation), and through general policies toward the economy. Kennedy and Reagan cut taxes to stimulate the economy; Federal Reserve Board, SEC, FDIC, JFK and Trade Expansion Act of 1962; dollar diplomacy

5. Responds to emergencies, natural and man-made, such as floods, riots, strikes, to maintain order in our society: Hoover and the Bonus Army.

D. Leader of free nations or president of the west

1. From 1815 to 1914 U.S. stayed out of European wars only because there were none.

2. Teddy Roosevelt asserted hegemony over Caribbean and Central America through the Roosevelt Corollary, Panama Canal; later, dollar diplomacy.

3. Wilson: Fourteen Points, League of Nations, World Court

4. 1920s—U.S. abdicated; 1930s—West leaderless

5. Second World War—FDR, Churchill, Stalin. By 1945 only two major countries were left.

6. Collective security: NATO, SEATO, CENTO, ANZUS, UN

7. Bipartisan foreign policy

8. Frustrating responsibility: de Gaulle, Suez Canal crisis, 1956; Eisenhower Doctrine; Vietnam; Korea; Bay of Pigs; Cuban missile crisis; Iran-Contra affair

9. Reagan, "The Cold War is over."

III. **Limits on the Power of the President**

A. Limits on permissibility

1. Must follow Constitution, international law; hampered by policies of our allies (French in Indochina; OAS and Cuban missile crisis).

2. Limited by his own judgment of action being accepted by military, Congress, public, allies, etc.

B. Limits on resources
1. Money, manpower, time to respond
2. U.S. is a superpower, but is not equally powerful everywhere. In 1968 the Pueblo, a U.S. spy ship, was captured off North Korea. We protested in the UN because within a few hours we could fly 25 jet fighters to the scene whereas North Korea could fly 625 comparable jet fighters.
3. Dropping an atomic bomb is not a viable option; our nuclear arsenal is more of a defense shield.
4. Unwillingness to commit resources: Hoover-Stimson Doctrine in Manchuria

C. Limits on time
1. Political timing of proposals may be dictated or hindered by events: Sputnik and education.
2. In early period of Cuban missile crisis almost all advisors urged an all-out attack on Cuba. Kennedy waited, and decided on a blockade to give Russians time to react.
3. Advisors frequently divided
4. Twenty-second Amendment limits time to carry out proposals, because a president is a lame duck after election to a second term.

D. Limits of previous commitments
1. Traditional party stands and constituencies
2. Treaties and laws
3. Past record in foreign policies, as abrupt changes may be unsettling
4. Existing precedents on what presidents have done in similar situations
5. Commitments made by subordinates in diplomatic situations, and promises to senators and congressmen
6. Political party platforms rank lowest of any commitments.

E. Limits on available information
1. Flow of information to presidents varies with personal style. JFK and LBJ absorbed much public media information; Nixon and Reagan preferred short summaries from their staff.
2. Usually too much information, except for foreign affairs

DOCUMENTS AND THE DOCUMENT-BASED QUESTION

Documents and the Study of History

Documents are the building blocks of history. History rests upon evidence supplied by documentary proof. In the words of an old saying among historians, "no documents, no proof, no history." The analysis and evaluation of documents is the starting place for all historians. You had better be honest, for documents will be used by future historians to reevaluate your judgments.

To master the study of history you must master the study of documents. This task is not burdensome. History comes alive when you read a diary. You begin to understand that the characters in history are human beings with human weaknesses. Andrew Jackson held his cabinet meetings on Tuesdays because he considered Tuesday to be his lucky day. The struggle of a sturdy pioneer woman leaps out from the terse diary notation: "Got up at five, cut wood, cooked breakfast, cleaned stove, nine o'clock, delivered my son." In its finest moments history erases the years separating the experiences of human beings, and we become closer observers of one another.

The observations of eyewitnesses to an event are termed primary sources. Primary sources do not have to be original. A copy of the Declaration of Independence is a primary source because it exists in the same wording as the original.

Writing based upon the study of primary documents is a secondary source. A historian investigating the evolution of municipal governments from 1650 to 1825 reads various collections of laws for the colonies and early states. On the basis of his reading of primary sources he writes an interpretation explaining how municipal government changed from being mostly interested in promoting trade to being primarily interested in providing municipal services such as police protection, sewer drainage, clean water, and fire protection. The resulting book, *The Municipal Revolution in America: Origins of Modern Urban Government, 1650–1825,* by Jon C. Teaford, is a secondary source.

Beyond the secondary source is the tertiary or third-level source. You are all too familiar with this example, the textbook. No author can read all the primary and secondary sources in American history! A historian tries to absorb as much history as possible while writing a textbook. Any textbook is by its very nature inadequate in terms of absolute correctness of all factual information and conceptual interpretation. Even if the author became aware of new historical discoveries and interpretations, years may pass before the new ideas appear in his textbook. Rewriting time, publisher's costs, printing schedules, market purchasing cycles, and dozens of other intrusions combine to create a time lag between the arrival of new ideas and information and their appearance in standard textbooks. It's easy to add a few pages for the latest presidential election; it's much harder to rewrite a section on reform in the 1830s.

The advantage of the tertiary source is that it gives you a general idea of the particular topic you are interested in. Secondary sources give specific detailed information if you can find a secondary source on your topic. Primary sources give you the opportunity to be a historian and to experience all the excitement and challenge the historian feels when analyzing and synthesizing data.

Working with documents is exciting, provided you maintain a dash of skepticism. Being critical of what you see, you must be prepared to test the credibility and authenticity of the document. Many times the simple explanation is sufficient. Be prepared, though, to look beyond the obvious.

The first test of authenticity, called external criticism, tests the date of the document. Was that particular technology of papermaking known at that time? Chemical and carbon dating tests pinpoint the period when a document was written. Be leery of the 1876 centennial time capsule that contains a photocopy of the Declaration of Independence. Other questions must be asked. Were the expressions and literary style appropriate for the period? (Would you believe an archaeological dig that unearthed a gold ring stamped 752 b.c.?) Finally, are the facts corroborated by other sources? Doubt letters dated December 15, 1821, West Virginia, because West Virginia was not a state until 1863. A letter dated November 1492 in which Columbus refers to his discovery of the continent of South America would be suspect, for he died not knowing he had discovered a continent. For years historians smiled at the fable of George Washington and the cherry tree, an inspirational story concocted by a minister long after Washington's death. Then came the discovery of European pottery depicting Washington and his cherry tree. Carbon dating put the pottery in the 1790s! Was there some truth to the story? Was the story transmitted orally long before the old minister wrote it down? We may never know for insufficient proof.

Another area of concern involves possession. How did the document come to be located where it is now? Is the known travel route believable? A collection of correspondence between Dorothea Dix and James Buchanan recently was found in a trunk in the attic of one of Dix's descendants. This sounds plausible, but your attic doesn't. Every year gullible tourists in the Middle East buy "ancient" coins from their guides. Such transactions are illegal, but the guide found it last week while plowing his field and his grandmother needs money for an operation and, well, you know the rest. Most documents and artifacts are carefully cataloged in an archival collection, and similar to prized breeding animals, documents have pedigrees.

Everyone possesses a style of writing. We all have pet expressions and particular words we use repeatedly. A knowledgeable investigator can read a newly discovered manuscript and confidently pass judgment on its author. Today computer technology is just as knowledgeable. Three supporters of the adoption of the Constitution in 1788—John Jay, Alexander Hamilton, and James Madison—wrote a series of unsigned essays to convince several states, especially New York, to ratify the Constitution. The collection of eighty-five essays is called *The Federalist Papers*. We unfortunately didn't know who wrote some of the essays. Enter the computer, which counted and analyzed the frequency of certain words in the essays. The computer designated the probable author of all of the essays, including many substantiated by other sources. Whether we know it or not, we all have style.

A second area of investigation is termed internal criticism. Was the observer in a position to know or to observe? Was the observer knowledgeable in the area of his observation? Could he be biased? Any lawyer or judge will tell you that eyewitness testimony is often the least reliable evidence. A classic psychology class experiment involves the sudden disruption of the class by a group of thugs who run in to attack the professor at a lectern. The class watches in horror as the attackers flee. All of a sudden the professor jumps up and tells everyone to write down what happened. The variety is unbelievable!

Another test asks if the document matches other statements made by the author. This aspect is tricky. Fifty campaign speeches may not reveal as much as a single private letter, and all you can do is make an imperfect judgment. In the late 19th century businessmen frequently quoted on Abraham Lincoln's birthday a widely circulated Lincoln speech praising the free enterprise system. Lincoln scholars could not locate any copy of or reference to the speech in Lincoln's public or private papers. Confronted with the possibility of fraud one distributor of the speech blurted that this was the speech Lincoln would have said if he had said something on the topic. In this case the speech's usefulness outweighed its truthfulness.

Reading a document demands critical analysis. Documents contain facts and opinions from which *you* draw an inference. Even primary sources are biased. George III's comments on the truthfulness of the Declaration of Independence were probably unprintable.

Even simple documents present problems. For instance, newspapers tell us much about the life of ordinary people, but a study of the newspapers in the 1850s in Hamilton, Canada, revealed that less than one percent of the city's population was mentioned in the local newspaper within a one year period. Obviously there is much the newspaper doesn't tell us. In another case, restored homes give us a taste of life in another period, yet many are constantly torn down in the name of progress. Why were particular houses preserved? Do they represent the typical home of the period? (I once visited a restored home in a small town in the South. The guide proudly described the home as typical, with three floors for the family and a fourth floor for the slaves. Since seventy-five percent of the white families in the South did not own slaves, this house was hardly "typical.")

Ideology plays a role in determining what is printed. Before Hitler invaded Russia in June 1941, the great enemies of the Soviet Union were the capitalist powers. After the German invasion, the United States suddenly changed from ideological enemy to potential ally. You can imagine the entry under Franklin Roosevelt in Soviet encyclopedia editions before and after June 1941. In the United States, portraits on first class stamps portray the heroes of the incumbent administration. Democrats produce Democratic heroes, Republicans, Republican heroes. Ideology is never as insidious a factor in our politics as in the Soviet Union, but it is present. Watch films and newsreels produced during wars. The other side makes propaganda films; we produce patriotic films. Such are the passions of war.

Another difficulty with documents is misinterpretation. A slaveowner listening to his slaves singing while picking cotton announced smugly that his slaves were happy. He should have listened to the words. The words of one song exhorted slaves to "follow the drinking gourd." (The Big Dipper points to the North Star, the route north for a runaway slave.) You have probably heard the sad tale of the "Master gone away," in the "Blue-tailed Fly." The master's horse threw him after the slave stuck a burr under the saddle, and the same slave sadly laments his master's unexplicible death when his favorite horse bolted. Some listen to a slave song and find content and happiness; some find a message of rebellion and resistance. The song is the same, but not the response of the listener. Be alert.

Types of Documents

Documents and physical evidence surround us. Your personal history appears in diaries, memorabilia from grade school, photographs, and a favorite stuffed animal or doll. Society's documents range from official records to printed matter to physical remains to domestic furnishings to a wide variety of miscellaneous objects.

Visit a local public archive, a depository of governmental records. The variety of official records is astonishing. You may find any of the following: church records, court records, census records, cabinet meetings, voting records, city records, state records, police records, hospital records, legislative records and journals, city council minutes, collections of laws, surveys, government publications, diplomatic messages, and maps of municipal sewer lines. Printed material includes the following: speeches, pamphlets, campaign literature, essays, newspapers, books, magazines, autobiographies, city directories, telephone directories, novels, and poems. Manuscripts include letters, diaries, contracts, wills, estate inventories, ship's bills of lading, ship's passenger lists, or warehouse inventories.

Society itself produces physical remains for the historian. Among society's physical evidence are the following: building remains, wells, inscriptions, machinery, aqueducts, roadways, architectural styles, monuments, restored homes, farm equipment, pyramids, fortifications, and sculptures. The inside of a house might include pottery, furniture, cross-stitching, vases, weapons, appliances, cooking utensils, and photographs. Your list of potential sources for information is hardly exhausted. Don't forget coins, maps, films, newsreels, videotapes, folk songs, legends, tapes, records, and stamps.

Finally, the site of a historical event itself is a living document. You learn new definitions of devotion and courage by walking the path of Pickett's charge during the battle of Gettysburg. Harpers Ferry, Virginia, a restored town, is not much different from what it was that autumn night in 1859 when John Brown tried to incite a slave uprising. Textbooks brand Brown's effort a failure, in part because so few slaves joined him. Local historians at Harpers Ferry add a different ingredient to this tale. After the Civil War many former slaves in the area said that they had been waiting in the nearby hills for a sign of success before joining Brown. If you sit on the hillside above Harpers Ferry, you can almost hear the runaway slaves whispering in the hills. You gain a new sense of both what was and what might have been.

Advanced Placement Document-Based Question

An essay question based upon documents is a special kind of essay question. A normal essay question requires you to respond to the wording in the question. A document-based question requires you to answer a question by using documentary evidence and your knowledge of the time period or the events alluded to in the question. One example of a document-based question is comparing four different pictures of the battle of Lexington, drawn by four different generations. How did the pictures change? Why did they change? Which is more accurate? Another example of a document-based question is the inquiry methodology. Students receive a number of documents which they use to synthesize a conceptual hypothesis. In the previous example the questions guide the conceptualization. In the inquiry method the students are free to ask whatever questions they wish concerning the documents, and their own questions determine the path of their analysis.

A special type of document-based question is the AP examination document-based question. Whereas early versions invited information beyond that presented in the documents, the present questions demand additional information and understanding. Using only the documents is not enough. Now a student must be able to display historical knowledge of the time period in addition to using the documents to answer the question.

The most important step in answering a document-based question is to read the question. You are answering the question, not the documents. If you are to use the documents to answer the question, you had better understand the question first.

Bring to your analysis of the documents a tentative hypothesis to answer the question. If a question asks if the Articles of Confederation provided for an effective government, you should say to yourself, in some ways it did and in some ways it did not. As you read each document, look for information to support either point of view. Don't take a simplistic point of view to answer a question. Most questions in history are more complex than they seem at first. Was colonial society becoming more democratic between 1750 and 1780? A simple "yes" or "no" is insufficient. A more sophisticated conceptual framework suggests that in some ways it was and in some ways democracy may even have regressed in some manner.

Suspend your judgment as you read the documents, and be prepared to modify it. In 1984 the document-based question was: "President Franklin D. Roosevelt is commonly thought of as a liberal and President Herbert C. Hoover as a conservative. To what extent are these characterizations valid?" The question invites you, even demands you, to challenge this simple characterization. Do it.

Document-based questions are often change-over-time questions. In a change-over-time question a sense of chronology is important and a sense of change (or not) is mandatory.

Document-based questions often suggest a means for organization of your essay. Does the question ask for factors or categories? If so, organize your paragraphs by means of these factors or categories. One document-based question asked students to respond "with reference to the moral, political, constitutional, and practical concerns that shaped Indian policy between 1789 and the mid-1830s." A good answer considers all four concerns. Another asked students: "Consider with specific reference to the following three areas of policy: railroad land grants, control of interstate commerce, and antitrust activities." Address the three areas. If you do not feel comfortable enough to write a full paragraph on one of the factors or concerns, combine two in one paragraph, but don't ignore a factor.

Pay close attention to the organization of the document-based question. Many documents have "tags." The tag tells you the source of the document. Read the tag before you read the document. Understanding an unfamiliar document is easier if you know the author is, say, Karl Marx. Look at the tag for information about the author, such as a title (Senator, Reverend); a position (Senate Whip, president of the VFW, delegate to the Articles of Confederation Congress); a particular point of view he may represent (labor, South, business, upper class, Republican Party); and a date indicating chronological development.

Certain document-based questions contain "notes" explaining what happened chronologically between two documents or groups of documents. Others contain "historical settings" that present the historical background by relating events leading to the topic of the question. Read the notes and historical setting for information. Use information in the historical setting for your essay if necessary for transition or if you have linked it to your conceptual theme. Don't merely rephrase the historical setting and the notes. Neither the notes nor the historical setting constitute the answer to the question.

Advanced Placement graders have found over the years that students have a tendency to overemphasize the first document, Document A. It is *a* document, not *the* document. Consider all the documents in answering your question. No one document in a document-based question is absolutely necessary. An excellent answer may refer to several documents implicitly.

As you read each document ask yourself what facts, ideas, or concepts are expressed in the document? Try to get at least one idea from it. If it doesn't make sense to you, skip it and go back to it later. Look for contradictions or tensions between documents, and be prepared to explain them. The 1984 document-based question asked students to react to the common characterization of Hoover as a conservative and Franklin Roosevelt as a liberal. One document contained a Roosevelt speech in which he said, "I am that kind of conservative because I am that kind of liberal." Either FDR was schizophrenic or the definitions of liberal and conservative vary from person to person and situation to situation. (It is the latter.) Whereas the students were not required to wrestle with the definition of liberal and conservative in their essays, the better papers tried to come to grips with the contradictions in the two words.

Be skeptical as you read. Be a detective. Ask yourself: Is the document reliable, is there corroboration, and is the source biased? What are the author's underlying assumptions? An abolitionist writing about John Brown differed from a Southerner's report on the raid. Could the source have been designed with posterity more in mind than contemporaries? Woodrow Wilson, assessing blame for the defeat of the Versailles Treaty, played the role of the prophet by foreseeing the Second World War. Finally, the context of references is important. Don't project modern values into the documents. The reference to tyranny in the Declaration of Independence doesn't make George III a fascist or a totalitarian dictator.

How to Analyze Documents

Many of the following examples are based upon former Advanced Placement document-based questions. The principles of how to analyze documents apply to any document.

I. Visuals

   A. Pictures and photographs

      1. Subject: What person, event, or subject is represented?
      2. Time and place: When and where is the subject taking place?
      3. Point of view: Is the artist or photographer trying to convey a particular point of view?
      4. Emotional impact: What is the general impression?
      5. Form of expression: What kind of picture—drawing, painting, etc.—is it?
      6. Any symbolism present: Justice blindfolded in a John Brown lithograph with the Virginia state flag in the background with the state motto, "Thus always to Tyrants." Painting, "The Bridge," by Joseph Stella, a mass of entangling wires and cables, some forming church-style windows (technology a new religion?)

   B. Cartoon

      1. Who are the characters in the cartoon? Are they realistic or exaggerated? What are their expressions?
      2. What symbols—flags, Uncle Sam, unemployed, etc.—are there?
      3. What is the overall idea or impression of the cartoon?
      4. Title or caption

   C. Poster

      1. Who published it, for what possible reasons? (It may reflect a biased view.)
      2. Title
      3. Intended for what audience?
      4. Purpose of the poster or the evidence

   D. Diagrams and flowcharts

      1. They are used to summarize an important idea and to illustrate the ideas's parts or components.
      2. Check the title.
      3. Examine the parts.
      4. Labels

   E. Maps

      1. Maps deal with a specific time period.
      2. A map focuses on a specific topic, event, or development in history, often a change-over-time illustration (Compromise of 1850).

    3. Places the subject in a specific location
    4. Check the title.
    5. Check the key or legend.
    6. Remember the differences between geographic maps and electoral vote maps.

F. Charts

    1. They usually illustrate a relationship between two subjects. Decide what those two subjects or ideas are (time and voting, residence and prohibitionist leadership, population and money supply) and their relationship (increases, decreases, no change, directly or indirectly related).

    2. Check title and category titles.

    3. Are the numbers percentages or absolute? Don't refigure the numbers. (It is stupid to claim that twins born to a family of four represent a 100% increase in the number of children in the family. The chart-makers used the numbers, either absolute or percent, to convey an idea, not to teach mathematics.)

    4. Be careful: Large money and population figures are often given in abbreviated form such as thousands. Thus, a 62,000 population figure may really be 62,000,000.

    5. Were the changes illustrated significant? (65% to 67% is not.)

    6. Remember that the chart illustrates a trend for only a specific period.

    7. Remember the possible influence of major events on the time period indicated (voting statistics in 1770–1790 and the Revolutionary War).

    8. Be aware of the chart with a collapsed X or Y axis (1770–1775, 1784–1792). It is intended to indicate that an insignificant period was purposefully left out of the chart.

G. Graphs

    1. Read the key.
    2. Notice the title.
    3. Look for dates.
    4. Graphs use statistical data to present historical comparisons or changes over time.
    5. Circle or pie graph: Each circle represents the total quantity, e.g., 100% of the population. Note that the portions of the circle represent a percentage.

Bar graph: read both axes. One usually represents a percentage or quantity and the other usually a time period. Note that the bars are drawn to scale to make a comparison.

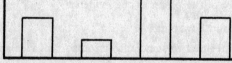

Line graph: Read both axes. Unlike a bar graph, which shows a subject at a specific time, a line graph can show trends over every part of the time period, and often shows several trends at once.

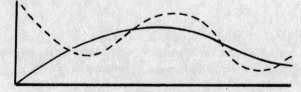

II. Printed Materials

A. Newspapers

1. Editorial or article (abolitionist sympathizer Horace Greeley on John Brown's raid). You should be aware that before the 20th century it is hard to differentiate between an article and editorial opinion.
2. Interview
3. Evidence of the newspaper's economic or political bias (urban, rural, South, *Wall Street Journal*)
4. Letter to the editor
5. Be aware that an editorial or article may either reflect mass opinion or be an attempt to influence or to create mass opinion.

B. Magazine or pamphlet

1. Same checks as under newspapers
2. What is the normal audience of the magazine (*McCall's, Field and Stream*)?

C. Book

1. Is it contemporary or not, an eyewitness to an event or second-hand comment (Frank Norris's *The Octopus*)?
2. A disinterested observer (*Uncle Tom's Cabin*; James B. Weaver, *A Call to Action*)
3. Politically partisan, based on evidence or opinion?
4. Remember that the preface is a personal statement.
5. Novels can be symbolic.
6. A review of a book is the reviewer's opinion, not the author's.
7. A recollection of an event long after it happened (Eisenhower recalling a meeting with President Truman three years earlier.)
8. Memoirs—a selective and personal view that is rarely self-critical.

D. Poem

1. Poems are meant to use language as art rather than to give information.
2. Usually illustrates a spiritual or symbolic view of a period, event, or idea.

III. Personal Documents

A. Speech

1. To what audience?
2. Rough draft (It may be more truculent.)
3. Official speech or informal (inaugural address, State of the Union Address)
4. Campaign speech (FDR versus Hoover)
5. Ask yourself, based on what you know about the speaker, is this a view you would expect him to take, such as Andrew Carnegie's opposition to the Treaty of 1898?

B. Letter

1. Official or personal
2. To a subordinate or a superior
3. What is the relationship between the two people?
4. Private or public (John Adams to his wife)
5. From an organization (VFW on immigration)
6. Is the date significant (a letter to a delegate during the Constitutional Convention, or a letter written during Shays's Rebellion)?

C. Diary

1. Personal
2. After or before the fact
3. Remember that a diary is usually not self-critical.

IV. Political Documents

A. Party platform

1. A presidential candidate may or may not agree with the platform.
2. A political platform is often a compromise document, although third party platforms are more truculent.
3. A convention declaration such as Seneca Falls, 1848, may describe present conditions, indicate a degree of stridency, or show the organization's goals and expectations, such as the Populist Party platform, 1892.

B. List of groups supporting legislation

1. What organizations are represented?
2. Any pattern to support or opposition, any common characteristics (South, urban, immigrant, slave states, Midwest, former Populist states)
3. Any surprises or unusual alliances (Carnegie and Bryan in opposition to the Treaty of 1898)

V. Public Records

A. Laws, proclamations, executive orders

1. Why was the law passed; what does it represent? Remember, laws are passed as solutions to a problem, as the representation of a group's ideal (prohibition), as a guide for future behavior (Puritan laws on church attendance), or as a response to public pressure for what is perceived as a problem (Sherman Antitrust Act).
2. Some laws are more symbolic in their passage than in their enforcement (Volstead Act, Sherman Antitrust Act)
3. Commentary on the laws similar to a textbook on laws (Blackstone's *Commentaries on the Laws of England*)
4. Federal, state, or local law?

B. Court decision

1. Does it declare a law unconstitutional, and if so, what new problems does it create (Dred Scott)?
2. Does the decision support the views of a particular section, party, or class (NRA)?
3. Was the decision enforced or obeyed (Brown, Indian removal)?
4. Narrow or broad interpretation in the decision
5. Note the division in the decisions: 5–4, 9–0, 6–3. Was it close?
6. Trial transcript—Scopes trial, Darrow versus Bryan

C. Legislative debate, Congressional Record, speech in Congress, testimony before a congressional committee

1. Was the speech for constituent consumption or for colleagues?
2. Any other evidence of influence of the speaker among his colleagues (Henry Clay would be more respected than George M. Dallas.)
3. Is the person known for other activities (Carnegie and the Treaty of 1898)?
4. What point of view or organization does a person testifying before Congress represent (a railroad vice-president testifying on long and short haul rate differentials)

D. Government agency report

1. Federal, state, or local
2. How does it reflect the general tone of government at the time (1920s versus 1930s)?
3. Be aware that agency reports are rarely critical of themselves.

4. A report may be intended to lay a basis for future expansion in scope or powers or increased funding.

E. Others

1. Diplomatic correspondence such as instructions from the secretary of state to treaty negotiators or correspondence to Congress or an official about ongoing negotiations.
2. Official letters (from the Rhode Island state assembly to Congress)
3. Treaties—provisions, how do the provisions compare with prior agreements, or cause future consequences (Yalta Agreements).

Document-Based Questions from Previous AP Examinations

Previous document-based questions have covered a wide range of topics in American history. The best way to prepare for a DBQ is to study American history. You should also remember that the DBQ is, in reality, a document-based essay question. All the rules for writing good essays apply to the DBQ.

Some DBQs require a student to use a specific act or action as a basis for generalizing about the ideas and events surrounding that action. Past DBQs have asked students to explain the reasons for the 1924 Immigration Act, and the reasons for the approval of the Treaty of Paris in 1899. Both questions require some awareness of the forces at work in Congress. Another DBQ looked at the factors involved in the Jacksonian Indian removal. The defeat of the Crittenden Compromise proposal in 1860 was the basis of another question. A recent DBQ used the dropping of the atomic bomb in 1945 as a focal point for the military and diplomatic history of the Second World War and the postwar period, 1939–1947.

A different type of DBQ asks a student to be aware of the events and characteristics of a period. Such DBQs concerned the beginning of the Civil War, agrarian discontent in the late 19th century, the era of the Articles of Confederation, the issues of the 1790s, the rise of Prohibition in the Progressive era, and cultural conflict in the Twenties.

The third type of DBQ centers around a concept in a particular period of history. One DBQ looked at democracy in the colonial era. Another used laissez-faire in the late 19th century as a focus. Still another asked for changes in the status of middle-class women over a century. In each case the student must understand the concept and the historical period. Any good American history student should have a firm understanding of the different forms of democracy, the theory and practice of laissez-faire, and the role of status and social class. Finally, one DBQ tested the student's knowledge of the political philosophies of liberalism and conservatism, using Franklin D. Roosevelt and Herbert Hoover as a focus.

THREE SAMPLE
DOCUMENT-BASED
QUESTIONS

The instructions in the AP examination booklet state that you must include additional information from the period in your essay answering the document-based question. As in any essay there are two different levels of factual and conceptual information. There are quality facts and concepts, and quantity facts and concepts. Not all of them are equal in importance. For example, a student might include the Sumner-Brooks affair in an essay on the causes of the Civil War, but forget to include slavery in the territories, the Dred Scott decision, the rise of the Republican Party, etc. Make certain you have covered the most significant concepts and provided quality facts to buttress your conceptual points.

First Sample DBQ

Suggested writing time—40 minutes

Percent of Section II score—50

Directions: The following question requires you to construct an essay that integrates your interpretation of Documents A-N and your knowledge of the period referred to in the question. In the essay you should strive to support your assertions both by citing key pieces of evidence from the documents and by drawing on your knowledge of the period.

1. "American foreign policy leading up to involvement in the Second World War was greatly influenced by the continuing debate over the 'lessons' of the 1914–1929 period." Assess the validity of this statement by considering the issues of American foreign policy in the period from 1914 to 1929 and the appropriateness of these "lessons" to the period from 1930 to 1941.

DOCUMENT A

Fifteen years ago came the Armistice and we all thought it was to be a new world. It is! But a lot worse than it was before.

Ten million men were killed and many more maimed, fifty billion dollars' worth of property destroyed, the world saddled with debts.

And for what? Would it have been any worse if Germany had won? Ask yourself honestly. No one knows.

Is this old world as safe for democracy as it was before all these lives were lost?

Source: editorial, William Allen White, Kansas editor, 1933

DOCUMENT B

American newspapers said in 1921 that the only American book 'supremely popular' in Europe was Uncle Sam's pocketbook; in 1923 that we had become a leading member of the 'League of Donations'; in 1928 that Europe counted too much on being 'Yank-ed' out of economic difficulties; in 1932 that our being expected to 'succor' Europe suggested too strongly 'sucker'; in 1933 that whenever an international conference met 'to get at the bottom of things,' one of the things is Uncle Sam's pocket.

Source: Thomas A. Bailey, *The Man in the Street, 1948*

DOCUMENT C

"SAMUEL! YOU'RE NOT GOING TO ANOTHER LODGE MEETING!"

Source: The Saturday Evening Post, January, 1938

DOCUMENT D

Mr. Con Says No:

"Outraged by Nazi barbarism and Japanese megalomania, we are already emotionally drifting, as in 1914–17, toward the same maelstrom. Since Munich, American anti-dictatorship sentiment is just as hot as anti-German sentiment in 1916. England is again casting sheep's eyes at us—witness Churchill's short-wave radio appeal to America, Eden's recent visit, recent English mutterings about maybe paying a little on the war debt. In the name of saving freedom our liberals are again deserting anti-military principles. In sum, we are already hard at what Charles A. Beard, most distinguished of American liberal historians, calls the 'demonology' of naïvely splitting the world into blacks and whites and letting our emotions warp us into betting everything on the side of the angels. They were queer angels in 1919—witness the peace treaties they drew up. Also, in 1931, when they ran out cynically on American efforts to get Japan to respect the Kellogg treaty outlawing war. Also when they permitted the rape of Ethiopia."

Source: "Pro and Con: Should We Act to Curb Aggressor Nations?" *Readers Digest,* March, 1939

DOCUMENT E

Mr. Pro Says Yes:

"Parallels with 1914–17 are miserably misleading here. Immature sympathies, Allied propaganda, interests with a financial stake in the Allied cause, had a lot to do with involving us then. Now the hard core of the matter is a natural horror at the bloody rape of China, the sadistic persecutions in Germany. There is no need for artificial propaganda against dictators. The brute facts of their behavior are an irresistible call to action."

Source: "Pro and Con: Should We Act to Curb Aggressor Nations?" *Readers Digest,* March, 1939

DOCUMENT F

Some of the factors at work 25 years ago are now present in much greater force; others are absent or are replaced by factors powerfully at work in the opposite direction. The first and the most overwhelming difference of all is, of course, the fact that we now have the experience of the past 25 years behind us. This clearly works both ways. It has given us a knowledge of modern war, a horror of and disillusion with it and a desire to have none of it, unlike anything we knew in 1914. It has also given us memories—of the blood shed at St. Mihiel and the Argonne, of the victory parade through the Arc de Triomphe, of the Hall of Mirrors at Versailles—that link our emotions, our policies and in a real sense our national interests much more closely with France and Great Britain than they were linked a quarter of a century ago. It has given us a conscious place upon the world stage of which we were at that time unaware, and a far more vivid sense of the degree in which any great war in Europe must affect the United States.

Source: Walter Millis, "1939 Is Not 1914,"
Life, November 6, 1939

DOCUMENT G

The new war is raising much the same detailed issues as did the old, but against this different background they come with a different impact and so far, at least, they have been handled differently. Once more we have acquiesced as the British have snuffed out our trade with Germany, and it seems certain that we shall be even less inclined than before to embarrass the Allied war effort by insisting upon its restoration. But the trade itself is of much less relative importance to us than was our trade with the Central Powers in 1914....

Even if a desire for the business and a wish to give further assistance to the Allies should break down the cash and carry restrictions and the Johnson act, there would still be the bitter memories of past foreign lending to discourage the rebuilding of a war-supply industry on credit. And even if a considerable industry of the sort should nevertheless develop, it might have no great effect in urging us on into war. Businessmen and bankers now know by hard experience what it means to resign the rushing profits of neutrality for the colossal taxation and rigorous controls of wartime. Few things seem to me more certain than that, if the United States does become a belligerent, it will not be for business reasons or under the impulse of an industrial and financial community which probably has more ground than any other group to dread the social and economic dislocations that full-scale participation in a great war must bring.

Source: Walter Millis, "1939 Is Not 1914,"
Life November 6, 1939

DOCUMENT H

During the first six weeks of the war—(Americans) gave the impression of struggling desperately against an inner urge to succumb to some force stronger than themselves.... This attitude was not so much one of normal abhorrence for a form of human activity which is extremely unpleasant, to say the least, as of mystic dread, as if going to war were a sin. One of the basic elements of Americanism—which is a permanent diffidence and protest against Europe as a whole—found a new expression: in spite of the desire to see Hitler defeated, and in spite also of the general conviction that the Allies had to go to war to achieve this end, the very fact that war existed in Europe reawakened the traditional tendency of the Americans to condemn Europe *en bloc* because it was at war.

Source: Raoul de Roussy de Sales, French journalist, "America Looks at the War," *The Atlantic Monthly,* February, 1940

DOCUMENT I

In other words, strenuous efforts were made to demonstrate, now that the fight was on, that not one side alone should be blamed, and to remind the Americans that the French and the English were greatly responsible, through their past errors, for having produced Hitler and therefore the war.

The attitude of the liberals was the most interesting of all. Any man who adopts a certain philosophy of life has to pay for it. The liberal bears a cross just like the fanatic, but the cross of the liberal is particularly troublesome because it means living most of the time in a maze of totally insoluble problems.

The liberals all over the world, but particularly in America, are bearing their cross of confusion with increased uneasiness these days. The flower of American intellect, they led the world crusade against Hitler and Fascism. Bravely they accepted the eventuality of war. Freedom, they said, is worth dying for. They sang the glory of the Ethiopians and of the Chinese. They wept over Austria. They mourned the treachery that lost Spain to Franco and Czechoslovakia to Hitler. When the showdown approached, last August, they began to waver. The cross of confusion weighed on their shoulders.

Source: Raoul de Roussy de Sales, French journalist, "America Looks at the War," *The Atlantic Monthly*, February, 1940

DOCUMENT J

The present war is a continuation of the old struggle among western nations for the material benefits of the world. It is a struggle by the German people to gain territory and power. It is a struggle by the English and French to prevent another European nation from becoming strong enough to demand a share in influence and empire.

The last war demonstrated the fallacy of sending American soldiers to European battlefields. The victory we helped to win brought neither order nor justice in its wake, and these interminable wars continue unabated and with modern fury. We cannot impose a peace by force upon strong nations who do not themselves desire it, and the records of both sides show little indication of such a desire, except when it is to their own material advantage. Whether one reads a history of England, Germany, or France, the wish for conquest, when opportunity arose, has always overshadowed the wish for peace.

Source: Charles A. Lindbergh, "What Substitute for War?" *The Atlantic Monthly*, February, 1940

DOCUMENT K

What meaning has the European war for us in 1940? Compare 1914–1917 with the period 1939–1940. Now, as then, most of the world is at war. Again we are neutral; again our neutrality is tilted to favor one side; again we contemplate the consequences to ourselves if that side should lose. What are some of those consequences?

... We must look ahead to the time when Britain and France may be crushed, and a large part of the world may fall under the dominance of Nazi Germany and Soviet Russia.

... We will not, we say, fight unless our vital interests are attacked. It follows, therefore, that the possible disappearance of Britain and France, along with their empires, is not a vital interest of America. Remember how Britain acted from 1931 to the end of 1939. Manchuria was no vital interest of hers. It was in distant Asia, and Japan would be reasonable. Ethiopia, Spain, Austria, Czechoslovakia, were not vital interests of Britain. The destruction by Hitler of the treaties of Locarno and Versailles, and the march into the Rhineland, were merely the whimsies of an unpredictable and dangerous man who might do unpredictable and dangerous things if he were asked—or compelled—to conform to the canons of Western civilization, one of which is a decent respect for the opinion of mankind. Such a policy—or lack of it—is, as we now know, suicidal. In a close-knit, interdependent world it is the equivalent of saying that if my neighbor is being murdered I must refrain both from helping him and from calling the police. After all, the homicide is private to the murderer and the dead man's family, and any intervention on my part means the abandonment of an 'objective attitude' whose preservation is more important than the preservation of life or the law or even, eventually, my own safety.

Source: David L. Cohn, "The Road Not Taken," *The Atlantic Monthly,* March, 1940

DOCUMENT L

If the British Empire, with all the weight of its democratic economic power and its military strength and naval force, should fall, the United States would be alone in a warlike world.... If war is not checked and thwarted in Great Britain, war will come inevitably to the United States. Because our first line of defense lies around the coast of Britain, in this crisis, we should turn to Great Britain in her hour of danger and agony with such neighborly help as public opinion in the United States may seem legally to justify.... Whoever is fighting for liberty is defending America.

Source: speech, William Allen White, Kansas editor, 1940

DOCUMENT M

Last week a Gallup poll pointed up a major shift in U.S. opinion. A 1937 poll had reported that 64% of U.S. citizens thought it had been a mistake for the U.S. to go into World War I; only 28% thought not. To the same question last week, 42% thought that U.S. entrance into World War I had not been a mistake, 39% still believed it was.

With the beginning of the Blitzkrieg, U.S. opinion on its part in World War I began to change. Many a circumstance, many a circumstantial report did much to remind U.S. citizens that the cause fought for 23 years ago was strikingly familiar to the cause being fought for in Europe today. Many have come to believe that the U.S. mistake was made, not in winning the war, but in losing the peace.

Source: Time magazine, December 23, 1940

DOCUMENT N

The President of the United States of America and the Prime Minister, Mr. Churchill, representing His Majesty's Government in the United Kingdom, being met together, deem it right to make known certain common principles in the national policies of their respective countries on which they base their hopes for a better future for the world.

First, their countries seek no aggrandizement, territorial or other.

Second, they desire to see no territorial changes that do not accord with the freely expressed wishes of the peoples concerned.

Third, they respect the right of all peoples to choose the form of government under which they will live; and they wish to see sovereign rights and self-government restored to those who have been forcibly deprived of them.

Fourth, they will endeavor, with due respect for their existing obligations, to further the enjoyment of all States, great or small, victor or vanquished, of access, on equal terms, to the trade and to the raw materials of the world which are needed for their economic prosperity.

Fifth, they desire to bring about the fullest collaboration between all nations in the economic field with the object of securing for all improved labor standards, economic adjustment and social security.

. . .

Eighth, they believe that all of the nations of the world, for realistic as well as spiritual reasons, must come to the abandonment of the use of force. Since no future peace can be maintained if land, sea or air armaments continue to be employed by nations which threaten, or may threaten aggression outside of their frontiers, they believe, pending the establishment of a wider and permanent system of general security, that the disarmament of such nations is essential. They will likewise aid and encourage all other practicable measures which will lighten for peace-loving peoples the crushing burden of armaments."

Source: The Atlantic Charter

In answering the document-based question on the "lessons" of the 1914 to 1929 period, you should, before reading a single document, make two columns. Into the first should go the issues of the early period, into the second those of the later period. After rereading the question five times note that the question concerns the "issues," not necessarily the events. Better answers organize around collective security, neutrality, disarmament, relations with Europe, etc. As you read through the documents, put issues and events in the appropriate columns in abbreviated form. After you are done, look at the columns to see what outside information you can add. The following are mentioned fleetingly or not at all: Washington Naval Disarmament Conference; Five, Four, and Nine Power Treaties; World Court; Quarantine Speech; Panay incident; Dawes and Young Plans; specifics of the 1930s neutrality acts; America First Committee; Lend-Lease; destroyers deal, etc.

DBQs are graded on a 1–15 scale. The best essay using *only* the documents usually receives a score no higher than a 7, and often is much lower. What I am telling you is simple: Bring in outside information; follow the instructions. You may use some issues and events outside the time period if you can relate them to the period. For example, "Unlike the period after the Second World War, no forum such as the United Nations existed to impose meaningful sanctions on aggressors. The League of Nations was toothless." These sentences indicate your comparative awareness of the effectiveness of the two world organizations.

Second Sample DBQ

Suggested writing time—40 minutes

Percent of Section II score—50

> **Directions:** *The following question requires you to construct an essay that integrates your interpretation of Documents A–N and your knowledge of the period referred to in the question. In the essay you should strive to support your assertions both by citing key pieces of evidence from the documents and by drawing on your knowledge of the period.*

2. "Between 1880 and 1915 labor leaders voiced sharp disagreement over the proper goals and strategies workers should follow to improve their position in American society." Assess the validity of this statement by contrasting the different goals and strategies advocated by labor leaders between 1880 and 1915. Include an assessment of their vision of the future of American society and the degree of success their approach achieved between 1880 and 1915.

DOCUMENT A

Question, a senator: I was only asking in regard to your ultimate ends.

Answer, Strasser: We have no ultimate ends. We are going on from day to day. We are fighting only for immediate objects—objects that can be realized in a few years.

Question, a senator: You want something better to eat and to wear, and better houses to live in?

Answer, Strasser: Yes; we want to dress better and to live better, and become better off and better citizens generally.

Question, a senator: I see that you are a little sensitive lest it should be thought that you are a mere theorizer. I do not look upon you in that light at all.

Answer, Strasser: Well, we say in our constitution that we are opposed to theorists, and I have to represent the organization here. We are all practical men.

> *Source:* testimony by Adolph Strasser, President of the Cigar Makers' Union and a founder of the American Federation of Labor, before a U.S. Senate Committee, 1883

DOCUMENT B

The many must act, and they must act together in a system of cooperation that will stop the grinding process.

Under the competitive system labor has no share in what it develops. It has to take what the master deals out to it; but once it receives a share in what it creates, industry will become part of him who produces, and the secret of content is found.

> *Source:* Terence V. Powderly, *Thirty Years of Labor*, 1889

DOCUMENT C

It has always been, and is at the present time, my policy to advocate conciliation and arbitration in the settlements of disputes.... Thousands of men who have become disgusted with the ruinous policy of the strike, as the only remedy for ills we complain of were drawn to us because we proclaimed to mankind that we had discarded the strike until all else had failed.... No matter what advantage we gain by the strike, it is only medicating the symptoms; it does not penetrate the system, and therefore fails in effecting a cure.... You must submit to injustice at the hands of the employer in patience for a while longer. Bide well your time. Make no display of organization or strength until you have every man and woman in your department organized, and then do not strike, but study, not only your own condition, but that of your employer. Find out how much you are justly entitled to, and the tribunal of arbitration will settle the rest.

> *Source:* Terence V. Powderly, quoted in a publication by the Missouri Bureau of Labor Statistics and Inspection, 1887

DOCUMENT D

The two movements were inherently different. Trade unions endeavored to organize for collective responsibility persons with common trade problems. They sought economic betterment in order to place in the hands of wage-earners the means to wider opportunities. The Knights of Labor was a social or fraternal organization. It was based upon a principle of cooperation and its purpose was reform. The K. of L. prided itself upon being something higher and grander than a trade union or political party."

> *Source:* Samuel Gompers, *Seventy Years of Life and Labor: An Autobiography*, 1925

DOCUMENT E

John D. Rockefeller's great fortune is built upon your ignorance. When you know enough to know what your interest is you will support the great party that is organized upon the principle of collective ownership of the means of life....

Now, we Socialists propose that society in its collective capacity shall produce, not for profit, but in abundance to satisfy human wants; that every man shall have the inalienable right to work, and receive the full equivalent of all he produces.

Source: Eugene V. Debs, *Debs: His Life, Writings and Speeches,* 1908

DOCUMENT F

It is well known that the Knights of Labor was not instituted with the view to action in the matter of regulating wages. The objects included education, the bettering of the material condition of the members by means of such schemes as co-operation, etc., and the elevation of labor by legislation through political action, but not taken, however, in a partisan way. The plan of the organization did not include the management of strikes or aught else pertaining to wages and terms of labor, and it is not surprising, therefore, that the machinery has not proven equal to those occasions, when the Knights went outside of their original objects. It would be a blessing to all concerned if the Knights of Labor shall resolve to first principles and devote undivided attention thereto.

Source: National Labor Tribune, July 7, 1883

DOCUMENT G

The working people find that improvements in the methods of production and distribution are constantly being made, and unless they occasionally strike, or have the power to enter upon a strike, the improvements will all go to the employer and all the injuries to the employees. A strike is an effort on the part of the workers to obtain some of the improvements that have occurred resultant from bygone and present genius of our intelligence, of our mental progress. We are producing wealth today at a greater ratio than ever in the history of mankind, and a strike on the part of workers is, first, against deterioration in their condition, and, second, to be participants in some of the improvements.

Source: Samuel Gompers, President of the American Federation of Labor, testimony before a House of Representatives Committee, 1899

DOCUMENT H

The "pure and simple" trade union of the past does not answer the requirements of today, and they who insist that it does are blind to the changes going on about them, and out of harmony with the progressive forces of the age....

A modern industrial plant has a hundred trades and parts of trades represented in its working force. To have these workers parcelled out to a hundred unions is to divide and not to organize them, to give them over to factions and petty leadership and leave them an easy prey to the machinations of the enemy. The dominant craft should control the plant or, rather, the union, and it should embrace the entire working force. This is the industrial plan, the modern method applied to modern conditions, and it will in time prevail.

Source: Eugene V. Debs, *Debs: His Life, Writings and Speeches,* 1908

DOCUMENT I

The advocates of the so-called industrial system of labor organizations urge that an effective strike can only be conducted when all workmen, regardless of trade, calling or occupation, are affected. That this is not borne out by the history of strikes in the whole labor movement is easily demonstrable. Though here and there such strikes have been temporarily successful, in the main they have been fraught with injury to all. The so-called industrial system of organization implies sympathetic strikes, and these time and experience have demonstrated that as a general proposition they should be discarded, while strikes of particular trades or callings have had the largest number of successes and the minimum of defeats.

Source: Convention Declaration, AFL, 1903

DOCUMENT J

The Socialist party is to the workingman politically what the trade union is to him industrially; the former is the party of his class, while the latter is the union of his trade.

The difference between them is that while the trade union is confined to the trade, the Socialist party embraces the entire working class, and while the union is limited to bettering conditions under the wage system, the party is organized to conquer the political power of the nation, wipe out the wage system and make the workers themselves the masters of the earth.

Source: Eugene V. Debs, *Debs: His Life, Writings and Speeches,* 1908

DOCUMENT K

I want to tell you, Socialists, that I have studied your philosophy; read your works upon economics, and not the meanest of them; studied your standard works, both in English and German—have not only read, but studied them. I have heard your orators and watched the work of your movement the world over. I have kept close watch upon your doctrines for thirty years; have been closely associated with many of you, and know how you think and what you propose. I know, too, what you have up your sleeve. And I want to say that I am entirely at variance with your philosophy. I declare it to you, I am not only at variance with your doctrines, but with your philosophy. Economically, you are unsound; socially, you are wrong; industrially, you are an impossibility.

Source: Samuel Gompers, speech, AFL convention, 1903

DOCUMENT L

Teacher of important and much-needed reforms, she [Knights of Labor] had been obliged to practice differently from her teachings. Advocating arbitration and conciliation as first steps in labor disputes she had been forced to take upon her shoulders the responsibilities of the aggressor first and, when hope of arbitrating and conciliation failed, to beg of the opposing side to do what we should have applied for in the first instance. Advising against strikes, we have been in the midst of them. Urging important reforms we have been forced to yield our time and attention to petty disputes until we were placed in a position where we have frequently been misunderstood by the employee as well as the employer. While not a political party we have been forced into the attitude of taking political action.

Source: Terence V. Powderly, 1893

DOCUMENT M

Resolved, that the A.F. of L. most firmly and unequivocally favors the independent use of the ballot by the trade unionists and workers, united regardless of party, that we may elect men from our own ranks to make new laws and administer them along the lines laid down in the legislative demands of the A. F. of L., and at the same time secure an impartial judiciary that will not govern us by arbitrary injunctions of the courts, nor act as pliant tools of corporate wealth. That as our efforts are centered against all forms of industrial slavery and economic wrong, we must also direct our utmost energies to remove all forms of political servitude and party slavery, to the end that the working people may act as a unit at the polls at every election.

Source: Convention Declaration, AFL, 1897

DOCUMENT N

Hillquit: Then, inform me upon this matter: In your political work of the labor movement is the American Federation of Labor guided by a general social philosophy, or is it not?

Gompers: It is guided by the history of the past, drawing its lessons from history, to know of the condition by which the working people are surrounded and confronted; to work along the lines of least resistance; to accomplish the best results in improving the condition of the working people, men and women and children, today and tomorrow and tomorrow—and tomorrow's tomorrow; and each day making it a better day than the one that had gone before. That is the guiding principle and philosophy and aim of the labor movement—in order to secure a better life for all.

Source: Debate between Samuel Gompers, President of the American Federation of Labor, and Morris Hillquit, Socialist Party official, before a Senate Committee investigating industrial relations, 1914

The labor leaders DBQ gives you four conceptual points around which to organize your essay: goals, strategies, vision of the future, and degree of success. You could also organize your essay around the different approaches advocated. The only difficulty with this organizational scheme is that you must be certain to contrast the four. The four approaches to improving the position of workers in American society were the American Federation of Labor, the Knights of Labor, the American Railway Union, and the Socialist Party. Gompers and Strasser are identified with the AFL; Hillquit and Debs (in Document E) are associated with the Socialist Party. Powderly is never clearly identified with the Knights of Labor; this association on your part is an example of the minimum level of outside information demanded by the DBQ. The toughest labor leader and program to remember is the American Railway Union, the short-lived industrial union led by Eugene Debs before he became a socialist. Understanding the differences between Debs before and after the Pullman strike, which destroyed the American Railway Union, is considered significant outside information by the grader. A good American history student is already prepared to differentiate clearly between the approaches to unionism advocated in this period. He already knows the four approaches. This DBQ will simply jog his memory. Since every student must do the DBQ, should you encounter one you don't feel quite knowledgeable about, quickly check the sources for the documents before reading a single document. The sources alone will help conceptualize your approach to reading the documents for information and ideas.

Before you begin reading the documents and after you have read the question five times, you should jot down the four concepts on a piece of scrap paper. As you read each document you should categorize the documents under the appropriate concept. Document A, for example, gives the goals of the AFL, usually summarized as "pure and simple" trade unionism, or "more." As a historian once explained, the AFL never argued over how to bake the pie, they just argued over how to slice it and how large a piece they should get. Unlike the Socialist Party, the AFL was never an anticapitalist movement.

Much of the outside information in the labor leaders DBQ should concern the degree of success. Notice that you must supply outside information about the great capitalists and the major strikes. Some of the outside information to include is as follows: the 1877 railroad strike, the Homestead strike, the Pullman strike, anarchists, the eight hour movement, the Haymarket Square riot, the National Civic Federation, Pinkertons, etc. An example of outside information beyond the time period that is permissible and adds to your essay is the following: "The AFL opposed organizing all the workers in an industry under one union. They were forced to face the issue again in the 1930s with the birth of the CIO. Debs was right after all, at least for some industries."

Third Sample DBQ

Suggested writing time—40 minutes

Percentage of Section II score—50

Directions: *The following question requires you to construct an essay that integrates your interpretation of Documents A-L and your knowledge of the period referred to in the question. In the essay you should strive to support your assertions both by citing key pieces of evidence from the documents and by drawing on your knowledge of the period.*

On July 14, 1848, the following announcement appeared in the Seneca (NY) *County Courier*, calling the first pre-Civil War woman's rights convention.

Woman's Rights Convention—A convention to discuss the social, civil and religious rights of woman will be held in the Wesleyan Chapel, Seneca Falls, New York, on Wednesday and Thursday, the 19th and 20th of July current; commencing at 10 a.m.

3. "What factors led to the woman's rights movement in this era and what goals were women seeking?"

DOCUMENT A

I now fully understood the practical difficulties most women had to contend with in the isolated household, and the impossibility of woman's best development if in contact, the chief part of her life, with servants and children. . . . Emerson says: "A healthy discontent is the first step to progress." The general discontent I felt with woman's portion as wife, mother, housekeeper, physician, and spiritual guide, the chaotic condition into which everything fell without her constant supervision, and the wearied, anxious look of the majority of women, impressed me with the strong feeling that some active measures should be taken to remedy the wrongs of society in general and of women in particular. My experiences at the World Anti-Slavery Convention, all I had read of the legal status of women, and the oppression I saw everywhere, together swept across my soul, intensified now by many personal experiences. It seemed as if all the elements had conspired to impel me to some onward step. I could not see what to do or where to begin—my only thought was a public meeting for protest and discussion.

Source: Elizabeth Cady Stanton, *Eighty Years and More,* 1898

DOCUMENT B

Thus far woman has struggled through life with bandaged eyes, accepting the dogma of her weakness and inability to take care of herself not only physically but intellectually. . . . But there is now awakened in her a consciousness that she is defrauded of her legitimate Rights and that she never can fulfill her mission until she is placed in that position to which she feels herself called by the divinity within. Hitherto she has surrendered her person and her individuality to man, but she can no longer do this and not feel that she is outraging her nature and her God . . . Woman by surrendering herself to the tutelage of man may in many cases live at her ease, but she will live the life of a slave, by asserting and claiming her natural Rights she assumes the prerogative which every free intelligence ought to assume, that she is the arbiter of her own destiny. . . . Self-reliance only can create true and exalted women. . . .

Source: Sarah M. Grimké, essay, "Sisters of Charity" 1838

DOCUMENT C

Beloved Sisters—We beg leave to call your attention to the importance of petitioning Congress, at its next session, for the abolition of slavery in the District of Columbia. It has been recommended that a single form of petition for females, should be circulated throughout the state, instead of using different forms in every town and country. . . . You will oblige us by giving to these petitions as rapid and as extensive a circulation as possible, and returning them with their signatures, to the Secretary of the Female A.S.S. for Muskingham County, as early as the 1st of October. We wish the signatures may be written in a fair legible hand, with their appropriate titles of Mrs. or Miss, that it may appear what proportion of them are adults. . . .

Source: Maria A. Sturges, Corresponding Secretary Of the Female A.S.S. for Muskingham Co., "Address to Females in the State of Ohio" 1836

DOCUMENT D

It will scarely be denied, I presume, that as a general rule, men do not desire the improvement of women. . . . I have myself heard men, who knew for themselves the value of intellectual culture, say they cared very little for a wife who could not make a pudding, and smile with contempt at the ardent thirst for knowledge exhibited by some women.

But all this is miserable wit and worse philosophy. It exhibits that passion for the gratification of a pampered appetite, which is beneath those who claim to be so far above us, and may justly be placed on a par with the policy of the slaveholder, who says that men will be better slaves, if they are not permitted to learn to read. . . .

Source: Sarah M. Grimké, essay, "Intellect of Woman" 1838

DOCUMENT E

. . . all society was built on the theory that men, not women, earned money and that men alone supported the family. . . . But I do not believe that there was any community in which the souls of some women were not beating their wings in rebellion. For my own obscure self I can say that every fiber of my being rebelled, although silently, all the hours that I sat and sewed gloves for a miserable pittance which, as it was earned, could never be mine. I wanted to work, but I wanted to choose my task and I wanted to collect my wages. That was my form of rebellion against the life into which I was born.

Source: Charolette Woodward, a 19 year old who worked at a nearby glove factory explaining why she attended the Seneca Falls Convention

DOCUMENT F

Effect of Factory Labor on Females in Boott Mill, No. 2

(effect of work on health)

where employed	number of females	average age	years employed	improved	as good	not as good
carding room	20	23	5	3	12	5
spinning room	47	28	4	14	29	4
dressing room	25	26	7	2	16	7
weaving room	111	22	3	10	62	39
	203			29	119	55

Source: Testimony by Mr. French, agent of the Boott Mills, before the Massachusetts state legislature, 1845

DOCUMENT G

"Why, yes: I calculate 'tain't of much account to have a woman if she ain't of no use. I lived up hyur two year, and had to have another man's woman do all my washin and mendin and so on, and at last I got tired o' totin my plunder back and forth, and thought I might as well get a woman of my own. There's a heap of things beside these, that she'll do better than I can, I reckon; every man ought to have a woman to do his cookin and such like, 'kase it's easier for them than it is for us. They take to it kind o' naturally."

I could scarcely believe that there was no more human vein in the animal, and determined to sound him a little deeper.

"And had you no choice made among your acquaintances? Was there no one person of whom you thought more than another?" said I.

"Yas, there was a gal I used to know that was stouter and bigger than this one. I should a got her if I could, but she'd got married and gone off over the Massissippi, somewhar."

The cold-hearted fellow! It was a perfectly business matter with him.

"Did you select this one solely on account of her size?" said I.

"Why, pretty much," he replied; "I reckon women are some like horses and oxen, the biggest can do the most work, and that's what I want one for."

Source: Eliza Farnham, from "Conversation With a Newly-Wed Westerner," in her travel book, *Life in Prairie Land*, 1846.

DOCUMENT H

I was disappointed when I came to seek a profession worthy of an immortal being—every employment was closed to me, except those of the teacher, the seamstress, and the housekeeper. In education, in marriage, in religion, in everything, disappointment is the lot of woman. It shall be the business of my life to deepen this disappointment in every woman's heart until she bows down to it no longer. I wish that women, instead of being walking show-cases, instead of begging of their fathers and brothers the latest and gayest new bonnet, would ask of them their rights . . . the same society that drives forth the young man, keeps woman at home—a dependent—working little cats on worsted, and little dogs on punctured paper; but if she goes heartily and bravely to give herself to some worthy purpose, she is out of her sphere and she loses caste. Women working in tailor-shops are paid one-third as much as men. Some one in Philadelphia has stated that women make fine shirts for twelve and a half cents apiece; that no woman can make more than nine a week, and the sum thus earned, after deducting rent, fuel, etc., leaves her just three and a half cents a day for bread.

Source: Lucy Stone, speech, National Women's Rights Convention, 1855

DOCUMENT I

. . . It is very well known that thousands nay, millions of women in this country are condemned to most menial drudgery, such as men would scorn to engage in, and that for one-fourth wages; that thousands of women toil at avocations which public opinion pretends to assign to men. They plough, harrow, reap, dig, make hay, rake, bind grain, thrash, chop wood, milk, churn, do any thing that is hard work, physical labor, and who says any thing against it? But let one presume to use her mental powers—let her aspire to turn editor, public speaker, doctor, lawyer—take up any profession or avocation which is deemed honorable and requires talent, and O! bring Cologne, get a cambric kerchief and a feather fan, unloose his corsets and take off his cravat! What a fainting fit Mr. Propriety has taken!

The efficient remedy for this class of evils is education; an equal education! . . . If you wish to maintain your proper position in society, to command the respect of your friends now, and husbands and children in future, you should read, read—think, study, try to be wise, to know your own places and keep them, your own duties and do them. You should try to understand every thing you see and hear; to act and judge for yourselves; to remember you have a soul of your own to account for;—a mind of your own to improve. When you once get these ideas fixed, and learn to act upon them, no man or set of men, no laws, customs, or combination of them can seriously oppress you. Ignorance, folly, and levity, are more or less essential to the character of a slave.

Source: Jane Swisshelm, *Letters to Country Girls*, 1853

DOCUMENT J

Teachers, Massachusetts Public Schools, 1837-1844

	1837 school year	1844 school year
Male Teachers	2370	2529
Female Teachers	3591	4581

Source: Horace Mann, Eighth Annual Report of the Secretary of the Board of Education, 1844

DOCUMENT K

Mr. Mandeville, Tax Collector: Sir—Enclosed I return my tax bill, without paying it. My reason for doing so, is, that women suffer taxation, and yet have no representation, which is not only unjust to one half the adult population, but is contrary to our theory of government. For years some women have been paying their taxes under protest, but still taxes are imposed, and representation is not granted. The only course now left us is to refuse to pay the tax. We know well what the immediate result of this refusal must be.

But we believe that when the attention of men is called to the wide difference between their theory of government and its practice, in this particular, that they cannot fail to see the mistake they now make, by imposing taxes on women, while they refuse them the right of suffrage, and that the sense of justice which is in all good men, will lead them to correct it. Then we shall cheerfully pay our taxes—not till then.

Respectfully, Lucy Stone

Source: Lucy Stone, letter, 1858

DOCUMENT L

It was my privilege to celebrate May day by officiating at a wedding in a farm-house among the hills of West Brookfield, Massachusetts. The bridegroom (Henry B. Blackwell) was a man of tried worth, a leader in the Western Anti-Slavery Movement; and the bride (Lucy Stone) was one whose fair name is known throughout the nation; one whose rare intellectual qualities are excelled by the private beauty of her heart and life.

I never perform the marriage ceremony without a renewed sense of the iniquity of our present system of laws in respect to marriage; a system by which "man and wife are one, and that one is the husband." It was with my hearty concurrence, therefore, that the following protest was read and signed, as a part of the nuptial ceremony; and I send it to you, that others may be induced to do likewise.

Rev. Thomas Wentworth Higginson

While acknowledging our mutual affection by publicly assuming the relation of husband and wife, yet in justice to ourselves and great principle, we deem it a duty to declare that this act on our part implies no sanction of, nor promise of voluntary obedience to such of the present laws of marriage, as refuse to recognize the wife as an independent, rational being, while they confer upon the husband an injurious and unnatural superiority, investing him with legal powers which no honorable man would exercise, and which no man should possess. We protest especially against the laws which give to the husband:

1. The custody of the wife's person.
2. The exclusive control and guardianship of their children.
3. The sole ownership of her personal, and use of her real estate, unless previously settled upon her, or placed in the hands of trustees, as in the case of minors, lunatics, and idiots.
4. The absolute right to the product of her industry.
5. Also against laws which give to the widower so much larger and more permanent an interest in the property of his deceased wife, than they give to the widow in that of the deceased husband.
6. Finally, against the whole system by which "the legal existence of the wife is suspended during marriage," so that in most States, she neither has a legal part in the choice of her residence, nor can she make a will, nor sue or be sued in her own name, nor inherit property.

Source: newspaper, *Worcester Spy*, 1855

Among the factors or causes you could see in this DBQ are the following: (1) the separation of work and home due to industrialization and the accompanying consequences—isolation, rise of the middle class, work outside the home; (2) frustration at the inability to develop intellectually through education; (3) economic concerns limiting or opening careers (women's sphere and teaching), factory working conditions, lack of control over one's own wages, wage discrimination; (4) the influence as example and as activity of the antislavery movement; (5) the general reform atmosphere of this era, transcendentalism and the public school movement; and, (6) concern over the contrast between the ideals and the reality of American society—second class status, suffrage, taxation, legal position, and marriage laws. A good answer to this DBQ would develop three to five factors as causes of the woman's movement and show how the movement worked to accomplish these goals.

Outside information could come from the issues and events of the antislavery movement, other reforms and reformers, transcendentalism, economic changes and their impact, the "cult of true womanhood," other women as reformers—Lucretia Mott, Dorothea Dix, Margaret Fuller, the public education movement, and political events or issues referred to in the documents, such as the Compromise of 1850 outlawing the slave trade in Washington, DC (Document C). Remember, you must bring in outside information for the DBQ. You know more than you think you do, so stop, get control of yourself, and decide what potential outside information you could use and how you could best use it. Just use it!

The woman's rights movement DBQ asks a two-part question: what factors led to the movement and what goals were women seeking? As soon as you read the question you should try to organize your answer. The immediate approach that springs to mind is one paragraph on causes and one on goals, sandwiched between an introduction and a conclusion. The difficulty with this attack is that it assumes an unchanging set of factors and goals. In many movements in history the goals either change over the course of time or the goals acquire a different priority. This is why you need at least a minimum sense of chronology when writing a history essay. Were the factors all of equal weight? Were some more important than others? Did new ingredients appear as the movement gained strength? Were the goals consistent? Did they shift over a period of time?

In selecting your organizational scheme, it would be better to recognize that goals often come out of causes. Something happens to give commitment to the accomplishment of an objective. Therefore, a preferred approach would be to use three to five factors or causes to show what goals were pursued to accomplish these objectives. Arrange your factors in either descending or ascending order of importance (I prefer the first), and include the remaining factors somewhere in your essay. This will show that you are aware of the other factors, that you considered them, and that you relegated them to a minor significance.

THREE SAMPLE
MULTIPLE-CHOICE TESTS

All of the following multiple-choice tests are designed to provide an experience similar to the actual Advanced Placement test, and follow the chronological and topical test specifications for the College Board Advanced Placement examination. The following chart gives the topical specifications for both the AP examination and for the three tests in this book, designated Test A, Test B, and Test C.

Topical Content Specifications for the Multiple-Choice Section of the AP Test

Content of Question	AP Test	Test A	Test B	Test C
Political history and government	42%	41%	40%	40%
Economic history	13%	13%	14%	13%
Social history	12%	12%	14%	14%
Diplomatic history	17%	19%	17%	19%
Intellectual and cultural history	16%	15%	15%	14%

The chronological specifications for the examination are broader than the unit divisions presented in this book. By combining this book's unit designations we approximate the examination's chronological specifications.

Chronological Content Specifications for the Multiple-Choice Section of the AP Test

Chronology	AP Test	Test A	Test B	Test C
1607–1789	15%	13%	14%	13%
1790–1916	45%	51%	50%	51%
1917–present	30%	26%	26%	27%
cross periods	10%	10%	10%	9%

The small imbalance is caused by the difference between the dating used for the examination and that used for the units in this book. The College Board Advanced Placement specifications define the colonial period as 1607 to 1789; this book defines it as 1607 to 1783. The College Board Advanced Placement's middle period is defined as 1789 to 1914; this book uses 1783 to 1920. The last College Board Advanced Placement period is 1915 to the present; this book uses 1920 to the present. The three practice examinations almost exactly parallel the Advanced Placement chronological specifications.

The topical content specifications come from an out-of-print College Board publication entitled, *The History Examinations of the College Board, 1980–1982*, which analyzed the actual content of eight different College Board examinations. The specifications given in the College Board publication, *Advanced Placement Course Description: History*, are as follows:

> "Both the multiple-choice and the free-response sections cover the period from the first colonial settlements to the present, although the majority of questions are on the 19th and 20th centuries. In the multiple-choice section approximately one-sixth of the questions deal with the period through 1789, one-half with the period 1790–1914, and one-third with the period 1915–present. Whereas the multiple-choice section may include a few questions on the period since 1970, neither the DBQ nor any of the five essay questions in Part B will deal exclusively with this period."

> *Reprinted with permission from Advanced Placement Course Description: History, © 1990 by College Entrance Examination Board, New York.*

Both the 1984 and the 1988 American History Advanced Placement examinations have been published. My personal analysis of the topical and chronological content specifications for each examination is as follows. Obviously, these two examinations parallel College Board AP guidelines.

Topical Content Specifications for the Multiple-Choice Section of the 1984 and 1988 AP Tests

Content of Question	1984 AP Test	1988 AP Test
Political history and government	42%	42%
Economic history	13%	15%
Social history	13%	12%
Diplomatic history	18%	19%
Intellectual and cultural history	14%	12%

Chronological Content Specifications for the Multiple-Choice Section of the 1984 and 1988 AP Tests

Chronology	1984 AP Test	1988 AP Test
1607-1789	14%	15%
1790-1916	48%	48%
1917-present	30%	30%
cross periods	8%	7%

Another College Board publication, the Chief Reader's report, *Grading the Advanced Placement Examination in American History*, gives the topical specifications as 33% for political institutions and behavior and public policy, and 16-17% for each of the following: social change, economic change, diplomacy and international relations, and cultural and intellectual developments. This book has chosen to follow the more exact specifications given in *The History*

Examinations of the College Board, 1980-1982. The lesson for the student planning to take the AP test is simple: Do not neglect any area of American history!

The most mysterious portion of the AP test is the multiple choice section. The one hundred multiple choice questions are seen only by the students. This section is collected by the examination proctor prior to beginning the essay and DBQ. All the multiple choice tests are shipped back to Educational Testing Service. Every AP teacher or student would love to be able to see all of the multiple choice questions given over a long period of time. As part of a research project my friend and AP colleague, Dr. Michael Henry of Parkdale High School, Riverdale, Maryland, was permitted to do exactly that. His review of 2,035 multiple choice questions given between 1960 and 1984 provides for all of us a rare look at the AP examination.[1] His findings confirmed a long-held theory among veteran AP teachers. The best preparation for the examination is a good course in American History! Sorry, gang, in some parts of life there simply are no shortcuts!

Dr. Michael Henry conducted his research to seek any shifts in emphasis among the types of questions or the categories of questions. He devised six different categories, which are as follows:

Primary document questions concerned reading passages from original sources such as diaries, letters, speeches, court cases, treaties, state and national laws, executive agreements, political party platforms and official government documents. Sources were direct quotations at the time the event occurred. They were not paraphrased or secondary accounts or interpretations. These questions featured documents as stimulus materials and were answered by reference to a written passage.

Historiographic questions concerned the history of history. They included passages from historians' works and their interpretations of history. These questions consisted of written passages and paraphrased materials that were interpretations rather than first-hand accounts of historical events or phenomena.

Symbolic representation questions concerned the interpretation of cartoons, graphs, and maps. Questions featured one of these three graphics and could not be answered independently of the specific cartoon, graph or map.

Arts and humanities questions concerned American literature, architecture, painting and sculpturing. They sometimes referred to a written passage or a picture, but they clearly related to a literary or artistic work.

Social science questions did not include stimulus materials such as reading passages, graphs, cartoons, and maps. They were answered without reference to such data. They concerned concepts, facts and skills from economics, sociology, anthropology and psychology. They related to such areas as earning a living, taxation, financial issues, industrialization, social groups and social relations.

Traditional questions did not feature stimulus materials such as reading passages, maps, cartoons or graphs and were answered without reference to such data. They concerned historically-oriented political, diplomatic, and military issues.

Since he was permitted to see the old AP tests only under ETS supervision, only Dr. Henry applied this categorization scheme to the questions. Thus, the judgment as to which category to place a specific question was his, and his alone. Another researcher applying the same

[1] Michael S. Henry, "The Advanced Placement American History Examination: How Has It Changed?" *The Social Studies*, July/August 1987, pp. 159–162.

criteria might have come up with slightly different percentages for the categories. But, in all likelihood, a single researcher consistently applying the same criteria would accurately define and identify any long range trends. This is exactly what Dr. Henry was trying to do and his research sheds great light on the most mysterious part of the American History AP examination—the multiple choice questions. The following chart summarizes the long-range trends in the multiple choice questions. Please note that the number of multiple choice questions on the AP test has changed over the period since 1960.

Distribution of Multiple-Choice Questions by Five-Year Periods, 1960-1984

Years	Total No. of Questions	Primary Documents	Historiography	Social Science	Arts and Humanities	Symbolic Representation	Traditional
1960-64	300	118 (39.2%)	2 (1.0%)	43 (14.2%)	4 (1.3%)	37 (12.3%)	96 (32.0%)
1965-69	375	130 (34.6%)	1 (0.5%)	62 (16.5%)	10 (2.6%)	55 (14.6%)	117 (31.2%)
1970-74	375	107 (28.6%)	17 (4.5%)	59 (15.8%)	14 (3.7%)	53 (14.1%)	125 (33.3%)
1975-79	485	108 (22.3%)	15 (3.1%)	121 (24.9%)	25 (5.2%)	32 (6.6%)	184 (37.9%)
1980-84	500	65 (13.0%)	8 (1.6%)	137 (27.4%)	39 (7.8%)	39 (7.8%)	212 (42.4%)

My summary of Dr. Henry's findings is as follows:

1. As you would expect in an introductory course, historiography is not that important. I have always felt that only four historiographic items must be in the college survey or secondary advanced placement course: Charles A. Beard's *An Economic Interpretation of the Constitution;* the phrase, "the Critical Period"; Frederick Jackson Turner's theories; and the two schools of historiography (but not necessarily the historians) of the interpretations of Reconstruction following the Civil War.

2. The decrease in primary document questions seems to parallel the introduction of the document-based question in 1973. Thus, the real percentage of document questions remained relatively stable over the 1960–1984 period.

3. The increased use of social science questions reflects the rise of two areas of textbook interest not present in 1960, women and minorities. And, in addition, the 1960s and 1970s saw an increase in interest within the history profession in economics, psychology, sociology, urbanization, etc.; in short, in areas influenced by social science concepts. Any good advanced placement textbook now contains sufficient social history to adequately prepare students for this type of question.

4. The increase in the proportion of arts and the humanities questions reflects the influence of American Studies and the emphasis on more interdisciplinary approaches in American history.

5. There are no "fads" or "hot" topics. This is a traditional examination. Don't try to outguess the test developers. Don't say to yourself, "Immigration is a hot political topic this year. I'll bet there will be 15-20 multiple choice questions on immigration!" You're in for a shock. Please note the increasing emphasis on traditional questions over the whole period, 1960–1984. In the earlier years there were more essay questions and fewer multiple choice. When the number of multiple choice questions expanded, the test developers tended to put more traditional questions into the test.

6. After reflecting on his review of 2035 multiple choice questions, Dr. Henry concluded that the advanced placement test always adhered "to the factual-oriented items that examined students' understanding of historical events, personalities, dates, and specific phenomenon. . . ." Study American history; that's what you will be tested on!!! There are no gimmicks. You have reached the point in your life where your academic potential or raw ability no longer matters. One doesn't take an AP examination on one's ability to figure out the correct answer. It means more to know the correct answer. That only comes from study, and lots of it.

The three complete multiple-choice tests in this book fall well within the guidelines concerning the number of negative questions; that is, questions that use *except, incorrect, but, least,* or *not.* No more than twenty-five percent of the Advanced Placement examination multiple-choice questions are negative questions. Approximately twenty-two percent of the multiple-choice questions in this book are negative questions. When you encounter a negative question it may help if you reword the question in your mind. If it asks "Which of the following is *not,*" say to yourself, "four of these are." Then identify the four that are true. This turns the question into the more frequently encountered positive wording.

The following breakdown of the three practice tests is provided to permit you to do the multiple choice questions chronologically. As you study American history in your course you can use the unit questions for review. At the end of the year, in preparation for the Advanced Placement examination, you may take these multiple-choice tests by units or all at once to duplicate the coming experience. For example, you may want to do all the colonial questions together. Or you may feel that you especially need review in one particular period.

Unit One, 1607–1763

Test A: 1, 8, 12, 42, 51, 55, 60, 77, 91
Test B: 2, 19, 27, 57, 59, 62, 74, 83
Test C: 1, 18, 33, 37, 48, 56, 94

Unit Two, 1763–1783

Test A: 31, 48, 58, 76
Test B: 17, 41, 55, 71, 77, 91
Text C: 30, 51, 66, 71, 74, 83

Unit Three, 1783–1800

Test A: 10, 17, 19, 21, 37, 54, 64, 72, 81, 84, 88
Test B: 6, 9, 20, 35, 44, 54, 67, 94
Test C: 8, 14, 21, 28, 34, 52, 61, 82, 85, 93

Unit Four, 1800–1840

Test A: 5, 13, 18, 23, 52, 56, 93, 95
Test B: 1, 5, 18, 30, 31, 53, 56, 78, 88, 90
Test C: 4, 15, 25, 36, 39, 41, 53, 65, 81, 89, 91, 95

Unit Five, 1840–1877

Test A: 3, 9, 11, 33, 40, 47, 61, 82, 87, 97
Test B: 4, 16, 33, 34, 46, 61, 63, 69, 79, 86, 97
Test C: 3, 6, 12, 20, 22, 49, 88, 90

Unit Six, 1865–1900

Test A: 14, 22, 26, 32, 49, 65, 67, 73, 79, 83, 90
Test B: 8, 10, 21, 32, 45, 47, 49, 66, 70, 75, 89, 99
Test C: 13, 16, 17, 24, 27, 38, 40, 42, 54, 59, 64, 68, 92

Unit Seven, 1900–1920

Test A: 6, 25, 30, 39, 44, 50, 63, 68, 69, 85, 94
Test B: 11, 15, 29, 48, 64, 73, 87, 93, 95
Test C: 7, 23, 29, 32, 55, 58, 62, 80

Unit Eight, 1920–1940

Test A: 4, 15, 28, 41, 45, 74, 78, 92, 96, 100
Test B: 7, 14, 26, 36, 38, 40, 51, 68, 80, 84
Test C: 2, 9, 11, 19, 43, 45, 70, 72, 75, 78, 98, 99

Unit Nine, 1940–1960

Test A: 20, 24, 27, 35, 43, 57, 59, 62, 75, 80, 99
Test B: 3, 12, 24, 37, 42, 76, 85, 100
Test C: 47, 50, 60, 76, 87, 97, 100

Unit Ten, 1960–1980s

Test A: 2, 36, 53, 70, 86
Test B: 13, 23, 28, 43, 50, 81, 92, 96
Test C: 5, 31, 44, 69, 77, 84, 86, 96

Cross Periods

Test A: 7, 16, 29, 34, 38, 46, 66, 71, 89, 98
Test B: 22, 25, 39, 52, 58, 60, 65, 72, 82, 98
Test C: 10, 26, 35, 46, 57, 63, 67, 73, 79

The three hundred multiple-choice questions in this book were designed to supplement three College Board publications that your teacher can order. The College Board "Acorn" book entitled "Advanced Placement Course Description, History" has thirty-five sample multiple-choice questions. Your Advanced Placement teacher can also obtain a copy of the entire 1984 and 1988 Advanced Placement American history examinations, which contain the one hundred multiple-choice questions given on the 1984 and 1988 AP examinations. The course description book and the 1984 and 1988 American History Examinations are available from Advanced Placement Program, CN6670, Princeton, New Jersey, 08541-6670. There is a charge for all three publications. None of the subject matter in the 1984 or 1988 multiple choice section of the AP examination is duplicated in this book. By combining all four resources you can see 535 sample AP type multiple-choice questions before you take the AP examination in May. It can only help!

Explanations of all answers appear at the end of each Sample Test.

SAMPLE TEST A
Answer Sheet

1 Ⓐ Ⓑ Ⓒ Ⓓ Ⓔ   21 Ⓐ Ⓑ Ⓒ Ⓓ Ⓔ   41 Ⓐ Ⓑ Ⓒ Ⓓ Ⓔ   61 Ⓐ Ⓑ Ⓒ Ⓓ Ⓔ   81 Ⓐ Ⓑ Ⓒ Ⓓ Ⓔ

2 Ⓐ Ⓑ Ⓒ Ⓓ Ⓔ   22 Ⓐ Ⓑ Ⓒ Ⓓ Ⓔ   42 Ⓐ Ⓑ Ⓒ Ⓓ Ⓔ   62 Ⓐ Ⓑ Ⓒ Ⓓ Ⓔ   82 Ⓐ Ⓑ Ⓒ Ⓓ Ⓔ

3 Ⓐ Ⓑ Ⓒ Ⓓ Ⓔ   23 Ⓐ Ⓑ Ⓒ Ⓓ Ⓔ   43 Ⓐ Ⓑ Ⓒ Ⓓ Ⓔ   63 Ⓐ Ⓑ Ⓒ Ⓓ Ⓔ   83 Ⓐ Ⓑ Ⓒ Ⓓ Ⓔ

4 Ⓐ Ⓑ Ⓒ Ⓓ Ⓔ   24 Ⓐ Ⓑ Ⓒ Ⓓ Ⓔ   44 Ⓐ Ⓑ Ⓒ Ⓓ Ⓔ   64 Ⓐ Ⓑ Ⓒ Ⓓ Ⓔ   84 Ⓐ Ⓑ Ⓒ Ⓓ Ⓔ

5 Ⓐ Ⓑ Ⓒ Ⓓ Ⓔ   25 Ⓐ Ⓑ Ⓒ Ⓓ Ⓔ   45 Ⓐ Ⓑ Ⓒ Ⓓ Ⓔ   65 Ⓐ Ⓑ Ⓒ Ⓓ Ⓔ   85 Ⓐ Ⓑ Ⓒ Ⓓ Ⓔ

6 Ⓐ Ⓑ Ⓒ Ⓓ Ⓔ   26 Ⓐ Ⓑ Ⓒ Ⓓ Ⓔ   46 Ⓐ Ⓑ Ⓒ Ⓓ Ⓔ   66 Ⓐ Ⓑ Ⓒ Ⓓ Ⓔ   86 Ⓐ Ⓑ Ⓒ Ⓓ Ⓔ

7 Ⓐ Ⓑ Ⓒ Ⓓ Ⓔ   27 Ⓐ Ⓑ Ⓒ Ⓓ Ⓔ   47 Ⓐ Ⓑ Ⓒ Ⓓ Ⓔ   67 Ⓐ Ⓑ Ⓒ Ⓓ Ⓔ   87 Ⓐ Ⓑ Ⓒ Ⓓ Ⓔ

8 Ⓐ Ⓑ Ⓒ Ⓓ Ⓔ   28 Ⓐ Ⓑ Ⓒ Ⓓ Ⓔ   48 Ⓐ Ⓑ Ⓒ Ⓓ Ⓔ   68 Ⓐ Ⓑ Ⓒ Ⓓ Ⓔ   88 Ⓐ Ⓑ Ⓒ Ⓓ Ⓔ

9 Ⓐ Ⓑ Ⓒ Ⓓ Ⓔ   29 Ⓐ Ⓑ Ⓒ Ⓓ Ⓔ   49 Ⓐ Ⓑ Ⓒ Ⓓ Ⓔ   69 Ⓐ Ⓑ Ⓒ Ⓓ Ⓔ   89 Ⓐ Ⓑ Ⓒ Ⓓ Ⓔ

10 Ⓐ Ⓑ Ⓒ Ⓓ Ⓔ   30 Ⓐ Ⓑ Ⓒ Ⓓ Ⓔ   50 Ⓐ Ⓑ Ⓒ Ⓓ Ⓔ   70 Ⓐ Ⓑ Ⓒ Ⓓ Ⓔ   90 Ⓐ Ⓑ Ⓒ Ⓓ Ⓔ

11 Ⓐ Ⓑ Ⓒ Ⓓ Ⓔ   31 Ⓐ Ⓑ Ⓒ Ⓓ Ⓔ   51 Ⓐ Ⓑ Ⓒ Ⓓ Ⓔ   71 Ⓐ Ⓑ Ⓒ Ⓓ Ⓔ   91 Ⓐ Ⓑ Ⓒ Ⓓ Ⓔ

12 Ⓐ Ⓑ Ⓒ Ⓓ Ⓔ   32 Ⓐ Ⓑ Ⓒ Ⓓ Ⓔ   52 Ⓐ Ⓑ Ⓒ Ⓓ Ⓔ   72 Ⓐ Ⓑ Ⓒ Ⓓ Ⓔ   92 Ⓐ Ⓑ Ⓒ Ⓓ Ⓔ

13 Ⓐ Ⓑ Ⓒ Ⓓ Ⓔ   33 Ⓐ Ⓑ Ⓒ Ⓓ Ⓔ   53 Ⓐ Ⓑ Ⓒ Ⓓ Ⓔ   73 Ⓐ Ⓑ Ⓒ Ⓓ Ⓔ   93 Ⓐ Ⓑ Ⓒ Ⓓ Ⓔ

14 Ⓐ Ⓑ Ⓒ Ⓓ Ⓔ   34 Ⓐ Ⓑ Ⓒ Ⓓ Ⓔ   54 Ⓐ Ⓑ Ⓒ Ⓓ Ⓔ   74 Ⓐ Ⓑ Ⓒ Ⓓ Ⓔ   94 Ⓐ Ⓑ Ⓒ Ⓓ Ⓔ

15 Ⓐ Ⓑ Ⓒ Ⓓ Ⓔ   35 Ⓐ Ⓑ Ⓒ Ⓓ Ⓔ   55 Ⓐ Ⓑ Ⓒ Ⓓ Ⓔ   75 Ⓐ Ⓑ Ⓒ Ⓓ Ⓔ   95 Ⓐ Ⓑ Ⓒ Ⓓ Ⓔ

16 Ⓐ Ⓑ Ⓒ Ⓓ Ⓔ   36 Ⓐ Ⓑ Ⓒ Ⓓ Ⓔ   56 Ⓐ Ⓑ Ⓒ Ⓓ Ⓔ   76 Ⓐ Ⓑ Ⓒ Ⓓ Ⓔ   96 Ⓐ Ⓑ Ⓒ Ⓓ Ⓔ

17 Ⓐ Ⓑ Ⓒ Ⓓ Ⓔ   37 Ⓐ Ⓑ Ⓒ Ⓓ Ⓔ   57 Ⓐ Ⓑ Ⓒ Ⓓ Ⓔ   77 Ⓐ Ⓑ Ⓒ Ⓓ Ⓔ   97 Ⓐ Ⓑ Ⓒ Ⓓ Ⓔ

18 Ⓐ Ⓑ Ⓒ Ⓓ Ⓔ   38 Ⓐ Ⓑ Ⓒ Ⓓ Ⓔ   58 Ⓐ Ⓑ Ⓒ Ⓓ Ⓔ   78 Ⓐ Ⓑ Ⓒ Ⓓ Ⓔ   98 Ⓐ Ⓑ Ⓒ Ⓓ Ⓔ

19 Ⓐ Ⓑ Ⓒ Ⓓ Ⓔ   39 Ⓐ Ⓑ Ⓒ Ⓓ Ⓔ   59 Ⓐ Ⓑ Ⓒ Ⓓ Ⓔ   79 Ⓐ Ⓑ Ⓒ Ⓓ Ⓔ   99 Ⓐ Ⓑ Ⓒ Ⓓ Ⓔ

20 Ⓐ Ⓑ Ⓒ Ⓓ Ⓔ   40 Ⓐ Ⓑ Ⓒ Ⓓ Ⓔ   60 Ⓐ Ⓑ Ⓒ Ⓓ Ⓔ   80 Ⓐ Ⓑ Ⓒ Ⓓ Ⓔ   100 Ⓐ Ⓑ Ⓒ Ⓓ Ⓔ

SAMPLE TEST B
Answer Sheet

1 Ⓐ Ⓑ Ⓒ Ⓓ Ⓔ   21 Ⓐ Ⓑ Ⓒ Ⓓ Ⓔ   41 Ⓐ Ⓑ Ⓒ Ⓓ Ⓔ   61 Ⓐ Ⓑ Ⓒ Ⓓ Ⓔ   81 Ⓐ Ⓑ Ⓒ Ⓓ Ⓔ

2 Ⓐ Ⓑ Ⓒ Ⓓ Ⓔ   22 Ⓐ Ⓑ Ⓒ Ⓓ Ⓔ   42 Ⓐ Ⓑ Ⓒ Ⓓ Ⓔ   62 Ⓐ Ⓑ Ⓒ Ⓓ Ⓔ   82 Ⓐ Ⓑ Ⓒ Ⓓ Ⓔ

3 Ⓐ Ⓑ Ⓒ Ⓓ Ⓔ   23 Ⓐ Ⓑ Ⓒ Ⓓ Ⓔ   43 Ⓐ Ⓑ Ⓒ Ⓓ Ⓔ   63 Ⓐ Ⓑ Ⓒ Ⓓ Ⓔ   83 Ⓐ Ⓑ Ⓒ Ⓓ Ⓔ

4 Ⓐ Ⓑ Ⓒ Ⓓ Ⓔ   24 Ⓐ Ⓑ Ⓒ Ⓓ Ⓔ   44 Ⓐ Ⓑ Ⓒ Ⓓ Ⓔ   64 Ⓐ Ⓑ Ⓒ Ⓓ Ⓔ   84 Ⓐ Ⓑ Ⓒ Ⓓ Ⓔ

5 Ⓐ Ⓑ Ⓒ Ⓓ Ⓔ   25 Ⓐ Ⓑ Ⓒ Ⓓ Ⓔ   45 Ⓐ Ⓑ Ⓒ Ⓓ Ⓔ   65 Ⓐ Ⓑ Ⓒ Ⓓ Ⓔ   85 Ⓐ Ⓑ Ⓒ Ⓓ Ⓔ

6 Ⓐ Ⓑ Ⓒ Ⓓ Ⓔ   26 Ⓐ Ⓑ Ⓒ Ⓓ Ⓔ   46 Ⓐ Ⓑ Ⓒ Ⓓ Ⓔ   66 Ⓐ Ⓑ Ⓒ Ⓓ Ⓔ   86 Ⓐ Ⓑ Ⓒ Ⓓ Ⓔ

7 Ⓐ Ⓑ Ⓒ Ⓓ Ⓔ   27 Ⓐ Ⓑ Ⓒ Ⓓ Ⓔ   47 Ⓐ Ⓑ Ⓒ Ⓓ Ⓔ   67 Ⓐ Ⓑ Ⓒ Ⓓ Ⓔ   87 Ⓐ Ⓑ Ⓒ Ⓓ Ⓔ

8 Ⓐ Ⓑ Ⓒ Ⓓ Ⓔ   28 Ⓐ Ⓑ Ⓒ Ⓓ Ⓔ   48 Ⓐ Ⓑ Ⓒ Ⓓ Ⓔ   68 Ⓐ Ⓑ Ⓒ Ⓓ Ⓔ   88 Ⓐ Ⓑ Ⓒ Ⓓ Ⓔ

9 Ⓐ Ⓑ Ⓒ Ⓓ Ⓔ   29 Ⓐ Ⓑ Ⓒ Ⓓ Ⓔ   49 Ⓐ Ⓑ Ⓒ Ⓓ Ⓔ   69 Ⓐ Ⓑ Ⓒ Ⓓ Ⓔ   89 Ⓐ Ⓑ Ⓒ Ⓓ Ⓔ

10 Ⓐ Ⓑ Ⓒ Ⓓ Ⓔ   30 Ⓐ Ⓑ Ⓒ Ⓓ Ⓔ   50 Ⓐ Ⓑ Ⓒ Ⓓ Ⓔ   70 Ⓐ Ⓑ Ⓒ Ⓓ Ⓔ   90 Ⓐ Ⓑ Ⓒ Ⓓ Ⓔ

11 Ⓐ Ⓑ Ⓒ Ⓓ Ⓔ   31 Ⓐ Ⓑ Ⓒ Ⓓ Ⓔ   51 Ⓐ Ⓑ Ⓒ Ⓓ Ⓔ   71 Ⓐ Ⓑ Ⓒ Ⓓ Ⓔ   91 Ⓐ Ⓑ Ⓒ Ⓓ Ⓔ

12 Ⓐ Ⓑ Ⓒ Ⓓ Ⓔ   32 Ⓐ Ⓑ Ⓒ Ⓓ Ⓔ   52 Ⓐ Ⓑ Ⓒ Ⓓ Ⓔ   72 Ⓐ Ⓑ Ⓒ Ⓓ Ⓔ   92 Ⓐ Ⓑ Ⓒ Ⓓ Ⓔ

13 Ⓐ Ⓑ Ⓒ Ⓓ Ⓔ   33 Ⓐ Ⓑ Ⓒ Ⓓ Ⓔ   53 Ⓐ Ⓑ Ⓒ Ⓓ Ⓔ   73 Ⓐ Ⓑ Ⓒ Ⓓ Ⓔ   93 Ⓐ Ⓑ Ⓒ Ⓓ Ⓔ

14 Ⓐ Ⓑ Ⓒ Ⓓ Ⓔ   34 Ⓐ Ⓑ Ⓒ Ⓓ Ⓔ   54 Ⓐ Ⓑ Ⓒ Ⓓ Ⓔ   74 Ⓐ Ⓑ Ⓒ Ⓓ Ⓔ   94 Ⓐ Ⓑ Ⓒ Ⓓ Ⓔ

15 Ⓐ Ⓑ Ⓒ Ⓓ Ⓔ   35 Ⓐ Ⓑ Ⓒ Ⓓ Ⓔ   55 Ⓐ Ⓑ Ⓒ Ⓓ Ⓔ   75 Ⓐ Ⓑ Ⓒ Ⓓ Ⓔ   95 Ⓐ Ⓑ Ⓒ Ⓓ Ⓔ

16 Ⓐ Ⓑ Ⓒ Ⓓ Ⓔ   36 Ⓐ Ⓑ Ⓒ Ⓓ Ⓔ   56 Ⓐ Ⓑ Ⓒ Ⓓ Ⓔ   76 Ⓐ Ⓑ Ⓒ Ⓓ Ⓔ   96 Ⓐ Ⓑ Ⓒ Ⓓ Ⓔ

17 Ⓐ Ⓑ Ⓒ Ⓓ Ⓔ   37 Ⓐ Ⓑ Ⓒ Ⓓ Ⓔ   57 Ⓐ Ⓑ Ⓒ Ⓓ Ⓔ   77 Ⓐ Ⓑ Ⓒ Ⓓ Ⓔ   97 Ⓐ Ⓑ Ⓒ Ⓓ Ⓔ

18 Ⓐ Ⓑ Ⓒ Ⓓ Ⓔ   38 Ⓐ Ⓑ Ⓒ Ⓓ Ⓔ   58 Ⓐ Ⓑ Ⓒ Ⓓ Ⓔ   78 Ⓐ Ⓑ Ⓒ Ⓓ Ⓔ   98 Ⓐ Ⓑ Ⓒ Ⓓ Ⓔ

19 Ⓐ Ⓑ Ⓒ Ⓓ Ⓔ   39 Ⓐ Ⓑ Ⓒ Ⓓ Ⓔ   59 Ⓐ Ⓑ Ⓒ Ⓓ Ⓔ   79 Ⓐ Ⓑ Ⓒ Ⓓ Ⓔ   99 Ⓐ Ⓑ Ⓒ Ⓓ Ⓔ

20 Ⓐ Ⓑ Ⓒ Ⓓ Ⓔ   40 Ⓐ Ⓑ Ⓒ Ⓓ Ⓔ   60 Ⓐ Ⓑ Ⓒ Ⓓ Ⓔ   80 Ⓐ Ⓑ Ⓒ Ⓓ Ⓔ   100 Ⓐ Ⓑ Ⓒ Ⓓ Ⓔ

SAMPLE TEST C
Answer Sheet

1 Ⓐ Ⓑ Ⓒ Ⓓ Ⓔ   21 Ⓐ Ⓑ Ⓒ Ⓓ Ⓔ   41 Ⓐ Ⓑ Ⓒ Ⓓ Ⓔ   61 Ⓐ Ⓑ Ⓒ Ⓓ Ⓔ   81 Ⓐ Ⓑ Ⓒ Ⓓ Ⓔ

2 Ⓐ Ⓑ Ⓒ Ⓓ Ⓔ   22 Ⓐ Ⓑ Ⓒ Ⓓ Ⓔ   42 Ⓐ Ⓑ Ⓒ Ⓓ Ⓔ   62 Ⓐ Ⓑ Ⓒ Ⓓ Ⓔ   82 Ⓐ Ⓑ Ⓒ Ⓓ Ⓔ

3 Ⓐ Ⓑ Ⓒ Ⓓ Ⓔ   23 Ⓐ Ⓑ Ⓒ Ⓓ Ⓔ   43 Ⓐ Ⓑ Ⓒ Ⓓ Ⓔ   63 Ⓐ Ⓑ Ⓒ Ⓓ Ⓔ   83 Ⓐ Ⓑ Ⓒ Ⓓ Ⓔ

4 Ⓐ Ⓑ Ⓒ Ⓓ Ⓔ   24 Ⓐ Ⓑ Ⓒ Ⓓ Ⓔ   44 Ⓐ Ⓑ Ⓒ Ⓓ Ⓔ   64 Ⓐ Ⓑ Ⓒ Ⓓ Ⓔ   84 Ⓐ Ⓑ Ⓒ Ⓓ Ⓔ

5 Ⓐ Ⓑ Ⓒ Ⓓ Ⓔ   25 Ⓐ Ⓑ Ⓒ Ⓓ Ⓔ   45 Ⓐ Ⓑ Ⓒ Ⓓ Ⓔ   65 Ⓐ Ⓑ Ⓒ Ⓓ Ⓔ   85 Ⓐ Ⓑ Ⓒ Ⓓ Ⓔ

6 Ⓐ Ⓑ Ⓒ Ⓓ Ⓔ   26 Ⓐ Ⓑ Ⓒ Ⓓ Ⓔ   46 Ⓐ Ⓑ Ⓒ Ⓓ Ⓔ   66 Ⓐ Ⓑ Ⓒ Ⓓ Ⓔ   86 Ⓐ Ⓑ Ⓒ Ⓓ Ⓔ

7 Ⓐ Ⓑ Ⓒ Ⓓ Ⓔ   27 Ⓐ Ⓑ Ⓒ Ⓓ Ⓔ   47 Ⓐ Ⓑ Ⓒ Ⓓ Ⓔ   67 Ⓐ Ⓑ Ⓒ Ⓓ Ⓔ   87 Ⓐ Ⓑ Ⓒ Ⓓ Ⓔ

8 Ⓐ Ⓑ Ⓒ Ⓓ Ⓔ   28 Ⓐ Ⓑ Ⓒ Ⓓ Ⓔ   48 Ⓐ Ⓑ Ⓒ Ⓓ Ⓔ   68 Ⓐ Ⓑ Ⓒ Ⓓ Ⓔ   88 Ⓐ Ⓑ Ⓒ Ⓓ Ⓔ

9 Ⓐ Ⓑ Ⓒ Ⓓ Ⓔ   29 Ⓐ Ⓑ Ⓒ Ⓓ Ⓔ   49 Ⓐ Ⓑ Ⓒ Ⓓ Ⓔ   69 Ⓐ Ⓑ Ⓒ Ⓓ Ⓔ   89 Ⓐ Ⓑ Ⓒ Ⓓ Ⓔ

10 Ⓐ Ⓑ Ⓒ Ⓓ Ⓔ   30 Ⓐ Ⓑ Ⓒ Ⓓ Ⓔ   50 Ⓐ Ⓑ Ⓒ Ⓓ Ⓔ   70 Ⓐ Ⓑ Ⓒ Ⓓ Ⓔ   90 Ⓐ Ⓑ Ⓒ Ⓓ Ⓔ

11 Ⓐ Ⓑ Ⓒ Ⓓ Ⓔ   31 Ⓐ Ⓑ Ⓒ Ⓓ Ⓔ   51 Ⓐ Ⓑ Ⓒ Ⓓ Ⓔ   71 Ⓐ Ⓑ Ⓒ Ⓓ Ⓔ   91 Ⓐ Ⓑ Ⓒ Ⓓ Ⓔ

12 Ⓐ Ⓑ Ⓒ Ⓓ Ⓔ   32 Ⓐ Ⓑ Ⓒ Ⓓ Ⓔ   52 Ⓐ Ⓑ Ⓒ Ⓓ Ⓔ   72 Ⓐ Ⓑ Ⓒ Ⓓ Ⓔ   92 Ⓐ Ⓑ Ⓒ Ⓓ Ⓔ

13 Ⓐ Ⓑ Ⓒ Ⓓ Ⓔ   33 Ⓐ Ⓑ Ⓒ Ⓓ Ⓔ   53 Ⓐ Ⓑ Ⓒ Ⓓ Ⓔ   73 Ⓐ Ⓑ Ⓒ Ⓓ Ⓔ   93 Ⓐ Ⓑ Ⓒ Ⓓ Ⓔ

14 Ⓐ Ⓑ Ⓒ Ⓓ Ⓔ   34 Ⓐ Ⓑ Ⓒ Ⓓ Ⓔ   54 Ⓐ Ⓑ Ⓒ Ⓓ Ⓔ   74 Ⓐ Ⓑ Ⓒ Ⓓ Ⓔ   94 Ⓐ Ⓑ Ⓒ Ⓓ Ⓔ

15 Ⓐ Ⓑ Ⓒ Ⓓ Ⓔ   35 Ⓐ Ⓑ Ⓒ Ⓓ Ⓔ   55 Ⓐ Ⓑ Ⓒ Ⓓ Ⓔ   75 Ⓐ Ⓑ Ⓒ Ⓓ Ⓔ   95 Ⓐ Ⓑ Ⓒ Ⓓ Ⓔ

16 Ⓐ Ⓑ Ⓒ Ⓓ Ⓔ   36 Ⓐ Ⓑ Ⓒ Ⓓ Ⓔ   56 Ⓐ Ⓑ Ⓒ Ⓓ Ⓔ   76 Ⓐ Ⓑ Ⓒ Ⓓ Ⓔ   96 Ⓐ Ⓑ Ⓒ Ⓓ Ⓔ

17 Ⓐ Ⓑ Ⓒ Ⓓ Ⓔ   37 Ⓐ Ⓑ Ⓒ Ⓓ Ⓔ   57 Ⓐ Ⓑ Ⓒ Ⓓ Ⓔ   77 Ⓐ Ⓑ Ⓒ Ⓓ Ⓔ   97 Ⓐ Ⓑ Ⓒ Ⓓ Ⓔ

18 Ⓐ Ⓑ Ⓒ Ⓓ Ⓔ   38 Ⓐ Ⓑ Ⓒ Ⓓ Ⓔ   58 Ⓐ Ⓑ Ⓒ Ⓓ Ⓔ   78 Ⓐ Ⓑ Ⓒ Ⓓ Ⓔ   98 Ⓐ Ⓑ Ⓒ Ⓓ Ⓔ

19 Ⓐ Ⓑ Ⓒ Ⓓ Ⓔ   39 Ⓐ Ⓑ Ⓒ Ⓓ Ⓔ   59 Ⓐ Ⓑ Ⓒ Ⓓ Ⓔ   79 Ⓐ Ⓑ Ⓒ Ⓓ Ⓔ   99 Ⓐ Ⓑ Ⓒ Ⓓ Ⓔ

20 Ⓐ Ⓑ Ⓒ Ⓓ Ⓔ   40 Ⓐ Ⓑ Ⓒ Ⓓ Ⓔ   60 Ⓐ Ⓑ Ⓒ Ⓓ Ⓔ   80 Ⓐ Ⓑ Ⓒ Ⓓ Ⓔ   100 Ⓐ Ⓑ Ⓒ Ⓓ Ⓔ

Sample Test A

AMERICAN HISTORY

SECTION I

Time—1 hour and 15 minutes

100 questions

Directions: *Each of the questions or incomplete statements below is followed by five suggested answers or completions. Select the one that is best in each case and then blacken the corresponding space on the answer sheet.*

1. Which of the following colonial powers exercised the least amount of control over the commercial and political practices in their colonies?

   (A) Portugal
   (B) The Netherlands
   (C) Great Britain
   (D) France
   (E) Spain

2. Four of the following were important sources behind the rise of the women's liberation movement in the 1960s. Which was *not* a contribution to the women's movement?

   (A) Women became dissatisfied with their roles in the black civil rights movement.
   (B) Antiwar protests radicalized women.
   (C) The number of women in the labor force had greatly increased while job discrimination remained.
   (D) Dissatisfaction arose over the image of the suburban housewife.
   (E) Anger grew from the failure to achieve ratification of the Equal Rights Amendment.

3. In the election of 1844,

   (A) Polk narrowly won on a platform of expansion, a lower tariff, and the Independent Treasury system
   (B) Polk won a large election mandate for Manifest Destiny
   (C) the Whig Party kept control of the White House

   (D) Van Buren defeated Clay over the Bank issue
   (E) Van Buren and Clay agreed to support Manifest Destiny

4. All of the following are considered by historians as causes of the depression in 1929 *except*

   (A) economic weaknesses in the agricultural sector of the economy
   (B) maldistribution of income
   (C) the depressed condition of Europe's economy
   (D) boom and bust cycles on the stock market
   (E) harsh federal government regulation of industries

5. In his message to Congress on December 2, 1823, Monroe asserted:

   (A) Any new European colonization required United States approval, including the transfer of colonies from one European power to another.
   (B) A long range American policy goal was the removal of all European colonies from the New World.
   (C) As a New World power the United States was entitled to participate in conferences involving major European powers.
   (D) The political systems of the Old World were so different from those of the New World that any attempt to extend European political systems to the New World was dangerous to the United States.
   (E) The United States sympathized with Spain's attempt to reacquire her lost South American colonies, but would not tolerate any other European power acquiring them.

183

6. "Political parties exist to secure responsible government and to execute the will of the people.

"From these great tasks both of the old parties have turned aside. Instead of instruments to promote the general welfare, they have become the tools of corrupt interests which use them impartially to serve their selfish purposes. Behind the ostensible government sits enthroned an invisible government owing no allegiance and acknowledging no responsibility to the people.

"To destroy this invisible government, to dissolve the unholy alliance between corrupt business and corrupt politics is the first task of the statesmanship of the day.

"The deliberate betrayal of its trust by the Republican party, the fatal incapacity of the Democratic party to deal with the new issues of the time, have compelled the people to forge a new instrument of government through which to give effect to their will in laws and institutions.

"Unhampered by tradition, uncorrupted by power, undismayed by the magnitude of the task, the new party offers itself as the instrument of the people to sweep away old abuses, to build a new and nobler commonwealth."

This party platform is from the
(A) Populist Party, 1892
(B) Union Party, 1864
(C) Communist Party, 1932
(D) Progressive Party, 1912
(E) Dixiecrat Party, 1948

7. Traditional United States diplomatic policy as defined by our first Secretary of State, Thomas Jefferson, was to recognize a new foreign government if the new government satisfied two criteria: first, if the new government was actually in control and capable of fulfilling its international obligations; and second, if the new government had popular support. Which president departed from this policy twice?
(A) Reagan in regard to El Salvador and Nicaragua
(B) Wilson in regard to Mexico and the Soviet Union
(C) Truman in regard to China and Israel
(D) Theodore Roosevelt in regard to Panama and the Dominican Republic
(E) McKinley in regard to Cuba and the Philippines

Spain	France	Great Britain

8. This map shows European land claims in
(A) 1713
(B) 1763
(C) 1783
(D) 1689
(E) 1500

9. *Uncle Tom's Cabin* by Harriet Beecher Stowe
(A) set off a storm of protest from the South
(B) was written by a Southern woman
(C) initially sold very few copies
(D) told a purposefully distorted story to stir up passions
(E) was published during the debate over the Compromise of 1850

10. Some actions by Congress require a simple majority; others require a two-thirds vote; and others require a three-fourths vote. Some actions apply to only one house of the Congress. Which of the following statements about votes in Congress is incorrect?

(A) A majority vote in both the House of Representatives and the Senate is needed to declare war.
(B) A two-thirds vote in both the House of Representatives and the Senate is needed to pass a bill over the president's veto.

(C) A two-thirds vote in only the Senate is needed to remove a president from office by impeachment.

(D) A two-thirds vote in only the Senate is needed to ratify a treaty.

(E) A two-thirds vote in both the House of Representatives and the Senate is needed to approve the appointment of cabinet members and federal judges.

11. Which of the following is *not* correctly paired?

(A) Cyrus McCormick—*Commonwealth* vs. *Hunt* case
(B) Boston Associates—Lowell factories
(C) Cyrus Field—undersea telegraph cable
(D) Eli Whitney—interchangeable parts
(E) Samuel Slater—Pawtucket mill

12. In the early colonial period a "Separatist" was defined as a person

(A) who left England to seek economic gain in the New World
(B) who wished to break away from the impure Church of England
(C) who left the Massachusetts Bay colony for religious freedom in Rhode Island
(D) who earned his freedom after working for another person for four to seven years
(E) who had served his apprenticeship

13. When Lincoln met Harriet Beecher Stowe he reportedly said, "So you're the little lady who started the war." Actually an earlier female could also lay claim to that honor. She precipitated a crisis in Jackson's cabinet that forced Vice-President Calhoun out of office, and cemented him more deeply into a position as spokesman for the slave South. Who was the earlier woman who also "started the war"?

(A) Elizabeth Cady Stanton
(B) Abigail Adams
(C) Peggy Eaton
(D) Rachel Donelson
(E) Mercy Otis Warren

14. "The language of the amendment itself does not support the theory that it was passed for the benefit of corporations. . . . Thus, the words 'life' and 'liberty' do not apply to corporations, and of course they could not have been so intended to apply. However, the decisions of this Court . . . hold that corporations are included in this clause in so far as the word 'property' is concerned. In other words this clause is construed to mean as follows:

" 'Nor shall any State deprive any *human being* of life, liberty, or property without due process of law; nor shall any State deprive any corporation of property without due process of law.'

"The last clause of this second sentence of section 1 reads: 'Nor deny to any person within its jurisdiction the equal protection of the laws.' As used here, 'person' has been construed to include corporations." This quotation from a dissenting opinion in a Supreme Court case in the 1930s attacked previous judicial interpretations of an amendment to the Constitution. The amendment was the

(A) Twenty-first Amendment
(B) First Amendment
(C) Thirteenth Amendment
(D) Fifth Amendment
(E) Fourteenth Amendment

15. When President Franklin Roosevelt took the oath of office in 1933 the most pressing problem he faced was

(A) the opposition of Father Coughlin, Huey Long, and Dr. Townsend
(B) the Manchurian crisis
(C) Hitler's invasion of Poland
(D) organizing his Brain Trust
(E) the banking crisis

16. Which third party candidate received the highest popular vote and the highest electoral vote for President?

(A) George Wallace, American Independent Party, 1968
(B) Eugene V. Debs, Socialist Party, 1912
(C) James Weaver, Populist Party, 1892
(D) Robert LaFollette, Progressive Party, 1924
(E) John Anderson, Independent, 1980

17. Which of the following was *not* associated with our foreign relations with France in the 1790s?

(A) XYZ affair
(B) Citizen Genêt
(C) undeclared naval war, 1798
(D) Treaty of 1778
(E) Barbary pirates

18. Andrew Jackson opposed the second Bank of the U.S. for many reasons. Which of the following is *not* a reason why Jackson opposed the Bank of the U.S.?

    (A) the ability of the Bank to influence congressmen through loans
    (B) the influence of the Bank over the lending policies of state banks
    (C) the inability of the Bank to provide a sound currency
    (D) the concentration of the Bank's stock in the hands of wealthy individuals in the Northeast and in Europe
    (E) the Bank was a monopoly and it was unconstitutional

19. Which political leader endorsed the philosophy that the political and social future of the United States was more secure if the United States emphasized agriculture instead of industry?

    (A) Thomas Jefferson
    (B) Alexander Hamilton
    (C) Henry Clay
    (D) Daniel Webster
    (E) Eugene V. Debs

20. Four of the following are concerned with the Monroe Doctrine in some form. Which had nothing to do with it?

    (A) Act of Chapultepec
    (B) Dawes Plan and Young Plan
    (C) Act of Havana
    (D) Montevideo Pact
    (E) Clark Memorandum

21. The Constitution was written to make it difficult for the majority of the population to impress their will on the federal government. Which of the following gave the people the most impact on the federal government?

    (A) length of the term of office for federal judges
    (B) length of the term of office for members of the House of Representatives
    (C) choosing the president by the Electoral College
    (D) the method of electing U.S. senators
    (E) having one-third of the Senate elected every two years

22. "When one becomes a member of society, he necessarily parts with some rights or priv-ileges. . . . This does not confer power upon the whole people to control rights which are purely and exclusively private; but it does authorize the establishment of laws requiring each citizen to so conduct himself, and so use his own property, as not unnecessarily to injure another. . . . Property does become clothed with a public interest when used in a manner to make it of public consequence, and affect the community at large. When, therefore, one devotes his property to a use in which the public has an interest, he, in effect, grants to the public an interest in that use, and must submit to be controlled by the public for the common good."
    This quotation from the decision by Chief Justice Waite approved a state law to fix maximum rates for railroad grain storage. This 1876 case was

    (A) *Muller v. Oregon*
    (B) *McCulloch v. Maryland*
    (C) *Lochner v. New York*
    (D) *Munn v. Illinois*
    (E) *Cohens v. Virginia*

23. Henry David Thoreau's essay on "Civil Disobe-dience" profoundly influenced which set of leaders?

    (A) Daniel Webster and Henry Clay
    (B) John Calhoun and Horace Mann
    (C) Mahatma Gandhi and Martin Luther King, Jr.
    (D) Abraham Lincoln and Jefferson Davis
    (E) Stephen Douglas and Frederick Douglass

24. "We conclude that in the field of public education the doctrine of 'separate but equal' has no place. Separate educational facilities are inherently unequal. Therefore, we hold that the plaintiffs and others similarly situated for whom the actions have been brought are, by reason of the segregation complained of, deprived of the equal protection of the laws guaranteed by the Fourteenth Amendment." This quotation is from the Supreme Court case of

    (A) *School District of Abington v. Schempp*
    (B) *Brown v. The Board of Education of Topeka*
    (C) *Plessy v. Ferguson*
    (D) *Bakke v. Regents of the University of California*
    (E) *West Virginia Board of Education v. Barnette*

25. Which of the following statements concerning child labor laws and court decisions is incorrect?

    (A) In *Bailey* v. *Drexel Furniture Co.* the Supreme Court invalidated the 1919 Child Labor Act on the grounds that the taxing provisions of the law went beyond the power to tax and were instead an attempt to regulate employment standards, which was clearly a police power of the states.

    (B) In *Hammer* v. *Dagenhart* the Supreme Court invalidated the 1916 Child Labor Act on the grounds that child labor could only be regulated under the police power of the states, not by Congress under the commerce clause.

    (C) The Child Labor Act of 1919, based upon the powers of Congress to tax, levied a special high tax on products produced by child labor, ten percent of a company's net profit.

    (D) The 1916 Keating-Owen Child Labor Act, based upon the commerce clause of the Constitution, prohibited the interstate shipment of products produced by child labor.

    (E) In *Adkins* v. *Children's Hospital* the Supreme Court invalidated the Maximum Hours Act of 1918, which prohibited the employment of children living in the District of Columbia. Since Congress is the legislature for the District of Columbia, which is not a state, the Supreme Court could not claim this was an infringement on the states' police power. Instead the act was invalidated as infringing upon the Fifth Amendment, the liberty of an individual to enter into a contract.

26. Which of the following statements about 19th century politics is correct?

    (A) Between Lincoln's election in 1860 and Wilson's election in 1912, the Republican Party dominated national politics, winning the presidency in all but eight years and always having a comfortable margin in the Senate and the House.

    (B) Andrew Johnson and Chester A. Arthur were the only presidents between 1860 and 1912 who were assassinated.

    (C) Between 1860 and 1912 only Grover Cleveland and Theodore Roosevelt were

elected to successive terms in the White House.

    (D) Between 1860 and 1896 most national presidential elections were hotly contested and narrow victories for the winner, either in popular vote or electoral vote.

    (E) Between 1860 and 1896 the Republican and Democratic parties cornered all the popular enthusiasm, and third parties never attracted a sizeable following nor won electoral votes.

27. Which outgoing president warned the nation in a farewell speech to beware of "the military-industrial complex," the result of the need for a sophisticated technological military and the subsequent development of a permanent, politically-oriented arms industry dependent on military purchases?

    (A) Jimmy Carter
    (B) Richard Nixon
    (C) Harry Truman
    (D) Dwight Eisenhower
    (E) Lyndon Johnson

28. Which work was representative of the Harlem Renaissance?

    (A) Langston Hughes, "Song to A Negro Wash-Woman" and "The Negro Artist and the Racial Mountain"
    (B) W.E.B. DuBois, *The Philadelphia Negro*
    (C) *The Autobiography of Malcolm X*
    (D) Gunnar Myrdal, *An American Dilemma*
    (E) John Howard Griffin, *Black Like Me*

29. Four of the following correctly describe how these states came under the authority of the United States government. Which one is incorrect?

    (A) Texas: joint resolution by Congress
    (B) Arizona and New Mexico: treaty after a war and then purchase of a small section from Mexico
    (C) Louisiana: purchase from France
    (D) Florida: treaty from Spain
    (E) Alaska: military protectorate, then annexation

30. Which of the following were events in our foreign relations with Japan?

    I. Burlingame Treaty
    II. San Francisco School Board incident
    III. Gentlemen's Agreement
    IV. Tampico landing
    V. Insular Cases

    (A) II and III only
    (B) I, II, III, and V only
    (C) I, III, and V only
    (D) II, III, and V only
    (E) II and IV only

31. George Washington once said, "There are combustibles in every state which a spark might set afire." What event in American history was he describing?

    (A) election of 1796
    (B) Stamp Act
    (C) Shays' Rebellion
    (D) Newburgh conspiracy
    (E) Whiskey Rebellion

32. He is best remembered for his writings about war, slums, and prostitution. A realist, his writings suggest that man is swept along by his environment, unable to control the forces around him. The author is

    (A) Henry David Thoreau
    (B) Ralph Waldo Emerson
    (C) Stephen Crane
    (D) F. Scott Fitzgerald
    (E) Carl Sandburg

33. "Of the thousand things that the. . .has done no balance sheet can ever be made. How it helped the ministers of the church, and saved the blacks from robbery! How it made all show respect for the Negro's rights! How it taught all the people the meaning of the law! It settled neighborhood quarrels, brought about friendly relations between employers and workers, improved education, helped freedmen become landowners, broke up bands of outlaws, taught equal rights, and in such ways carried the light of the North into the dark places of the South." What is the author of this 1866 quotation referring to?

    (A) adoption of the Black Codes
    (B) the Freedmen's Bureau
    (C) end of the Jim Crow laws

(D) signing of the Emancipation Proclamation
(E) period after the *Brown* v. *Bd. of Education* decision

34. If the Populists had been transported by magic back into an earlier period of American history they would have most likely joined

    (A) Ku Klux Klan
    (B) Shays's Rebellion
    (C) Knights of Labor
    (D) Whiskey Rebellion
    (E) Federalist Party

35. Which of the following were generally considered antilabor by organized labor?

    I. Taft-Hartley Act, 1947
    II. Landrum-Griffin Act, 1959
    III. Fair Labor Standards Act, 1938
    IV. Wagner Act, 1935

    (A) I only
    (B) I and IV only
    (C) III and IV only
    (D) I and II only
    (E) II, III, and IV only

36. All but one of the following are true about the Vietnam War. Which statement is *not* correct?

    (A) Johnson used the domino theory to justify the need for American action.
    (B) In the 1950s the United States supported a dictatorship in South Vietnam.
    (C) The United States did not permit national elections as specified by the Geneva Accords of 1955 to be held in South Vietnam.
    (D) The war effort encountered widespread popular opposition within the United States.
    (E) The United States withdrawal in 1973 ended the fighting between North Vietnam and South Vietnam.

37. Which of the following were associated with the Federalist Party in the 1790s?

    I. They sympathized with Great Britain rather than France in European disputes.
    II. They favored strict interpretation of the Constitution.
    III. They disapproved of the Alien and Sedition Acts.
    IV. Alexander Hamilton and John Adams were two of their party leaders.

V. They favored paying the national debt at par to current holders of bonds.

(A) I, III, IV, and V only
(B) II and III only
(C) I, IV, and V only
(D) II, III, and IV only
(E) I, III, and IV only

38. The high death rates during travel, the extensive quantity of land, the successive waves of immigrants, the harsh conditions of life, and the hostility of the weather all combined to produce by the end of the period a society that accepted a high degree of social disorder, accepted a high degree of personal risk, and glorified youth and vitality over age and wisdom. What era in American history is described?

(A) the Twenties
(B) Reconstruction
(C) The Transportation Revolution
(D) the Revolutionary War
(E) the colonial era

39. "The fact is that a reformer can't last in politics. He can make a show for a while, but he always comes down like a rocket. Politics is as much a regular business as the grocery or dry-goods or the drug business. You've got to be trained up to it or you're sure to fall. . . .

"I've been studyin' the political game for forty-five years, and I don't know it all yet. I'm learnin' somethin' all the time. How, then, can you expect what they call 'business men' to turn politics all at once and make a success of it? It is just as if I went up to Columbia University and started to teach Greek. They usually last about as long in politics as I would last at Columbia."

This quotation represents the viewpoint of a late 19th century

(A) big city ward politician
(B) Populist
(C) AFL labor organizer
(D) Progressive
(E) Chautauqua lecturer

40. "Provided, that, as an express and fundamental condition to the acquisition of any territory from the Republic of Mexico by the United States, by virtue of any treaty which may be negotiated between them, and to the use by the Executive of the moneys herein appropriated, neither slavery nor involuntary servitude shall ever exist in any part of said territory, except for crime, whereof the party shall first be duly convicted." This brief proposal, introduced in Congress by Representative David Wilmot,

(A) was in retaliation for the gag rule
(B) became part of the Treaty of Guadelupe Hildago, which ended the Mexican War
(C) was incorporated into the Compromise of 1850
(D) stirred a heated debate between North and South over slavery in the territories
(E) outlawed slavery in California

41. To people living in the decade of the 1920s, which came to symbolize immoral decadence?

(A) the Muller v. Oregon case
(B) the Sacco and Vanzetti trial
(C) the Scopes trial
(D) the Leopold and Loeb trial
(E) the sit-down strikes

42. Most of the thirteen original colonies

(A) started as proprietary colonies and became royal colonies by the 1750s
(B) were within their first twenty years successful in terms of their original plans
(C) started as charter colonies and became royal colonies by the 1750s
(D) were formed as royal colonies
(E) purchased their charters from their proprietors

43. "Red China is not the powerful nation seeking to dominate the world. Frankly, in the opinion of the Joint Chiefs of Staff, this strategy would involve us in the wrong war, at the wrong place, at the wrong time, and with the wrong enemy." This quotation from a speech before a congressional hearing by General Omar Bradley, the Chairman of the Joint Chiefs of Staff, concerned

(A) U.S. recognition of the government of Taiwan
(B) U.S. response to the Japanese invasion of China in the 1930s
(C) the application of the Hoover-Stimson Doctrine to Manchuria
(D) U.S. policy in regard to enlarging the scope of the Korean War
(E) the U.S. decision to support the government of South Vietnam

44. "The fortunes amassed through corporate organization are now so large . . . as to make it a matter of necessity to give to . . . the government, which represents the people as a whole, some effective power of supervision over their corporate use. . . . I am in no sense hostile to corporations. This is an age of combination, and any effort to prevent all combination will be not only useless, but in the end vicious, because of the contempt for law which the failure to enforce law inevitably produces. We should, moreover, recognize in cordial and ample fashion the immense good effected by corporate agencies in a country such as ours, . . . The corporation has come to stay, just as the trade-union has come to stay. Each can do and has done great good. Each should be favored as long as it does good. But each should be sharply checked where it acts against law and justice."
Who gave this speech around 1900 outlining his philosophy toward corporations?

(A) Woodrow Wilson
(B) Andrew Carnegie
(C) Theodore Roosevelt
(D) J. Pierpont Morgan
(E) William Jennings Bryan

45. Franklin Roosevelt's court packing plan and his interference in the congressional elections of 1938 both evoked harsh criticism of the New Deal. One result of the uproar was the

(A) development of new programs to combat the Depression, such as the Agricultural Adjustment Act, the Civilian Conservation Corps, and the Reconstruction Finance Corporation
(B) creation of two new political parties out of the Democratic Party—the Progressives and the Dixiecrats
(C) end of the administration's farm price-support program
(D) creation of a conservative congressional coalition of Southern Democrats and conservative Republicans that effectively blocked liberal legislation
(E) Supreme Court's invalidation of more New Deal legislation

46. Created in haste it was a wartime government, "a league of friendship," suffering many pressures from the beginning. It lacked the power to enforce its laws, to tax directly, and to regulate internal commerce. Which government is described?

(A) the colonies during the French and Indian War
(B) the Articles of Confederation
(C) the first decade under the Constitution
(D) the Northwest Ordinance
(E) the League of Nations

47. Historians' opinions are colored by the political issues of their times. The following have been suggested by historians as a cause of the Civil War. Which is *least* associated with a particular time period and climate of historical writing?

(A) dispute over slavery
(B) constitutional dispute over states' rights
(C) needless emotional fanaticism on both sides
(D) struggle between two competing economic groups or classes for control of the federal government
(E) impact of sectional antagonism upon the national political party system

48. Born in England of Quaker parents, he participated in both the American and the French revolutions through his inflammatory writings. Who is described?

(A) Marquis de Lafayette
(B) Thaddeus Kosciusko
(C) Baron von Steuben
(D) Thomas Paine
(E) John Paul Jones

49. "Our greatest danger is that in the great leap from slavery to freedom we may overlook the fact that the masses of us are to live by the productions of our hands, and fail to keep in mind that we shall prosper in proportion as we learn to dignify and glorify common labour and put brains and skill into the common occupations of life. . . . No race can prosper till it learns that there is as much dignity in tilling a field as in writing a poem. It is at the bottom of life we must begin, and not at the top. Nor should we permit our grievances to overshadow our opportunities.
"The wisest among my race understand that the agitation of questions of social equality is

the extremest folly, and that progress in the enjoyment of all privileges that will come to us must be the result of severe and constant struggle rather than of artificial forcing. . . . The opportunity to earn a dollar in a factory just now is worth infinitely more than the opportunity to spend a dollar in an opera-house."

These passages represent the philosophy of

(A) Marcus Garvey
(B) Booker T. Washington
(C) Malcolm X
(D) W.E.B. DuBois
(E) Martin Luther King, Jr.

50. In December 1918, ex-President Theodore Roosevelt issued a public statement that said, "Our allies and our enemies and Mr. Wilson himself should all understand that Mr. Wilson has no authority whatever to speak for the American people at this time. His leadership has just been emphatically repudiated by them. Mr. Wilson and his Fourteen Points . . . have ceased to have any shadow of right to be accepted as expressive of the will of the American people." What prompted Roosevelt to make this analysis?

(A) Wilson's stroke negated his ability to lead the nation.
(B) Article X of the Versailles Treaty angered a majority of the Senate.
(C) The Republican Party had just won control of the Senate in an election in which Wilson had appealed for the public to elect Democrats to the Senate.
(D) The isolationists from both parties in the Senate constituted a majority, ensuring defeat of the treaty.
(E) Wilson refused Theodore Roosevelt's advice to include a prominent Republican in the treaty delegation.

51. Which of the following statements concerning the British colonial system prior to 1763 is *not* true?

(A) The colonial system was a secondary concern to Great Britain. British political attention focused more on the many changes within the British government from 1603 to the 1760s.

(B) The struggle of the British House of Commons for increased power provided a model for the lower houses of the colonial assemblies.
(C) The emergence of a two party system in British politics encouraged the acceptance of the concept of outspoken opposition to the government.
(D) Responsibility for governing and controlling the colonies rested clearly and completely in one part of the British government—the Board of Trade.
(E) India was considered to be a more valuable colony than all the North American colonies.

52. At the end of the War of 1812 Daniel Webster opposed the protective tariff. Fifteen years later he had switched his position to favoring protective tariffs. Why?

(A) British dumping of low priced products after the War of 1812 ruined many American industries.
(B) The base of the New England economy changed from shipping and commerce to industrial production.
(C) The Jeffersonian Democrats, who had originally opposed the concept of a protective tariff, changed to supporting protective tariffs and forced the Federalist Party to adopt the opposite position.
(D) Anger over Calhoun's "Exposition and Protest" turned most Northerners in favor of free trade.
(E) Webster supported Clay's American System in exchange for Clay's support of Webster's proposal for a second Bank of the United States.

53. Since the Second World War the Soviet Union has had difficulty presenting communism as a unified movement, a monolithic workers' international. Which of the following satellites has disputed the leadership of the Soviet Union the *least*?

(A) China
(B) Yugoslavia
(C) Albania
(D) Hungary
(E) Cuba

54. Which is *not* true concerning the Alien and Sedition Acts?

   (A) They were used by the president to silence his political opponents, the Federalist newspaper editors.

   (B) They gave the president the power to imprison or to deport aliens dangerous to the national welfare.

   (C) They raised the residency requirement from five to fourteen years for naturalized citizenship.

   (D) They provided fines and imprisonment for those who spoke or published "false, scandalous, and malicious writing or writings against the government of the United States" or Congress or the president.

   (E) They grew out of the public anger at the undeclared naval war with France, the XYZ affair, the influx of Irish and French fleeing the abortive Irish Revolution of 1798, and the French Revolution of the 1790s.

55. The historian investigating the origins of slavery in the colonial period encounters little documentary evidence to establish the date when the two essentials of slavery—lifetime service and inherited status—first appeared. Even less information provides clues to why black slavery was established. Which of the following has *not* been advanced as an explanation for the development of slavery in colonial America?

   (A) need for labor

   (B) inability of Indians to serve as a labor source

   (C) black slavery in Great Britain as an example

   (D) prejudice towards blacks

   (E) heathen status of blacks

56. It began as a debate over federal land policy and ended as a debate over states' rights and the nature of the federal union. What is described?

   (A) Constitutional Convention, 1787

   (B) Webster-Hayne debate

   (C) Lodge-Wilson debate

   (D) Lincoln-Douglas debates

   (E) Kennedy-Nixon debates

57. This map shows the

   (A) nations who fought with the United States in the Second World War

   (B) members of NATO, the North Atlantic Treaty Organization

   (C) nations conquered by Axis powers in the Second World War

   (D) members of the Warsaw Pact

   (E) Allies in the First World War

58. Designed as an attempt to secure the loyalty of the French to their new rulers, this act broke new ground in toleration and statesmanship. Unfortunately for the British, the Americans saw only sinister designs. The act was the

   (A) Treaty of Paris, 1783

   (B) Tea Act

   (C) Statute of Westminister

   (D) Declaratory Act

   (E) Quebec Act

59. On October 4, 1957, the Soviet Union launched the first man-made satellite, Sputnik (fellow traveler of the earth). The event jolted Americans into doing all the following *except*

   (A) passing the National Defense Education Act, 1958

   (B) pouring more money into the National Aeronautics and Space Administration budget

(C) taking a critical look at our education system

(D) putting a special emphasis on improving the teaching of science, mathematics, and foreign languages

(E) hiring German rocket experts from the Second World War to work on United States rocket research

60. The high wages enjoyed by colonial workers were primarily caused by

(A) little competition from English craftsmen

(B) monopolies granted by town councils

(C) restrictions of the guild system

(D) existence of so much land

(E) laws against manufacturing

61. "The North has acquired a decided ascendency over every department of this Government and through it a control over all the powers of the system. A single section governed by the will of the numerical majority, has now, in fact, the control of the Government and the entire powers of the system. What was once a constitutional federal republic, is now converted, in reality, into one as absolute as that of the Autocrat of Russia, and as despotic in its tendency as any absolute government that ever existed.

"As, then, the North has the absolute control over the Government, it is manifest that on all questions between it and the South, where there is a diversity of interests, the interest of the latter will be sacrificed to the former, however oppressive the effects may be; as the South possesses no means by which it can resist, through the action of the Government."

(A) This statement was made in support of the Virginia Plan at the Constitutional Convention, 1787.

(B) This statement is from the preamble to the Populist Party platform, 1892.

(C) The author of this statement suggested a concurrent majority to protect the interests of the South, 1850.

(D) This statement was part of the announcement of the Monroe Doctrine, December 2, 1823.

(E) This statement was written in response to the Alien and Sedition Acts, 1798.

62. Truman aided the cause of civil rights by

(A) denouncing Southern support in the 1948 presidential election

(B) desegregating the armed forces

(C) integrating the public schools

(D) ordering nondiscrimination in all defense contracts

(E) integrating restaurants, movie theaters, and interstate travel

63. "That the United States hereby disclaims any disposition or intention to exercise sovereignty, jurisdiction, or control over said Island except for the pacification thereof, and asserts its determination, when that is accomplished, to leave the government and control of the Island to its people." This quotation is

(A) the Teller Amendment

(B) part of the Treaty of Paris, 1898

(C) from the Ostend Manifesto

(D) the Platt Amendment

(E) the speech in which General MacArthur promised to return to the Philippines

64. The ideas of an Englishman and a Frenchman strongly influenced the Founding Fathers when they wrote the Constitution. They were

(A) John Locke and de Tocqueville

(B) Edmund Burke and Lafayette

(C) Alexander Hamilton and Montesquieu

(D) James Madison and Lafayette

(E) John Locke and Montesquieu

65. A violent act aided its creation. Its beginnings were meager. Most successive presidents expanded it to protect their own. It used merit for promotion, and was run by a commission. What is described?

(A) United States Army

(B) civil service

(C) postal service

(D) National Aeronautics and Space Administration

(E) American Federation of Labor

66. Which of the following describes something that happened during the five years after the

end of the fighting in both the First and the Second World wars?

(A) The political party which did not control the White House won control of Congress.

(B) The United States entered into treaties of alliance with our allies to prevent future wars.

(C) Postwar conferences were held which wrote peace treaties.

(D) The United States sent economic aid to rebuild the European economy.

(E) A depression hindered the transition of the economy from wartime to peacetime.

67. Of the five routes shown, which was the first railroad to be completed?

(A) Great Northern
(B) Northern Pacific
(C) Central Pacific and Union Pacific
(D) Atchison, Topeka and Santa Fe
(E) Southern Pacific

68. Which two railroads shown were the target of Theodore Roosevelt's trust busting?

(A) Southern Pacific and Northern Pacific
(B) Central Pacific and Union Pacific
(C) Great Northern and Northern Pacific
(D) Atchison, Topeka and Santa Fe and the Southern Pacific
(E) Central Pacific, Union Pacific and the Atchison, Topeka and Santa Fe

69. Which of the following was *not* a reform mayor during the Progressive era?

(A) Tom Johnson in Cleveland
(B) Samuel "Golden Rule" Jones in Toledo

(C) Hazen Pingree in Detroit
(D) Lincoln Steffens in Philadelphia
(E) Seth Low in New York City

70. Which post-Second World War ally threatened the solidarity of the Western alliance by opposing Great Britain's entry into the Common Market and by forcing the removal from its soil of NATO headquarters?

(A) France
(B) China
(C) Japan
(D) Germany
(E) the United Nations

71. Jeffersonian Democracy and Jacksonian Democracy most differed in

(A) the belief that it was essential to limit federal spending

(B) the belief that the Constitution limited the sphere of the federal government's powers

(C) the degree to which Jefferson and Jackson contributed to the movements which carried their names

(D) the belief that the winning political party was justified in using the spoils system to remove federal officeholders

(E) their faith in the wisdom and goodness of the common people

72. The first amendments to the Constitution, the Bill of Rights, were added to protect

(A) the states from the power of the federal government

(B) individual citizens from the power of the federal government and state governments

(C) individual citizens from the power of the federal government

(D) the individual citizens from the power of the state governments

(E) minorities from the majority

73. Horatio Alger wrote over one hundred books aimed at American youth. His message is most accurately described as which of the following?

(A) Rags to riches is possible for a hardworking young man.

(B) Rugged individualism is the best philosophy for American business.

(C) Luck and chance play a major role in the rise from rags to respectibility.

(D) Andrew Carnegie and John D. Rockefeller were examples of the typical business tycoons in terms of their origins and their success.

(E) The best way to success is to strike out on your own and start your own business.

74. The New Deal of Franklin Roosevelt inaugurated the "welfare state," which theoretically establishes a floor below which society will not permit its citizens to fall and a ceiling above which individuals should not be permitted to rise. Four of the following are aspects of the "welfare state." Which is *not?*

(A) veterans' benefits

(B) unemployment compensation

(C) personal progressive income tax

(D) aid to dependent children

(E) corporate progressive income tax

75. Which of the following is an idea of Woodrow Wilson's that came to be an accepted part of United States foreign policy after 1945?

(A) Nonrecognition of revolutionary governments will lead to the downfall of such offensive governments.

(B) The security of the United States is best preserved through collective security.

(C) Isolation has kept us out of past European wars and will keep us out of future European wars.

(D) The World Court is the best forum to settle international disputes.

(E) Arbitration treaties between nations provide a much needed period for tempers to cool.

76. Which of the following were characteristics of new state constitutions written during the Revolutionary War?

I. A Bill of Rights was included.

II. The principles of separation of powers and checks and balances were incorporated.

III. A weak executive was provided for.

IV. The abolition of all property qualifications for suffrage.

(A) I, II, III, IV

(B) I, III, and IV only

(C) II, III, and IV only

(D) II and IV only

(E) I, II, and III only

77. Which of the following was an attempt by the Puritans to enlarge church membership in order to include those faithful members who had not become one of the visible saints, or "elect"?

(A) Cambridge Platform, 1648

(B) Child Petition, 1646

(C) Massachusetts Body of Liberties, 1641

(D) Half-Way Covenant, 1662

(E) Mayflower Compact, 1620

78. In 1938 Roosevelt called the South the nation's number one economic problem. The report of the National Emergency Council on the Economic Condition of the South supported his assessment. Which of the following was *not* an economic problem in the South during this period?

(A) badly eroded soil

(B) reliance on crops such as cotton and tobacco that extracted many nutrients from the soil

(C) over one-half of the farms were farmed by tenant farmers who cared little for the long range consequences of their farming methods

(D) an overreliance on federal government crop price supports through the sale abroad of surpluses by the Federal Farm Board

(E) the destruction of large areas of the Southern forests, reducing their ability to slow down rainwater runoff

79. "It occurred to me that woman, having received from her Creator the same intellectual constitution as man, has the same right as man to intellectual culture and development.

"I considered that the mothers of a country mold the character of its citizens, determine its institutions, and shape its destiny.

"Next to the influence of the mother is that of the female teacher, who is employed to train young children at a period when impressions are most vivid and lasting.

"It also seemed to me that if woman were properly educated, some new avenues to useful and honorable employment, in entire harmony with the gentleness and modesty of her sex, might be opened to her." This statement of purpose envisioned by the founder of a newly created college for women was probably delivered

(A) in the 1920s, after women received the right to vote

(B) after the Civil War, reflecting expectations for women from the middle and upper classes

(C) in the 1960s, following the establishment of the National Organization for Women

(D) in the early 19th century, reflecting the need for female teachers

(E) after the Revolutionary War, reflecting the spirit of nationalism and self-help in education

80. The National Security Act of 1947 and the National Security Act of 1949 established which of the following?

   I. National Security Council
   II. Central Intelligence Agency
   III. Secretary of Defense
   IV. Joint Chiefs of Staff
   V. House Un-American Activities Committee

(A) I only
(B) I and II only
(C) I, II, and V only
(D) II and IV only
(E) I, II, III, and IV only

81. Secretary of the Treasury Alexander Hamilton proposed that the federal government do which of the following?

   I. Have a protective tariff rather than a revenue tariff
   II. Establish a national bank
   III. Promote development of industry
   IV. Pay off foreign and national debts
   V. Have the federal government assume state debts
   VI. Establish an excise tax

(A) II, IV, and VI only
(B) I, II, III, IV, V, and VI
(C) II, IV, V, and VI only
(D) II, III, IV, V, and VI only
(E) I, II, III, V, and VI only

82. Which of these strategic objectives did the North accomplish last during the Civil War?

(A) splitting the Confederacy by gaining control of the Mississippi River

(B) blockading Southern ports

(C) capturing the Confederate capital of Richmond

(D) isolating the South diplomatically, preventing an alliance with a European power

(E) splitting the Confederacy by marching through Georgia

83. Four of the following are designs or schemes in American diplomatic history which were not successful, although they may have been ultimately successful. Which is the only diplomatic endeavor that was successful and is matched to the correct presidential administration?

(A) annexation of Hawaii, Grover Cleveland

(B) Ostend Manifesto, Franklin Pierce

(C) All-Mexico Movement, James K. Polk

(D) annexation of Santo Domingo, Ulysses S. Grant

(E) Pan-American Union, Benjamin Harrison

84. Which of the following was a similarity between Shays' Rebellion and the Whiskey Rebellion?

(A) Both alarmed conservatives throughout the nation.

(B) George Washington put both down.

(C) Both were caused by a protest over taxes.

(D) Both occurred in Pennsylvania.

(E) Both occurred during the government of the Articles of Confederation.

85. She coined the phrase "birth control" and published a magazine appropriately named *Woman Rebel.* Who was this pioneer advocate of family planning in the Progressive era?

(A) Jane Addams
(B) Ida Tarbell
(C) Frances Willard
(D) Charolette Perkins Gilman
(E) Margaret Sanger

"It's More Than We've Ever Put Out Before"

© 1966 by Herblock in The Washington Post

86. This cartoon suggests that

(A) the cost for the war in Vietnam deprived cities of needed federal funds

(B) federal aid to urban areas was inadequate

(C) federal government programs were misdirected, not reaching those who needed it

(D) the public was opposed to federal aid to cities

(E) the financial future for cities would be better

87.   "With malice toward none, with charity for all, with firmness in the right as God gives us to see the right, let us strive on to finish the work we are in, to bind up the nation's wounds, to care for him who shall have borne the battle and for his widow and his orphan, to do all which may achieve and cherish a just and lasting peace among ourselves and with all nations."
These words were

(A) spoken by Wilson urging his Fourteen Points, 1917

(B) spoken by Lincoln during his Second Inaugural Address, 1865

(C) spoken by Washington in his farewell address to his troops, 1783

(D) spoken by Jefferson in his inaugural address, which also contained the phrase, "We are all Republicans, we are all Federalists."

(E) written by Calhoun (he was too ill to speak) during the debate over the Compromise of 1850

88. The electoral college system

(A) worked the way it was envisioned only in the first two elections

(B) foresaw the rise of political parties

(C) was copied from the British parliamentary system

(D) provides for a popularly elected president

(E) was part of the Great Compromise, giving disproportionate representation to the smaller states

89. In *Democracy in America* the French author Alexis de Tocqueville pointed out a potential defect of American democracy, the potential for the abuse of an individual's rights by an emotional democratic majority.

"I know no country in which there is so little true independence of mind and freedom of discussion as in America. . . . In America, the majority raises very formidable barriers to the liberty of opinion." This role of the tyranny of majority opinion in American history is illustrated by all of the following *except*

(A) the Alien and Sedition Acts

(B) the gag rule in the 1830s

(C) the imprisonment of Eugene V. Debs during the First World War

(D) McCarthyism

(E) antiwar demonstrations against the Vietnam War

90. The political cartoonist who ended Boss Tweed's career is credited with popularizing the donkey and the elephant as symbols for the Democratic and Republican parties. He was

(A) Richard Olney

(B) Thomas Reed

(C) James B. Duke

(D) Albert B. Fall

(E) Thomas Nast

91. The majority of people came to America in the colonial period for which of the following reasons?

    (A) to seek economic gain
    (B) to seek religious freedom
    (C) to avoid involvement in European wars
    (D) to gain political rights
    (E) to pursue the cultural arts

92. Prohibition became part of the Constitution in the Eighteenth Amendment. Many Americans, convinced that a new dawn had arrived, celebrated its arrival. Events in the 1920s illustrated that Prohibition was not working, that it produced undesirable results, yet millions of Americans continued to support Prohibition. Who were the staunchest supporters of Prohibition in the 1920s?

    (A) the three Republican presidents
    (B) organized crime figures
    (C) rural Americans and small town residents
    (D) big city immigrants
    (E) labor leaders and labor unions

93. *Marbury v. Madison* established the principle of "judicial review," by declaring an act of Congress unconstitutional. What was the second occasion when the Supreme Court declared an act of Congress unconstitutional?

    (A) the Dred Scott case
    (B) *Worcester v. Georgia*
    (C) *Cohens v. Virginia*
    (D) *McCulloch v. Maryland*
    (E) the Dartmouth College case

94. Which muckraking novel is *not* correctly linked to the topic of the novel?

    (A) *The Jungle*—meatpacking industry in Chicago
    (B) *The Octopus*—railroads and farmers
    (C) *Wealth Against Commonwealth*—Standard Oil Co.
    (D) *The Shame of the Cities*—corrupt urban charities
    (E) *The Bitter Cry of the Children*—use of child labor

95. The removal of the Cherokee Indians from Georgia pushed westward an Indian nation that had attempted to assimilate into white culture. In which of the following were the Cherokees the *least* successful in assimilating into white culture?

    (A) adopting white agricultural methods
    (B) establishing a government based upon a written constitution
    (C) adopting white religions
    (D) owning black slaves
    (E) adopting white patterns of land ownership

96. What is described? "The antitrust approach was abandoned in favor of regulating business by means of codes of fair practices, in the desire to balance production and consumption. The individual industry codes fixed production levels, wages, hours, and guaranteed workers the right to unionize."

    (A) New Frontier
    (B) Sherman Antitrust Act
    (C) President Nixon's wage and price controls
    (D) National Recovery Administration
    (E) Interstate Commerce Act

97. In the period from 1789 to the Civil War, what was the general trend in federal land policy in terms of price and the minimum number of acres that had to be purchased?

    (A) The price per acre rose and the minimum acreage was reduced.
    (B) The 1789 Homestead Act lowered the minimum acres to 160 and lowered the price to nothing, stimulating the settlement of the West.
    (C) The price per acre decreased and the minimum acreage was reduced.
    (D) The price per acre rose and the minimum acreage increased.
    (E) The price per acre decreased and the minimum acreage increased.

98. Four of the following were Native American (Indian) leaders who led their people in war against white settlers. Which one does *not* belong as a famous Native-American (Indian) chief?

    (A) King Philip
    (B) Osceola
    (C) Pontiac
    (D) Sacajawea
    (E) Tecumseh

99. In the policies they followed, Eisenhower, Nixon, and Reagan all emphasized
    (A) stricter regulation of big business
    (B) shifting some responsibilities from the federal government to the state and local governments
    (C) reducing American responsibilities as the leader of the coalition of free nations
    (D) expanding the New Deal's programs
    (E) reducing the federal deficit by cutting defense spending

100. Which congressional investigating committee concluded that American entry into the First World War resulted from the influence of big business and the munitions industry?
    (A) Pujo Committee
    (B) Nye Committee
    (C) McCarthy Committee
    (D) House Un-American Activities Committee
    (E) Kefauver Committee

ANSWERS

1. C	21. B	41. D	61. C	81. B
2. E	22. D	42. A	62. B	82. C
3. A	23. C	43. D	63. A	83. E
4. E	24. B	44. C	64. E	84. A
5. D	25. E	45. D	65. B	85. E
6. D	26. D	46. B	66. A	86. B
7. B	27. D	47. A	67. C	87. B
8. D	28. A	48. D	68. C	88. A
9. A	29. E	49. B	69. D	89. E
10. E	30. A	50. C	70. A	90. E
11. A	31. C	51. D	71. C	91. A
12. B	32. C	52. B	72. C	92. C
13. C	33. B	53. E	73. C	93. A
14. E	34. B	54. A	74. A	94. D
15. E	35. D	55. C	75. B	95. E
16. A	36. E	56. B	76. E	96. D
17. E	37. C	57. B	77. D	97. C
18. C	38. E	58. E	78. D	98. D
19. A	39. A	59. E	79. B	99. B
20. B	40. D	60. D	80. E	100. B

EXPLANATORY ANSWERS

1. **(C)** Spain, France, and Portugal all exercised tight control, in theory, over their colonies. The Netherlands controlled the economy and trade more than the political system. Great Britain exercised the least amount of control in theory and in practice. At one point the colonial-mother country relationship was described as "salutary neglect," or friendly neglect.

2. **(E)** Agitation for an Equal Rights Amendment began in the 1920s after women won the right to vote. The actual Equal Rights Amendment passed Congress only in 1972, and was never ratified by the required number of states. The ERA resulted from the women's movement of the 1960s.

3. **(A)** As the election of 1844 approached, Clay and Van Buren, the expected candidates, both agreed to downplay the volatile issue of expansion. Polk surprised the wily politicians by winning the Democratic nomination, the first so-called dark horse in the presidential sweepstakes. Polk (Democrat) went on to eke out a narrow victory over Clay (Whig) on a platform of expansion, a lower tariff, and the Independent Treasury system.

4. **(E)** The federal regulatory agencies in the 1920s existed more on paper than in reality. Conservatives dominated them and regulations were laxly enforced. The first four are among the many reasons for the Depression of 1929.

5. **(D)** This question requires a knowledge of what the Monroe Doctrine actually stated. First, any attempt by European powers to extend their monarchical political system to the Americas is dangerous to our uniquely republican principles. Second, there will not be any new European colonization in the American continents, or the transfer of colonies from one European power to another. Third, the United States will not interfere in existing European colonies in the Americas. Fourth, the United States will not participate in strictly internal European affairs.

6. **(D)** The stinging indictment of both major parties and the "holier-than-thou" attitude stamps the platform as the 1912 Progressive Party. It was probably the only presidential nominating convention in American history that sang, "Onward Christian Soldiers." The Progressives were fighting evil more than seeking mere public office. The quote lacks the truculence necessary for the Populist platform of 1892, which every student should read.

7. **(B)** Reagan supported the government in El Salvador but not the one in Nicaragua; however, the United States recognized both. Truman recognized Israel in 1948 but not China in 1949. Theodore Roosevelt recognized Panama immediately after the revolution in 1903. Debt repayment, not recognition, was the issue in the Dominican Republic. McKinley took over the Philippines and established a protectorate over Cuba. Wilson refused to recognize the Mexican government under Huerta, and fear of communism withheld recognition of the Soviet Union in 1917. The United States finally recognized the Soviet Union in 1933 in the hope of increasing trade.

8. **(D)** Jamaica was captured by the English in 1655. By 1713 England owned the Hudson Bay area. After 1763 the French were gone. The year 1783 doesn't fit because the United States had already been established.

9. **(A)** Published in 1852, *Uncle Tom's Cabin* set off a storm of Southern protest. Southerners claimed that the Yankee's book on slavery distorted the facts. Harriet Beecher Stowe had spent just a short time in Kentucky, but was well read in all the antislavery writings of the period. Her characters were fictional but quite real. *Uncle Tom's Cabin* was one of the three best selling novels of the 19th century. (The other two were *Ben-Hur* and *Looking Backward, 2000–1887*.) Her book sold 5,000 copies in two days and over 1.5 million in five years.

10. **(E)** Two-thirds approval of the Senate only is needed for ratifying the nominations of cabinet members and federal judges.

11. **(A)** Cyrus McCormick invented the mechanical reaper used to harvest wheat. Eli Whitney invented both the cotton gin and the principle of interchangeable parts for rifles.

12. **(B)** In the religious turmoil of 17th century England a Separatist wanted to disassociate himself from the Church of England, which was too corrupt and inert ever to correct its many wrongs. The Pilgrims were Separatists; the Puritans were not. The Puritans fought to purify the Church of England either by staying in England to fight or by going to New England to become such a brilliant example of the purified Church that the mother country would imitate New England. This is the "mission in the wilderness" or "city upon a hill" concept. This attitude helps explain why the Puritans would not tolerate shortcomings, for they were rescuing an entire nation.

13. **(C)** Peggy O'Neale married Jackson's Secretary of War, John Eaton. Her questionable background caused socially conscious wives of cabinet members to shun White House social functions. Jackson, remembering his wife's ill treatment, sided with his old Tennessee friend and his charming young wife. Eventually the entire cabinet was forced to resign in a face-saving gesture. Calhoun clearly saw that the presidency lay beyond his grasp, but not the defense of his beloved South.

14. **(E)** Justice Black wrote this dissenting opinion in *Connecticut General Life Insurance Co. v. Johnson*, 1938. He attacked the fifty-year-old Supreme Court interpretation that the Fourteenth Amendment prohibition against denying "any person of life, liberty, or property, without due process of law" applied to corporations. Corporations often used the Fourteenth Amendment to protect themselves in court against government regulations that took away their "property" rights.

15. **(E)** On March 4, 1933, thirty-eight states had closed their banks, and in the other states banks were severely restricted. Most historians would jokingly say that the Brain Trust (originally called the Brains Trust) was never organized. There was too much infighting for any semblance of organization. The fervent opposition of Father Coughlin, Huey Long, and Dr. Townsend came after the honeymoon of the Hundred Days. President Hoover and Secretary of State Stimson had wrestled with the Manchurian crisis in 1931–1932. Hitler invaded Poland in 1939, starting the Second World War.

16. **(A)** The winner by far is George Wallace in 1968, who received 9,906,473 popular votes and 46 electoral votes. The others received the following: Anderson, 5,581,379, and 0; Debs, 900,672 and 0; Weaver, 1,041,028 and 22; and LaFollette 4,822,856 and 13.

17. **(E)** The Barbary pirates had nothing to do with France. Don't let the 1778 date fool you. We were still allied with France under the Treaty of 1778.

18. **(C)** Even its opponents never questioned the Bank's record of providing a sound, stable currency. Despite Chief Justice Marshall's decision in *McCulloch* v. *Maryland*, Jackson considered the Bank of the United States to be unconstitutional. The other three were generally acknowledged by everyone at the time. Wealthy Bank stockholders and grateful congressmen enjoyed the plums that came their way.

19. **(A)** Clay, Hamilton, and Webster all endorsed industry and commerce over agriculture. Thomas Jefferson wrote in his *Notes on Virginia* (1785) that agriculture was the basis for a republican society. Manufacturing meant dependence on others, urban poor, and unruly mobs. Debs was a labor leader from a much later period.

20. **(B)** The Clark Memorandum in 1928 repudiated the Roosevelt Corollary. The Clark Memorandum asserted that the Monroe Doctrine existed to defend the Americas against European intervention, not to justify U.S. domination. We could still intervene, but the Monroe Doctrine didn't give us that right! The 1933 Montevideo Conference agreement denied the right of any American government to intervene in the external or internal affairs of another American government. The 1940 Act of Havana provided for the takeover of European colonies in the Americas if the mother country had fallen to European dictators. Its most important agreement was to declare an attack on one American republic to be an attack on all the American republics. In essence, the Monroe Doctrine was multilateralized. This position was restated in the Act of Chapultepec in 1945 with the additional provision that the signers agree to consult

with one another in the case of aggression. Unlike the Act of Havana, the Act of Chapultepec applied to any aggression, including one American republic against another. The Dawes and Young plans concerned German reparations in the 1920s.

21. **(B)** Federal judges are appointed for life in order to place them beyond popular control. Although federal judges may be impeached, this mechanism is rarely used. The electoral college was designed to put layers of knowledgeable republicans between the chaotic masses and the chief executive. The electoral college was an undemocratic feature of the Constitution, and the Founding Fathers were quite proud of it. United States senators serve for six years, and one-third of the Senate is up for reelection every two years. The Senate's purpose was to serve as a cooling mechanism for the potentially volatile House of Representatives. All the members of the House of Representatives are elected every two years, making the House the most popularly responsive part of the federal government.

22. **(D)** *Munn* v. *Illinois*, one of the Granger cases, concerned an 1873 Illinois law. Since the case involved intrastate, not interstate, commerce, the state of Illinois had not overstepped its authority and infringed upon the federal government's.

23. **(C)** Thoreau's essay served as a catalyst for Gandhi and Martin Luther King, Jr. Without the concept of disobedience to an unjust law, neither movement would have succeeded as it did.

24. **(B)** The quotation is from the Brown decision, which reversed the "separate but equal" decision of *Plessy* v. *Ferguson*. They both deserve a long look from students. The Schempp case involved school prayer. The West Virginia case concerned saluting the flag. The Bakke case involved reverse discrimination. A white was excluded from admission to a medical school because a certain percentage of admissions were held open for minorities. Bakke scored higher on the entrance exam than the minority applicants, but not high enough to qualify for the admission slots open for whites.

25. **(E)** *Adkins* v. *Children's Hospital* declared unconstitutional an act of Congress which authorized the Wage Board of the District of Columbia to establish minimum wages for women, not maximum hours for children.

26. **(D)** The Republicans won the presidency for all but eight years between 1860 and 1912, but rarely controlled both houses of Congress. A quick glance at the presidents gives the impression that Republicans dominated from 1860 to 1912. A closer look doesn't support that conclusion. Lincoln, Garfield, and McKinley were assassinated in this period. Lincoln, Grant, and McKinley were all reelected. Third parties won many popular and electoral votes between 1860 and 1896, especially the Greenback Labor Party in 1880 and the Populist Party in 1892. Lincoln in 1860, Hayes in 1876, Garfield in 1880, and Cleveland in 1892 all won the presidency with less than 50% of the total popular vote for all candidates. The electoral vote count in 1876 was Hayes 185, Tilden 184.

27. **(D)** In a farewell speech on January 17, 1961, Eisenhower raised the specter of "the military-industrial complex." Before 1940 the United States hadn't had a tradition of a standing army, but the days of the instant militia were gone. Thus, a grave fear existed that this new element in American life would somehow change American values over a period of time. We shall see. As one historian said, by 1960 the United States entered a new age, leaving the age of security. The oceans no longer protected us; missiles could cross the Atlantic Ocean in minutes.

28. **(A)** Langston Hughes is associated with the 1920s Harlem Renaissance, an era when white Americans discovered black poets, novelists, authors, etc. *The Philadelphia Negro*, published in 1899, was a pioneering sociological study of a black neighborhood in Philadelphia. Myrdal's *An American Dilemma*, published in 1944, was a comprehensive indictment of American race relations. *The Autobiography of Malcolm X* (1966) was a statement by an early black power advocate. John Howard Griffin's electrifying *Black Like Me* stunned white America when published in 1960. A white journalist, Griffin medically treated his skin to appear black. A white man inside a black body, he traveled throughout the South, and experienced what it meant to be black in the white man's world.

29. **(E)** Alaska was purchased for $7,200,000 from Russia in 1867 after the prodding of Secretary of State Seward.

30. **(A)** Following the San Francisco earthquake of 1906 the school board caused an uproar by designating a special school for older Japanese boys. The incident raised hackles in Japan that were finally pacified by the Gentleman's Agreement in 1907. Japan promised to no longer issue passports to Japanese headed for the United States, and the United States promised not to specifically exclude Japanese from American soil. The 1868 Burlingame Treaty between the United States and China recognized China's sovereignty and territorial integrity in exchange for continued Chinese immigration into the United States, with the stipulation of possible withholding of naturalization for Chinese immigrants. Woodrow Wilson landed the Marines at Tampico in 1914, part of the almost unfathomable strife between the United States and Mexico in this period. The Insular Cases in 1901 and 1902 concerned the question of the Constitution following the flag. Did natives of newly acquired territory automatically enjoy full rights under the Constitution? The Supreme Court ruled that not all constitutional rights applied.

31. **(C)** He was referring to Shays's Rebellion, which disturbed conservatives throughout the country. The Newburgh Conspiracy took place after the Revolutionary War had ended. Some army officers plotted to take over the despicably weak Congress and put George Washington in charge, but Washington put a stop to it. The Whiskey Rebellion was a local event. Shays's Rebellion was also local, but many areas looked ripe for similar uprisings, since law and order seemed to be breaking down.

32. **(C)** Stephen Crane lived a short but productive life. He is best remembered for *The Red Badge of Courage* and *Maggie: A Girl of the Streets*.

33. **(B)** In the period immediately following the Civil War the Freedman's Bureau improved the lot of thousands of newly freed black slaves.

34. **(B)** Like the Shayites the Populists believed that the political system was unresponsive and the judiciary was narrowly concerned with enforcing contracts and forcing the payment of debts. The Whiskey Rebellion was caused by taxes.

35. **(D)** Organized labor considered the Taft-Hartley Act and the Landrum-Griffin Act to be antilabor. The Taft-Hartley Act outlawed the closed shop (a worker had to belong to a union in order to get a job); permitted states to pass "right-to-work" laws banning the union shop (a worker had to join the union after he got the job); prohibited unions from making political contributions; provided for a sixty day "cooling off" period after a union-management agreement expired (declared by the president if he felt the strike could endanger the safety of the public); and prohibited communists from holding union offices.

Aimed at union corruption, the Landrum-Griffin Act regulated union elections and supervised union finances. Some picketing was restricted and most secondary boycotts eliminated.

The Fair Labor Standards Act created the minimum wage and maximum hours concept, and also ended child labor in interstate commerce. The Wagner Act gave unions the right to organize and bargain collectively, and outlawed a number of antilabor management practices. Also known as the National Labor Relations Act, the Wagner Act established the National Labor Relations Board, empowered to issue cease and desist orders and to adjudicate charges of unfair labor practices.

36. **(E)** Johnson believed the domino theory was valid. Just as a line of dominoes falls over after the first one goes, so would all the countries of Southeast Asia fall to communism. After the final French defeat in Vietnam at Dien Bien Phu in 1954, a meeting in Geneva salvaged something out of the situation. Vietnam was temporarily divided into North and South Vietnam. Within a few years national elections were supposed to have determined which single leader would rule Vietnam. The elections were never held in South Vietnam because Ho Chi Minh, the communist hero of the anti-French guerrilla forces, was certain to win. Thus, the United States backed the temporary government of Diem in South Vietnam, a notoriously repressive regime. The United States was eventually drawn into the civil war that developed in Vietnam, which finally ended in 1975, two years after all American troops had left Vietnam. Millions of Americans opposed our participation in the war because political leaders were unable to convince them that the Vietnam war was essential to our national security.

37. **(C)** The decade of the 1790s is crucial for students of American history. You must know the differences between the Federalists and the Democrats (also called Republicans or Democratic-Republicans or Jeffersonians). The Federalists saw in Great Britain a government and society that the United States should imitate. France represented radical revolution, Great Britain stable evolution. Federalists favored a loose interpretation of the Constitution. If it wasn't prohibited, you could do it. The Federalists, or most of them, sponsored the Alien and Sedition Acts to clamp down upon the radical Democratic-Republicans. The Federalist leaders were Adams, Hamilton, Jay, and Pinckney. Hamilton, secretary of the treasury under Washington, pushed through Congress his idea to pay the national debt at par.

38. **(E)** All of the clues point to the colonial era, such as high death rates, waves of immigrants, harsh conditions of life, etc.

39. **(A)** The quote is from the delightful little book, *Plunkitt of Tammany Hall,* first published in 1905. George Washington Plunkitt, ward boss of the New York City Fifteenth Assembly District, revealed his honest opinions to newspaperman William Riordon. The chapter on reformers in politics is entitled, "Reformers Only Mornin' Glories." Morning glories are flowers that bloom early in the day and quickly retreat.

40. **(D)** The Wilmot Proviso passed the House of Representatives but not the Senate, and aroused bitter feelings in the South. The Southern reaction proved to abolitionists that the Mexican War had been a plot to expand slavery. The Compromise of 1850 temporarily resolved the issue of slavery in the territories acquired from Mexico.

41. **(D)** Leopold and Loeb, two college students, killed a stranger for the thrill of it, shocking many who wondered about the continuation of old-fashioned values in the new urban society. Two other events associated with the Twenties, the Scopes trial and the Sacco and Vanzetti case, were strong symbols, but not of immoral decadence.

42. **(A)** Five of the original thirteen began as proprietary colonies and became royal colonies: North Carolina, South Carolina, Georgia, New York, and New Jersey. Three began as charter colonies and became royal colonies: Virginia, Massachusetts, and New Hampshire. Maryland began as a proprietary colony and became a royal colony, but was restored to proprietary status in 1715. Delaware and Pennsylvania remained proprietary colonies. Rhode Island and Connecticut were charter colonies.

43. **(D)** The quote represents the position of Truman and the Joint Chiefs of Staff in response to General MacArthur's suggestion to enlarge the scope of the Korean War by an attack on mainland China. Truman fired MacArthur for insubordination for publically questioning United States policy in Korea. In this episode MacArthur produced two well-known quotes. "There is no substitute for victory." "Old soldiers never die; they just fade away." Korea was a limited war, limited in objectives, tactics, scope, and weapons. Many Americans did not accept this new type of warfare. To the President and the Joint Chiefs of Staff the primary concern was Europe, not Asia; the principal enemy Russia, not China.

44. **(C)** Neither Carnegie nor Morgan advocated giving the federal government any control over corporations. Woodrow Wilson and William Jennings Bryan leaned toward a philosophy of laissez-faire competition. The conservative Theodore Roosevelt steered a middle course by differentiating between the bad and the reasonable corporation. The famous trustbuster in reality busted few trusts in comparison to other Progressives.

45. **(D)** Southern conservative Democrats and conservative Republicans joined forces to frustrate FDR. The alliance worked because congressional seniority rules put Southerners in charge of many committees. As committee chairmen the Southerners blocked, or forced changes in, liberal legislation. Congressional politics continued to operate this way for over forty years, leading one senator to write a book entitled, *Four Party Politics*. Our nation had four parties, not two. They were the Democrats, Republicans, and congressional Democrats and congressional Republicans.

    The AAA was passed in 1933, the CCC in 1933; the RFC had been passed under Hoover in 1932. The Progressive and Dixiecrat split came in 1948 when Truman ran for reelection. The Supreme Court, partially responding to public opinion, began to invalidate fewer New Deal measures. Farm price supports ended much later.

46. **(B)** The government described is the Articles of Confederation. The three powers mentioned—enforcing laws, taxing directly, and regulating commerce—were granted to the federal government under the Constitution. Neither the Northwest Ordinance nor the League of Nations were governments. The colonies did not coordinate their efforts and never had a unified government during the French and Indian War. Remember the Albany Plan of Union?

47. **(A)** Southern apologists writing immediately after the Civil War claimed that the war was a constitutional squabble over states' rights. This is why some Southerners still prefer calling it the War Between the States. Progressive era historians emphasized economic and class struggle as themes in American history. Charles Beard saw two competing classes which just happened to also have been divided geographically into a planter aristocracy and a rising industrial class. The First World War, fought to save the world for democracy, left many intellectuals disillusioned. Historians now saw a needless fanaticism in all wars, especially apparent in the 1850s. The rise of a congressional conservative coalition in the late 1930s and the Dixiecrat revolt of 1948 led to a reexamination of the impact of sectionalism on national political parties in the late 1930s and 1940s.

Slavery is the one interpretation that was always present as a secondary explanation or even primary cause of the Civil War. As Lincoln said in his second inaugural address, "All know that slavery was somehow the cause of the war." Historians may disagree over exactly how it caused the war; but it was the one indispensable ingredient of the Civil War.

48. **(D)** Three foreigners gave distinguished service to the American Revolution. Lafayette participated in both revolutions, but not as a pamphleteer. Von Steuben drilled the new troops at Valley Forge. Kosciusko served as the chief engineer in the army. John Paul Jones was the hero of the American navy and later led the Russian navy. Paine wrote *Common Sense* and other incendiary pamphlets. Distressed by the calm at the end of the American Revolution, he traveled to England to incite revolution. Bitterly disappointed, he revived when the mob stormed the Bastille. Unable to read or write French, he joined the French Revolution and was elected to the revolutionary legislature.

49. **(B)** These quotations are from the Atlanta Exposition Address by Booker T. Washington in 1895, nicknamed the "Atlanta Compromise." He stressed vocational preparation for eventual full citizenship rather than seeking political and social equality. Booker T. Washington secretly financed law suits against Jim Crow laws, but publically he counseled patience. W.E.B. DuBois offered opposing advice.

50. **(C)** Even after the Republican victory in the congressional election of 1918 Wilson continued on as before. Confident that his cause was just, Wilson failed to make mid-course corrections that might have secured the League of Nations treaty. The war ended November 11, 1918. Despite Democratic Party losses, the overwhelming majority of the country and the Senate favored some kind of system of collective security. Teddy Roosevelt was extremely bitter toward Wilson, and his analysis of the situation was personal rather than analytical.

51. **(D)** Most Americans feel insulted when they discover that we were not the most important part of the British colonial system. As a British historian once explained, the British empire was primarily Indian, naval, and then colonial. India and the quest to secure India was uppermost. Next came the needs of the navy for ports, supplies, etc., and other trade considerations. The imperial system was never systematic, and it was never important enough to be so. The British government underwent momentous alterations in the 1603–1760 period. The era between the accession of James I and George III was characterized by bitter struggles between king and Parliament and within Parliament itself between the House of Commons and the House of Lords. The concept of legitimate opposition developed during this struggle; outspoken disagreement with the government was not necessarily treason. No one institution within the British government held responsibility for the colonies. That responsibility was diffused throughout many different institutions, such as the Board of Trade, Parliament, the navy, etc.

52. **(B)** In 1815 Webster, like most New Englanders, feared that a high tariff would inhibit shipping and commerce. By 1830, though, the region's future clearly lay in industrialization more than shipping, and protective tariffs protected American industries from foreign competition. Choice (A) did occur, but nationalism was not the reason for Webster's switch. Only the first part of (C) is correct. Political parties never determine their stands based on that of their opponents, and the areas of agreement between parties far outnumber those of disagreement. Free trade is the opposite of a protective tariff. Clay's American system included a Bank of the United States and a high tariff,

with the proceeds being used to fund internal improvements. Webster didn't sell his support (or soul) to Clay nor to anyone else. (Ask your English teacher about the short story, "The Devil and Daniel Webster.")

53. **(E)** Yugoslavia initiated the opposition to Moscow-run international communism. Marshall Tito's native communist guerrillas had liberated Yugoslavia from the Germans, and the Second World War ended with no Soviet troops in Yugoslavia. This permitted the establishment of a strong, nationalist communist government which later rejected Moscow's dictates. Hungary revolted against Soviet rule in 1956, only to be viciously repressed. China proved too large to be a satellite and never was under Soviet domination. Almost more Asian than European, Albania broke with the Soviet Union over ideological differences, and sided more with Communist China. Cuba has never given the Soviet Union trouble, except to drain money out of the Soviet treasury to prop up the Castro government and economy.

54. **(A)** Choice (A) is not correct because of the word "Federalist." If the statement read "Republican" newspaper editors it would be correct.

55. **(C)** African blacks possessed two distinguishing features, racial color and heathen status, that set them apart from whites. Over a period of time this perception of differences combined with a severe labor shortage, especially in the South, to produce a form of servitude unique to the English. Black slavery never existed in Great Britain before a few slaves were brought from the colonies. Blacks came from a more advanced culture than the American Indians, who were impossible to enslave because Indian males simply refused to do a woman's task. To them, death was more honorable.

56. **(B)** The Webster-Hayne debate in 1830 began over federal land policy. New Englanders sought to slow the sale of western public land because as population shifted westward New England's political power dissipated. The South joined the West in a fierce counterattack. Senator Hayne of South Carolina brought up the issue of nullification and the nature of the union. Webster replied that our nation was one of *united* states, not united *states*. It was poor history, but he was probably correct in describing the actual political thinking of the day. He closed his speech with "Liberty and Union, now and forever, one and inseparable."

57. **(B)** The map shows a divided Germany, or post-Second World War Germany. The NATO nations are shown. The Warsaw Pact is the Eastern European counterpart to NATO.

58. **(E)** The Quebec Act solved a vexing problem for the British. It secured the loyalty of 60,000 Frenchmen in the new British possession of Canada by guaranteeing the right to practice their Catholic faith. It also rearranged the borders by shifting the southern border of Quebec down to the Ohio River. This seemed logical because the trade orientation of the Great Lakes was through the St. Lawrence River. Since England owned all the colonies involved, the action to them resembled rearranging furniture in one's own home.

Americans had a different perception. Their land claims and original charters (often conflicting) gave them the land north of the Ohio River, and the Quebec Act dampened the area's potential for land speculators. The Quebec Act indirectly attacked representative government by not providing for representative government in Quebec. Anti-Catholics saw omnious threats in the extension of Catholicism to the Ohio River. To them, the Anglican Church, always dangerously close to Catholicism, had joined papal forces to hem in Protestantism along the coast. From the British point of view the act was quite successful. French Canadians remained loyal to the British when the colonies rebelled despite intense American efforts.

59. **(E)** German scientists were already in the United States. The chief of the German V-2 program, Wernher Von Braun, and over one hundred twenty of his colleagues were seized after the Second World War and brought to the United States to run our rocket research program. The other four were reactions to Sputnik, espècially the feeling that American education needed a boost.

60. **(D)** The difficulty of obtaining land in Europe depressed wages. In America the availability of land raised wages because workers had an alternative. The prevailing system of values encouraged land ownership as the highest form of personal independence and security. Many towns had minimum hours and maximum wage laws for some craftsmen in order to hold down prices. Mercantile restrictions on manufacturing were inconsequential. The guild system belonged more to the Middle Ages.

61. **(C)** This quotation is from Senator John C. Calhoun's last speech to the Senate on March 4, 1850, concerning the Compromise of 1850. A colleague delivered the speech for the dying Calhoun. Several phrases pinpoint the date of the speech: "the North has acquired a decided ascendency over every department;" a single section has control over "the entire powers of the system;" and "the South possesses no means by which it can resist."

The theory of concurrent majority called for majority approval in both sections on major issues dividing the sections. Against a federal law a state could use either "state interposition" (nullification), or a state veto, which went in effect until overruled by three-fourths of the states meeting in a special convention.

62. **(B)** Truman desegregated the armed forces in 1948 by Executive Order 9981. He never left the Southern Democrats in 1948; they left him to form the Dixiecrat Party. Not until after the Brown case did desegregation of the public schools begin. Movies, restaurants, and interstate travel came later. Franklin Roosevelt had ordered nondiscrimination in defense contracts at the beginning of the Second World War in Executive Order 8802.

63. **(A)** The Teller Amendment was attached to the joint resolution declaring war on Spain in 1898; the United States eschewed any territorial designs on Cuba. Don't confuse the Teller Amendment with the Platt Amendment, part of an army appropriations bill after the Spanish-American War ended. The Platt Amendment, eventually incorporated into the Cuban constitution and into a treaty between the United States and Cuba, made Cuba into a U.S. protectorate.

64. **(E)** Montesquieu's *The Spirit of Laws* (1748) declared that "separation of powers" and "checks and balances" best protected individual liberties in a republic. John Locke's *Second Treatise on Government* (1689) expounded the theory that man in nature inherently possessed certain rights such as life, liberty, and property. Governments are established by choice in the manner of a contract. Should the government break its obligations to the contract, the people are released from their obligations to the government, or free to rebel. Thus the people are the ultimate source of political authority.

65. **(B)** Garfield's assassination led to the Pendleton Act, creating the federal civil service system run by the Civil Service Commission. To everyone's surprise the new president,

the former New York spoilsman Chester A. Arthur, placed nearly ten percent of the federal offices under civil service. Each succeeding President enlarged the coverage to protect some of his own appointments. The nonpartisan independence of system benefited from the alternating parties of the next several presidents: Cleveland, Democrat; Harrison, Republican; Cleveland, Democrat; and McKinley, Republican.

66. **(A)** The Republicans captured the House and Senate in 1918 and 1946, and made life more difficult for Woodrow Wilson and Harry Truman. The United States joined NATO, but rejected the League of Nations with its Article X and overtures from France for a treaty of alliance. Quickly, name the treaty that ended the Second World War! There was no treaty comparable to the Versailles Treaty that ended the First World War. The United Nations was supposed to tackle those arrangements but the Cold War got in the way. The United States sent massive aid to Europe after only the Second World War. No depression struck after the Second World War but one did after the First.

67. **(C)** The first transcontinental railroad was the Central Pacific Railroad built eastward to meet the westward construction of the Union Pacific Railroad. They met at Promontory, Utah, in 1869.

68. **(C)** The Northern Securities Company was a holding company which owned three-fourths of the stock of the Northern Pacific and the Great Northern Railroad. The two parallel lines owned most of the stock in the Chicago, Burlington and Quincy, which connected the Northern Pacific and the Great Northern Railroad.

69. **(D)** Lincoln Steffens wrote the muckraking exposé, *The Shame of the Cities*. His book contains the classic indictment of boss-ridden Philadelphia, "the most corrupt and the most contented."

70. **(A)** Under President Charles de Gaulle France experienced a revival of nationalism, and asserted its traditional role as a leader in European affairs. Great Britain was regarded as too involved with its former colonies and the United States to be a true European nation. Thus, for years France blocked Great Britain's entry into the economic organization of Europe, the Common Market. Moving the headquarters of NATO removed an obnoxious American presence from French soil.

71. **(C)** Jefferson and Madison organized their party and built their following. Jacksonian Democracy existed before Jackson entered the scene. It is named for him because he came to symbolize the movement, but he had nothing to do with its origins or philosophy. Take Jefferson's ideas out of Jeffersonian Democracy and little is left. On the contrary, you might have trouble finding Jackson's intellectual contributions in Jacksonian Democracy.

72. **(C)** The Bill of Rights protected individuals from the federal government. Not until the Fourteenth Amendment and subsequent court interpretations did its guarantees also apply to state governments. Choice (E) is enticing, but the Founding Fathers didn't think in terms of minorities. To them a minority was what was left over when the majority won an election. No one used minorities in the sense of racial and ethnic minorities.

73. **(C)** Horatio Alger is one of those rarely read, much quoted authors. The heroes in his books were poor boys or orphans who climbed the lower rungs of the ladder of material

success, or middle-class children suddenly on their own due to their father's death or misfortune. Alger's heroes attained middle-class respectability, not massive wealth. Carnegie and Rockefeller represent the exception in the 19th century, not the norm. Most wealthy business executives started near or at the top. (William Vanderbilt inherited only $90 million. Within a short time he had $200 million.) Alger's heroes worked for someone else. To a great extent Alger praised the character traits of the loyal employee: thrift, punctuality, subservience, loyalty, etc. The businessmen in Alger's books, like the young heroes, have internalized Christian virtues, which solidify their inner strength and guide their small philanthropic acts. But religion is never worn as a badge of righteousness. The youth in the 19th century liked the adventure and luck in Alger's books; their fathers liked the respectable middle-class values of family, charity, and loyalty. Rugged individualism was not a middle-class value.

74. **(A)** The progressive income tax, both personal and corporate, theoretically shifts an ever increasing burden upon those most able to pay, and helps redistribute income. Unemployment compensation is a right only for those who have worked that cushions their loss of income, and keeps them as consumers to prevent endangering other parts of the economy. Aid to dependent children protects a segment of the population that has no political voice or clout.

Veterans benefits have nothing to do with the welfare state. Veterans' benefits stem from political pressure by lobby groups in our population that have virtually no opposition. By the 1930s the cost of Civil War veterans' benefits had exceeded the cost of the Civil War itself.

75. **(B)** Wilson's advocacy of the League of Nations at the Versailles Conference was based upon the concept of collective security; that is, an attack on one is an attack on all. His ideas bore fruit in the United Nations, NATO, SEATO, etc. William Jennings Bryan staunchly supported arbitration treaties, but the concept never caught on.

76. **(E)** The original Constitution did not contain a Bill of Rights, but the state constitutions did. The belief that George III had corrupted Parliament caused the states to include a system of checks and balances, a separation of powers, and a weak executive. Property qualifications for voting remained. This generation still believed in the "stake in society" theory, that those who owned property in the society should run it.

77. **(D)** The Half-Way Covenant, agreed to by the Ministerial Association in 1657, was adopted by the Massachusetts Synod in 1662. Full church membership remained restricted to those who had undergone a conversion experience, evidence of God's seal through a covenant of grace. Members who had not been so stricken but who lived a good life were not entitled to partake fully in the sacraments and voting rights of the church, and neither were their children. Robert Child's petition to Parliament attacked the congregational organization of the churches, decried restricting voting to church members, and demanded closer adherence to the laws of England. The Massachusetts Body of Liberties established a code of laws for the colony, replacing the possibly arbitrary whims of the civil magistrates. The Cambridge Platform defined the organization of the Puritan churches. They were individually controlled yet subject to synod authority, and civil authorities enforced synod dictates. The Pilgrims adopted the Mayflower Compact, not the Puritans.

78. **(D)** The Federal Farm Board was part of the McNary-Haugen Bill twice vetoed by Coolidge. The other four were problems suffered by Southern agriculture.

79. **(B)** These remarks by Matthew Vassar in 1865 illustrate the dominant opinion of the purpose of female education in the post-Civil War era. As befitting her natural responsibilities, a woman should first be trained to be a good wife and mother. If she must work, teaching, which is a form of mothering and nurturing, was the appropriate occupation. Other jobs were also open to women, but she should only work in those positions in "harmony with the gentleness and modesty of her sex." One wonders at the response a pioneer wife would have made to Vassar's remarks.

80. **(E)** The National Security Acts of 1947 and 1949 created the National Security Council to advise the President; the Central Intelligence Agency to coordinate information gathered through espionage; the Secretary and Department of Defense to coordinate the navy, army, and air force; and the Joint Chiefs of Staff to facilitate interservice actions.

81. **(B)** Hamilton proposed all six measures although Congress did not enact all of his proposals. The first truly protective tariff did not come to pass until 1816. The promotion of industry remained as a Federalist attitude but was never a policy of the federal government.

82. **(C)** The capital of Richmond was not captured until near the end of the war.

83. **(E)** The Pan American Union, originally called the International Bureau of American Republics, began in 1889 under Benjamin Harrison's administration. Hawaii was eventually annexed but under McKinley. The other three were unsuccessful.

84. **(A)** The Whiskey Rebellion took place in 1794 in Pennsylvania. Shays's Rebellion took place in 1786 in Massachusetts during the Articles of Confederation. The Whiskey Rebellion protested against Hamilton's excise tax on whiskey, which was designed more to impress the inhabitants of the West with the power of the federal government than to raise revenue. Squeezed by creditors, Massachusetts farmers protested against court confiscations of their farms for nonpayment of debts. President Washington put down the Whiskey Rebellion, not Shays's Rebellion. Both uprisings alarmed conservatives across the nation.

85. **(E)** Margaret Sanger was the pioneering crusader for birth control. Frances Willard led the Women's Christian Temperance Union for almost twenty years, and also lobbied for women's suffrage. Ida Tarbell wrote a scathing exposé of John D. Rockefeller's ruthlessness in building the Standard Oil Company. Jane Addams founded Hull House in Chicago in 1889, launching the settlement house movement in the United States. She branched out from working among the urban poor to women's suffrage and the peace movement, and was the co-winner of the Nobel Peace Prize in 1931. Charlotte Perkins Gilman, best remembered for *Women and Economics,* wrote about the need for women to achieve equality in all of its meanings in the new industrial society.

86. **(B)** Lyndon Johnson offered new federal government programs to meet the needs of the cities in his Great Society, but urban problems were growing faster than increased spending for cities.

87. **(B)** The quotation is from Lincoln's masterful second inaugural address. His call for a just and lasting peace was answered by Reconstruction.

88. **(A)** The electoral college was not part of the Great Compromise, which established the Senate and House and their respective responsibilities. Some political scientists claim

that the electoral college does overrepresent small states because the state's electoral votes are determined by the number of senators and representatives. Since each state is guaranteed two senators the state's national percentage of the population may be less than its national percentage of the members of Congress. As a practical matter, though, the awarding of all of a state's electoral votes to the winner within that state tends to overemphasize larger states, and to actually diminish the importance of smaller states. Americans invented the electoral college system, a unique contribution to government. It sought to avoid a popularly elected leader because popular election always led to demagoguery or the rise of a personal following such as political parties. Unfortunately for its creators, the electoral college fell victim to partisan political parties after George Washington's first two elections to the presidency.

89. **(E)** The antiwar demonstrators in the 1960s encountered little resistance from the authorities except in a few cases. The overall tone of American society had become open and tolerant. The other four represent intolerant events and periods in American history.

90. **(E)** Thomas Nast first used the elephant and the donkey together in a cartoon for the 1880 presidential campaign, but he had often used the two separately. The donkey symbol was already over fifty years old at the time.

91. **(A)** Americans are much more religious and churchgoing today than they were in the colonial era. Despite the many elementary school stories of religious freedom, the truth is that very few colonists came for that reason. Most came to improve their economic situation.

92. **(C)** Prohibition was to a large degree a small town and middle-class movement directed against the large cities with their immigrant, working-class populations. Samuel Gompers, the labor leader, called prohibition class legislation, and to a certain extent it was. Labor union leaders opposed prohibition because the saloon was the workingman's relaxation. Organized crime loved prohibition because it provided a ready market for bootleg liquor. Harding, Coolidge, and Hoover were only lukewarm in their support of prohibition.

93. **(A)** The issue of the constitutionality of an act of Congress did not appear again until the Dred Scott case. The decision found the Missouri Compromise of 1820 unconstitutional because the 36° 30' line deprived citizens of their right to the use of their property without following due process of law. *Worcester* v. *Georgia* concerned federal treaty supremacy over a state law trying to push the Cherokee Indians westward. *Cohens* v. *Virginia* dealt with federal jurisdiction to review state court decisions to judge if they violated rights guaranteed under the Constitution. The decision in *McCulloch* v. *Maryland* asserted the national sovereignty of the federal government and the constitutionality of the Bank of the United States. Finally, the Dartmouth College case declared that the sanctity of a contract was beyond the will of the people as expressed through their state legislature.

94. **(D)** In *The Shame of the Cities* Lincoln Steffens exposed corrupt municipal governments. The authors of the books are as follows: Upton Sinclair, *The Jungle*; Frank Norris, *The Octopus*; Henry Demarest Lloyd, *Wealth Against Commonwealth*; and John Spargo, *The Bitter Cry of the Children*.

95. **(E)** To Indians land was something to use rather than to own. Land belonged to everyone; thus the tribal council controlled the land. In white culture individuals

owned land, and each individual controlled the use of his land. This was one aspect of white culture that Indians could not seem to grasp.

96. **(D)** The National Recovery Administration, or NRA (the Blue Eagle), tried a partnership approach to restablize the economy during the early years of the New Deal. Overproduction was the country's villain. Thus, production was controlled to reduce competition and prevent waste. The "sick chicken" Schechter case mercifully ended the hodgepodge of almost unenforceable regulations of the NRA.

97. **(C)** There were six land acts passed between 1785 and 1834. The first two set 640 acres as the minimum unit one had to purchase. The next four acts—1800, 1804, 1820, and 1834—each cut the minimum in half, to 320, 160, 80, and 40 acres. The minimum accepted auction price was set at $1 in 1785, raised to $2 in 1796, and lowered in 1820 to $1.25. The terms of sale at first permitted partial purchase on credit. By 1820, however, the terms were cash. In 1785 one had to buy 640 acres at a minimum of $1 for a total of $640, a sizeable sum in that day. By 1820 one had to purchase only 80 acres for $1.25 per acre; in 1832 only 40 acres. Thus, by 1832 one needed only $50 to purchase land. The Pre-emption Act in 1841 gave squatters the right to purchase land at the minimum auction price. In 1854 the Graduation Act permitted lands unsold at the minimum auction price to be sold below the minimum. Finally, in 1862 the Homestead Act gave 160 acres (320 to married couples) to any settler who lived on the land and improved it. Giving away public land was a culmination of a long trend, not a sudden new departure in policy.

98. **(D)** Sacajawea was the female guide who led the Lewis and Clark Expedition. King Philip (Metacomet) led an uprising against the New England settlements in 1675–1676. Pontiac's Rebellion paralyzed the western Pennsylvania frontier at the end of the French and Indian War. Tecumseh fought with the British against the Americans during the War of 1812. Osceola, a Seminole leader, plagued federal troops for years in central Florida before he was captured through treachery.

99. **(B)** None of these three Republican presidents advocated reducing the defense budget. They all recognized an increased American responsibility to leading the Free World, but the methods for carrying out that responsibility have varied. The three generally tried to reduce the scope of the New Deal programs. Despite a few spectacular antitrust suits, big business was not strictly regulated by them. The common thread among them was their desire to reduce the responsibilities for many federal social, educational, and welfare programs.

100. **(B)** The Pujo Committee, formed in response to the panic of 1907, investigated the "money trust." Many of their investigations bore fruit during the Wilson administration in the Federal Trade Commission, the Clayton Antitrust Act, and the Federal Reserve. The House Committee on Un-American Activities (HUAC) was organized before the Second World War to search for subversives within the federal government. Senator Joseph McCarthy's committee continued the search in the early 1950s, and concentrated on ferreting out communists and communist sympathizers in the federal government. In the late 1950s the Kefauver Committee investigated organized crime. The 1934 Nye Committee investigated American bank loans to the Allies and the profits of American arms manufacturers, giving the impression that the "merchants of death" manipulated our entry into the First World War both to protect and to make huge profits.

Sample Test B

AMERICAN HISTORY

SECTION I

Time—1 hour and 15 minutes

100 Questions

Directions: *Each of the questions or incomplete statements below is followed by five suggested answers or completions. Select the one that is best in each case and then blacken the corresponding space on the answer sheet.*

1. Between 1820 and 1860 five million immigrants arrived in the United States. Most of them came from

   (A) Eastern and Southern Europe
   (B) Germany and Ireland
   (C) Great Britain and Italy
   (D) Poland and Russia
   (E) Poland and Italy

2. One of the characteristics of colonial America was frequent rebellions or uprisings against the political authorities. Which of the following was *not* an uprising in the colonial period?

   (A) Leisler's Rebellion
   (B) Paxton Boys
   (C) Whiskey Rebellion
   (D) Bacon's Rebellion
   (E) the Regulator Movement

3. "When an epidemic of physical disease starts to spread, the community approves and joins in a quarantine of the patients in order to protect the health of the community against the spread of the disease. . . .

   "War is a contagion, whether it be declared or undeclared. It can engulf states and peoples remote from the original scene of the hostilities. We are determined to keep out of war, yet we cannot insure ourselves against the disastrous effects of war and the dangers of involvement. We are adopting such measures as will minimize our risk of involvement, but we cannot have complete protection in a world of disorder in which confidence and security have broken down.

   "If civilization is to survive, the principles of the Prince of Peace must be restored. Trust between nations must be revived."

   On October 5, 1937, the League of Nations found Japan in violation of the Kellogg-Briand Pact and the Nine Power Treaty for its invasion of China. On the same day the president tried to awaken the people in his "quarantine the aggressors" speech. Which president made this speech?

   (A) Herbert Hoover
   (B) Dwight Eisenhower
   (C) Harry Truman
   (D) Theodore Roosevelt
   (E) Franklin Roosevelt

4. The first led to the second in all of the following *except*

   (A) bleeding Kansas led to the Sumner-Brooks affair
   (B) the Compromise of 1850 led to the Nashville Convention
   (C) the Kansas-Nebraska Act led to the birth of the Republican Party
   (D) the Lincoln-Douglas debates led to the Dred Scott decision
   (E) the 1860 secession crisis led to the Crittenden Compromise proposal

5. Most of the canals built in the era of internal improvements, 1815–1850, were built by state and local government. Most railroads built after this era were funded by private individuals

and corporations. How do you explain this difference?

(A) Private enterprise is always superior to public enterprise.

(B) The canals were only moderately successful financially, prompting most state governments to invest their money elsewhere.

(C) After expanding too rapidly, state governments were caught in the panic of 1837, which forced many states to repudiate their debts and caused them to prohibit the further use of governmental expenditures for internal improvements.

(D) More funds could be raised by private funding, permitting large projects such as railroad lines.

(E) As interstate corporations railroads came under the control of the federal Interstate Commerce Commission, which excluded state and local governments from building railroads.

6.   "The body of the people, governed by habit, will still retain their respective peculiarities of speaking; and for want of schools and proper books, fall into many inaccuracies, which, incorporating with the language of the state where they live, may imperceptibly corrupt the national language. Nothing but the establishment of schools and some uniformity in the use of books, can annihilate differences in speaking and preserve the purity of the American tongue. A sameness of pronunciation is of considerable consequence in a political view . . . .

"As an independent nation, our honor requires us to have a system of our own, in language as well as government. Great Britain, whose children we are, and whose language we speak, should no longer be *our* standard." This quotation is from the writings of

(A) Noah Webster
(B) Mevil Dewey
(C) Horace Mann
(D) Daniel Webster
(E) George Washington

7.   Most of the rationale for conservative opposition to the New Deal came from the argument that New Deal programs

(A) raised taxes on the rich
(B) regulated the stock market

(C) diminished the liberty of the individual
(D) favored the wealthy
(E) favored agriculture over big business

8.   "Conceding, therefore, in the fullest manner, that colored persons, the descendants of Africans, are entitled by law, in this commonwealth, to equal rights, constitutional and political, civil and social, the question then arises, whether the regulation in question, which provides separate schools for colored children, is a violation of any of these rights.

"In the absence of special legislation on this subject, the law has vested the power in the (local school) committee to regulate the system of distribution and classification (of students). . . . The committee, apparently upon great deliberation, have come to the conclusion, that the good of both classes of schools will be best promoted, by maintaining the separate primary schools for colored and for white children, and we can perceive no ground to doubt, that this is the honest result of their experience and judgment."

This quotation is from the Massachusetts court decision in *Roberts* vs. *City of Boston*, 1849. It foreshadowed a later decision which involved the U.S. Supreme Court case of

(A) *Minor* v. *Happensett*
(B) *Plessy* v. *Ferguson*
(C) *Gideon* v. *Wainwright*
(D) *Korematsu* v. *U.S.*
(E) *Brown* v. *Board of Education*

9.   Which of the following is *not* true concerning the relationship between Congress and the federal courts?

(A) Congress has the power to remove a piece of legislation from the jurisdiction of the federal courts.

(B) The Senate must approve the appointment of federal judges.

(C) The House of Representatives may impeach federal judges.

(D) Congress has the power to reduce or increase the number of Supreme Court judges.

(E) A two-thirds vote of both the House of Representatives and the Senate overrides a Supreme Court decision declaring an act of Congress to be unconstitutional.

10. All but one of the following is associated with the retail business in the three decades before 1910. Which is *not* associated with the retail business in this period?

    (A) Mail-order houses such as Montgomery, Ward & Co. and Sears, Roebuck & Co. expanded.

    (B) Brand name advertising such as Uneeda Biscuits began.

    (C) Chain stores such as the Atlantic and Pacific Co. (A & P) and Woolworth's 5 and 10 cent stores expanded.

    (D) Retailers concentrated more on rural than urban markets.

    (E) Mail-order houses opened retail stores in small and medium-sized cities.

11. McKinley officially urged the Senate to accept acquisition of the Philippines for all of the following reasons *except*

    (A) we couldn't give them back to Spain

    (B) someone else such as Germany may take the Philippines if we don't

    (C) the Filipinos were unfit for self-government

    (D) we were obligated to Christianize and civilize the Filipinos

    (E) the Philippines were a potential source for corporate business profits

National Debt of the United States Government

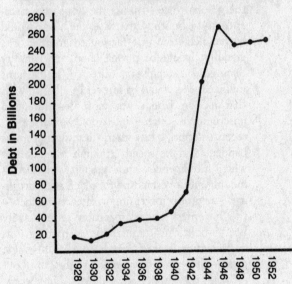

12. This graph indicates that

    (A) New Deal expenditures to fight the effects of the depression caused most of the increase in the national debt

    (B) the national debt grew mostly because of wartime expenditures

    (C) the rise in the national debt coincided with the Cold War

    (D) the national debt increased most when Republican presidents occupied the White House

    (E) expenditures for welfare and social programs caused the increase in the national debt

13. Which author shocked the American public in a best seller that warned against the misuse of chemical insecticides and pesticides such as DDT?

    (A) Rachel Carson

    (B) Betty Friedan

    (C) Jonas Salk

    (D) J. Robert Oppenheimer

    (E) Ralph Nader

14. How do you explain the hero worship of Charles Lindbergh and Babe Ruth during the 1920s?

    (A) Both men did something no one else had ever done before.

    (B) They showed the accomplishments possible through team effort.

    (C) They showed that individualism was still alive in a modern America of the corporation and the team player.

    (D) Their exploits took people's minds off the depression.

    (E) Both were associated with the isolationist cause to keep America out of Hitler's wars.

15. Many years after the Progressive movement the Kansas editor, William Allen White, jokingly remarked, "All we Progressives did was catch the Populists in swimming and steal all their clothing except the frayed underdrawers of Free Silver." Which Populist reform was *not* part of Progressivism?

    (A) direct primaries

    (B) an income tax

    (C) direct election of senators

    (D) initiative, referendum, recall

    (E) government ownership of railroads

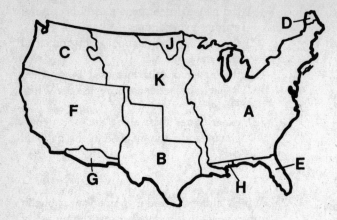

16. Which of the following statements is *not* correct? The U.S. acquired

(A) K and G by purchase.
(B) B by annexation.
(C) H and E by seizing it or by threatening to seize it.
(D) J and D through negotiated treaties.
(E) F and C by war conquest.

17. The British considered the Sugar Act of 1764 to be an improvement over the Molasses Act of 1733 because

(A) the tax rate was reduced
(B) a determined effort was made to collect the new tax
(C) the price of molasses was reduced, stimulating the rum trade
(D) the earlier act was part of the mercantilist philosophy
(E) colonial sugar was cheaper

18. He created an embarrassing crisis for the United States government. A general in the U.S. Army, he invaded Spanish territory with a state militia when we were not at war with Spain, and hanged two British citizens. His actions almost led to war with Great Britain and Spain. Cooler heads prevailed, though, and Spain, realizing she could not defend her possession, eventually ceded it to the United States. He was

(A) James Madison
(B) John Quincy Adams
(C) Commodore Dewey
(D) Theodore Roosevelt
(E) Andrew Jackson

19. Their thinking was dominated by the word covenant, one a covenant between God and the church and the other between the governed and the government. Who is described?

(A) Maryland Catholics
(B) Baptists in Rhode Island
(C) Pilgrims in Plymouth
(D) Puritans in Massachusetts
(E) Quakers in Pennsylvania

20. The Treaty of Alliance of 1778 with

(A) France was officially ended by Washington's Neutrality Proclamation
(B) France ended with the defeat of the British in 1783
(C) Great Britain ended when the countries declared war in 1812
(D) France ended with the Convention of 1800
(E) France is the only peacetime alliance the United States has ever had

21. "The clear and unmistakable domination of the white race, dominating not through violence, not through party alliance, but through the integrity of its own vote and the largeness of its sympathy and justice through which it shall compel the support of the better classes of the colored race—that is the hope and assurance of the South. Otherwise, the Negro would be bandied from one faction to another. His credulity would be played upon, his cupidity tempted, his impulses misdirected, his passions inflamed. He would be forever in alliance with that faction which was most desperate and unscrupulous. Such a state would be worse than reconstruction, for then intelligence was banded, and its speedy triumph assured. But with intelligence and property divided—bidding and overbidding for place and patronage—irritation increasing with each conflict—the bitterness and desperation seizing every heart—political debauchery deepening, as each faction staked its all in the miserable game—there would be no end to this, until our suffrage was hopelessly sullied, our people forever divided, and our most sacred rights surrendered." This passage was part of a speech delivered at the Dallas State Fair, October 26, 1887. This speech prophetically foresaw the

(A) difficulty that the Populists would encounter trying to build up a coalition of poor blacks and poor whites in the South

(B) conditions of Reconstruction

(C) impact the Spanish-American War had on Southern racial thinking

(D) end of school segregation and the use of force, as in the dispatching of federal troops to Little Rock, Arkansas, to integrate public schools

(E) rise of the Democratic Solid South, the political expression of the unity of whites in the South

22. Which of the following gained a reputation as an architect rather than as a painter?

(A) Gilbert Stuart
(B) Henry Sargent
(C) Frank Lloyd Wright
(D) James Whistler
(E) John Singleton Copley

23. Which of the following statements is *not* true concerning women in the 1970s compared to those in the 1920s?

(A) A higher percentage of women graduated from high school and college compared to the 1920s.

(B) There were more women doctors and lawyers compared to the 1920s.

(C) The percentage of women in the labor force was higher compared to the 1920s.

(D) There were more children being born, as measured by children per thousand fertile women, than in the 1920s.

(E) There were more women living as single persons in houses and apartments than in the 1920s.

24. A rabid anticommunist, he exploited the nation's fear of internal subversion in the early 1950s. His sensational charges of "fellow travelers" and "card-carrying Communists" excited the nation, but his irresponsibile charges quickly turned public opinion against him. Who is described?

(A) Adlai Stevenson
(B) Douglas MacArthur
(C) Jimmy Hoffa
(D) Joseph McCarthy
(E) Richard Nixon

25. Four of the following tried to restrict the powers of the president. Which doesn't belong with the others?

(A) Bricker Amendment, 1952
(B) War Powers Resolution, 1973
(C) Hartford Convention, 1814
(D) Gulf of Tonkin Resolution, 1964
(E) Ludlow Amendment, 1930s

26. "To be not only a best-seller in America but to be really beloved, a novelist must assert that all American men are tall, handsome, rich, honest, and powerful at golf; that all country towns are filled with neighbors who do nothing from day to day save go about being kind to one another; that although American girls may be wild, they change always into perfect wives and mothers; and that, geographically, America is composed solely of New York, which is inhabited entirely by millionaires; of the West, which keeps unchanged all the boisterous heroism of 1870; and of the South, where every one lives on a plantation perpetually glossy with moonlight and scented with magnolias. . . .

"We still most revere the writers for the popular magazines who in a hearty and edifying chorus chant that the America of a hundred and twenty million population is still as simple, as pastoral, as it was when it had but forty million; that in an industrial plant with ten thousand employees, the relationship between the worker and the manager is still as neighborly and uncomplex as in a factory of 1840, with five employees; that the relationships between father and son, between husband and wife, are precisely the same in an apartment in a thirty-story palace today, with three motor cars awaiting the family below and five books on the library shelves and a divorce imminent in the family next week, as were those relationships in a rose-veiled five-room cottage in 1880; that, in fine, America has gone through the revolutionary change from rustic colony to world-empire without having in the least altered the bucolic and Puritanic simplicity of Uncle Sam." This quotation is from the 1930 Nobel Prize acceptance speech by an American author whose literary themes attacked materialism and the small town mentality. Who is the author?

(A) Sinclair Lewis
(B) Upton Sinclair
(C) Theodore Dreiser
(D) H.L. Mencken
(E) F. Scott Fitzgerald

27. Which was *not* a result of the French and Indian War (Seven Years' War)?

(A) France lost Canada.
(B) Great Britain incurred high war costs.
(C) Great Britain gained Louisiana.
(D) Great Britain saw a need to tighten its administrative system.
(E) Great Britain made a decision to reinvigorate the mercantile system.

28. Some third-party presidential candidates have used a campaign strategy of trying to prevent either major party candidate from winning a majority of the electoral college votes. According to the Constitution, the House of Representatives, voting by states, would select the next president. The third-party candidates hoped at that time to possess a solid bloc of states in one section of the country to deliver to whichever candidate was willing to give in to their policies. Which of the following followed this campaign strategy?

(A) J. Strom Thurmond, 1948
(B) George Wallace, 1968
(C) Aaron Burr, 1800
(D) John Quincy Adams, 1824
(E) Theodore Roosevelt, 1912

29. The Federal Reserve Act of 1913

(A) set up a banking system that successfully prevented future depressions
(B) was intended to create a more elastic currency
(C) ended the National Bank system started in 1863
(D) represented a victory for Wall Street bankers and financiers
(E) was similar to a suggestion proposed by Theodore Roosevelt during his administration

30. List the following in their correct chronological order.

I. Nullification crisis
II. Tariff of Abominations
III. South Carolina Exposition and Protest
IV. Compromise Tariff of 1833

(A) I, II, III, IV
(B) I, IV, II, III
(C) III, IV, I, II
(D) II, III, I, IV
(E) I, III, II, IV

31. "There are at the present time two great nations in the world . . . the Russians and the Americans. . . . They have suddenly placed themselves in the front rank among the nations. . . .

"All other nations seem to have nearly reached their natural limits, and they have only to maintain their power; but these are still in the act of growth. All the others have stopped, or continue to advance with extreme difficulty; these alone are proceeding with ease and celerity along a path to which no limit can be perceived. The American struggles against the obstacles that nature opposes to him; the adversaries of the Russian are men. The former combats the wilderness and savage life; the latter, civilization with all its arms. The conquests of the American are therefore gained by the plowshare; those of the Russian by the sword. The Anglo-American relies upon personal interest to accomplish his ends and gives free scope to the unguided strength and common sense of the people; the Russian centers all the authority of society in a single arm. The principal instrument of the former is freedom; of the latter, servitude. Their starting-point is different and their courses are not the same; yet each of them seems marked out by the will of Heaven to sway the destinies of half the globe." This astounding statement is from a book, *Democracy in America*, published early in the 19th century by a foreign observer. The author was

(A) Jenny Lind
(B) James Bryce
(C) Francis Trollope
(D) Lafayette
(E) Alexis de Tocqueville

32. In *The American Commonwealth* James Bryce, a British citizen, pointed out the defects of the

American political system. He found "a certain apathy among the luxurious classes . . . disgusted by the superficial vulgarities of public life" and "laxity in the management of public business." "The tone of public life is lower than one expects to find in so great a nation." ". . . in no country is the ideal side of public life . . . so ignored by the mass and repudiated by the leaders." City government was "the one conspicuous failure of the United States." Bryce's observations were corroborated in a novel written by Charles Dudley Warner and Mark Twain. What period of American history was Bryce describing?

(A) the Progressive era
(B) the 1920s
(C) the Gilded Age
(D) the 1960s
(E) the years from 1830 to 1860

33.　"What, to the American slave, is your Fourth of July? I answer; a day that reveals to him, more than all other days in the year, the gross injustice and cruelty to which he is the constant victim. To him, your celebration is a sham; your boasted liberty, an unholy license; your national greatness, swelling vanity; your sounds of rejoicing are empty and heartless; your denunciation of tyrants, brass-fronted impudence; your shouts of liberty and equality, hollow mockery; your prayers and hymns, your sermons and thanksgivings, with all your religious parade and solemnity, are, to him, mere bombast, fraud, deception, impiety, and hypocrisy—a thin veil to cover up crimes which would disgrace a nation of savages. There is not a nation on the earth guilty of practices more shocking and bloody than are the people of the United States, at this very hour.

　"Go where you may, search where you will, roam through all the monarchies and despotisms of the Old World, travel through South America, search out every abuse, and when you have found the last, lay your facts by the side of the everyday practices of this nation, and you will say with me that, for revolting barbarity and shameless hypocrisy, America reigns without a rival." This stinging speech, entitled "The Meaning of July Fourth for the Negro," was delivered at Rochester, New York in 1852 by

(A) Elijah Lovejoy
(B) Denmark Vesey

(C) Frederick Douglass
(D) Nat Turner
(E) William Lloyd Garrison

34. Out of over one thousand individual items identified in the 1860 tariff customs reports, one city was the leader in all but seven American exports and all but twenty-four foreign imports. Which of the following was this leading U.S. seaport?

(A) Boston
(B) Philadelphia
(C) Baltimore
(D) New Orleans
(E) New York City

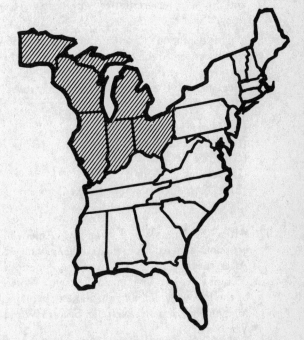

35. Which of the following are associated between 1776 and 1800 with the shaded area on the map?

　I. Northwest Ordinance
　II. Land Ordinance of 1785
　III. Whiskey Rebellion
　IV. squabbles among the states over western land claims
　V. the admission of two of the first three states to join the original thirteen

(A) I, II, IV, and V only
(B) I, III, IV, and V only
(C) I, II, III, and IV only
(D) I, II, and IV only
(E) II, III, and V only

36. "Not only, as we have shown, is the federal power over external affairs in origin and essential character different from that over internal affairs, but participation in the exercise of the power is significantly limited. In this vast external realm, with its important, complicated, delicate and manifold problems, the President alone has the power to speak or listen as a representative of the nation. He *makes* treaties with the advice and consent of the Senate; but he alone negotiates. Into the field of negotiation the Senate cannot intrude; and Congress itself is powerless to invade it. As Marshall said . . . 'The President is the sole organ of the nation in its external relations, and its sole representative with foreign nations.' "

This quotation is from a court case in 1936, which confirmed the complete authority of the President over foreign affairs. As a President once stated, "I am American foreign policy." What was the court case?

(A) *Marbury* v. *Madison*
(B) the Insular cases
(C) *Baker* v. *Carr*
(D) *Schenck* v. *U.S.*
(E) *U.S.* v. *Curtiss-Wright Export Corp.*

37. After the First World War the American economy suffered from high unemployment. After the Second World War the American economy avoided high unemployment. Which of the following did *not* contribute to avoiding high unemployment after the Second World War?

(A) The G.I. Bill took thousands of veterans out of the labor market.
(B) Many women left the labor force because they considered their Second World War service to be a temporary patriotic duty.
(C) The Employment Act of 1946 committed the federal government to following policies to achieve full employment.
(D) The depression following the Second World War was not as severe as the one following the First.
(E) Maintaining a peacetime army after the Second World War required many in the armed forces, unlike the experience after the First World War.

38. The Democratic Party candidate, John W. Davis, received 8,386,503 votes (28.8% of the popular vote) and 136 electoral votes. A third party candidate, Robert La Follette, received 4,822,856 votes (16.6% of the popular vote) and 13 electoral votes. Who won this election?

(A) Wilson in 1912
(B) Lincoln in 1860
(C) Truman in 1948
(D) Coolidge in 1924
(E) Roosevelt in 1912

39. What do the "sick chicken" Schechter decision and Jefferson's opposition to Hamilton's Bank of the United States proposal have in common?

(A) Both involved the "necessary and proper" or elastic clause.
(B) Both involved opposition to direct taxation by the federal government.
(C) Both involved attempts to control inflation through banking.
(D) Both involved the issue of federal control of interstate commerce.
(E) Both involved the question of Congress illegally delegating its powers, to the NRA and to the Bank.

40. John Dewey was associated with

(A) the establishment of the junior high school
(B) campaigning for child labor laws
(C) the "back-to-basics" movement
(D) progressive education
(E) the establishment of tax-supported public schools

41. Which of the following is in correct chronological order?

(A) Pontiac's Rebellion, Proclamation of 1763, Boston Massacre, Boston Tea Party
(B) Boston Tea Party, Boston Massacre, Stamp Act, Olive Branch Petition
(C) Stamp Act, Proclamation of 1763, Quebec Act, battles of Lexington and Concord
(D) Boston Massacre, Boston Tea Party, Declaration of Independence, Stamp Act
(E) Quebec Act, Townshend Acts, Stamp Act, Stamp Act Congress

42. Which of the following were manifestations of the small town anti-urban impulse of the 1920s?

    I. prohibition
    II. fundamentalism
    III. immigration restriction
    IV. Ku Klux Klan
    V. election of 1928

    (A) I, II, and III only
    (B) I, II, III, IV, and V
    (C) II, III, and V only
    (D) II, III, and IV only
    (E) I, II, III, and IV only

43. In a ringing speech John F. Kennedy said that those who don't understand what the confrontation between the Soviet Union and the Western democracies was all about should visit "an island of freedom in a Communist Sea . . . . a beacon of hope behind the Iron Curtain, an escape hatch for refugees . . . the great testing place of Western courage and will." To what was Kennedy referring?

    (A) South Korea
    (B) West Berlin
    (C) South Vietnam
    (D) Laos
    (E) Cuba

44. Which best explains the rise of political parties in the 1790s?

    (A) Hamilton and Jefferson's personal dislike for one another
    (B) a continuation of the Loyalist-Revolutionaries split of the Revolutionary War era
    (C) a continuation of the division of those for and against (the Antifederalists) the ratification of the Constitution
    (D) the desire of Washington for two distinct viewpoints on policy issues so that he could evaluate the issues to select the better course of action
    (E) differing ideology and viewpoints accented by disagreements over the establishment of a national bank; the payment of the foreign, national, and state debts; our foreign policies; and the Alien and Sedition Acts

45. In 1850 the federal government owned 1.4 billion acres of unoccupied land in the West.

Including the acreage granted by state governments, the railroads received over 223 million acres in land grants in the next thirty years to encourage the building of railroads. Which of the following statements is *not* true concerning land grants to the railroads?

    (A) Corruption of public officials accompanied land grants.
    (B) Most of the railroads were built without government funds.
    (C) Railroad land grants accomplished the objective of the government—to bring the area under settlement as quickly as possible.
    (D) Granting government subsidies to private industry represented a break with previous laissez-faire practices.
    (E) The federal government paid subsidies based on the terrain the railroad crossed.

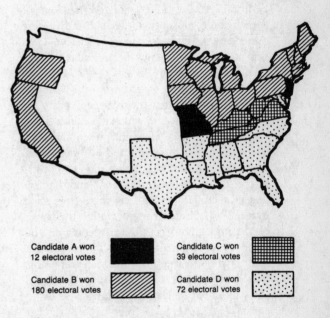

Candidate A won 12 electoral votes

Candidate C won 39 electoral votes

Candidate B won 180 electoral votes

Candidate D won 72 electoral votes

46. This map shows the election of

    (A) 1824
    (B) 1860
    (C) 1912
    (D) 1800
    (E) 1948

47. In the late 19th century numerous protest books appeared which became best sellers. What is the best explanation for the commercial success of *Progress and Proverty, Looking Backward, 2000–1887,* and *Coin's Financial School?*

(A) These works represented a continuation of the Transcendentalist theme in American literature.

(B) These works promoted the popular new idea of socialism.

(C) These works reflected widespread concern over the maldistribution of wealth accompanying industrialization.

(D) These works supported the theme of the Social Gospel.

(E) These works provided insight into the methods of the entrepreneurs that were imitated by small businessmen.

48. *Schenck* v. *U.S.* (1919) and *Abrams* v. *U.S.* (1919) both involved the question of whether or not the Espionage Act of 1917 and the Sedition Act of 1918 violated freedom of speech and press guaranteed by the First Amendment. The decision in *Schenck* v. *U.S.* was unanimous; Schenck's conviction was upheld. The decision in *Abrams* v. *U.S.* was 7-2. One Supreme Court justice wrote the Schenck opinion, asserting that the true test of every act is "the circumstances in which it is done." Does the act constitute a "clear and present danger?" The same justice dissented in the Abrams case, claiming that Abrams's action did not constitute a "clear and present danger," and that the best protection for our society was a "free trade in ideas—that the best test of truth is the power of the thought to get itself accepted in the competition of the market. . . ." Who was this justice who drew a fine line defending free speech and press?

(A) Oliver Wendell Holmes, Jr.
(B) Earl Warren
(C) Hugo Black
(D) Louis Brandeis
(E) William Howard Taft

49.   "I am tired of fighting. . . . The old men are all killed. It is the young men who say yes and no. He who led the young men is dead. It is cold and we have no blankets. The little children are freezing to death. My people, some of them, have run away to the hills and have no blankets, no food; no one knows where they are, perhaps freezing to death. I want time to look for my children and see how many of them I can find. Maybe I shall find them among the dead. . . . I am tired; my heart is sick and sad. From where the sun now stands, I will fight no more forever." These words were spoken by

(A) General Robert E. Lee after surrendering at Appomattox Courthouse
(B) Aguinaldo after the U.S. ended the Philippine revolt
(C) Chief Joseph after the final defeat of the Nez Percé Indians
(D) William Bradford after the first winter in Plymouth
(E) General Sam Houston after the Battle of the Alamo

50. It was the scene of the last major Native American (Indian) battle against the U.S. Army in 1890. It was also the site of an Indian protest confrontation in 1973. The site was

(A) My Lai
(B) Wounded Knee
(C) Little Big Horn
(D) Sand Creek
(E) Watts

51. A major difference between the first New Deal and the second New Deal was that the second New Deal

(A) was much more successful in reducing unemployment
(B) stressed a closer working partnership with big business
(C) emphasized a regulated economy more than a planned economy
(D) supported legislation to secure civil rights for blacks
(E) was more concerned with revising the banking system

52. Which of the following is most opposed to the concept of imperialism?

(A) the Northwest Ordinance
(B) the Treaty of Paris, 1898
(C) the writings of Alfred Thayer Mahan
(D) dollar diplomacy
(E) Manifest Destiny

Occupations of fathers of graduates of Chelsea High School, 1858–1864, and of fathers of students entering Somerville High School, 1856–1861.

OCCUPATION	CHELSEA	SOMERVILLE
Upper middle class		
Professional and public employee	2	11
Owner of business, store, manufacturing operation, or financial concern (merchant or broker)	19	44
Business employee	3	8
Master mariner, shipping master, shipwright, shipsmith	5	2
Total	29	65
Middle Class		
Artisan	11	26
Farmer	0	9
Total	11	35
Lower Class		
Operative	0	0
Farm laborer	0	1
Laborer	0	0
Total	0	1
No occupation listed for parent	3	10
Total	43	111

53. Which is the best conclusion to draw from this table?

(A) Most of the youths of the two towns were illiterate.

(B) The push to establish high schools came primarily from the working classes.

(C) Most of the students in elementary schools came from the upper class.

(D) The availability of high schools in this period represented more a symbolic than a real opportunity for the lower class.

(E) Young males worked, thus mostly girls were encouraged to go to high school.

54. The Constitution was based upon many sources—the colonial experience, the Revolutionary War, the Articles of Confederation, the imperial relationship, the British example, and political theory. On one topic, the concept of sovereignty, the Founding Fathers

(A) broke new ground by deciding that sovereignty lay with the people, not the states, and that sovereignty could be divided by the people between the federal government and the states

(B) provided for the settlement of future disputes by giving the federal courts the power of judical review

(C) laid the basis for the Civil War by granting sovereignty to the states similar to what had been in existence under the Articles of Confederation

(D) continued the practice of the imperial system by vesting sovereignty in the executive branch

(E) united the new nation by placing sovereignty under the legislative branch, similar to British political theory

55. The British parliament enacted which of the following to enforce mercantilist theories?

(A) Half-Way Covenant, 1662; Woolens Act, 1699; Hat Act, 1732

(B) Navigation Act, 1651; Enumerated Commodities Act, 1660; Staple Act, 1663

(C) The Fundamental Orders of Connecticut, 1638; Act of Toleration, 1649; Navigation Act, 1651

(D) Iron Act, 1750; Sugar Act, 1764; Stamp Act 1765

(E) Stamp Act, 1765; Quebec Act, 1774; Olive Branch Petition, 1775

56. "From the commencement of our government Congress has passed acts to regulate trade and intercourse with the Indians, which treat them as nations, respect their rights, and manifest a firm purpose to afford that protection which treaties stipulate. All these acts, and especially that of 1802, which is still in force, manifestly consider the several Indian nations as distinct political communities. . . .

"The Cherokee Nation, then, is a distinct community, occupying its own territory, with boundaries accurately described, in which the laws of Georgia can have no force, and which the citizens of Georgia have no right to enter but with the assent of the Cherokees themselves or in conformity with treaties and with the acts of Congress. The whole intercourse between the United States and this nation is, by our Constitution and laws, vested in the government of the United States. . . .

"The Acts of Georgia are repugnant to the Constitution, laws, and treaties of the United States." Chief Justice John Marshall based his opinion in this case,, *Worcester* v. *Georgia*, on

(A) the supremacy of the Constitution and treaties over state laws

(B) federal control of interstate trade and commerce

(C) the doctrine of states' rights

(D) the advanced civilized state of the Cherokee Indians

(E) the Tenth Amendment

57. The existence of the New World offered an opportunity for Europeans to start a society free from the mistakes inherited from the past. One of the themes of colonial history is unfortunately the extent to which the American environment forced changes in careful European plans. Which of the following pairs of colonies most clearly exemplify the extent to which American conditions changed the original plans of the colony's founders?

(A) Connecticut and New Jersey

(B) Massachusetts and Connecticut

(C) Pennsylvania and Massachusetts

(D) Georgia and the Carolinas

(E) Virginia and Pennsylvania

58.   "[The members of a trade union] should know that the labor movement means more, infinitely more, than a paltry increase in wages and the strike necessary to secure it; that while it engages to do all that possibly can be done to better the working conditions of its members, its highest object is to overthrow the capitalist system of private ownership of the tools of labor, abolish wage-slavery and achieve the freedom of the whole working class and, in fact, of all mankind. . . .

"The Socialist party is to the workingman politically what the trade union is to him industrially; the former is the party of his class, while the latter is the union of his trade.

"The difference between them is that while the trade union is confined to the trade, the Socialist party embraces the entire working class, and while the union is limited to bettering conditions under the wage system, the party is organized to conquer the political power of the nation, wipe out the wage system and make the workers themselves the master of the earth." These quotes

(A) were written by Eugene V. Debs when criticizing the aims and objectives of the AFL, the American Federation of Labor

(B) came from a speech by Earl Browder, twice

the Communist party candidate for the presidency

(C) refuted the thinking of the abolitionist and social reformer, Wendell Phillips

(D) illustrate the dissatisfaction within the American Federation of Labor which led to the creation of the CIO, the Congress of Industrial Organizations

(E) are from the preamble to the constitution of the Americans for Democratic Action, (ADA)

59. There wasn't one but two colonial Souths: the Chesapeake society and the Carolina society. In four of the following respects these two Souths were alike. In which were they different?

(A) the percentage of black slaves

(B) the existence of towns as a focal point for social life

(C) the existence of indentured servants

(D) their fears of a slave revolt

(E) their dependence on export crops

60. Which best describes our foreign relations or policies for the entire 19th century?

(A) American foreign policy frequently became entwined in the issues raised by conflicts between European powers.

(B) Territorial acquisitions increased our overseas possessions.

(C) The United States maintained a small military and naval establishment because of our preoccupation with internal domestic issues, the protection afforded by the oceans, and the existence of weak neighbors on our borders.

(D) Much of our attention went to developing trade with Japan and to partitioning China into spheres of influence.

(E) We protected North, Central, and South America against European conquest.

61. Which is associated with events in the presidential elections of 1848, 1852, and 1856?

(A) The Whig Party virtually disappeared by 1856.

(B) Third parties advocating the end of slavery won electoral votes.

(C) The Republican Party, advocating the extinction of slavery, grew stronger and stronger.

(D) The Democratic Party was swept into the

White House in three victories over the Whig Party.

(E) Lincoln's election in 1856 caused South Carolina to secede.

62. Religious toleration developed by the end of the colonial period primarily because

(A) no church was strong enough to gain dominance
(B) the colonists saw the folly of Europe's bloody wars of religion
(C) of the example of the Puritans coming to America for religious freedom
(D) of Roger Williams's example of separating church and state to keep the government free from religious interference
(E) of the English tradition of strict separation of church and state

63. During the Civil War the Confederate government raised most of its funds by

(A) increasing taxes
(B) selling bonds
(C) selling cotton to Great Britain
(D) printing paper currency
(E) borrowing from European countries

64. Early in his administration Woodrow Wilson attacked what he called "the triple wall of privilege." He pushed three pieces of legislation through a reluctant Congress to break it. The three highlights of the early Wilson administration were the

(A) Underwood Tariff, Federal Reserve Act, and Clayton Act
(B) Adamson Act, Payne-Aldrich Tariff, and Elkins Act
(C) Volstead Act, act creating the Pujo Committee, and Interstate Commerce Act
(D) Sherman Antitrust Act, Interstate Commerce Act, and Federal Reserve Act
(E) Agricultural Adjustment Act, National Industrial Recovery Act, and Works Progress Administration

65. Which of the following did *not* involve relations between the United States and Cuba?

(A) Ostend Manifesto
(B) Platt Amendment
(C) the U.S.S. Maine
(D) missile crisis, 1962
(E) Roosevelt Corollary

66. "The black men of America have a duty to perform, a duty stern and delicate—a forward movement to oppose a part of the work of their greatest leader. So far as Mr. Washington preaches Thrift, Patience, and Industrial Training for the masses, we must hold up his hands and strive with him, rejoicing in his honors and glorying in the strength of this Joshua called of God and of man to lead the headless host. But so far as Mr. Washington apologizes for injustice, North or South, does not rightly value the privilege and duty of voting, belittles the emasculating effects of caste distinctions, and opposes the higher training and ambition of our brighter minds— so far as he, the South, or the Nation, does this—we must unceasingly and firmly oppose them." The author of this passage was

(A) W.E.B. DuBois
(B) Thomas Jefferson
(C) John C. Calhoun
(D) James Madison
(E) Martin Luther King, Jr.

67. The issue of loose versus strict interpretation of the Constitution first arose

(A) over Hamilton's proposal to create a Bank of the United States
(B) over Jefferson's decision to purchase Louisiana from Napoleon
(C) in the case of *Marbury* v. *Madison*
(D) over Hamilton's proposal to consolidate national, foreign, and state debts and to pay them off at face value
(E) in the 1796 presidential campaign between the Federalist and Jeffersonian parties

Percentage of all Farms Operated by Tenants

	1880	1900	1930
United States	26%	35%	42%
Region in Question	36%	47%	56%

68. One region of the country exceeded the nation's average of farms operated by tenants in 1880, 1900, and 1930. What farming region was heavily characterized by tenant farming in these years?

(A) New England
(B) South
(C) Great Plains
(D) Middle West
(E) California valleys

69. I. "This filthy enactment was made in the nineteenth century, by men who could read and write. I will not obey it, by God." Ralph Waldo Emerson

II. "This momentous question, like a fire bell in the night, awakened and filled me with terror." Thomas Jefferson

III. "On this subject I do not wish to think, or speak, or write, with moderation. . . . I am in earnest—I will not equivocate—I will not excuse—I will not retreat a single inch—AND I WILL BE HEARD." William Lloyd Garrison
These comments were made on the

(A) Fugitive Slave Act; admission of Missouri as a state; subject of slavery in the first issue of *The Liberator*

(B) adoption of the Constitution; secession crisis; irrepressible conflict speech

(C) Dred Scott decision; gag rule; *Sociology for the South*

(D) Dred Scott decision; Underground Railroad; debate on Three-Fifths Compromise

(E) Kansas-Nebraska Act; Nat Turner's Rebellion; John Brown's raid on Harpers Ferry

70. All but one of the following were aspects of urban growth between 1850 and 1900. Which does *not* belong with the other four?

(A) establishment of professional police forces

(B) introduction of building codes to prevent disastrous fires

(C) building of coordinated water and sewer systems

(D) urban park movement begun by Frederick Law Olmsted

(E) introduction of the city manager and commission forms of city government

71. In the colonial period, westward settlement in the Mohawk River valley west of Albany was

(A) blocked by the Iroquois Confederacy

(B) stopped by the Appalachian Mountains

(C) stimulated by the Erie Canal

(D) encouraged by the Northwest Ordinance

(E) accomplished by Scotch-Irish settlers

72. Which black American is incorrectly matched with his or her accomplishment?

(A) Phillis Wheatly—poet during the Revolutionary War

(B) Ralph Bunche—United Nations official who won the 1950 Nobel Peace Prize

(C) Benjamin Banneker—mathematician and surveyor who helped lay out the plans for Washington, D.C.

(D) Jackie Robinson—first black to play baseball in the major leagues

(E) George Washington Carver—escaped slave who helped other blacks escape via the Underground Railroad

73. Which have been advanced by historians as an explanation for, or as a description of, the Progressive movement?

I. The primary aspect of Progressivism was the urban masses who formed the backbone of the voting electorate and who supported reforms to improve the lot of the lower classes.

II. The leadership of Progressivism came from middle class urbanites and professionals who had experienced a decline in status with the rise of colossal fortunes.

III. Progressivism was a coalition of groups united by rising dissatisfaction with corporate and railroad arrogance.

IV. Progressivism was not a reform at all, but "political capitalism" in which conservative businessmen supported "reforms" to use government intervention to consolidate and entrench big business.

V. Progressivism was a part of the cyclical patterns of alternating periods of liberal reform and conservative reaction that frequently reappears in American history.

(A) II and V only

(B) II, III, and V only

(C) I, II, and V only

(D) III and V only

(E) I, II, III, IV, and V

74. In the 1790s Virginia and Maryland exported 130,000,000 pounds per year. In 1775, 165,000 barrels of another product passed through Charleston and Savannah. New England exported 2,700,000 gallons of its chief product in 1775. These three exports are, respectively,

(A) corn, indigo, and fish

(B) wheat, naval stores, and molasses

(C) rice, fish, and wheat

(D) tobacco, rice, and rum

(E) tobacco, naval stores, and fish

75. "The issue is Socialism versus Capitalism. I am for Socialism because I am for humanity. We have been cursed with the reign of gold long enough. Money constitutes no proper basis of civilization. The time has come to regenerate society—we are on the eve of a universal change." This passage was

 (A) delivered by William Jennings Bryan in his Cross of Gold speech
 (B) spoken by President Grover Cleveland responding to J. Pierpont Morgan's offer to rescue the U.S. Treasury by selling it gold
 (C) written by Eugene V. Debs after being imprisoned following the Pullman strike
 (D) part of the Populist Party platform in 1892
 (E) spoken by Franklin Roosevelt as part of his inaugural address, March 4, 1933

76. Which was the first wartime conference attended by the three leaders, Stalin, FDR, and Churchill?

 (A) Teheran
 (B) Yalta
 (C) Casablanca
 (D) Cairo
 (E) Atlantic Charter meeting

77. Which of the following ideas is *not* found in the preamble to the Declaration of Independence?

 (A) Governments exist to protect their citizens' inalienable rights.
 (B) When a government is oppressive the people have a right to revolt.
 (C) The government is the servant of the people, not their master.
 (D) Governments are founded on the popular consent of the governed.
 (E) Governments exist to give all people an equal opportunity to share in the wealth of the nation.

78. James Madison asked for a declaration of war against Great Britain in 1812 for four reasons. Which was *not* included in his address to Congress?

 (A) blockading of American ports
 (B) impressment of American seamen
 (C) inciting Indians to attack settlers
 (D) the opportunity to grab part of Canada
 (E) violation of American neutral rights

79. What is the correct chronological order for the following disputes with Great Britain?

 I. Webster-Ashburton Treaty
 II. Caroline affair
 III. Laird rams
 IV. Trent affair

 (A) I, II, III, IV
 (B) III, I, II, IV
 (C) II, I, IV, III
 (D) I, II, IV, III
 (E) IV, II, III, I

80. "At this time, among all the peoples of the world, the group that suffers most from injustice, the group that is denied most of those rights that belong to all humanity, is the black group. . . . We of the UNIA believe that what is good for the other folks is good for us. . . . We [want] a kind of government that will place our race in control, even as other races are in control of their own government. . . . You and I can live in the United States of America for 100 years, and our generations may live for 200 years or for 5,000 more years, and as long as there is a black and white population, when the majority is on the side of the white race, you and I will never get political justice or get political equality in this country." These words are from a speech by the black leader who founded the Universal Negro Improvement Association (UNIA). Who was this "Black Moses"?

 (A) A. Phillip Randolph
 (B) Robert C. Weaver
 (C) Thurgood Marshall
 (D) Marcus Garvey
 (E) Ralph Bunche

81. Which Supreme Court decisions concerned the principle that the Sixth and Fourteenth amendments guaranteed the right to legal counsel in criminal prosecutions and that the Fifth Amendment guaranteed the right to remain silent and not to incriminate oneself?

 I. *Gideon* v. *Wainwright*, 1963
 II. *Escobedo* v. *Illinois*, 1964
 III. *Miranda* v. *Arizona*, 1966
 IV. *Baker* v. *Carr*, 1962
 V. Bakke case, 1978

 (A) I and V only
 (B) II, III, and IV only
 (C) I, IV, and V only
 (D) I, II, and III only
 (E) II, III, and V only

82. He studied Puritanism because one of his 17th century ancestors had played an important role in the Salem witch trials. In a novel he satirized the spirit of Puritanism through his tale of Arthur Dimmesdale, Roger Chillingworth, and Hester Prynne. Who was this author?

    (A) Nathaniel Hawthorne in *The Scarlet Letter*
    (B) William Dean Howells in *The Rise of Silas Lapham*
    (C) George Santayana in *The Last Puritan*
    (D) Sinclair Lewis in *Main Street*
    (E) Theodore Dreiser in *Sister Carrie*

83. Political theory in the colonial period said that the ideal government was a "mixed government" that contained elements of democracy, aristocracy, and monarchy. The glue that held the mixture together was "deference," which was the belief in

    (A) universal suffrage for white males
    (B) popular sovereignty
    (C) the acceptance of majority rule
    (D) yielding to the leadership of the superior upper class
    (E) the consent of the governed

Unemployment Statistics, 1929–1939

Year	Total Labor Force	Number Unemployed	Percent Unemployed
1929	49,180,000	1,550,000	3.2
1930	49,820,000	4,340,000	8.7
1931	50,420,000	8,020,000	15.9
1932	51,000,000	12,060,000	23.6
1933	51,590,000	12,830,000	24.9
1934	52,230,000	11,340,000	21.7
1935	52,870,000	10,610,000	20.1
1936	53,440,000	9,030,000	16.9
1937	54,000,000	7,700,000	14.3
1938	54,610,000	10,390,000	19.0
1939	55,230,000	9,480,000	17.2

84. These unemployment statistics indicate that

    (A) the number of new jobs grew by 17.2%
    (B) Hoover's second term was the worst period of the Depression
    (C) New Deal programs helped to counter the effects of the Depression, but did not end them
    (D) the use of Keynesian economics brought the United States out of the Depression
    (E) the economy went downhill after the NRA was declared unconstitutional

85. The first is famous for bitterly opposing Woodrow Wilson's League of Nations. The second, although originally an isolationist, reversed his thinking during the Second World War and became a strong advocate of the United Nations. Who were these two leading Republican senators?

    (A) Charles Evans Hughes and Richard Nixon
    (B) Henry Cabot Lodge and Arthur Vandenberg
    (C) Hiram Johnson and Robert Taft
    (D) William Borah and Harry Truman
    (E) Robert La Follette and Joseph McCarthy

86. Which of the following most accurately describes the relationship between the abolitionists and political parties between 1830 and 1860?

    (A) Since political action proved ineffectual, most abolitionists depended on moral persuasion to advance their cause.
    (B) Enough voters supported the Free Soil Party and the Liberty Party to hold the balance that determined victors in presidential elections.
    (C) Abolitionists infiltrated the major political parties and gained positions of influence which they used to change their party's position to favoring gradual emancipation for slaves.
    (D) Most abolitionists were attracted to the Know-Nothing Party political position on slavery, which advocated the creation of a new state for blacks in the Appalachian Mountains in the South.
    (E) Disdaining the issue at the national level, abolitionists successfully achieved major victories for blacks in the Northern states in voting and civil rights.

87. As late as 1914 six states still had no compulsory school attendance laws. Why?

    (A) All six were located in the South where child labor was needed for farming and textile mills.
    (B) All six were located in areas of high immigration, and they could not afford compulsory attendance laws because of the high number of immigrant children.

(C) All six were frontier states, and scattered settlements made compulsory attendance laws impractical.

(D) All six were industrial states, and the Dewey philosophy of "learning by doing" proved impractical in them because of the great demand for vocational training schools.

(E) Compulsory attendance laws threatened Jim Crow segregation in the South; therefore, six Southern states refused to jeopardize their segregated schools by enacting compulsory attendance laws.

88. Chief Justice John Marshall asserted that only Congress, not the states, possessed the power to control interstate commerce. The case was

(A) *Marbury v. Madison*
(B) the Slaughterhouse cases
(C) *McCulloch v. Maryland*
(D) *Cohens v. Virginia*
(E) *Gibbons v. Ogden*

89.   "If the church cannot bring business under Christ's law of solidarity and service, it will find his law not merely neglected in practice, but flouted in theory. With many the Darwinian theory has proved a welcome justification of things as they are. It is right and fitting that thousands should perish to evolve the higher type of the modern business man. Those who are manifestly surviving in the present struggle for existence can console themselves with the thought that they are the fittest, and there is no contradicting the laws of the universe. Thus an atomistic philosophy crowds out the Christian faith in solidarity. The law of the cross is superseded by the law of tooth and nail. It is not even ideal and desirable 'to seek and to save the lost,' because it keeps the weak and unfit alive. . . .

"The gospel, to have full power over an age, must be the highest expression of the moral and religious truths held by that age. If it lags behind and deals in outgrown conceptions of life and duty, it will lose power over the ablest minds and the young men first, and gradually over all. In our thought to-day the social problems irresistibly take the lead. If the Church has no live and bold thought on this dominant question of modern life, its teaching authority on all other questions will dwindle and be despised. It cannot afford to have young men sniff the air as in a stuffy room when they enter the sphere of religious thought. When the world is in travail with a higher ideal of justice, the Church dare not ignore it if it would retain its moral leadership." This is a statement of the philosophy behind

(A) Social Darwinism
(B) the Social Gospel
(C) the Single Tax
(D) Populism
(E) Fundamentalism

90. The two routes pictured, routes "A" and "B,"

(A) were parts of the Underground Railroad carrying slaves to freedom in Canada
(B) were financed by the federal government to provide internal improvements
(C) were originally vetoed by Andrew Jackson in the Maysville veto
(D) were state projects which stimulated imitation by other states
(E) marked the beginning of the "transportation revolution"

Collection of Customs Revenues

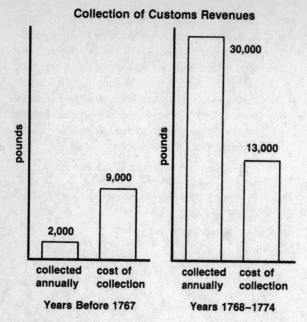

Years Before 1767

Years 1768–1774

91. These charts illustrate

(A) the unfairness of mercantilism before 1767
(B) British neglect of the mercantile system before 1767
(C) the reasons behind the Boston Massacre incident
(D) the impact of Hamilton's protective tariffs
(E) the increase in the national debt during the Confederation period

92.   "Even though we face the difficulties of today and tomorrow, I still have a dream. . . . I have a dream that one day this nation will rise up and live out the true meaning of its creed: 'We hold these truths to be self-evident, that all men are created equal.'

"I have a dream that one day on the red hills of Georgia the sons of former slaves and the sons of former slaveowners will be able to sit down together at the table of brotherhood. I have a dream that one day even the state of Mississippi, a state sweltering with the people's injustice, sweltering with the heat of oppresion, will be transferred into an oasis of freedom and justice.

"I have a dream that my four little children will one day live in a nation where they will not be judged by the color of their skin but by the content of their character. . . .

"I have a dream that one day every valley shall be exalted, every hill and mountain shall be made low, the rough places will be made plain and the crooked places will be made

straight, and the glory of the Lord shall be revealed and flesh shall see it together.

"This is our hope."

This speech was delivered by

(A) Stokely Carmichael
(B) Lyndon Johnson
(C) Martin Luther King, Jr.
(D) John F. Kennedy
(E) Malcolm X

93. When the First World War broke out in 1914 Woodrow Wilson asked the American people to be neutral in thought as well as deed. U.S. policy failed to remain neutral because of which of the following?

I. Our foreign policy assumed that American neutral rights would be respected.
II. Our foreign policy assumed that the United States government could pursue a truly neutral policy.
III. Allied control of the seas effectively blocked evenhanded trade with belligerents.
IV. Germany was unwilling to accept the sovereignty of the League of Nations.
V. New methods of warfare tainted the image of Germany.

(A) III and V only
(B) I, II, III, and V only
(C) II, III, and IV only
(D) I, II, III, IV, and V
(E) I, III, and V only

94. The positions of loose construction and strict construction of the Constitution were first established in letters written by Hamilton and Jefferson to President Washington. The letters concerned

(A) the issue of creating a Bank of the U.S.
(B) our obligations to France under the Treaty of 1778
(C) consolidating the national, state, and foreign debt and paying them at face value
(D) an appropriate response to the Whiskey Rebellion
(E) Jefferson's decision to purchase Louisiana

95. Upton Sinclair's chief purpose in writing *The Jungle* was to

(A) awaken the public to the horribly unsanitary conditions in meat-packing plants

(B) aid the plea for better housing for immigrant stockyard workers

(C) rally public support for the Meat Inspection Act and the Pure Food and Drug Act, both of which were tied up in the Senate

(D) join other muckrakers in attacking the political corruption within the municipal government of Chicago

(E) advance the cause of socialism and fight against "wage slavery"

96. The "War on Poverty" fought illiteracy and unemployment under Lyndon Johnson. Four of the following kept the "War on Poverty" from achieving victory in the next twenty years. Which did *not* contribute to the demise of the efforts to reduce poverty?

(A) Two basic industries, steel and automobile, switched to more automation and suffered from fierce foreign competition, resulting in increased layoffs.

(B) Millions of illegal immigrants entered the United States from poverty-stricken Mexico and war-torn Central America.

(C) An increase in divorces lowered the living standards for millions of children and women.

(D) Reduced Social Security benefits raised the number of elderly people among the poor.

(E) The Vietnam War diverted the commitment to domestic concerns.

97. The Compromise of 1850 provided for the

(A) establishment of the 36° 30' line to divide slave and free territories

(B) admission of Missouri as a slave state and Maine as a free state

(C) ending of the importation of slaves into the United States as provided by the Constitution

(D) absorption of the Confederate debt after the Civil War

(E) addition of a free state without adding a new slave state

98. The Constitution obligates the federal government to guarantee a republican form of government in each state. Which incident most closely involved the question of "a republican government" within a state?

(A) Populist Party state victories in 1892

(B) Dorr's Rebellion in Rhode Island in 1841–1842

(C) federal troops sent to the Pullman strike, 1894

(D) federal takeover of the Arkansas state government during the school integration crisis in 1957

(E) takeover of automobile plants during the sit-down strikes in the 1930s

99. By the end of the 1880s

(A) immigrants from Eastern and Southern Europe began to outnumber those from Northern and Western Europe

(B) Chinese immigration began to increase

(C) the Irish fleeing the potato famine began to arrive

(D) most immigrants were becoming farmers

(E) the first immigration quota act was passed, based on the census of 1890

100.   "The Communist threat is a global one. Its successful advance in one sector threatens the destruction of every other sector. . . .

"Apart from the military need, as I saw it, to neutralize sanctuary protection given the enemy north of the Yalu, I felt that military necessity in the conduct of the war made necessary:

(1) The intensification of our economic blockade against China.

(2) The imposition of a naval blockade against the China coast.

(3) Removal of restrictions on air reconnaissance of China's coastal areas and of Manchuria.

(4) Removal of restrictions on the forces of the Republic of China on Formosa, with logistical support to contribute to their effective operations against the Chinese mainland. . . .

"War's very object is victory, not prolonged indecision."

Who made this speech on April 19, 1951?

(A) Harry Truman after the invasion of South Korea

(B) Republican candidate Thomas Dewey after the fall of China to the communists

(C) General Westmoreland during the Vietnam War

(D) General MacArthur after being relieved of his command in the Korean War

(E) Harry Truman issuing the Truman Doctrine

ANSWERS

1. B	21. A	41. A	61. A	81. D
2. C	22. C	42. B	62. A	82. A
3. E	23. D	43. B	63. D	83. D
4. D	24. D	44. E	64. A	84. C
5. C	25. D	45. D	65. E	85. B
6. A	26. A	46. B	66. A	86. A
7. C	27. C	47. C	67. A	87. A
8. B	28. B	48. A	68. B	88. E
9. E	29. B	49. C	69. A	89. B
10. D	30. D	50. B	70. E	90. E
11. E	31. E	51. C	71. A	91. B
12. B	32. C	52. A	72. E	92. C
13. A	33. C	53. D	73. E	93. B
14. C	34. E	54. A	74. D	94. A
15. E	35. D	55. B	75. C	95. E
16. E	36. E	56. A	76. A	96. D
17. B	37. D	57. D	77. E	97. E
18. E	38. D	58. A	78. D	98. B
19. D	39. E	59. B	79. C	99. A
20. D	40. D	60. C	80. D	100. D

EXPLANATORY ANSWERS

1. **(B)** This is the peak period for Irish and German immigration. The Irish fled crowded Ireland and the potato famine. The Germans left poor agricultural conditions and the failed revolution of 1848.

2. **(C)** All these rebellions pitted the lower classes against their superiors. Leisler's Rebellion took place in New York City in the 1690s, a period of turmoil throughout the colonies. Bacon's Rebellion in 1676 has been interpreted as a frontier versus tidewater uprising and as the early forerunner to the spirit of 1776. The Paxton Boys in Pennsylvania and the Regulators in the Carolinas were both frontier protests against colonial governments too preoccupied with Eastern concerns. The Whiskey Rebellion took place in 1795 after the colonial era.

3. **(E)** The president was Franklin D. Roosevelt. The speech is often seen as a turning point in American foreign policy even though the general public remained isolationist in sentiment.

4. **(D)** The Lincoln-Douglas debates took place in 1858 after the Dred Scott decision in 1857. Lincoln nailed Douglas by asking him if he supported both the Dred Scott decision, which Southerners applauded , and popular sovereignty, a term popularized by Douglas. The Dred Scott decision had said slaves could go anywhere; Douglas' answer, called the Freeport Doctrine, was that settlers in the territories could as a practical matter exclude slaves. Douglas's leaning toward popular sovereignty antagonized the South and cost him the nomination of a unified Democratic Party in 1860.

5. **(C)** Don't be fooled by that old myth that laissez-faire has always characterized the U.S. economy. In the pre-Civil War period many state and local governments owned stock in corporations. One historian has characterized the economy in this era as a "mixed economy." The Depression of 1837 disrupted many grandiose projects and reduced the income generated by roads and canals. Many states repudiated their debt in order to escape the financial morass. Burned by this experience, many states prohibited their own governments from investing in corporate stock. Thus the railroads were mostly funded by private funds.

6. **(A)** Noah Webster, "the father of American lexicography," advocated American usage and spelling of the English language. "America must be as independent in literature as she is in politics, as famous for arts as for arms." His spelling book sold over 60 million copies. His *An American Dictionary of the English Language* (1828) was the authoritative American dictionary. Daniel Webster, the famous politician, was not related to Noah. Mevil Dewey began the Dewey Decimal System of classifying library books and established the first school for training librarians. Horace Mann was a famous Massachusetts educator.

7. **(C)** Conservatives saw in the New Deal a creeping socialism that would put us on the road to serfdom and destroy individual liberty. Read campaign speeches from the 1936 presidential race, especially material from the Liberty League.

8. **(B)** The case of *Plessy* v. *Ferguson* produced the "separate but equal" doctrine, and essentially put the stamp of judicial approval on segregation. *Brown* v. *Board of Education* overturned Plessy. *Minor* v. *Happensett*, (1875) ruled that voting was not an inherent right of citizenship. Women could be citizens but still be deprived of voting rights. The Korematsu case upheld the removal of the Japanese from the West Coast in the beginning of the Second World War. *Gideon* v. *Wainwright* ensured a poor defendant's right to free counsel in state felony cases.

9. **(E)** There are two methods of overriding a Supreme Court decision declaring an act of Congress unconstitutional. One is to pass an amendment to the Constitution. For example, the Sixteenth Amendment, permitting income taxes, negated the decision in *Pollock* v. *Farmers' Loan and Trust Co.*, which had declared income taxes unconstitutional. The second method is to have the Supreme Court reverse its decision. *Brown* v. *Board of Education of Topeka* overturned the "separate but equal" doctrine in *Plessy* v. *Ferguson.*

   The other choices are powers Congress has over the Supreme Court. Article III, section 2, gives Congress the authority to remove a piece of legislation from court review. The Reconstruction Act is an example of this. Congress reduced the number of Supreme Court judges under Andrew Johnson to forestall the possibility that he might make an appointment to the Supreme Court. FDR's court packing plan pressed unsuccessfully for an enlargement of the Supreme Court.

10. **(D)** Retailers concentrated on expanding urban markets, not the static rural markets, although mail order catalogs opened new vistas for rural folks.

11. **(E)** Economic gain is often offered as a reason for American imperialist expansion, but McKinley did not present it in his address to the Senate. Many industrialists such as Andrew Carnegie opposed acquisition of the Philippines.

12. **(B)** The huge increase in the national debt this century has come from war and the threat of war. Spending for social programs has added very little to the total federal budget deficit.

13. **(A)** Rachel Carson's *Silent Spring,* (1962) alerted the world to the dangers of pesticides, especially DDT, which was banned ten years later. Betty Friedan wrote *The Feminine Mystique* (1963) which helped launch the women's movement. Jonas Salk discovered a vaccine for polio. Robert Oppenheimer led the Manhattan Project that developed the atomic bomb during the Second World War. Ralph Nader was a driving force behind the consumer revolt of the 1960s. He accused the automobile industry of producing unsafe cars in *Unsafe at Any Speed,* (1965).

14. **(C)** Ruth and Lindbergh proved that individualism could still triumph. Corporations sponsored entries in the race to be the first single pilot across the Atlantic, but Lindbergh beat them all. Babe Ruth violated every training rule in existence, and some not in existence. The contemporary maxim was "follow the rules and be a team player." Ruth didn't and yet he still excelled. Choice A is distracting, for their adulation far exceeded their accomplishments. Lindbergh later became a spokesman for the isolationist cause, and, some would say, the German cause. Ruth did not.

15. **(E)** Populists wanted government ownership of the railroads, but Progressives never did. Progressivism tended to be much more political than Populism. The two key words in Progressivism are efficiency and democracy.

16. **(E)** The Mexican Cession (F) was a prize of war, but the Oregon territory (C) was acquired by treaty from Great Britain in 1846.

17. **(B)** The tax rate was reduced from six pence to three, but that was not the most significant part of the Revenue Act of 1764 (the Sugar Act). The British were determined to collect this tax and to inaugurate a new policy of enforcing trade and navigation laws.

18. **(E)** Andrew Jackson chased Seminole Indians into Florida in 1818, precipitating a crisis. His actions raised many eyebrows, but secured Florida for the United States. Ironically, Jackson's future political opponent, John Quincy Adams, supported him, and his future vice-president, John C. Calhoun, condemned him. In 1818 Calhoun was the secretary of war and Adams the secretary of state.

19. **(D)** Covenant thinking and covenant theology dominated Puritanism. As one historian stated, a Puritan sermon was like a lawyer's brief, logically proving a legalistic relationship. Your obligation was to hold up your end of the contract, or suffer the consequences forever in you-know-where!

20. **(D)** The Treaty of 1778, an alliance between France and the United States, ended with the Convention of 1800. After using massive French help to win the Revolutionary War the United States, following self-interest, avoided helping France in its wars with Great Britain in the 1790s. Washington's Neutrality Proclamation of 1793 wiggled out of our commitment but not out of the alliance. After the undeclared naval war of 1798 further strained U.S.-French relations it became possible to break off the perpetual alliance of 1778. The United States has had many peacetime alliances since NATO.

21. **(A)** By the 1880s Southern whites en bloc supported Democratic candidates in order to negate the black vote, and to overwhelm Republicans. Political contests took place during Democratic primaries, not at the general elections, hence the nickname, Solid South. If whites had ever been divided, the beneficiary would have been blacks, who would have found themselves courted by competing groups or classes of whites. This happened during the rise of Populism when low-class whites sought the support of the predominantly low-class blacks.

22. **(C)** The architect is Frank Lloyd Wright. He believed that form should follow function, and that the internal use of a building should guide its design.

23. **(D)** Whether through birth control, family planning, or the pill, there are fewer births per thousand fertile women than in the 1920s.

24. **(D)** Senator Joseph McCarthy, a Republican from Wisconsin, raised eyebrows and passions with his sensational charges of twenty years of treason. The Republican Party found his accusations useful during Eisenhower's 1952 campaign, but its opinion quickly changed when McCarthy added the first year of Eisenhower's administration to the charge of twenty years of treason. The Senate eventually censured McCarthy and his methods, ending his influence.

25. **(D)** The Gulf of Tonkin Resolution in 1964 gave Lyndon Johnson carte blanche authorization to use military force in Southeast Asia. Only two senators opposed this nationalistic response to apparent attacks on U.S. destroyers off the coast of Vietnam in the Gulf of Tonkin. Dissatisfaction over the consequences of their grant of power led Congress to pass the War Powers Act in 1973, which limited the time period during which a president could commit American troops to combat situations. The Hartford Convention, the Ludlow Amendment, and the Bricker Amendment all tried unsuccessfully to restrict presidential control of foreign policy.

26. **(A)** Sinclair Lewis used his acceptance speech to take a stab at the stuffy establishment of American letters. His award shocked the academic literary gentry, and his speech did not appease them. He recognized how much America had changed.

27. **(C)** The French lost Louisiana in the French and Indian War (Seven Years' War, Great War for Empire) but not to the British. Anxious to end the fighting, France gave Louisiana to her ally Spain, as compensation for Spain's losses. From the American point of view the two chief results of the war were the cession of Canada to Great Britain and the huge debt the British incurred, forcing a reevaluation of the porous system for collecting customs duties.

28. **(B)** George Wallace knew that he couldn't win the presidency in 1968. He hoped no one would win. His control of the states of the old Confederacy would give him approximately twelve states, half what one of the other candidates would need to win in the House of Representatives. At that point profitable deals were possible.

    The only other third party candidate listed is Strom Thurmond. He sought to deny victory for Truman and to teach the Democrats that they must be more respectful of white Southern feelings on racial issues.

29. **(B)** The Federal Reserve Act (Owen-Glass Act) created a new banking system to solve the dilemma of inelastic currency. The Federal Reserve Board controlled the decentral-

ized system through twelve districts. Banks established under the 1863 National Bank System were required to join the Federal Reserve.

The new system was unable to prevent the great crash of 1929 and subsequent downturns in the economy. Wall Street tenaciously fought against the proposed system in the six-month-long congressional debate. Whereas Theodore Roosevelt avoided volatile issues like the tariff and currency inelasticity, Wilson charged ahead and won in both areas.

30. **(D)** The South Carolina Exposition and Protest was directed against the Tariff of Abominations; the protest followed the tariff. The controversy simmered for several years before leading to the nullification crisis of 1831–1833 resolved by the Compromise of 1833, which included the Tariff of 1833 and the Force Bill.

31. **(E)** Alexis de Tocqueville wrote the insightful *Democracy in America*. Frances Trollope, an English novelist, wrote a delightfully unflattering book, *The Domestic Manners of the Americans* (1832), pungently describing crude American social customs to bemused or angered readers. James Bryce tried to explain the actual workings of the American political system in *The American Commonwealth* (1888), still widely quoted as an accurate analysis. Jenny Lind, the "Swedish Nightingale," captivated American audiences in her concert tour from 1850 to 1852. Promoted by P.T. Barnum, she captured the public's imagination, and even inspired a collection of trunks and furniture.

32. **(C)** Mark Twain and Charles Dudley Warner entitled their novel, *The Gilded Age*. To gild means to cover something with a thin layer of gold. The outside looks nice in appearance, but it covers something inferior. The political values and practices of the age earned the title, "The Gilded Age."

33. **(C)** Denmark Vesey was a free black executed in 1822 for plotting a revolt in Charleston, South Carolina. Nat Turner's Virginia uprising in 1831 ended with his hanging. Elijah Lovejoy, an abolitionist newspaper editor, was killed in 1837 trying to defend his printing press against an angry mob. Choosing between Douglass and Garrison is difficult. The speech follows Garrison's truculent vein, but the first paragraph indicates that the speaker feels himself to be outside American society itself, not just American mainstream thought. Hence the choice is Douglass.

34. **(E)** An excellent harbor, proximity to European markets, a good location for business headquarters, and a wide hinterland all combined to make New York City the primary United States seaport and not just in this period of history.

35. **(D)** The Whiskey Rebellion took place in Western Pennsylvania in the 1790s. The first states to join the union after the original thirteen were Vermont in 1791, Kentucky in 1792, and Tennessee in 1796, all outside the Northwest Territory.

36. **(E)** The company violated a presidential order prohibiting the sale of weapons or munitions to Bolivia or Paraguay, who were at war. Curtiss-Wright had been selling airplanes to Bolivia and smuggled fifteen machine guns for airplanes into Bolivia. The Insular cases involved the question of constitutional rights applying to people in newly acquired American territories. The Marbury case established judicial review. *Baker* v. *Carr*, *Wesberry* v. *Sanders*, and *Reynolds* v. *Simms* involved state legislative and congressional reapportionment. The Schenck case upheld the Espionage Act of 1917. Justice Holmes presented his famous "clear and present danger" test in the unanimous decision.

37. **(D)** The economy suffered inflation after the Second World War but not depression. The booming economy surprised many.

38. **(D)** La Follette headed the Progressive Party ticket in 1924. The winner was Republican Calvin Coolidge. Republican prosperity and Coolidge's distance from the Harding scandals made him unbeatable. Already occupying the White House after Harding's death also helped.

39. **(E)** For Congress to give its functions and responsibilities to another branch of the government is unconstitutional. Even if another branch can do a more efficient job, Congress cannot relinquish its authority and responsibility. Jefferson argued against the claim that the Bank would facilitate the tax collection function of the federal government. One of the reasons the Supreme Court ruled against the NRA was that the NRA Act delegated legislative powers to an agency under the control of the executive branch.

40. **(D)** John Dewey revolutionized educational theory with his book, *The School and Society* (1899), which advocated "learning by doing." Repetitious rote learning must be replaced with practical knowledge; each course should reflect a student's needs, not a teacher's abstract standards. He gave a boost to vocational education. In addition, Dewey argued that every child should be guided to reach his full potential. His ideas came to be called "progressive education."

41. **(A)** The correct order is as follows: Pontiac's Rebellion; Proclamation of 1763; Stamp Act, 1765; Stamp Act Congress, 1765; Townshend Acts, 1767; Boston Massacre, 1770; Boston Tea Party, 1773; Quebec Act, 1774; Lexington and Concord, 1775; Olive Branch Petition, 1775; and the Declaration of Independence, 1776.

42. **(B)** Prohibition, fundamentalism, and immigration restriction were all small town attacks against corrupt urban America. The Ku Klux Klan is much more complicated because there are actually three Klans: the anti-black organization after the Civil War; the pro-small town movement in the 1920s; and the anticommunist Klan of the 1950s and 1960s. All contained the same elements, but their emphasis shifted. The 1920s Klan was a fraternalistic glorification of the values of small town America. In the election of 1928 Herbert Hoover ran against Al Smith, the son of immigrants, a Catholic, and a wet. Rural America and small town America voted for Hoover to save the USA from a horrible fate!

43. **(B)** All of these have been testing grounds of Western courage and will. Two clues indicate Berlin, "an island of freedom" and "behind the Iron Curtain." Berlin is entirely within East Germany. Both Germany and Berlin were divided temporarily after the Second World War into French, British, American, and Russian zones. The temporary arrangement solidified with the growth of the Cold War. The French, British, and American zones in Germany merged to form West Germany in 1949. Before the Berlin Wall it was possible for an Eastern European to get a passport to visit West Berlin. Once there one simply took a plane to West Germany and freedom.

44. **(E)** Some historians have seen the origins of political parties in the personal clash between Hamilton and Jefferson. Although they disliked one another, this alone didn't generate political parties. Historians by nature are always looking for the roots of something. In a nutshell this is the "germ theory of history," the belief that everything grows from a source, and with sufficient investigation we can find that source. Thus

some historians see the continuation of splits in the Revolutionary War era and the Confederation period. But political parties need programs on issues, fundamental ideologies, continuous organization, central leadership, and a cadre of faithful workers. These all came into existence as the issues of the 1790s sparked controversies.

45. **(D)** Government grants varied with the terrain; the rougher the terrain the higher the grant. The scandalous Crédit Mobilier was only the most notorious example of political corruption. Contrary to popular myth, private funds built the majority of the railroads. Land grants enticed railroads to build lines across barren prairies. The normal progression elsewhere was for a sufficient population to settle in an area, and lure investors into building a railroad to the new settlement. In the Great Plains there never would have been settlement without prior railroad construction. Government policy was to move settlers into vacant lands; the railroads became the means to entice settlers. Once and for all, the prevailing philosophy in 19th century America was laissez-faire; the prevailing practice was government help such as bonds, stock subscriptions, tariffs, etc.

46. **(B)** There are few presidential elections in U.S. history in which four candidates received electoral votes. The clear sectional vote indicates that this is the election of 1860. The Republican Lincoln won the North and the Democrat Breckinridge took the South. Bell and Douglas divided the middle.

47. **(C)** These three represent the most famous and best written protest works. There were thousands of pamphlets speeches, etc., and the vast majority, as in the three works mentioned, addressed the bewildering mystery of how a society could produce simultaneously so much wealth and poverty.

48. **(A)** Oliver Wendell Holmes, Jr. spent thirty years on the Supreme Court where he became famous for the clarity and sharpness of his dissents, many of which later formed the basis for majority opinions.

49. **(C)** This widely quoted speech was delivered by Chief Joseph after the final defeat of the Nez Percé Indians in 1877.

50. **(B)** Wounded Knee and Sand Creek were both white massacres of virtually defenseless Indians. Wounded Knee, the last major battle between whites and Indians, was the scene of a militant "Red Power" demonstration in 1973 led by members of AIM, the American Indian Movement. The confrontation symbolized the new militant attitude of many young Indian radicals. The Sioux wiped out Custer at Little Big Horn in 1876. My Lai was the site of an American massacre of a Vietnamese village during the Vietnam War. Watts, a black neighborhood in Los Angeles, erupted in 1965, symbolizing black disgust with the pace of civil rights.

51. **(C)** One major characteristic of the second New Deal was the shift from a cooperative, planned partnership approach with big business to a more hostile, regulated approach. The National Recovery Administration belongs to the first New Deal. The Second World War, not the New Deal, solved the unemployment dilemma. The banking crisis was part of the Hundred Days. Despite personal sympathy for the plight of blacks, FDR felt that an open civil rights effort would jeopardize his congressional Southern support for New Deal legislation.

52. **(A)** The Northwest Ordinance promised America's "colonies," the Northwest territories, that they would not be colonies forever. Eventually they would be states equal to the original thirteen.

53. **(D)** Choices (A), (B), and (E) may be true, but the chart doesn't provide information to support any of them. Literacy was high in the United States, but most students attended school for a total of only two to five years. The working class was only one source of the push for establishing schools. Many historians also attribute a custodial purpose to the early school reformers; they wanted to keep the students out of the labor market and confined within a caretaker institution. No information indicates the sex of the students. Choice (E) sounds plausible, but we don't know. Choice (C) refers to elementary schools, not high schools.

    Another twenty-five years passed before half the lower classes or working classes attended high school, and much longer before half graduated.

54. **(A)** The great contribution the Founding Fathers made to political theory was the idea that sovereignty was divisible. Before the Constitution sovereignty lay with one person (the sovereign), a body such as a council or legislature, or in a class or category of society. The Constitution divided sovereignty, granting some to the states, most to the federal government, and ultimate sovereignty to the people. If the people decide to change *their* government, they may.

    Some constitutional scholars claim that the Founding Fathers tacitly gave their consent to judicial review. It is one of those historical questions that will probably never be answered. We have all the historical documents that could possibly deal with the question, and a new diary or letter is unlikely.

55. **(B)** This question demands that you understand the theories behind mercantilism. Always select the best answer. Questions occasionally contain excellent distracters, the term for the wrong answers. In (A) both the Woolens Act and the Hat Act apply, but not the Half-Way Covenant, a milestone in Puritan religious doctrine. In (C) the Maryland Act of Toleration was political and religious while the Fundamental Orders of Connecticut was the first written constitution. The Iron Act and the Sugar Act are enticing in (D), but the Stamp Act was to raise revenue. None of the choices in (E) are economic or mercantilist.

56. **(A)** *Worcester v. Georgia* was a contest between a Georgia law and a federal treaty. As Marshall interpreted the Constitution a federal treaty always took precedence over a state law. (See Article VI of the Constitution.) Georgia defied Marshall with the support of President Jackson, who reportedly said, "John Marshall has made his decision, now let him enforce it!" Executive power, the power to enforce laws, lies with the president, who in this case chose not to. The Georgia law had tried to restrict the activities of white missionaries on Indian lands within Georgia. Georgia was trying to push the Indians westward, a policy supported by Jackson, federal treaty or no.

57. **(D)** The creation of a group of idealists headed by James Oglethorpe, Georgia never fulfilled its founders' vision. Liquor and slavery were banned, small farming plots laid out, and a silk industry started. Within a short time all changed. The Fundamental Constitutions of Carolina (1669) envisioned for North and South Carolina an orderly feudal society complete with serfs, tenants, and nobles. Even after four revisions the Fundamental Constitutions were never put into effect.

58. **(A)** Eugene V. Debs was the spokesman for the Socialist Party. The Socialists criticized Samuel Gompers and the American Federation of Labor for concentrating only on

economic gains for workers. The Socialist Party's objectives included the overthrow of the capitalist system. The AFL never criticized capitalism; it just argued for a bigger slice of the pie. Many radical writers have called the AFL one of the strongest supporters of capitalism.

59. **(B)** Charleston and Savannah served as urban centers for the lower South. The Chesapeake Bay permitted ships to visit virtually every tidewater plantation. Despite the well-known restoration of Williamsburg, the Chesapeake South lacked urban centers of social and economic vitality.

60. **(C)** There were few European conflicts to get involved in. The Crimean War, Austro-Prussian War, and Franco-Prussian War were short conflicts confined to Europe. We were also not much involved in European imperialism in Africa and the Far East because most of our territorial acquisitions were contiguous to the United States. We did acquire some minor possessions—Guam, Midway, Samoa, Hawaii, the Philippines—but not until late in the century. The United States forced Japan open, but we never parlayed it into much trade because the Japanese didn't want us. The United States played an outsider's role in the partitioning of China.

Don't be overly impressed by the Monroe Doctrine. After it was announced in 1823 it lay dormant for much of the century. We did chase the French out of Mexico and helped push the British out of part of Venezuela and the Mosquito Coast; but we seemed to many Latin Americans to protect only so that we could seize. We tried to buy or take Cuba and Santo Domingo (the Dominican Republic), and invaded Canada and Mexico in the 19th century.

61. **(A)** Antislavery parties campaigned unsuccessfully in this period. The chief characteristic of the three elections was the death of the Whig Party after 1852 and the sudden birth of the Republican Party in 1854, caused by Northern concern over the Kansas-Nebraska Act. The Republican Party never called for the extinction of slavery. The Whigs won in 1848 with Zachary Taylor. Millard Fillmore became president when Taylor died in July 1850.

62. **(A)** Religion was only one reason for Europe's so-called wars of religion. Nationalism, economic rivalry, dynastic control, and the balance of power also played a role. For many policy makers of this era religion was similar to modern Cold War ideology. Wars over religion were bloody, but far from foolish to contemporaries. Puritans came for freedom from religious persecution, not religious freedom for everyone. Roger Williams wanted to separate church and state to maintain purity of the church, not the state. The English have never separated church and state, although they practice religious freedom.

63. **(D)** Southern financial strategy relied on the easiest method to raise funds, printing money. Wild inflation resulted and made Confederate dollars virtually worthless.

64. **(A)** Wilson pushed for legislative reforms in tariff, banking, and antitrust laws. Theodore Roosevelt was reluctant to fight Congress on these issues, but Wilson was not.

65. **(E)** The Roosevelt Corollary was directed at the Dominican Republic. Cuba was already a semiprotectorate of the U.S. by this time.

66. **(A)** Several hints point to W.E.B. DuBois. The first is the opposition to (Booker T.) Washington, who emphasized thrift, patience, and vocational education at Tuskegee

Institute. The author emphasizes the importance of voting, attacks the racial caste system of Jim Crow, and proposes the education of the "talented tenth," the upper ten percent of the negro race. Finally, he urges using "every civilized and peaceful method," including court suits, demonstrations, newsletters, etc., to fight for black civil rights. Booker T. Washington opposed such methods in public, although he secretly helped finance legal challenges to Jim Crow laws.

67. **(A)** President Washington was uncertain about the constitutionality of the Bank of the United States, which passed Congress on February 8, 1791, and asked for written opinions. The best two came from Secretary of the Treasury Hamilton and Secretary of State Jefferson. They remain the classic statements of loose and strict construction of the Constitution. Washington followed Hamilton's thinking and signed the bill creating the Bank. Hamilton's position was poured into judicial concrete in the McCulloch decision in 1819. In purchasing Louisiana in 1803 Jefferson swallowed his strict interpretation stance. The Constitution does not indicate who, if anyone, may purchase new territory for the United States. There wasn't time to pass a constitutional amendment to give the president authority, and the deal was too good to pass up!

68. **(B)** In all three years the most backward agricultural section of the nation was the South. The South was labor rich and land poor, forcing farmers to work as tenants.

69. **(A)** In the first quote Emerson vented his anger at the Fugitive Slave Act, part of the Compromise of 1850. The second quote was Jefferson's prophetic reaction to the bitterness over the admission of Missouri as a slave state, eventually resolved in the Compromise of 1820. William Lloyd Garrison's first issue of the *Liberator* carried his uncompromising approach to abolition. More quotable than influential, he guaranteed that his position in the abolitionist movement would be overemphasized.

70. **(E)** The city manager and commission forms of government belong to the later Progressive Era. Galveston, Texas invented the commission form of government after a hurricane struck the city in 1900. Divided responsibility sped recovery. Staunton, Virginia first used the city manager plan in 1908. Following a disastrous flood in 1910 Dayton, Ohio adopted the city manager plan, widely publicizing it as an efficient municipal government.

71. **(A)** The Iroquois Confederacy prevented settlers from moving westward. There is a natural break in the Appalachian Mountains in northern New York, where the route of the Erie Canal was built between 1817 and 1825. The Northwest Ordinance of 1785 applied to the old Northwest Territory: Ohio, Indiana, Illinois, Michigan, Wisconsin, and part of Minnesota. The bulk of the Scotch-Irish settled in western Pennsylvania and, following the Shenandoah Valley, the back country of the South.

72. **(E)** George Washington Carver was a distinguished scientist at Tuskegee Institute, run by Booker T. Washington. Hoping to draw black farmers out of the vicious cycle of cotton production, Carver invented over three hundred products for peanuts, including peanut butter.

73. **(E)** All have been advanced as the causes or characteristics of Progressivism. The following historians are associated with each description: Joseph Huthmacher: urban lower classes; George Mowry and Richard Hofstadter: middle class status; David Thelan: corporate arrogance; Gabriel Kolko: political capitalism; and Arthur Schlesinger, Jr.: alternating cycles of reform and reaction.

74. **(D)** Corn was a major crop in Virginia and Maryland, but tobacco was the chief export. Barrels of rice passed through Charleston and Savannah. Molasses was imported into New England to make rum, the chief export. Fish was also a major New England export, but was not shipped in gallons!

75. **(C)** Do not be fooled by the references to gold in the passage; Bryan and Morgan are incorrect. The only socialist among the choices is Eugene V. Debs. Imprisoned after the fiasco of the Pullman strike in 1894, Debs read socialist literature and emerged from jail a confirmed socialist. He helped organize the Socialist Party in 1901. His most successful campaign for the presidency garnered almost one million votes while he was an inmate in the Atlanta Federal Penitentiary, sentenced under the Sedition Act of 1918.

76. **(A)** In chronological order, the wartime conferences are the following. The Atlantic Charter meeting in August 1941 took place before U.S. participation in the Second World War. Churchill and FDR issued a statement of principles, and committed themselves to cooperation between the United States and Great Britain. In February 1943 at the Casablanca Conference FDR and Churchill announced that the war would continue until the unconditional surrender of the Axis powers. In November 1943 FDR, Churchill, and Chiang Kai-shek conferred in Cairo on the war against Japan, and agreed upon postwar territorial changes in the Far East. In December 1943 FDR and Churchill met with Stalin for the first time. The most important agreement at Teheran was the American and British pledge to finally open a second front against Germany. In February 1945 an ailing FDR met with Stalin and Churchill at Yalta to make arrangements for the postwar world. A call was issued for a San Francisco meeting to establish the United Nations. The Yalta agreements were later heavily criticized as too favorable to the Soviet Union, but one should not read history backwards. At the time the agreements seemed essential. The United States needed Soviet help to defeat Japan, for it was estimated that the war against Japan would go on for two or three more years. The atomic bomb was not even tested until July 16, 1945. Japan's weakness far exceeded expectations. We no longer needed Russian help, but it was too late to redefine the Yalta agreements. The Russians were also granted dominance in Eastern Europe, but there was not much else FDR could have done, since the Russian army already occupied the area.

77. **(E)** Reread the Declaration of Independence. Only (E) is missing. Governments exist to provide equality of opportunity in a negative sense of not giving special privileges to a few, but nowhere does the Declaration of Independence assert everyone's right to an equal share of the wealth of the nation. It is primarily a political document.

78. **(D)** The official declaration didn't mention Canada. Americans were of two minds in regard to Canada: some wanted to take it and others wished to invade it as a means of punishing the British.

79. **(C)** The Caroline affair in 1837–1838 strained U.S.-British relations. American supporters of an abortive Canadian revolution transported supplies to the rebels on the ship Caroline. Canadian militia crossed to the American side of the Niagara River and burned it. Passions and retaliations continued for several years. The Webster-Ashburton Treaty in 1842 settled the border between Maine and New Brunswick, a sticky situation dating from the Revolutionary War. In the Trent affair in 1861 a U.S. ship stopped the British steamer Trent and removed two Confederate commissioners, James Mason and John Slidell. Secretary of State Seward later ordered the two released because even if the two were guilty of treason, the United States didn't have the right

to commandeer a British ship in order to capture them. The Laird rams were Confederate ships being built in a private British shipyard for the South in 1863. After the U.S. minister, Charles Francis Adams, complained, the British government seized the ships as a violation of Great Britain's neutrality.

80. **(D)** Marcus Garvey formed the Universal Negro Improvement Association and the African Communities League in Jamaica in 1914. After moving to Harlem in 1916 Garvey became a symbol of black pride and nationalism. He devised a black, green, and red flag for blacks. His movement floundered after several bad business ventures and his conviction for mail fraud. The other black leaders came after Garvey. A. Phillip Randolph organized the Brotherhood of Sleeping Car Porters and Maids in 1925. Robert C. Weaver was the first black cabinet member, appointed secretary of the new Department of Housing and Urban Development in 1966. Thurgood Marshall was the first black appointed to the Supreme Court. Ralph Bunche held several top positions in the United Nations, and won the Nobel Peace Prize in 1950 for his work during the Arab-Israeli conflict following the creation of Israel.

81. **(D)** The Gideon case granted the right of free counsel for poor defendants accused in state felony prosecutions. The Escobedo and Miranda cases dealt with the right to counsel and protection against self-incrimination. *Baker* v. *Carr* involved legislative reapportionment. The Bakke case concerned reverse discrimination.

82. **(A)** The characters are from *The Scarlet Letter.* Hester Prynne is found guilty of adultery for bearing the child of Arthur Dimmesdale, one of the ministers. Her husband, believed lost at sea, returns on the day of her public condemnation because she refuses to name the child's father. He forces her to help conceal his identity while he takes a new name, Roger Chillingworth. The crux of the novel revolves around the different types of sin each exemplifies: Chillingworth in the unpardonable pursuit of the father; Dimmesdale in the suffering of secret sin; and Prynne in the penitent yet proud sinner.

83. **(D)** Deference was the belief that everyone knew his place and acted accordingly. As long as colonists lived in relatively confined areas everyone knew everyone else, and therefore, knew their positions socially and politically. Popular sovereignty, associated with the 1850s, referred to the people in the territories deciding the status, slave or free, for their territory.

84. **(C)** The number of new jobs in the economy is 55,230,000 minus 49,180,000, or 6,050,000, a 12.3% growth. Hoover never had a second term. The Schechter "sick chicken" case declared the NRA unconstitutional in 1935. The economy was improving after that date, but the improvement had nothing to do with the decision. FDR never endorsed Keynesian economics; in many respects he remained an old-fashioned fiscal conservative in his thinking. The New Deal brought hope and work to many people in many sections of the economy, but statistics show that the New Deal alone did not solve the problem of employment. The Second World War solved it.

85. **(B)** Republican Senator Henry Cabot Lodge helped keep the United States out of the League of Nations after the First World War. Republican Senator Arthur H. Vandenberg helped put the United States into the United Nations after the Second World War.

86. **(A)** National political action proved to be futile, and forced abolitionists to depend on moral persuasion. The Know-Nothings focused their attention only on the immigrant

flood. They never advocated a black sanctuary, although John Brown raised the issue. Every Northern state considered the question of black suffrage in the period before the Civil War. All either rejected it or took voting rights away from blacks. The North was no paradise for free blacks or escaped slaves, but at least they didn't have slavery.

87. **(A)** Compulsory attendance laws drew children out of the labor market. Therefore, you would not find compulsory attendance laws where children were heavily employed as in the South.

88. **(E)** Marshall's decision in *Gibbons* v. *Ogden* (1824) asserted congressional control over interstate commerce even in the absence of federal legislation. The case involved a New York state grant of a monopoly for steamship navigation between New York and New Jersey. The Marbury case concerned judicial review. McCulloch established the constitutionality of the Bank of the U.S., and therefore of a liberal interpretation of the elastic clause. The Cohens case established federal review of state court decisions. The Slaughterhouse Case in 1873 began the narrow interpretation of the Fourteenth Amendment in regard to civil rights for blacks.

89. **(B)** The quotations are from the Rev. Walter Rauschenbusch, professor of church history at Rochester Theological Seminary from 1902 to 1918. His book, *Christianity and the Social Crisis,* (1907) established him as one of the leaders of the Social Gospel movement. As the highest creature on the evolutionary ladder the principles of that ladder did not necessarily apply to man.

90. **(E)** These two projects set off the "transportation revolution." Route A is the Erie Canal, financed entirely by the state of New York. The federal government funded Route B, the National Road. Jackson vetoed the Maysville Road project because it lay entirely within a single state, Kentucky. Jackson's enemy, Henry Clay, sponsored the bill, which helped doom the proposal. At the time there were hundreds of proposals in Congress for federal funding for internal improvements.

91. **(B)** Before 1767 it cost the British more to collect the customs duties than they collected! After 1767 the British made a determined effort to collect their taxes, and the resulting ill will helped fuel the revolutionary spirit.

92. **(C)** The Rev. Martin Luther King, Jr., delivered this famous speech in 1963 on the steps of the Lincoln Memorial, climaxing the massive March on Washington. He was awarded the Nobel Peace Prize in 1964.

93. **(B)** For many reasons complete neutrality proved impossible to maintain after 1914. Choices I, II, III, and V all contributed to what eventually was a distinctly unneutral American position toward Germany. The League of Nations was established after the First World War.

94. **(A)** Jefferson's letter of February 15, 1791, and Hamilton's letter of February 23, 1791, were two of three opinions Washington requested on the constitutionality of the Bank of the U.S. Attorney General Randolph actually submitted two letters, one against the bank and one equivocal. Jefferson's letter and Hamilton's letter are the classic summaries of the strict and loose construction theories.

95. **(E)** Upton Sinclair wrote *The Jungle* to dramatize the plight of the workers. As Sinclair later complained, "I aimed at the public's heart and hit it in the stomach." He hoped to

arouse the public's sympathy for immigrant workers. Often mentioned and rarely read by students, *The Jungle* should be read as a work of literature and as a work of protest rather than as an exposé.

96. **(D)** Social Security benefits were expanded and cut the poverty rate in half among those 65 and older.

97. **(E)** California entered the Union as a free state in 1850, but no slave state entered to maintain the balance in the Senate. The Missouri Compromise in 1820 brought in Missouri as a slave state and Maine as a free state, and also established the 36° 30′ line dividing the slave and free territories to the Rocky Mountains. A provision in the original Constitution ended the slave trade in 1808. The Confederate debt went unpaid after the Civil War.

98. **(B)** Until the 1840s Rhode Island continued to operate her state government under the 1663 colonial charter, which restricted suffrage to property owners and their eldest sons. Rebuffed by legal and constitutional efforts to expand suffrage, Thomas Dorr led a popular uprising that gave Rhode Island two governors, two legislatures, and a very small armed confrontation. The federal government avoided getting involved in the ensuing political mess. Luckily, the dissidents won their original demand for expanded suffrage in a few years. None of the other choices involve the fundamental nature of state governments.

99. **(A)** By the end of the 1880s immigrants from Southern and Eastern Europe outnumbered any other group. The Irish who fled the potato famine came in the 1840s. Chinese immigration disappeared in the 1880s following the 1882 Chinese Exclusion Act. By the 1880s the majority of immigrants lived in large cities, giving a distinct flavor to urban America. The second immigration act of 1924 used 1890 as a base for calculating the percentage of immigrants from each country permitted into the United States.

100. **(D)** General MacArthur disputed the concept of a limited war, and argued for an attack against the Chinese mainland. Truman relieved him of his command for publically criticizing the Commander in Chief. In a speech before Congress, MacArthur delivered his famous, "In war there can be no substitute for victory." But in the nuclear age, it's possible there can be no victory.

Sample Test C

AMERICAN HISTORY

SECTION I

Time—1 hour and 15 minutes

100 Questions

Directions: Each of the questions or incomplete statements below is followed by five suggested answers or completions. Select the one that is best in each case and then blacken the corresponding space on the answer sheet.

1. More than any other, this colony was the lengthened shadow of one man. He offered easy land terms of 50 free acres; laid out his principal city in checkerboard fashion to prevent a disaster similar to the Great Fire of London; and offered a sincere trust in humanity and religious freedom in his "Holy Experiment." What colony and founder is described?

   (A) New York—Peter Stuyvesant
   (B) Georgia—James Oglethorpe
   (C) Pennsylvania—William Penn
   (D) Maryland—Lord Baltimore
   (E) Massachusetts Bay—John Winthrop

2. The treaties that came out of the Washington Disarmament Conference in the early 1920s—the Five Power Naval Disarmament Treaty, the Four Power Treaty, and the Nine Power Treaty—were consistent with previous American foreign policy in regard to the

   (A) Open Door Notes
   (B) Stimson Doctrine
   (C) mediation of the Russo-Japanese War
   (D) Versailles Treaty
   (E) Monroe Doctrine

3. The most important influence on the institution of slavery was the

   (A) cotton gin
   (B) gag rule
   (C) American Colonization Society
   (D) Underground Railroad
   (E) "Three-fifths" Compromise

4. "There are, in this case, all the essential constituent parts of a contract. There is something to be contracted about; there are parties, and there are plain terms in which the agreement of the parties, on the subject of the contract, is expressed. There are mutual considerations and inducements. The charter recites, that the founder, on his part, has agreed to establish his seminary in New Hampshire, and to enlarge it, beyond its original design, among other things, for the benefit of that province; and thereupon a charter is given to him and his associates, designated by himself, promising and assuring to them, under the plighted faith of the state, the right of . . . administering its concerns, in the manner provided in the charter. There is a complete and perfect grant to them of all the power of superintendence, visitation, and government. Is this not a contract?" This quotation

   (A) is from Calhoun's Exposition and Protest opposing the Tariff of Abominations
   (B) is from Marshall's decison in *Gibbons v. Ogden*
   (C) is from a speech in favor of the Morrill Land-Grant College Act
   (D) illustrates the emotions and arguments of the Great Awakening
   (E) is from Daniel Webster's argument before the Supreme Court in the Dartmouth College case

5. If all of these five were transported back to the antebellum period, which would be most likely to approve of the "Cult of True Womanhood?"

    (A) Phyllis Schlafly
    (B) Betty Friedan
    (C) Carrie Nation
    (D) Gloria Steinem
    (E) Shirley Chisholm

6. Who practiced polygamy, organized an authoritarian political community, and separated themselves from outsiders?

    (A) Shakers
    (B) Mormons
    (C) Christian Scientists
    (D) Quakers
    (E) the Amish

7. "If a nation shows that it knows how to act with reasonable efficiency and decency in social and political matters, if it keeps order and pays its obligations, it need fear no interference from the United States. Chronic wrongdoing, or an impotence which results in a general loosening of the ties of civilized society, may in America, as elsewhere, ultimately require intervention by some civilized nation, and in the Western Hemisphere the adherence of the United States to the Monroe Doctrine may force the United States, however reluctantly, in flagrant cases of such wrongdoing or impotence, to the exercise of an international police power." What foreign policy was based upon this statement?

    (A) dollar diplomacy
    (B) "watchful waiting" in Mexico
    (C) Good Neighbor policy
    (D) Open Door policy
    (E) Roosevelt Corollary

8. The Great Compromise during the writing of the Constitution involved

    (A) the creation of three separate branches of government—executive, legislative, and judicial
    (B) determining whether sovereignty rested with the states or the federal government
    (C) the respective powers of the House and Senate and representation in the Senate and the House

    (D) ending the slave trade after twenty years
    (E) whether or not only a majority vote was needed to tax imports

9. Bruce Barton's *The Man Nobody Knows* (1925) differed from William Stead's *If Christ Came to Chicago* (1894) and Charles Sheldon's *In His Steps* (1897) in that the first book

    (A) was part of the Social Gospel movement
    (B) reconciled business ethics and Christian teachings
    (C) condemned big businessmen for not doing enough to aid the poor
    (D) concerned advertising and politics, whereas the other two concerned religion
    (E) was part of the muckraking tradition

10. "But the injuries and disadvantages we sustain by that connection are without number, and our duty to mankind at large, as well as to ourselves, instruct us to renounce the alliance [with Great Britain as colonies]: because any submission to or dependence on Great Britain, tends directly to involve this continent in European wars and quarrels. As Europe is our market for trade, we ought to form no partial connection with any part of it . . . England and America . . . belong to different systems. England to Europe: America to itself."
    This quotation from Thomas Paine's *Common Sense* foresaw the

    (A) NATO and SEATO alliances
    (B) Monroe Doctrine
    (C) Atlantic Charter
    (D) end of the French and Indian War
    (E) Roosevelt Corollary

11. This act guaranteed the right of labor unions to organize and to bargain collectively, and created the National Labor Relations Board to ensure fair and open campaigning by unions for initial union recognition and organization. Which act is described?

    (A) Clayton Act
    (B) Norris-LaGuardia Act
    (C) Taft-Hartley Act
    (D) Landrum-Griffin Act
    (E) Wagner Act

12. The legacy of Reconstruction included

    (A) the Solid South and the rise of the Redeemers or Bourbons
    (B) constitutional amendments to ensure black civil rights sometime in the future
    (C) the crop lien system and sharecropping
    (D) expenditures for badly needed schools and roads
    (E) all of the above

13. All of the following except one contributed to the adoption of Jim Crow laws in the South in the 1890s. Which of the following did *not*?

    (A) a decline in the commitment of Northern liberals to civil rights for blacks
    (B) the inability of the Southern Redeemer conservative governments to maintain control of Southern state governments
    (C) the adoption of racism by Southern Populist radicals to counter conservative Redeemer use of racism to win political support
    (D) civil rights marches and agitation by Southern blacks, provoking white retaliation
    (E) a series of Supreme Court decisions weakening the protection of civil rights granted by the Fourteenth Amendment

14. "His Catholic Majesty will permit the citizens of the United States, for the space of three years from this time, to deposit their merchandizes and effects in the port of New-Orleans, and to export them from thence without paying any duty than a fair price for the hire of the stores, and His Majesty promises either to continue this permission, if he finds during that time that it is not prejudicial to the interests of Spain, or if he should not agree to continue it there, he will assign to them, on another part of the banks of the Mississippi, an equivalent establishment." This quotation is from

    (A) the Treaty of Paris (1763) ending the French and Indian War (Seven Years' War)
    (B) the Treaty of Paris 1783
    (C) Pinckney's Treaty with Spain
    (D) the Clayton-Bulwer Treaty
    (E) the Jay-Gardoqui Treaty

15. President Martin Van Buren endorsed the Independent Treasury plan that

    (A) ordered payment of land purchases in specie
    (B) advocated the creation of a new Bank of the U.S.
    (C) advocated the creation of a Federal Reserve banking network
    (D) provided for federal depositories independent of private or state banks
    (E) deposited federal revenues in "pet banks"

16. Who defended his business practices as a necessary survival of the fittest? "The American Beauty Rose can be produced in the splendor and fragrance which bring cheer to its beholder only by sacrificing the early buds which grow up around it. This is not an evil tendency in business. It is merely the working out of a law of nature and a law of God."

    (A) Matthew Josephson
    (B) J. Pierpont Morgan
    (C) John D. Rockefeller
    (D) William Jennings Bryan
    (E) Andrew Carnegie

17. Which was *not* part of the politics of 1865 to 1900?

    (A) waving the bloody shirt
    (B) the Grand Army of the Republic
    (C) Crédit Mobilier
    (D) Mugwumps
    (E) Loco-Focos

18. It is impossible for us to know how many colonists attended church services. We do know, however, how many church buildings existed in 1775. The largest single denomination had only 668 out of 3142 buildings. Knowing what you do about religion in colonial America, which of the following would be arranged in order from highest number to lowest number of church buildings?

    (A) Congregational, Anglican, Quaker, Catholic
    (B) Anglican, Catholic, Mennonite, Quaker
    (C) Catholic, Huguenot, Methodist, Congregational
    (D) Quaker, Lutheran, Jewish synagogues, Dunker
    (E) Catholic, Presbyterian, Anglican, Moravian

19. Franklin Roosevelt put together a coalition of different groups that became the backbone of the Democratic Party for the next thirty years. FDR's Democratic coalition included all of the following *except*

    (A) Southerners
    (B) suburbanites
    (C) blacks
    (D) urban machines
    (E) labor

20. All of the following contributed to the causes of the Mexican War *except*

    (A) the election of 1844
    (B) the spot resolutions
    (C) Mexican anger over the Republic of Texas
    (D) American designs on California
    (E) private claims of U.S. citizens against Mexico

21. According to the census of 1790, of the four largest ethnic groups in the United States, which of the following gives the correct order for describing the ethnic groups from the largest to the smallest?

    (A) English, black, Scots and Scotch-Irish, German
    (B) English, German, Scots and Scotch-Irish, black
    (C) English, Scots and Scotch-Irish, black, German
    (D) Scots and Scotch-Irish, English, German, black
    (E) German, English, Scots and Scotch-Irish, black

22. The 1850s were marked by intense North-South debate over the issue of slavery in the territories, yet the census of 1860 listed only seven slaves in the Nebraska territory and two in the Kansas territory. What explains the contradiction between the actual number of slaves in the Kansas and Nebraska territories and the intensity of the dispute?

    (A) Slaveholders expected to move into Kansas and Nebraska when opposition to slavery in that area decreased.
    (B) The issue of slavery in the territories had become an important symbol to both sections and an indication of the future direction of the economy and the nation.

    (C) The Lecompton Constitution safeguarding slaveholders had not yet been adopted.
    (D) John Brown's raid on Harpers Ferry led to the Pottawatomie massacre, causing slaveholders to retreat to Missouri.
    (E) Slavery was tied to cotton production, which was impractical in the Kansas and Nebraska territories.

23. In his early political career he was a Republican state representative in the New York state legislature, an unsuccessful candidate for mayor of New York City, a member of the United States Civil Service Commission, and the head of the New York City Board of Police Commissioners. Who is described?

    (A) Lyndon Johnson
    (B) Woodrow Wilson
    (C) Theodore Roosevelt
    (D) John F. Kennedy
    (E) William Jennings Bryan

24. "The price which society pays for the law of competition, like the price it pays for cheap comforts and luxuries, is also great; but the advantages of this law are also greater still, for it is to this law that we owe our wonderful material development, which brings improved conditions in its train. But, whether the law be benign or not, we must say of it, as we say of the change in the conditions of men to which we have referred: It is here; we cannot evade it; no substitutes for it have been found; and while the law may be sometimes hard for the individual, it is best for the race, because it insures the survival of the fittest in every department. We accept and welcome, therefore, as conditions to which we must accommodate ourselves, great inequality of environment, the concentration of business, industrial and commercial, in the hands of a few, and the law of competition between these, as being not only beneficial, but essential for the future progress of the race." Which of the following would *not* have supported this statement?

    (A) William Graham Sumner
    (B) Herbert Spencer
    (C) Henry George
    (D) John D. Rockefeller
    (E) Andrew Carnegie

25. In 1811 there were 88 state banks; in 1816, 256. What explains the increase in the number of state banks from 1811 to 1816?

    (A) The needs of the wartime economy during the War of 1812 demanded it.
    (B) The restraining influence of the first Bank ended when its charter expired.
    (C) Regional trade was stimulated by the building of canals.
    (D) Federalists replaced the Democrats, and changed federal banking policies.
    (E) New banks were established under the National Banking system.

26. Which famous American woman is *not* correctly matched to her accomplishments?

    (A) Jane Addams founded Hull House, the first settlement house in America.
    (B) Mary Lyon, pioneering woman educator, founded Mount Holyoke.
    (C) Susan B. Anthony advocated women's suffrage.
    (D) Frances Willard advocated better treatment of the insane before the Civil War.
    (E) Frances Perkins was the first woman cabinet member, Secretary of Labor under FDR.

27.   Executive Office, State of _____
                                        July 6, 18__

    Hon. XXXX, President of the United States, Sir: "Your answer to my protest involves some startling conclusions and ignores and evades the question at issue—that is, that the principle of local self-government is just as fundamental in our institutions as is that of Federal supremacy. . . .

    "You calmly assume that the executive has the legal right to order Federal troops into any community of the United States, in the first instance, whenever there is the slightest disturbance, and that he can do this without any regard to the question as to whether that community is able and ready to enforce the law itself. Inasmuch as the executive is the sole judge of the question as to whether any disturbance exists in any part of the country, this assumption means that the executive can send Federal troops into any community in the

    United States at at his pleasure, and keep them there as long as he chooses. . . .

    "You say that troops were ordered in . . . upon the demand of the post-office department, and upon representations of the judicial officers of the United States that process of the courts could not be served, and upon proof that conspiracies existed."

    This letter was written by a state governor to

    (A) Cleveland during the Pullman strike
    (B) Eisenhower during the Little Rock crisis
    (C) Washington during the Whiskey Rebellion
    (D) Jackson during the nullification crisis
    (E) Truman after he dismissed General MacArthur

28. Which of the following statements contradicts Jefferson's philosophy of government?

    (A) That government is best which governs the least.
    (B) The presidency should have little pomposity or ceremony.
    (C) A strong army is essential to defend liberty.
    (D) Freedom of speech is essential in a republic.
    (E) The will of the majority must by accepted.

29. In the 1912 presidential campaign Woodrow Wilson urged his New Freedom, Theodore Roosevelt his New Nationalism. Which of the following statements about these two economic philosophies is correct?

    (A) Wilson won the election and put his philosophy into legislation and into practice.
    (B) Roosevelt won the election and put his philosophy into legislation and into practice.
    (C) In the next seventy years the federal government's approach to big business and antitrust followed New Nationalism philosophy.
    (D) New Deal economic policies were mainly a continuation of New Freedom policies.
    (E) They were both copied from Eugene V. Debs' program for the economy.

State Representation in 18th Century Representative Bodies

(The number of representatives from the colonies/states who signed the following documents and who served in the First Congress.)

	Albany Plan of Union	Dec. of Indep.	Art. of Confed.	Const. of 1787	First Congress under the Const.
NH	2	3	2	2	3
Mass	7	5	6	2	8
Conn	5	4	5	2	5
RI	2	2	3	0	1
NY	4	4	4	1	6
NJ	3	5	2	4	4
PA	6	9	5	8	8
DE	0	3	3	5	1
MD	4	4	2	3	6
Vir	7	7	5	3	10
NC	4	3	3	3	5
SC	4	4	5	4	5
GA	0	3	3	2	3

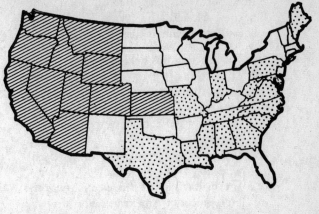

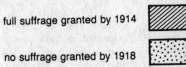

full suffrage granted by 1914

no suffrage granted by 1918

30. What is the best conclusion to draw from these figures?

(A) Colonists followed virtual representation in practice despite their protests to Great Britain.

(B) Representation in political conventions was apportioned by population as much as possible.

(C) Drawing a conclusion is difficult because for personal and political reasons some delegates did not sign the documents.

(D) The majority of the delegates to the Constitutional Convention did not sign that document.

(E) Most of the signers of one document signed the other documents.

31. The Camp David Accords, agreed to under the leadership of President Carter, led to peace in the Middle East between

(A) Iran and Iraq
(B) Afganistan and the Soviet Union
(C) Lebanon and Israel
(D) Israel and Egypt
(E) the Soviet Union and the United States

32. The proper title for this map is

(A) "Women's Suffrage Movement"
(B) "Manhood Suffrage in the Era of Jacksonian Democracy"
(C) "Black Suffrage During Reconstruction"
(D) "Jim Crow Laws and Black Suffrage"
(E) "Suffrage Laws and the Populist Movement"

33. Which of the following statements concerning mercantilism is accurate?

(A) Laissez-faire was a basic concept in mercantilism.

(B) Mercantilism seriously retarded the development of a wide range of colonial industries.

(C) Americans were economically hurt by the laws requiring all imperial trade to be carried in British ships manned by British sailors.

(D) The British government controlled and directed economic activities to benefit the national state more than the colonies or individual British citizens.

(E) A nation increased its national wealth by importing more goods than it exported.

34. The following is the electoral college vote for president in the second race between John Adams and Thomas Jefferson: Jefferson, 73;

Aaron Burr, 73; John Adams, 65; Charles Pinckney, 64; and John Jay, 1. Which of the following statements is true?

(A) This election was held in 1796.
(B) This election led to the adoption of the Twelfth Amendment.
(C) Because of the tie the president was selected by the Senate, as specified by the Constitution.
(D) This presidential campaign was Jefferson's reelection to the presidency.
(E) The major issue of this election was the impressment of American sailors.

35. The first talking motion picture was

(A) *The Jazz Singer*
(B) *Rebel Without a Cause*
(C) *Gone With the Wind*
(D) *Birth of a Nation*
(E) *Bridge On the River Kwai*

36. Which statement describes American social structure in the Age of Jackson, 1820–1850?

(A) American society became more aristocratic.
(B) Social mobility increased and economic equality increased.
(C) Social mobility increased and economic inequality increased.
(D) There was social rigidity and an increase in economic inequality.
(E) There was social rigidity and an increase in economic equality.

37. The Mayflower Compact is significant in American political thought because

(A) in it the people regard themselves as the source of political power
(B) in it the people agreed to be bound by the will of the majority
(C) it was copied for the Massachusetts Bay Charter
(D) in it church and state are separated
(E) in it were provisions guaranteeing civil rights for women and blacks

38. The Dawes Act

(A) made Native Americans (Indians) citizens
(B) established the reservation system
(C) pushed the Native Americans (Indians) further west
(D) failed in its intended purpose
(E) led to the publication of *A Century of Dishonor*

Percentage Margin of Victory by the Winning Presidential Candidate Over His Nearest Opponent, by States

	1828	1832	1836	1840	1844
Massachusetts	66	30	9	16	12
Connecticut	50	20	1	11	5
New York	2	4	9	4	1
Pennsylvania	33	16	4	1	2
Virginia	38	50	13	1	6
North Carolina	47	70	6	15	5
Kentucky	1	9	6	29	8
Tennessee	90	90	16	11	1
Mississippi	60	77	2	7	13
Indiana	13	34	12	12	2
Illinois	34	37	10	2	12
Missouri	41	32	21	14	17
Total Average	36%	36%	11%	11%	9%

Percentage of Adult White Males Voting in Presidential Elections

1824: 26.5%	1836: 55.2%
1828: 56.3%	1840: 78.0%
1832: 54.9%	1844: 74.9%

39. The figures from these two tables support the statement that

(A) Andrew Jackson's campaign in 1840 and 1844 stimulated high voter interest.
(B) Voter participation increased as presidential elections within individual states became more hotly contested.
(C) Jacksonian Democracy dramatically increased the number of voters.
(D) Issue-oriented presidential campaigns such as the election of 1840 stimulated high voter turnout.
(E) The antislavery movement changed voting patterns.

40. Which labor group pursued limited objectives, excluded intellectuals, avoided politics, and avoided broad social aims?

    (A) American Federation of Labor
    (B) Knights of Labor
    (C) American Railway Union
    (D) National Labor Union
    (E) Socialist Party

41. Who glorified America in *Leaves of Grass?*

    (A) Nathaniel Hawthorne
    (B) James Fenimore Cooper
    (C) Henry Wadsworth Longfellow
    (D) Walt Whitman
    (E) Joseph Smith

42. "The fruits of the toil of millions are boldly stolen to build up colossal fortunes for a few, unprecedented in the history of mankind; and the possessors of these, in turn, despise the Republic and endanger liberty. From the same prolific womb of governmental injustice we breed the two great classes—tramps and millionaires. . . .

    "We have witnessed for more than a quarter of a century the struggles of the two great political parties for power and plunder, while grievous wrongs have been inflicted upon the suffering people. We charge that the controlling influences dominating both these parties have permitted the existing dreadful conditions to develop without serious effort to prevent or restrain them. Neither do they now promise us any substantial reform." These quotes are from a political party platform that was part of the presidential election of

    (A) 1932
    (B) 1924
    (C) 1912
    (D) 1892
    (E) 1948

43. Four of the following contributed to the passage of the immigration acts of 1921 and 1924. Which did *not?*

    (A) results of I.Q. tests given to American soldiers during the First World War

    (B) resentment of workers against foreign immigrants' taking jobs away from Americans by their willingness to work for low wages
    (C) a belief, caused by two short postwar depressions, that the nation's pool of labor was already overcrowded
    (D) the belief that those immigrants already in the country were not adequately Americanized
    (E) a desire to resume after the First World War the prewar policy of restrictive quotas

44. Which is true of both the Korean War and the Vietnam War?

    (A) Both led to a change in the party occupying the White House.
    (B) It is possible to establish the day on which the first enemy military action took place in each war.
    (C) In both wars the United States took over after a long unsuccessful struggle by an ally.
    (D) The United Nations entered both wars, and branded North Korea and North Vietnam as aggressors.
    (E) The United States had stated clearly that it would defend South Korea and South Vietnam if attacked.

45. Which New Deal agency no longer exists?

    (A) Agricultural Adjustment Administration (AAA)
    (B) Securities and Exchange Commission (SEC)
    (C) Federal Housing Administration (FHA)
    (D) Federal Deposit Insurance Corporation (FDIC)
    (E) Tennessee Valley Authority (TVA)

46. "A modern industrial plant has a hundred trades and parts of trades represented in its working force. To have these workers parcelled out to a hundred unions is to divide and not to organize them, to give them over to factions and petty leadership and leave them an easy prey to the machinations of the enemy. The dominant craft should control the plant or, the union, and it should embrace the entire working force. This is the industrial plan, the

modern method applied to modern conditions, and it will in time prevail."

(A) This passage is from the 1881 preamble to the constitution of the American Federation of Labor.
(B) This passage explains the role of industrial company unions in the 1920s.
(C) This criticism was delivered against the American Railway Union during the Pullman strike.
(D) This quotation is from the Taft-Hartley Act.
(E) This criticism was answered by the formation of the CIO in the 1930s.

47. "The Dixiecrats deserted him over the issue of civil rights for blacks. Thousands of his potential supporters swung to Henry Wallace's Progressive Party. His major opponent came from New York and had been the presidential candidate four years before. And, yet, somehow he won." Who is referred to?

(A) Jimmy Carter in 1976
(B) Richard Nixon in 1968
(C) Franklin D. Roosevelt in 1932
(D) John F. Kennedy in 1960
(E) Harry Truman in 1948

48. Established churches (tax-supported) existed in all of the colonies *except*

(A) New Jersey and Massachusetts
(B) Pennsylvania and Rhode Island
(C) Virginia and South Carolina
(D) Maryland and Pennsylvania
(E) New York and Rhode Island

49. The Thirteenth, Fourteenth, and Fifteenth Amendments to the Constitution

(A) were necessary to secure the civil rights of the freedmen
(B) completed the political proposals of William Lloyd Garrison
(C) were widely supported in the North
(D) were passed because of Andrew Johnson's strong support
(E) were passed and ratified as a group

50. All of the following were crises during the Eisenhower administration *except* the

(A) U-2 spy plane incident
(B) building of the Berlin Wall

(C) tension between Red China and Nationalist China in the Taiwan Straits
(D) Suez Canal crisis
(E) Lebanon crisis leading to the Eisenhower Doctrine

51. In 1774 Jefferson wrote that although "single acts of tyranny may be ascribed to the accidental opinion of a day . . . a series of oppressions begun at a distinguished period and pursued unalterably through every change of ministers too plainly prove a deliberate and systematic plan of reducing us to slavery." Which of the following was *not* cited in this period as "deliberate and systematic" efforts to attack liberty?

(A) Boston Massacre and the massacre in St. Georges fields
(B) missionaries sent by the Society for the Propagation of the Gospel
(C) Stamp Act
(D) John Wilkes' being denied a seat in Parliament
(E) British refusal to evacuate the Northwest posts

52. "Whereas it appears that a state of war exists between Austria, Prussia, Sardinia, Great Britain, and the United Netherlands on the one part and France on the other, and the duty and interest of the United States require that they should with sincerity and good faith adopt and pursue a conduct friendly and impartial toward the belligerent powers:

"I have therefore thought fit by these presents to declare the disposition of the United States to observe the conduct aforesaid toward those powers respectively, and to exhort and warn the citizens of the United States carefully to avoid all acts and proceeding whatsoever which may in any manner tend to contravene such disposition." This quotation is from

(A) a speech by Franklin Roosevelt after the beginning of the Second World War in Europe
(B) the Good Neighbor policy of Hoover, which was endorsed by Franklin Roosevelt
(C) Wilson's declaration at the outbreak of the First World War
(D) Washington's Neutrality Proclamation
(E) Jefferson's embargo on foreign trade

53. The dotted lines on the map represent the

    (A) canal routes used by entrepreneurs
    (B) National Road linking the states together
    (C) new territory in the Louisiana Purchase
    (D) extent of the frontier line for 1800 and 1830
    (E) lines for the Proclamation of 1763

54. "The sympathies of the Democratic Party, as shown by the platform, are on the side of the struggling masses who have ever been the foundation of the Democratic party. There are two ideas of government. There are those who believe that, if you will only legislate to make the well-to-do prosperous, their prosperity will leak through on those below. The Democratic idea, however, has been that if you legislate to make the masses prosperous, their prosperity will find its way up through every class which rests upon them.

    "You come to us and tell us that the great cities are in favor of the gold standard; we reply that the great cities rest upon our broad and fertile prairies. Burn down your cities and leave our farms, and your cities will spring up again as if by magic; but destroy our farms and the grass will grow in the streets of every city in the country."
This speech came from

    (A) the campaign of William Jennings Bryan for the presidency in 1896
    (B) the campaign of Franklin D. Roosevelt for the presidency in 1932
    (C) the campaign of Theodore Roosevelt for the presidency in 1912
    (D) the attempt by McNary and Haugen to secure price supports for farmers in the 1920s
    (E) FDR in support of a second Agricultural Adjustment Act after the first was declared unconstitutional

55. "It is inconsistent with the spirit of neutrality for a neutral nation to make loans to belligerent nations, for money is the worst of all contrabands—it commands all other things . . . as a neutral government does all in its power to discourage its citizens from enlisting in the armies of other countries, it should discourage those who by loaning money would do more than they could by enlisting. The government withdraws the protection of citizenship from those who do enlist under other flags—why should it give protection to money when it enters foreign military service?" This attitude by Secretary of State Bryan was later echoed in the

    (A) Marshall Plan
    (B) Fourteen Points
    (C) Nye Committee investigations
    (D) Atlantic Charter
    (E) Lend-Lease Act

56. A historian compared tax lists for the years 1687 and 1771. What changes do you think he found in the Boston of 1771 compared to the Boston of 1687?

    (A) an increase in the number of indentured servants entering Boston from abroad
    (B) a decline in the number of people considered poor and propertyless
    (C) a more stratified social structure
    (D) an economy controlled by large landowners rather than by merchants
    (E) a stable population with little geographical, occupational, economic, or generational mobility

57. All of the following curtailed freedom of speech or expression *except*

   (A) Lincoln's suspension of habeas corpus during the Civil War
   (B) the gag rule in the 1830s and early 1840s
   (C) the Sedition Act, 1918
   (D) McCarthyism during the 1950s
   (E) British writs of assistance in the early 1760s

58. Four of the following were considered to be conservationists. Who was *not* considered a friend of conservation?

   (A) John Muir
   (B) Theodore Roosevelt
   (C) Gifford Pinchot
   (D) Franklin Roosevelt
   (E) Richard Ballinger

59. "Every contract, combination in the form of trust or otherwise, or conspiracy, in restraint of trade or commerce among the several States, or with foreign nations, is hereby declared to be illegal. Every person who shall make any such contract or engage in any such combination or conspiracy, shall be deemed guilty of a misdemeanor, and, on conviction thereof, shall be punished. . . .

   "Every person who shall monopolize, or attempt to monopolize, or combine or conspire with any other person or persons, to monopolize any part of the trade or commerce among the several States, or with foreign nations, shall be deemed guilty of a misdemeanor, and, on conviction thereof, shall be punished."

   The law from which this quotation is taken

   (A) proved difficult to enforce against big business
   (B) passed Congress by a close vote after a bitter struggle
   (C) represented a new departure and a new direction in governmental policy
   (D) continued the tradition of the Clayton Antitrust Act
   (E) was part of the New Deal legislation

60. Why was the United Nations able to defend South Korea when it was attacked?

   (A) The Soviet Union was boycotting it in protest of its refusal to give a seat to Communist China.
   (B) The Soviet Union did not use its veto power because it was concerned about the rise of Communist China as a rival.
   (C) The Korean War was a local struggle, and neither the United States nor the Soviet Union considered it part of the Cold War.
   (D) The Soviet Union was boycotting it in order to test its response to a carefully orchestrated scheme—the preplanned invasion by a communist country into an ally of the West.
   (E) South Korea was entitled to protection as a member of the United Nations.

61. Which of the following statements about the process of amending the Constitution is correct?

   (A) The original Constitution did not provide for a means of amendment.
   (B) The Constitution can be amended by a two-thirds vote of both the Senate and House of Representatives and by the approval of two-thirds of the state legislatures.
   (C) The states can bypass the federal government by forcing Congress to call a national convention to propose an amendment (if requested by the legislatures of two-thirds of the states) and by approving the proposed amendment with three-fourths of the state conventions.
   (D) Proposed constitutional amendments need the approval of the House of Representatives and the Senate and the president's signature before amendments can be submitted to the states for ratification.
   (E) Through the power of judicial review the federal courts have the power to declare an amendment unconstitutional.

62. Little remembered by later generations, this politician was Secretary of War, 1899–1904; Secretary of State, 1905–1909; a Republican senator from New York, 1909–1915; and the winner of the Nobel Peace Prize in 1912. His greatest accomplishment was the moderniza-

tion of the army's organization. He created the General Staff of the Army, which was directly responsible to the Secretary of War and to the president, and established the Army War College. These two institutions were responsible for policy making within the confines of clear civilian control. Who was the able administrator who reorganized the Army?

(A) William Howard Taft
(B) Theodore Roosevelt
(C) John J. Pershing
(D) Elihu Root
(E) Franklin D. Roosevelt

63.   "All men are, by nature, equal and free: No one has a right to any authority over another without his consent: all lawful government is founded on the consent of those who are subject to it: Such consent was given with a view to ensure and to increase the happiness of the governed, above what they could enjoy in an independent and unconnected state of nature." This quotation from James Wilson is an example of the

(A) doctrine of nullification
(B) philosophy of natural rights
(C) philosophy of rugged individualism
(D) Southern states' rights point of view
(E) rhetoric of Populism

64.   "The existence of an area of free land, its continuous recession, and the advance of American settlement westward, explain American development." Which of the following is *not* part of the theories of the author of this quotation?

(A) The westward movement influenced the development of American character.
(B) Our frontier was a steady movement away from the influence of Europe.
(C) Successive waves of frontiers—a trader's frontier, a rancher's frontier, a miner's frontier, and a farmer's frontier—swept over the unsettled lands during the westward movement.
(D) Part of our frontier heritage was the acquisition of habits of wastefulness in regard to national resources.

(E) The frontier produced two economic classes, and therefore the underlying cause of all major events in American history was economic.

65.   As defined by John C. Calhoun, the doctrine of nullification

(A) said that both the highest federal court and the highest state court had to agree on the constitutionality of a federal law
(B) gave a majority of states voting in their state legislatures the power to declare an act of Congress null and void
(C) stated that any individual state could on its own authority declare a federal law unconstitutional and therefore unenforceable
(D) called for two presidents, one from the North and one from the South, either of whom could nullify a federal law
(E) applied only to tariff laws and revenue laws

66.   Four of the following were characteristics of the colonial economy and colonial politics which continued into the Revolution and Confederation era. Which did *not* continue into the latter era?

(A) tension between debtors and creditors
(B) a scarcity of currency
(C) tension between Westerners and Easterners
(D) constitutional struggles between the lower house of the state assemblies and the governors
(E) disputes among the states over western land claims

67.   United States foreign policy in the 1920s most resembled the decade from 1800 to 1810 in which of the following?

(A) territorial expansion
(B) involvement in the armed conflicts of Europe
(C) commitment to the pursuit of diplomacy by peaceful means
(D) interest in events in the Pacific
(E) disarmament

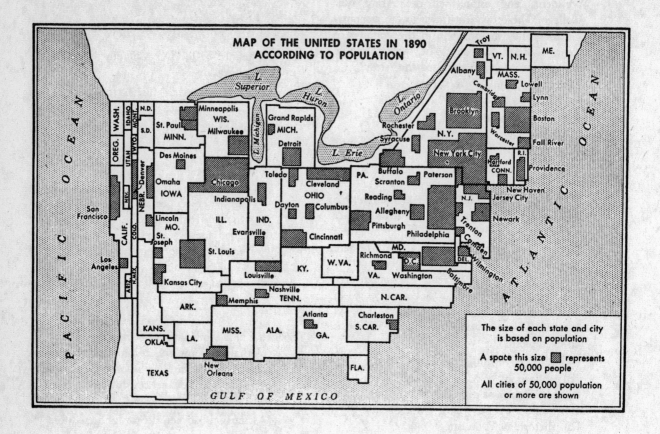

68. The map above
    (A) illustrates the division between the frost-belt and the sunbelt
    (B) illustrates why so many presidential candidates came from the Midwest in the latter half of the 19th century
    (C) graphically distorts the approximate electoral vote
    (D) shows why the Populist Party worried professional politicians in the Democratic and Republican parties
    (E) is distorted to overrepresent the wealthy states

69. After the Second World War older black organizations were challenged by the rise of new, more militant groups. Which of the following belong to postwar militant black organizations?
    (A) National Association for the Advancement of Colored People (NAACP) and Student Nonviolent Coordinating Committee (SNCC)
    (B) Southern Christian Leadership Conference (SCLC) and Student Nonviolent Coordinating Committee (SNCC)
    (C) Urban League and Congress of Racial Equality (CORE)
    (D) Southern Christian Leadership Conference (SCLC) and Urban League
    (E) National Association for the Advancement of Colored People (NAACP), Southern Christian Leadership Conference (SCLC), and Congress of Racial Equality (CORE)

(Courtesy of The Art Institute of Chicago)

70. Who painted this stern-faced father and daughter?
(A) John James Audubon
(B) Ben Shahn
(C) Andrew Wyeth
(D) Grant Wood
(E) Thomas Eakins

71. The Intolerable Acts, also called the Repressive Acts,
(A) closed all American ports until the tea from the Boston Tea Party was paid for
(B) punished the colonists for the Stamp Act Congress
(C) extended the Canadian border down to the Ohio River
(D) led to the First Continental Congress
(E) were in retaliation for the Boston Massacre

72. "Scientific management" was the practice of using time measurement to break down all the components of a job in order to discover the best method to do that job. Who was most responsible for the "scientific management" movement in the early 20th century?

(A) John D. Rockefeller
(B) Andrew Carnegie
(C) John Dewey
(D) J.P. Morgan
(E) Frederick W. Taylor

73. The Supreme Court case of *Myers* v. *U.S.* in 1925 said that the president had the power to fire anyone appointed to a position in the executive branch, even a position which required Senate approval for appointment. This decision vindicated the position taken by
(A) Andrew Jackson in regard to the spoils system
(B) Jefferson in regard to impeaching Federalist judges
(C) Wilson in regard to the Versailles Treaty
(D) Andrew Johnson in opposition to Radical Republicans
(E) the Hartford Convention during the War of 1812

74. "Neither of the two parties shall conclude either truce or peace with Great Britain without the formal consent of the other first obtained; and they mutually engage not to lay down their arms until the independence of the United States shall have been formally or tacitly assured by the treaty or treaties that shall terminate the war." This passage is Article VIII of the Treaty of Alliance of 1778 between France and the United States. The United States did not keep its pledge to France as stipulated in Article VIII. It instead signed a peace treaty without conferring with France. Why?
(A) It did not want to get involved with the French Revolution.
(B) It discovered that France and her ally Spain were eager to prevent it from gaining control of the territory extending from the Appalachian Mountains to the Mississippi River.
(C) Since French military and naval aid did not amount to much help, it did not feel obligated to follow the treaty.
(D) No British troops were left in the United States after the capture of Cornwallis's army, and the British quickly gave in before we had an opportunity to consult with our ally, France.
(E) Washington's Neutrality Proclamation, April 22, 1793, abrogated the Treaty of 1778.

75. The conservative branch of the Republican Party recaptured the White House in the 1920s. How did they deal with the Progressive legacy of federal regulatory legislation?

    (A) They quietly permitted the legislation which created the regulatory agencies to expire.

    (B) They supported new legislation to weaken the powers of the regulatory agencies.

    (C) They captured the regulatory agencies by appointing conservatives as members.

    (D) They joined forces with New Dealers to improve and to update the old regulatory legislation.

    (E) They abolished the federal regulatory agencies.

76. The center of the manufacturing of cotton textiles switched from New England to the South between the 1880s and the 1930s because

    (A) New England Irish and Italian immigrants refused to work in the textile mills

    (B) New England changed its textile emphasis to wool production

    (C) cheap Southern labor and lower taxes enticed the textile industry to move to the South

    (D) the Arab oil embargo drove New England industrial costs too high

    (E) blacks were once again permitted to work in the textile mills as they had during slavery

77. Why did Lyndon Johnson make a decision not to run for election in 1968?

    (A) He lost in the early New Hampshire Democratic primary to Senator Eugene McCarthy.

    (B) His deescalation of the American involvement in Vietnam angered too many people, and jeopardized his reelection.

    (C) His previous presidential election had been very close, giving him grounds to suspect defeat if this election was going to be close.

    (D) The objectives of the War on Poverty and the war in Vietnam had been achieved.

    (E) His potential Republican opponent, Richard Nixon, looked unbeatable.

78. "The [signers of the treaty] solemnly declare in the names of their respective peoples that they condemn recourse to war for the solution of international controversies, and renounce it as an instrument of national policy in their relations with one another.

    The [signers of the treaty] agree that the settlement or solution of all disputes or conflicts of whatever nature or of whatever origin they may be, which may arise among them, shall never be sought except by pacific means." This quotation is from the

    (A) Yalta Agreement
    (B) Truman Doctrine
    (C) SALT I Agreement
    (D) Nuclear Test Ban Treaty
    (E) Kellogg-Briand Treaty

79. Which two presidential candidates were bitterly attacked because they were Catholics?

    (A) Thomas Dewey and Adlai Stevenson
    (B) Walter Mondale and Lyndon Johnson
    (C) Al Smith and John F. Kennedy
    (D) Herbert Hoover and Dwight David Eisenhower
    (E) Jimmy Carter and John F. Kennedy

80. "Once lead this people into war and they'll forget there ever was such a thing as tolerance. To fight you must be brutal and ruthless, and the spirit of ruthless brutality will enter into every fiber of our national life, infecting Congress, the courts, the policeman on the beat, the man in the street." Wilson's prophecy came true in regard to all of the following *except*

    (A) the Chicago race riot, 1919
    (B) the Palmer raids
    (C) the Espionage Act of 1917 and the Sedition Act of 1918
    (D) the reaction to the steel strike of 1919
    (E) the Volstead Act

81. Four of the following correctly match a reformer to the area of reform. Which is incorrectly matched?

    (A) Dorothea Dix—treatment of the mentally ill
    (B) Lucretia Mott—women's rights
    (C) Horace Mann—education
    (D) Neal Dow—temperance
    (E) Rober B. Taney—labor unions

82. In order for a bill to become a law it must

    (A) be approved by the president
    (B) be approved by the House and the Senate
    (C) be reviewed by the federal courts under the power of judicial review
    (D) be supported by the majority party
    (E) originate in the House of Representatives

83. Why was there so much colonial opposition to the Tea Act of 1773?

    (A) The East India Company was granted a monopoly control over the sale of tea in the colonies.
    (B) The act raised taxes on tea.
    (C) British troops accompanied the British merchants who came to sell the tea.
    (D) The tea tax was passed in retaliation for the Boston Tea Party.
    (E) The act raised the price of tea.

84. Which of the following is *not* correctly linked to an event which occurred during his presidential administration?

    (A) Peace Corps started—JFK
    (B) Marshall Plan—FDR
    (C) U-2 incident—Eisenhower
    (D) Iranian hostage crisis—Carter
    (E) SALT I Agreement—Nixon

85. After the Constitution was written in 1787 it was sent to the states for ratification. Virginia narrowly approved the Constitution, 89-79. Who was the Virginia delegate who fought in Virginia against ratifying the Constitution because it lacked a Bill of Rights? His fight earned him the title, "Father of the Bill of Rights."

    (A) Thomas Jefferson
    (B) George Washington
    (C) John Adams
    (D) George Mason
    (E) Sam Adams

86. "*Pervasive discrimination and segregation* in employment, education and housing, which have resulted in the continuing exclusion of great numbers of Negroes from the benefits of economic progress.

"*Black in-migration and white exodus*, which have produced the massive and growing concentrations of impoverished Negroes in our major cities, creating a growing crisis of deteriorating facilities and services and unmet human needs.

"*The black ghettos*, where segregation and poverty converge on the young to destroy opportunity and enforce failure. Crime, drug addiction, dependency on welfare, and bitterness and resentment against society in general and white society in particular are the result." This quotation from the *Report on Civil Disorders* identified the reasons behind the race riots in the 1960s. The report was the work of the

(A) Urban League
(B) Kerner Commission
(C) NAACP
(D) Warren Commission
(E) Niagara Movement

87. "In the future days, which we seek to make secure, we look forward to a world founded upon four essential human freedoms.

"The first is freedom of speech and expression, everywhere in the world.

"The second is freedom of every person to worship God in his own way, everywhere in the world.

"The third is freedom from want, which, translated into world terms, means economic understanding which will secure to every nation a healthy peacetime life for its inhabitants, everywhere in the world.

"The fourth is freedom from fear—which, translated into world terms, means a worldwide reduction of armaments to such a point and in such a thorough fashion that no nation will be in a position to commit an act of physical aggression against any neighbor—anywhere in the world."
Who gave this "Four Freedoms" speech?

(A) Wendell Wilkie
(B) Woodrow Wilson
(C) Franklin Roosevelt
(D) Winston Churchill
(E) Herbert Hoover

88. After Southern congressmen and senators had withdrawn, the Republicans during the Civil War passed significant legislation that the Southerners had opposed. Which of the following was part of this legislation?

    I. transcontinental railroad
    II. Morrill Land-Grant College Act
    III. Morrill Tariff
    IV. Homestead Act
    V. Federal Reserve Act

    (A) I, II, III, and IV only
    (B) II, III, and IV only
    (C) II, IV, and V only
    (D) I, II, III, IV, and V
    (E) I, III, and IV only

89. Both France and Great Britain violated American neutral rights in the years preceding the War of 1812. What consideration influenced the United States to go to war against Great Britain rather than France?

    (A) British violations caused the loss of American lives; the French violations only cost property losses.
    (B) The Federalist Party, which controlled Congress, tended to be anti-British.
    (C) It was easier for the U.S. to attack British territory than to attack French territory.
    (D) The French respected our embargo, the British did not.
    (E) President Adams had already chastised France in the undeclared naval war of the late 1790s; this time he decided to attack Great Britain.

90. Which of the following was *not* used by Southerners in defense of the institution of slavery?

    (A) Northern wage workers toiling in the factories were treated more inhumanely.
    (B) The curse on Cain for killing his brother began the degradation of blacks.
    (C) Slavery was essential to the agricultural system of the South, which produced crops requiring extensive hand labor.
    (D) Slavery existed in the Bible and was never criticized by Christ, the Disciples, or the Old Testament prophets.
    (E) The Constitution protected slavery in the South, and abolished it only north of the Ohio River and the Mason-Dixon line.

91. In just one year, 1807–1808, American imports dropped from $138 million to $57 million. American exports dropped from $108 million to $22 million. Why?

    (A) Britain tightened its impressment of American sailors, driving American shipping from the seas.
    (B) Macon's Bill No. 2 restricted American trade to every nation except Great Britain and France.
    (C) Jefferson's embargo curtailed American shipping.
    (D) Napoleon's Berlin and Milan decrees cut continental Europe off from American shipping.
    (E) The undeclared naval war with France made shipping too dangerous.

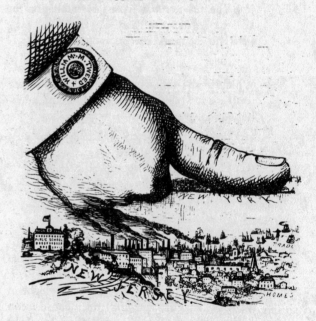

92. Who drew this 19th century political cartoon attacking boss rule in New York City?

    (A) William Seward
    (B) Thomas Nast
    (C) William Marcy Tweed
    (D) Fiorello La Guardia
    (E) Seth Low

93. Which historian first labeled the years immediately preceding the writing and adopting of the Constitution the "critical period" of American history?

    (A) Frederick Jackson Turner
    (B) John Fiske

(C) Charles A. Beard
(D) George F. Kennan
(E) W.E.B. DuBois

94. Which colony was established as a buffer against the Spanish colonies and to give the poor and unfortunate a chance for a new start in life?

(A) Maryland
(B) Georgia
(C) Nova Scotia
(D) Pennsylvania
(E) Plymouth

95.   "That the further introduction of slavery or involuntary servitude be prohibited, except for the punishment of crimes, whereof the party shall have been fully convicted; and that all children born within the said State, after the admission thereof into the Union, shall be free at the age of twenty-five years." This brief amendment to a piece of pending legislation concerning the admission of a new state set off a crisis. What is the amendment and what was the crisis?

(A) Wilmot Proviso, Compromise of 1850
(B) South Carolina Exposition and Protest, Compromise of 1833
(C) end of slavery proposed in Virginia legislature debates, 1831–1832, admission of West Virginia
(D) Tallmadge Amendment, Missouri Compromise
(E) popular sovereignty for the territories, Kansas-Nebraska Act

96. In his sociological study, *The Levittowners*, about a planned suburb in New York, Herbert Gans found a local society characterized by "the equality of men and women, the power of the child over his parents, the importance of voluntary association, the social functions of the church, and the rejection of high culture" and "the adherence to the traditional virtues: individual honesty, thrift, religiously inspired morality, Franklinesque individualism, and Victorian prudery." His description of suburban society is most reminiscent of

(A) Sloan Wilson's *The Man in the Gray Flannel Suit*
(B) Alexis de Tocqueville's *Democracy in America*

(C) Theodore Dreiser's *Sister Carrie*
(D) William H. Whyte's *The Organization Man*
(E) Willa Cather's *My Antonia*

97. Which of the following was *not* an influential book that affected American economic thinking?

(A) John Kenneth Galbraith, *The Affluent Society*
(B) John Maynard Keynes, *The General Theory of Employment, Interest and Money*
(C) Adam Smith, *The Wealth of Nations*
(D) Thorstein Veblen, *The Theory of the Leisure Class*
(E) Gunnar Myrdal, *An American Dilemma*

98. Which of the following is *not* true concerning the WPA (Works Progress Administration) and the PWA (Public Works Administration)?

(A) Harry Hopkins ran the WPA.
(B) The philosophy of the PWA was to build large construction projects such as the Grand Coulee Dam to stimulate private enterprise through the purchase of materials and the building of an industrial infrastructure.
(C) The philosophy of the WPA was to employ, usually on small jobs, as many people as possible, as quickly as possible; the productivity of the work was not as important as getting people a job and an income.
(D) Harold Ickes ran the PWA.
(E) The PWA projects included the Federal Arts Program, which employed thousands of artists, entertainers, and writers.

99. "Brother, Can You Spare a Dime?" and "Can I Sleep in Your Barn Tonight, Mister?" were popular hit songs during

(A) 1917
(B) the Civil War
(C) the Second World War
(D) 1932
(E) the 1960s

100. The OPA during the Second World War was similar to which of the following?

(A) President Nixon's wage freeze
(B) Manhatten Project
(C) Atomic Energy Commission
(D) NATO
(E) CARE

ANSWERS

1. C	21. A	41. D	61. C	81. E
2. A	22. B	42. D	62. D	82. B
3. A	23. C	43. E	63. B	83. A
4. E	24. C	44. A	64. E	84. B
5. A	25. B	45. A	65. C	85. D
6. B	26. D	46. E	66. D	86. B
7. E	27. A	47. E	67. C	87. C
8. C	28. C	48. B	68. B	88. A
9. B	29. C	49. A	69. B	89. C
10. B	30. C	50. B	70. D	90. E
11. E	31. D	51. E	71. D	91. C
12. E	32. A	52. D	72. E	92. B
13. D	33. D	53. D	73. D	93. B
14. C	34. B	54. A	74. B	94. B
15. D	35. A	55. C	75. C	95. D
16. C	36. D	56. C	76. C	96. B
17. E	37. B	57. E	77. A	97. E
18. A	38. D	58. E	78. E	98. E
19. B	39. B	59. A	79. C	99. D
20. B	40. A	60. A	80. E	100. A

EXPLANATORY ANSWERS

1. **(C)** William Penn founded his "Holy Experiment" in Pennsylvania. The American environment usually forced drastic alterations in the original plans of the founders. Pennsylvania was an exception.

2. **(A)** American policy in the Far East was based upon the philosophy of the Open Door Notes: maintain an autonomous China with all nations having equal trade access. Japan offered the greatest threat to China and to U.S. possessions in the Far East, and for this reason the treaties tried to curtail Japanese power.

3. **(A)** Before the cotton gin (short for engine) many Southerners speculated how the South could get rid of its useless slave system. Eli Whitney's invention made the question intellectual speculation for the foreseeable future. The cotton gin cemented both cotton and slavery in the South.

4. **(E)** The Dartmouth College case, *Dartmouth College* v. *Woodward* (1819) concerned an attempt by the New Hampshire legislature to replace the board of trustees of Dartmouth College, and in effect to take control of the institution. The Supreme Court invalidated the seizure, finding the original charter to be a contract beyond the power of the legislature to alter unilaterally. In his argument before the Supreme Court Daniel Webster made his famous remark, "It is, sir, as I have said, a small college, and yet there are those that love it."

5. **(A)** "The Cult of True Womanhood" emphasized domesticity, piety, purity, and submissiveness as the attributes of a true woman. The modern antifeminist, Phyllis Schlafly, would approve of these virtues. Betty Friedan, author of *The Feminine Mystique* (1963), was the first president of NOW, the National Organization for Women. Gloria Steinem has also been a feminist leader. Carrie Nation was a militant prohibitionist who went from town to town with her trusty axe, busting up one bar after another. Shirley Chisholm, the first black woman elected to the House of Representatives in 1968, once said that being a woman presented more obstacles to her career than being black.

6. **(B)** Polygamy separates Mormons from the others. Shakers separated the sexes, even married couples. Christian Scientists eschewed modern medicine for God's healing power through prayer. The Mormons left for Utah, then a territory of Mexico, to find a home where no one would ever bother them. In quick succession came the Mexican War, the Mexican Cession, and the California gold rush, and their isolation evaporated.

7. **(E)** Theodore Roosevelt's Corollary to the Monroe Doctrine (1904) asserted that the United States had the right to intervene to punish "chronic wrongdoing," meaning fiscal mismanagement of international borrowing. The Monroe Doctrine had said European powers could not intervene; the Roosevelt Corollary said the United States could.

8. **(C)** The Great Compromise, or Connecticut Compromise, established a two house federal legislature with the numbers in the Senate based on equal representation for each state and those in the House of Representatives based on population. It reconciled the conflict between the Virginia Plan and New Jersey Plan. The other choices involved other compromises made during the writing of the Constitution.

9. **(B)** Bruce Barton was an advertising genius who invented Betty Crocker, a nonexistent specialist in the new field of home economics. He also wrote *The Man Nobody Knows*, which depicted Christ as the ultimate businessman who created a world-class organization with twelve associates plucked off the streets. Barton was trying to link business methods and Christian doctrines and practices. In the other two books the authors suggested that Christ would be shocked at the attitudes and conditions of modern life, and indirectly laid the blame upon the values and practices of businessmen.

10. **(B)** Two of Paine's ideas are expressed in the Monroe Doctrine in 1823: European ideas differ from New World republican values; and the New World should have as little as possible to do with Europe. One of the sources for isolationist sentiment was the belief, even then, that the United States would be contaminated by Europe. Purity lay westward into the American continent.

11. **(E)** This New Deal law was the Wagner Act, also known as the National Labor Relations Act, which passed Congress in 1935. The Supreme Court found the act constitutional in the case of *NLRB* v. *Jones and Laughlin Steel Corp*. The Clayton Act (1914), nicknamed labor's Magna Carta, exempted labor organizations from antitrust laws, although subsequent court decisions weakened that protection. The Norris-LaGuardia Act (1932) prohibited yellow dog contracts and restricted injunctions in regard to boycotts, picketing, and strikes. The Taft-Hartley Act (1947) outlawed closed shops, permitted right-to-work laws (which could locally get rid of the union shop), and established a cooling off period for strikes involving the nation's security (deemed so by a federal judge). The Landrum-Griffin Act (1959) attempted to control labor union corruption and to ensure internal democratic procedures within unions.

12. **(E)** Political Reconstruction ended when the Bourbons, or Redeemers, took control of state governments. For almost one hundred years afterwards the South voted Democratic hence the term Solid South. Impoverished land-rich planters and the abundance of poor whites and ex-slaves combined to create sharecrop farming in the South. The planters, who had controlled prewar state legislatures, spent very little in order to keep their own taxes down. This attitude had helped make the prewar South backward, and in many respects the South had been an underdeveloped country preoccupied with race. Much good came out of Reconstruction. Many schools and roads were built. Another legacy was the constitutional promise to grant civil rights to blacks. It may not sound like much of an achievement, but thereafter blacks had only to get whites to obey existing laws, not to rewrite the laws. That is why the American experience cannot be compared with events in South Africa.

13. **(D)** In the late 19th century Northern liberals began to acquiesce to Southern racism. Many were exhausted by their unsuccessful effort to secure civil rights; others were seduced by the racist implications of imperialism and Darwinism. The Redeemer governments proved to be even more corrupt than the Reconstruction governments they rescued the South from. Challenged by the rising Populist movement, the Redeemers raised the specter of race over and over to maintain their power. Poor whites abandoned their black allies and proved even more effective racists. Meanwhile successive Supreme Court decisions weakened the commitment to civil rights. The Slaughterhouse Cases (1873) and the Civil Rights Cases (1883) helped create the atmosphere that led to the Plessy decision.

14. **(C)** Pinckney's Treaty granted the United States the right of deposit at New Orleans in the 1790s. In the 1850 Clayton-Bulwer Treaty the United States and Great Britain promised not to build an isthmian canal without the other's permission. In the proposed Jay-Gardoqui Treaty under the Articles of Confederation in the 1780s the United States surrendered the right of navigation on the lower Mississippi River in exchange for increased commerce with Spain. The treaty never materialized due to Southern opposition.

15. **(D)** After the destruction of the second Bank of the U.S., provision had to be made for federal monies. Jackson's policy of depositing federal funds in pet banks was too politically oriented. Van Buren's Independent Treasury Act (1840) created subtreasuries controlled by the federal government. Each subtreasury served as a depository for federal funds; none operated as a bank nor performed any banking functions. One year later the Whigs repealed it, but Polk revived it in 1846. With minor changes it lasted until the Federal Reserve Act in 1913.

16. **(C)** John D. Rockefeller defended his business practices with this famous quote. A cartoonist pictured Rockefeller pulling all the buds off a rose bush except for one, his Standard Oil Company.

17. **(E)** "Waving the bloody shirt" was a favorite tactic of Republican candidates in the post-Civil War era. "Vote as you shot." As one wag explained it, not every Democrat was a traitor, but every traitor (Southerner) was a Democrat. Therefore, as a voter you should vote Republican and only Republican. The GAR, or Grand Army of the Republic, was an organization of Union veterans. Their pension demands solved the vexing problem of how to spend the huge treasury surplus built up by high tariff rates. The Crédit Mobilier scandal accompanied the building of the first transcontinental railroad. Mugwumps were high-principled Republicans who could not bring themselves

to support the unscrupulous Blaine in 1884. Instead they threw their support to the Democrat Cleveland. The Loco-Foco faction of the Democratic Party in the Jackson period supported economic reforms against banks, monopolies, and tariffs. Loco-Focos were mostly New York radicals.

18. **(A)** In 1775 one-half of the colonists lived in New England, the home of the Puritan, or Congregational, Church. The Anglican Church, or Church of England (Episcopal Church), was the official church in six colonies. Most Quakers lived in heavily populated Pennsylvania and New Jersey. Catholic historians refer to the colonial era as the penal period, for at one time or the other every colony had some form of anti-Catholic legislation. Very few Catholics lived in colonial America. The ranking for the churches named in the question is as follows:

Congregational: 668	Catholic: 56
Presbyterian: 588	Moravian: 31
Anglican: 495	Dunker: 24
Quaker: 310	Mennonite: 16
Lutheran: 150	Huguenot: 7
Methodist: 65	Jewish synagogues: 5

The complete list is in Clinton Rossiter's *The First American Republic,* a paperback edition of part of a larger work, *Seedtime of the Republic.*

19. **(B)** Suburbia was always the citadel of Republicans. As suburban areas grew in the 1950s–1970s the Republican Party's strength increased. If intellectuals and academics were added to the remaining four you would have the nucleus of FDR's coalition.

20. **(B)** The spot resolutions were attempts by Whigs in Congress to embarrass President Polk after he had asked for a declaration of war based upon the claim that Mexico had "shed American blood upon American soil." Whig Congressman Abraham Lincoln and others introduced resolutions asking the president to point out the "spot" on the map where American blood had been shed. The "spot" of the incident, of course, lay entirely within disputed territory, not on American soil.

21. **(A)** The largest ethnic group is the English. Blacks were second. Historians estimate that in colonial America blacks made up as much as twenty-five percent of the total population. Nineteenth century European white immigration reduced the percentage of blacks in American society. The natives of Scotland are Scots, not Scotch. The Scots who left Scotland for Northern Ireland and then later migrated to America are called Scotch-Irish.

22. **(B)** Choice (E) is tricky. It explains why some historians consider the issue of slavery in Kansas and Nebraska to be foolish, but doesn't explain why Northerners and Southerners became so upset over a "foolish" issue. The future direction and tone of the nation was being decided. Slavery became a powerful symbol meaning different things to people in each sections. Don't assume that slavery could never have been adapted to a use other than agriculture. The Lecompton Constitution, which proposed that Kansas enter the Union as a slave state, was ultimately rejected by the voters of Kansas. John Brown's raid on Pottawatomie Creek took place in 1856 prior to his 1859 raid on Harpers Ferry.

23. **(C)** The accomplishments described were part of the early political career of Theodore Roosevelt.

24. **(C)** This paragraph is from "Wealth," an essay written by Andrew Carnegie in 1889. His position that competition is essential to society would have been enthusiastically supported by all except Henry George. William Graham Sumner, a Yale professor, is best remembered for *What Social Classes Owe to Each Other* (1883). Herbert Spencer, and English proponent of Darwinism and good friend of Carnegie, published his ideas in *Social Statics*. John D. Rockefeller wiped out competition in an innovative, ruthless style. Henry George's *Progress and Poverty* championed the single tax to resolve the widening gap between wealth and poverty. The single tax would absorb all unearned increment on land value, and end the necessity for any other tax. Thus, taxes would be paid by society's increased wealth, not by any individual.

25. **(B)** The first Bank of the U.S. was chartered in 1791 for twenty years. When Jefferson won the presidency, he and his followers merely tolerated the Federalist Bank, and in 1811 quietly let it die. To their dismay they learned the economic value of the Bank in providing a reliable currency. They swallowed their ideology and chartered the second Bank of the U.S. in 1816, again with a twenty-year charter.

26. **(D)** Frances Willard was for years the driving force behind the WCTU, the Women's Christian Temperance Union. She also worked to obtain women's suffrage.

27. **(A)** This letter was written by Governor John Peter Altgeld to President Cleveland. The best clue is the reference to the federal mail, the pretext for Cleveland's ordering of federal troops to put down the Pullman strike. The issue of constitutionality in federal-state confrontations is invariably raised by the losing state.

28. **(C)** Jefferson disapproved of a large federal army, believing that the state militias could effectively defend the United States from invasion. Jefferson believed a strong army was a threat to liberty because of a possible coup led by generals. The defense of Washington, D.C. in the War of 1812 proved otherwise.

29. **(C)** New Nationalism emphasized regulating big business; New Freedom wanted to break up monopolies. Wilson won the election and pushed the Clayton Antitrust Act and the Federal Trade Commission through Congress. He slowly shifted his approach in practice, however, to regulation rather than antimonopoly. For the next seventy years the policy of the federal government was one of regulation of big business. Despite some spectacular, isolated antitrust suits the federal government's approach toward business has been regulation rather than antitrust. One historian wrote an article in the 1950s entitled, "Whatever Happened to the Antitrust Movement?" Debs was the candidate of the Socialist Party. His prescription for American business differed radically.

30. **(C)** The British political system espoused virtual representation, every member of Parliament represented every British citizen everywhere. The Americans practiced actual representation, each member of a legislative body represented the people who put him there. Now you see why the British couldn't make any sense of the American argument of "No taxation without representation." Each colony or state is generally represented at the meetings. The colonist followed actual representation, in theory and in practice. The First Congress under the Constitution is the only body apportioned by population. A comparison with the other numbers indicates that the colonists and states did not apportion their representative bodies strictly. Thirty-nine of the fifty-five delegates to the Constitutional Convention signed the Constitution, a majority. Most of the signers of the Declaration did not sign the Constitution. Only six—Benjamin

Franklin, George Read, James Wilson, George Clymer, Robert Morris, and Roger Sherman—signed both. Some historians have suggested that the Declaration was the work of radicals and the Constitution of conservatives. Too much can be made of this; the correct answer is probably the years between the two signings. The documents have almost a separate and individual existence. It is too artificial to try to uncover threads linking both of them together.

31. **(D)** President Carter personally mediated a peace agreement between two suspicious enemies, Egypt and Israel. The Camp David Accords in 1978 set the stage for a 1979 peace treaty. Egypt became the first Middle East Arab nation to accept the existence of Israel.

32. **(A)** The map shows "The Women's Suffrage Movement." Note that women's suffrage was a western movement beginning in Wyoming. The conservative Southern states held out the longest.

33. **(D)** Laissez-faire, first articulated by Adam Smith in his 1776 book, *The Wealth of Nations,* advocated a philosophy of freeing individuals from government restrictions so that each could pursue his self-interest. Mercantilism, an earlier philosophy, advocated governmental control of economic activity to increase the national wealth. A few industries were hampered by British restrictions but the number of restrictions was small and enforcement was lax. Examples are the restrictions in the Woolens Act (1699), the Hat Act (1732), and the Iron Act (1750). Before 1776 the colonists were British citizens. They benefited from the Navigation Acts' restricting trade to British ships and British crews. Seventy-five percent of colonial trade was carried in colonial ships. A nation gained wealth by exporting more than it imported, therefore maintaining a favorable balance of trade and piling up money in the treasury.

34. **(B)** This is the election of 1800, the second race between John Adams and Thomas Jefferson. Adams had won in 1796. The Constitution originally stipulated that each presidential elector was to vote for two individuals. The man who received the most votes, provided that he received more than half, was the president. The second highest number of votes was the vice-president, provided that he also received more than half the votes. The tie between Jefferson and Burr forced the election into the House of Representatives, which was controlled by the Federalists. After a long rancorous debate Jefferson won. Realizing that the election machinery needed correction, the Twelfth Amendment changed the means of selecting the president. Now the electors specified a vote for president and for vice-president, and no repetition of the election of 1800 was possible. The amendment also ended the possibility of a president and vice-president from different political factions, which had happened in 1796.

35. **(A)** An early full-length picture, *Birth of a Nation* in 1915 portrayed the Ku Klux Klan as a benevolent organization that saved the South during Reconstruction. The first talking motion picture, however, was *The Jazz Singer* in 1927, with Al Jolson. The other films are classics from later decades.

36. **(D)** The myth of the Jacksonian Era is that economic equality increased. It did not. Recent research indicates a rigidity in social mobility and an increase in economic inequality. The post-Civil War era was characterized more by social mobility.

37. **(B)** The Mayflower Compact was signed by forty-one male passengers aboard the Mayflower in November 1620. Since only about one-third of the passengers were

members of the Leyden congregation and the ship was outside the boundaries of its land grant, the leaders had no legitimate means of controlling the company. The agreement committed everyone to following majority rule in their civil government. This document is one of the cornerstones of American political theory. Plymouth itself was never much of a colony, being eventually absorbed by Massachusetts.

38. **(D)** The Dawes Severalty Act (1887) tried to dissolve the Indian tribes by dividing tribal lands among individual Indians, 160 acres per family, 80 acres to single adults. The word "severalty" means owning something free of joint interest; in other words, free from tribal limitations or restrictions. To prevent fraud the land could not be sold for twenty-five years. The act failed in its intended purpose of breaking up the tribes and turning Indians into individual farmers because the Indians didn't want to be individuals. Helen Hunt Jackson's eloquent book, *A Century of Dishonor* (1881) marked the beginning of the agitation which culminated with the Dawes Act. Whites made the cultural mistake of assuming that Indians really wanted to be like them. Indians were finally made full citizens in 1924.

39. **(B)** To say that one of the characteristics of Jacksonian Democracy was high voter turnout is too simplistic. Voter participation increased during the Jacksonian period only as presidential elections within each state became more hotly contested. Interest and excitement within each state increased as that particular state became part of the national political campaign. When each candidate seemed to have a fighting chance within a particular state, interest shot up. Not until the Whig Party generated a real threat to the Democrats did voter interest peak. High voter interest was not a cause of Jacksonian Democracy, it was a characteristic of Jacksonian Democracy.

40. **(A)** Samuel Gompers, the founder of the AFL, once summarized the AFL philosophy succinctly as "more" for its members. The AFL, fearing that the solidarity of the labor movement would be dissipated by ideological concerns, spurned involvement in larger issues.

41. **(D)** Walt Whitman published *Leaves of Grass* in 1855. Nicknamed the "Poet Laureate of Democracy," he broke tradition in style, rhyme, and subject. The poem is a long paean to all things American.

42. **(D)** The quote is from the Populist Party platform, July 4, 1892. Every student of American history should read the preamble to the Populist Party platform.

43. **(E)** Prior to the First World War there had never been a policy of restriction of immigrants. The other choices added fuel to the discussion of raising a fence around the Statue of Liberty. The fence went up in the 1921 act and was perfected in 1924.

44. **(A)** The wars played a major role in the outcome of the elections of 1952 and 1968, both of which replaced the party in the White House. In 1952 the Democrats lost to Eisenhower, in 1968 to Nixon. In both elections the incumbent Democratic president did not run for reelection. The Korean War began on a specific day, Vietnam did not. The United States took over after the French left Vietnam. The United Nations branded North Korea as the aggressor; no such action ever accompanied the Vietnam War. We had treaty obligations to defend South Vietnam but not South Korea. On the eve of North Korea's invasion the Secretary of State curiously excluded South Korea from the United States defense perimeter in the Far East. Truman reacted because he saw a repetition of the same events that sparked the Second World War.

45. **(A)** The Supreme Court declared the AAA unconstitutional in the case of *U.S.* v. *Butler.*

46. **(E)** This quotation from the writings of Eugene V. Debs was critical of the AFL organization of the work force by separate independent craft unions. The CIO, created in the 1930s, organized all workers, skilled and unskilled, in each industry into the same union. The CIO had an automobile workers union, a steel workers union, etc. The earlier American Railway Union with Debs as its president had followed this philosophy, but the newly organized ARU was wiped out by the Pullman strike. You should be able to differentiate all the different approaches to union organization.

47. **(E)** Harry Truman defied all odds by winning reelection in 1948. The Republican candidate, Thomas Dewey, was considered such a shoo-in that he had already begun to select his cabinet. The Democratic Party was split three ways, but somehow Truman triumphed in one of the greatest upsets ever.

48. **(B)** William Penn believed in the liberty of conscience. He had often been jailed in England for espousing such an utterly unthinkable idea. If people think for themselves, of what need are rulers? Roger Williams, kicked out of Massachusetts by the civil and religious authorities, also practiced religious toleration. The next best choice is Maryland and Pennsylvania because of the Maryland Act of Toleration in 1649. The law was actually a vain attempt by Catholics to protect their own freedom of worship in the face of overwhelming Protestant migration into Maryland. The Protestants gained control of the colonial assembly and virtually nullified the Act of Toleration five years after it had passed.

49. **(A)** William Lloyd Garrison was satisfied with the Emancipation Proclamation and the Thirteenth Amendment because all he sought was the immediate end of slavery. By the end of the Civil War the Thirteenth Amendment was widely supported in the North, but not the Fourteenth and Fifteenth. Slavery was a sin, but political or social equality was unacceptable to many in the North. Popular acceptance of the doctrine of the equality of the races is a mid-twentieth-century concept. Johnson disapproved of the Fourteenth and Fifteenth amendments, but the president plays no role whatsoever in the amending process. The later two amendments were passed because the actual implementation or operation of the previous one revealed specific defects that had to be corrected. The amendments went into effect as follows: Thirteenth, December 18, 1865; Fourteenth, July 28, 1868; and Fifteenth, March 30, 1870.

50. **(B)** The Berlin Wall was erected during Kennedy's administration in August 1961.

51. **(E)** By 1774 Americans thought they saw a pattern in British practices, a deliberate attempt to subvert liberty at home and in the colonies. John Wilkes and his friend Colonel Barre were popular radicals in England. Wilkes was elected to Parliament and denied his seat. Was this the beginning of a deliberate attack on the principle of representative government, the right of the people to choose their representatives? A group of Wilkes's supporters gathered at St. Georges fields near London. The authorities dispatched the mob (or were they good citizens exercising their right to assemble and petition the government?) with brutal force. News of the incident reached the colonies shortly before the Boston Massacre. Were the two "massacres" a new British policy? The Anglican Church sent missionaries to the colonies from the Society for the Propagation of the Gospel ostensibly to convert Indians. Why did the missionaries stay in Boston? The Anglican Church obviously meant to entice converts from the Congre-

gational and Presbyterian churches in New England. Were the British deliberately attacking religion in the colonies? The Stamp Act represented a new type of taxation, an internal tax that affected almost everyone, as compared to customs tariffs, which were collected at the port of entry. The issue of the Northwest posts came up after the Revolutionary War.

52. **(D)** This passage is from Washington's Neutrality Proclamation of April 22, 1793. The United States wanted to avoid getting involved in the European wars set off by the French Revolution. The Neutrality Proclamation is an excellent example of diplomatic double-talk: nowhere in the proclamation does Washington use the word "neutrality."

53. **(D)** The lines are the frontier line for 1800 and 1830. One hint is that Kentucky and Tennessee were two of the first three states added to the union.

54. **(A)** The quotation is from the famous Cross of Gold speech by William Jennings Bryan in the presidential campaign of 1896.

55. **(C)** In the 1930s the Nye Committee publicized the "merchants of death" interpretation of the reasons for United States involvement in the First World War. We entered to protect loans made by American banks to the Allies and to protect the profits of the arms manufacturers. The Johnson Debt Default Act (1934) prohibited new loans to any foreign government that never repaid their First World War debts. The neutrality acts of 1935, 1936, and 1937 tried to prevent a repetition of the U.S.'s becoming economically entangled with one side during a foreign war. They were one war too late.

56. **(C)** The colonial period lasted from 1607 to 1776. Many broad generalizations about colonial society need qualifications. By the 1770s the number of indentured servants among immigrants was much lower. In many respects the colonists were beginning to think of themselves as the Europeanized, crowded society. As cities grew the urban poor more than doubled in size, creating a shifting, propertyless mass of workers. Most broad generalizations concerning colonial society do not apply to the cities. Only five percent of the population lived in cities. From the beginning the sea trade dominated the Boston economy. By the 1770s the Boston social structure was more stratified, but one's position in that structure was not guaranteed. Geographic, occupational, and generational mobility opened theoretical opportunities for all.

57. **(E)** The writs of assistance tried to curtail smuggling, not speech. James Otis eloquently attacked the writs in a Massachusetts court suit, but British authorities upheld their use. The gag rule placated Southern congressmen by prohibiting the reading in Congress of abolitionist petitions. The offensive (to Southerners) petitions could still be presented to Congress, but not read. Lincoln's suspension of habeas corpus during the Civil War is not well known. He imprisoned 15,000 civilians for disloyalty or sedition, and suppressed over 300 newspapers for criticizing the war. The 1918 Sedition Act, actually an amendment to the Espionage Act of 1917, jailed pacifists and socialists for opposing the war effort. McCarthyism saw communists sprinkled throughout American society. They could be easily identified by their liberal leanings. If you were not a rabid anticommunist you were suspect.

58. **(E)** Naturalist John Muir was instrumental in the establishment of Yosemite National Park and the National Forest system. Both Roosevelts were well known conservationists in and out of the White House. Gifford Pinchot served as chief forester in Theodore Roosevelt's administration. He continued in his post in the Taft administration, but his

good friend and boss, James Garfield, was replaced as Secretary of the Interior by Richard Ballinger. The impetuous Pinchot clashed with Ballinger over his plans to sell federal land set aside for conservation. Ballinger was legally correct in his actions, but he seemed to be selling out the nation's conservation effort to corporation interests.

59. **(A)** This is from the Sherman Antitrust Act passed in 1890. The act sailed through the House of Representatives unanimously and through the Senate 52-1. Only innocuous laws pass Congress by these margins. The Sherman Act passed Congress so easily because it did not introduce new features into traditional interpretations of Anglo-American law. Combinations and conspiracies had always been illegal. The terms combination, trust, conspiracy, and monopolize were never defined in the act itself. What the Sherman Antitrust Act did was to establish a precedent for later, more effective legislation. The Clayton Antitrust Act in 1914 continued the tradition of the Sherman Act, not vice versa.

60. **(A)** The Soviet Union was boycotting the United Nations Security Council as a protest of the refusal of the United Nations to shift Nationalist China's (Taiwan) seat to Communist China. The invasion apparently took the Soviet Union by surprise. (A recent historian has suggested that it was all planned, but the evidence is still missing.) Unable to veto due to its absence, the Soviet Union watched helplessly as the machinery of the U.N. quickly operated in the manner envisioned by its founders. Dozens of U.N. members sent troops or supplies. None of the nations left "temporarily" divided by the Second World War received seats in the U.N. East and West Germany finally acquired seats in 1973. After conquering South Vietnam, Vietnam joined the U.N. in 1977. North and South Korea still don't belong.

61. **(C)** There are two methods of proposing an amendment to the Constitution and two methods of ratifying an amendment. An amendment is proposed by a two-thirds vote of each house of Congress, or by a national convention called by Congress when requested by two-thirds of the state legislatures. A proposed amendment can be ratified by three-fourths of the state legislatures or by the conventions of three-fourths of the states. The president plays no role in the amendment process. By definition, any part of the Constitution is constitutional, and an amendment can't be ruled unconstitutional.

62. **(D)** The administrator was Elihu Root. General John J. Pershing commanded the American Expeditionary Force (A.E.F.) during the First World War. Franklin Roosevelt served as Assistant Secretary of the Navy, a post also held by Theodore Roosevelt earlier. Taft was governor of the Philippines before becoming Roosevelt's Secretary of War.

63. **(B)** This quotation by James Wilson represents the philosophy of natural rights during the Revolutionary period. The most succinct summary is found in the preamble to the Declaration of Independence.

64. **(E)** The quotation is from the writings of historian Frederick Jackson Turner, who is most famous for his essay, "The Significance of the Frontier in American History." Choice (E) is part of an argument of Charles Beard, who stressed the economic interpretation of American history. Turner claimed that the frontier experience was the great equalizer of social classes. The demands of the environment stripped the veneer of culture and civilization, and made each man equal to another.

65. **(C)** Calhoun's doctrine of nullification gave a state the authority to declare an act of Congress null and void. The only means to overcome a state's nullification was for three-fourths of the states to meet in a special convention to pass a particular nullification ordinance. Calhoun was convinced that it would be too difficult to garner three-fourths of the states. Calhoun's theory of concurrent majority called for two presidents, one for each majority: the majority from the North and the majority (in the South) of the South. To Calhoun majority rule meant plunder of the minority. Only institutional safeguards could protect each majority, North or South.

66. **(D)** Currency problems and clashes between debtors and creditors continued into the latter period. Shays's Rebellion is just one example. Tension between the tidewater and the frontier regions is illustrated by the Paxton Boys, Regulators, legislative disputes over appropriations for fighting Indians, and the relocation of state capitals to inland locations. Disputes over western lands were not resolved until after the Confederation period. The one characteristic that changed was the fighting between the lower house and the governors. The lower house won because eleven states rewrote their constitutions by 1777 to provide a much weaker executive.

67. **(C)** The two decades are similar in their attempts to achieve American objectives by peaceful means. Between 1800 and 1810 Jefferson and Madison used the Embargo Act, the Nonintercourse Act, the Chesapeake affair, and Macon's Bill No. 2 to try to avoid war. The Washington Naval Disarmament Conference; the Four, Five, and Nine Power treaties; and the Kellogg-Briand Pact indicate the diplomatic objectives and methods in the Twenties.

68. **(B)** Any map distorted to reflect relative population by states also indicates the electoral college distortion. A quick glance at the map shows why Ohio was the "mother of presidents" and why so many presidential candidates came from the Midwest. It was a strong power base from which to build a political coalition. The map also shows why Populism never really had a chance at national power. The Populist states together were insignificant in total population.

69. **(B)** The NAACP and the Urban League were founded around 1910. CORE grew out of a meeting of Chicago militants in 1942. The post-Second World War organizations are the Southern Christian Leadership Conference (1957) and the Student Nonviolent Coordinating Committee (1960).

70. **(D)** This is Grant Wood's *American Gothic*, painted in 1930. Wood used his sister and his dentist to show the harsh and simple values of his Iowa neighbors.

71. **(D)** The Boston Massacre took place much earlier in 1770. After the Boston Tea Party in December 1773, the British responded with the Intolerable Acts, which closed the port of Boston; revoked the Massachusetts charter; took from the popularly elected assembly the power to appoint the governor's council, and gave it to the king; restricted town meetings to one a year; and moved trials for British officials out of Massachusetts. Widespread concern among the other colonies led to the convening of the First Continental Congress.

72. **(E)** Frederick W. Taylor was the father of scientific management, the application of time and motion studies to the office and the assembly line. His work carried the promise of human efficiency throughout the entire workplace. He created a new management type, the industrial engineer.

73. **(D)** Most of the articles of impeachment against Andrew Johnson concerned his violation of the Tenure of Office Act. This act expressly prohibited the president from firing any person appointed to a position which required Senate approval. Always willing to accept a belligerent challenge, Johnson promptly fired Secretary of War Stanton. Johnson was impeached and found not guilty by a 35-19 vote, since a two-thirds majority was necessary for conviction. He was saved by one vote.

74. **(B)** The American negotiators—Benjamin Franklin, John Jay, and John Adams—signed the separate peace because the French and Spanish seemed too eager to hem the infant United States along the Atlantic coast. Anxious to wean the United States from her alliance with France, the British offered generous boundary terms, including the area to the Mississippi River. Despite textbook exaggerations of George Rogers Clark's exploits, the U.S. claim to the trans-Appalachians was quite poor. The French Revolution didn't start until the end of the decade. The Peace of Paris took place in 1783 (with a preliminary treaty in 1782) long after the defeat at Yorktown in 1781. The United States would never have won the Revolutionary War without massive amounts of French aid and supplies. When General Cornwallis surrendered at Yorktown the British still had 50,000 soldiers in the colonies. The U.S. didn't defeat Great Britain; Great Britain intelligently gave up a hopeless cause.

75. **(C)** Conservative Old Guard Republicans took control of the regulatory agencies by putting conservatives on the boards and in the agencies. Conservatives in the Reagan administration have followed the same tactic. Trying to abolish the boards and agencies involves a fight with Congress. It is much easier to negate the effectiveness of agencies from the inside.

76. **(C)** Cheap labor and low taxes drew the textile industry out of New England and into the South. Each new wave of New England immigrants worked in factories and mills before being replaced with new and cheaper immigrants. Not a lack of labor but the cost of labor pulled textiles out of New England. Only a few slaves worked in industry in the South before the Civil War. The textile labor force was made up chiefly of poor whites.

77. **(A)** Lyndon Johnson lost the New Hampshire Democratic primary to Senator Eugene McCarthy of Wisconsin, an antiwar critic. The War on Poverty may have been over, but the Vietnam War was not. Johnson had creamed Barry Goldwater in 1964; victory in 1968 looked more difficult. Nixon won an overwhelming victory in his reelection bid in 1972, but his victory over Humphrey in 1968 was very close. Nixon later deescalated American involvement in Vietnam.

78. **(E)** The quote is from the Kellogg-Briand Treaty, drafted in 1928 and ratified by the Senate in January 1929, 85-1. The Kellogg-Briand Treaty outlawed war. That's why there have been no wars since 1929! Seriously, the Senate clearly understood that this treaty was a philosophical statement not binding on any nation because no one was responsible for enforcing the treaty. The same day the Senate approved the treaty it appropriated funds for fifteen new cruisers. This toothless document was resurrected for the Nuremberg Trials. One of the charges against the Nazi war criminals was violation of the Kellogg-Briand Pact.

79. **(C)** A whisper and smear campaign confronted both Al Smith in 1928 and John F. Kennedy in 1960. The truth is that no Democrat, Catholic or Protestant, could have beaten Hoover in 1928. In 1960 Kennedy's Catholicism apparently helped him more

than it hindered. Catholic ethnic voters tended to live in large urban areas, which increased Kennedy's urban vote total and gave him a better chance of capturing an entire state's electoral vote.

80. **(E)** The Espionage Act and the Sedition Act were both examples of governmental intolerance. The steel strike, the Boston police strike, the coal strike, the Seattle general strike, and the Palmer raids were all part of the Red Scare of 1918–1921, one of the periods of intolerance. Intolerant of only liquor, the Volstead Act implemented prohibition. Even habitual drinkers looked forward to prohibition as a great social experiment to build a better future society. Ten years later prohibition may have been revealed to be foolish, but it was not so considered at its inception.

81. **(E)** Roger B. Taney (pronounced Tawney) was the fourth Chief Justice of the Supreme Court, serving from 1836 to 1864. Helping Jackson during the Bank War, he drafted the bank veto message and removed the deposits from it. As Chief Justice he is best remembered for two decisions. The Charles River Bridge decision (1837) protected the community's rights from monopoly grants to corporations and entrepreneurs. The Dred Scott case (1857) invalidated the Missouri Compromise and the Compromise of 1850, and infuriated Northerners.

82. **(B)** In order to become a law a bill must pass the Senate and House in the exact same wording. The President may sign, veto or pocket veto. If Congress is in session the bill becomes a law within ten days of passage without the President's approval. He may elect to show his displeasure by not signing a bill, but it still becomes a law.

83. **(A)** Monopoly control over the sale of tea angered the colonists, particularly merchants. The tax remained steady for over six years at three pence per pound. The British troops were already here. Remember the Boston Massacre, March 5, 1770? The tea was consigned to American merchants for sale. The Boston Tea Party, December 16, 1773, was caused by anger over the Tea Act, not the reverse. Because the East India Company had been granted a monopoly it was able to lower the price of tea in the colonies, and the new price was lower than smuggled tea.

84. **(B)** The Marshall Plan was part of Truman's administration.

85. **(D)** That honor belongs to George Mason. He refused positions he was offered in the new government, standing stubbornly for the inclusion of a Bill of Rights in the Constitution. Virginia ratified the Constitution and then proposed that the first order of business for the new government be a consideration of a Bill of Rights. The amendments quickly passed.

86. **(B)** The Niagara Movement was the forerunner of the NAACP. The Warren Commission investigated the circumstances surrounding the assassination of John F. Kennedy. The Kerner Commission, headed by the governor of Illinois, looked at the reasons for black discontent in the 1960s.

87. **(C)** Franklin D. Roosevelt delivered this eloquent speech in January 1941. It remains today a succinct summary of the universal aspirations of people all over the globe.

88. **(A)** The Republican Party platform for the 1860 campaign specifically mentions four: a transcontinental railroad, a higher tariff, a national banking system, and a homestead act. The land-grant college idea had been pushed for years, especially by Midwest-

erners. Nicknamed the "Illinois idea," and sponsored by a Vermont senator, it finally passed Congress after the Southerners pulled out. Senator Jefferson Davis of Mississippi vehemently opposed the college land-grant law.

89. **(C)** Canada attracted the Americans in two ways, as a prize of war and as a means of attacking the British. No method existed for the U.S. to attack France unless we attacked only French shipping. Since Great Britain had virtually driven French shipping from the seas, our options were severely limited. British violations aggrieved the Americans more, for impressment was frustrating and humiliating. We were driven to war by steady diplomatic humiliation.

90. **(E)** Southerners defended slavery with the Bible. It is true that the institution of slavery is not criticized in the Bible. In ancient times a conquered people were enslaved as war booty as when the Jews were carried into Babylon. The Cain and Abel story was often used by Southerners. After confronting Cain for killing Abel, God punished Cain by putting a mark on him and his descendants. By reading between the lines and stretching their imaginations, Southerners reasoned that Cain was turned into a Negro for punishment. The comparison between the conditions for the worst Northern factory workers and the conditions for the best slaves was fair, and often used by Southerners. Very few could imagine anything other than an agricultural South. "King Cotton" blinded them to any other possible crop or industry. The Constitution did not specifically protect slavery in the South, although the Three-fifths clause and the 1808 date abolishing the slave trade seem to condone slavery. The Northwest Ordinance abolished slavery in the Old Northwest. Individual state action abolished slavery north of the Mason-Dixon line.

91. **(C)** All of these statements are true for the fifteen years preceding the War of 1812. In 1807–1808 Jefferson's embargo stymied shipping. Be able to put the changing American, French, and British policies prior to the War of 1812 in chronological order.

92. **(B)** The cartoonist Thomas Nast undermined Boss Tweed's control. Even illiterate New York City immigrants understood Nast's scathing cartoons.

93. **(B)** John Fiske wrote *The Critical Period of American History* in 1888 to counter the widespread popular notion that the recent Civil War was the most critical event in American history. The popular thinking of the time was that the U.S. had barely survived. Not so, said Fiske, it was an earlier period that had almost finished the United States as a nation, that during the Articles of Confederation. "The dangers from which we were saved in 1788 were even greater than the dangers from which we were saved in 1865. . . ."

94. **(B)** James Oglethorpe led a group of associates who founded Georgia in 1732 for the relief of jailed debtors and to fortify the southern frontier against Spanish Florida.

95. **(D)** New York Representative Tallmadge introduced this amendment in 1819 to limit the expansion of slavery. Note that no slave would have been freed under Tallmadge's provision. All children born of slaves would become free at twenty-five. The ensuing debate—both public and congressional—was settled by the Missouri Compromise.

96. **(B)** The emphasis on equality, voluntary association, the social character of churches, the rejection of culture, and the emphasis on public morals are also in *Democracy in America,* published in the 1830s.

97. **(E)** The full title of Myrdal's book is *An American Dilemma: The Negro Problem and Modern Democracy*. The book illustrated the huge gap between professed democratic ideals and actual practices, especially in regard to race relations. Adam Smith's *The Wealth of Nations* (1776) was the first to present laissez-faire systematically. Veblen's *The Theory of the Leisure Class* (1899) attacked the values of capitalism and business, differentiating between industry and business. He added "conspicuous consumption" to economic thinking when he linked status to consumption patterns. Keynesian economics advocated manipulating the economy through fiscal policy (governmental taxing and spending policies) and monetary policy (controlling the money supply). In bad economic times the government should use deficit spending to stimulate the economy. When the economy begins to move too fast a tax increase cools it off. *The General Theory of Employment, Interest and Money* was published in 1936, but his fundamental ideas had been published earlier. Galbraith's *The Affluent Society* (1958) questioned ignoring the quality of life in social, educational, and cultural matters inherent in the Keynesian emphasis on private production of material goods.

98. **(E)** The Federal Arts Program was part of the WPA, not the PWA. Ickes, the head of the PWA, thought that Hopkins deliberately selected the initials WPA to confuse everyone into giving him credit for PWA accomplishments. Millions of students trying to separate the two agencies have endorsed Ickes's conspiracy charge.

99. **(D)** These two songs were popular in 1932 because they conveyed the popular feelings of the period. If you can, find someone who lived through the Depression and ask him to tell you his personal history. You may be surprised at the depths of deprivation and fear in the early years of the Depression.

100. **(A)** The OPA was the Office of Price Administration, which fixed price ceilings and controlled rents during the Second World War. Your grandparents may still have some of the coin-like meat coupons from the OPA. Its purpose was to limit inflation. Nixon's wage and price controls also tried to limit inflation.

Index

F

G

H

X

Y